"Seyd in forme and reverence"

Essays on Chaucer and Chaucerians
in Memory of
Emerson Brown, Jr.

Emerson Brown
Jazz Clarinet
and
Mediaeval Philology

Drawing by Cindy Brown

"Seyd in forme and reverence"

*Essays on Chaucer and Chaucerians
in Memory of
Emerson Brown, Jr.*

EDITED BY

T. L. BURTON AND JOHN F. PLUMMER

The Chaucer Studio Press

First published 2005 by The Chaucer Studio Press
an imprint of The Chaucer Studio

Discipline of English
The University of Adelaide
SA 5005, Australia
and
Department of English
Brigham Young University
Provo
UT 84602-6218, U.S.A.

ISBN 0-8425-2631-5

Typeset at the University of Adelaide
Printed at Brigham Young University, Provo

Contents

Troilus and Criseyde and Henryson's Testament of Cresseid

Minor Poems

Oral Performance

Editing and Annotating

Philosophical and Scriptural Topics

Notes on Contributors

ACKNOWLEDGEMENTS

The Chaucer Studio Press and the editors of this volume wish to express their gratitude to the Faculty of Humanities and Social Sciences at the University of Adelaide and the College of Humanities at Brigham Young University, Provo, for research grants that have assisted in its preparation; to Rosamund Allen and Andrew Lynch for their expert and thorough reading of the essays contributed; to Anna Higgins for her careful subeditorial work in preparing the essays for publication; to Carie Jackson for the cover design; and to Cindy Brown for the drawing of Emerson Brown reproduced as the frontispiece.

NOTE ON THE TEXT

Except when otherwise stated the source of all quotations from Chaucer's works
is *The Riverside Chaucer*, 3rd. ed., General Ed. Larry D. Benson (Boston:
Houghton Mifflin, 1987).

Emerson L. Brown, Junior
Some Bio-Bibliographical Notes

JOHN F. PLUMMER

All of Emerson Brown's friends, colleagues and students (and those groups overlapped considerably) will remember him for the energy he brought to his teaching, scholarship, bike riding, jazz playing, and every other activity in which he engaged. He once confided in me that Dante had heaven wrong. "Heaven," he said, "is where we read medieval studies papers to each other all morning, ride bikes all afternoon, and play jazz all night." The eighteen essays gathered here represent, in a variety of different fashions, affectionate and respectful responses to that learning and energy.

Emerson Brown was born in 1934. He was educated at Hamilton College, where he received his BA in 1956. He then earned an MA at Syracuse University and PhD at Cornell University. He taught at the Inter American University in Puerto Rico from 1958–61, the University of Puerto Rico from 1961–69, and at Stanford University from 1969–75, whence he came to Vanderbilt in the Autumn of 1975.

At Vanderbilt Emerson taught courses in Chaucer, King Arthur and his Knights, the Medieval Dawn Song, and Dante. The enthusiam, learning, dedication and imagination he brought to his teaching earned Emerson the recognition of Vanderbilt's Jeffrey Nordhaus Award for Excellence in Undergraduate Teaching in 1992.

He was a member of the Medieval Academy, the Dante Society, International Arthurian Society, New Chaucer Society, and the Southeastern Medieval Association. His tireless support of and participation in the last was recognized by SEMA's 2002 meeting at Florida State University, where two special sessions of papers were dedicated to his memory, which papers in turn formed the seed of the present volume. He served on the editorial board of *Mediaevalia* and the Chaucer bibliographies of the University of Toronto Press, and he was an active supporter of and participant in recordings of The Chaucer Studio. A founding member of the scholarly team that produces the Variorum Chaucer editions, Emerson was both interested and learned in questions of textual criticism and editorial practice, producing several talks and essays on the editing of medieval texts, and arguing consistently that students and scholars alike have been poorly served by modern editions.

Emerson was the Vanderbilt University faculty advisor of Teach for America, and he actively encouraged his best students to consider a teaching career.

During the 1980s he took part in many workshops on teaching for high school teachers in Tennessee, Alabama, and Mississippi, funded by the Mellon Regional Faculty Development Program.

An avid outdoorsman, Emerson enjoyed hiking, and canoeing, and was particularly devoted to cycling; he rode 950 miles from Nashville to Clinton, N. Y. for his 25th class reunion at Hamilton. He also enjoyed playing jazz clarinet, performing with a number of bands. For many years he and a band made up of academics named "The Impaired Faculties" played for the cocktail party given each May by the English Department for graduating seniors and at the Sewanee Medieval Colloquium dinners. His illness forced early retirement upon him in 1997. He is warmly remembered by friends and colleagues at Vanderbilt for his enthusiasm, his devotion to teaching and learning, and his genial collegiality.

Emerson's publications, appearing in the most prestigious journals of medieval studies and English philology, were meticulously and expansively researched; they are marked by deep, rich, and detailed learning on the one hand, and a remarkable breadth of interest on the other, and the subjects covered in the course of his career—though centered in the middle ages—reached from classical antiquity to the twentieth century, from Epicurus to Dante, and Chaucer to Thomas Hardy and William Carlos Williams.

In rereading Emerson's work in preparation for this essay, I was struck by a set of methodological, theoretical, and temperamental threads which weave through his scholarship. The first of these is an insistence that a literary text is not complete in itself, "splendid in its ontological independence of both creator and public" ("Of Mice and Women," 63), but is rather dependent upon other texts and its audience (especially an audience familiar with those other texts) for its meaning. While not much interested in literary theory as a subject in itself, Emerson was fully aware that his methodology was characterized by attention to intertextuality and the role of learned, active readers and their responses, and it is a pleasant irony he no doubt enjoyed that he published much of this work, implicitly in opposition to the New Criticism, at Vanderbilt University, its birthplace.

This intertextual methodology manifests itself of course most clearly in his work on richly allusive classical and medieval texts. In his "Biblical Women in the *Merchant's Tale*: Feminism, Antifeminism, and Beyond," an important study of the resonances of exegesis in the multiple allusions to biblical women in the *Merchant's Tale*, Emerson tackled the difficult tonal valences of the Merchant's several allusions to biblical women. He argued that Chaucer's audience would have beeen familiar with the exegetical commentary on these figures both in its learned Latin and its popular vernacular forms, both of which understood these women to be both heroic and moral. The Merchant's attempts to use them ironically and sarcastically, emphasizing Judith's violence and Rebecca's counsel of deception to Jacob, lead to a complex resonance and dissonance: "The dubious example, the insincere hyperbole, the fragment of the commonplace taken out of context—all these techniques shock us into exercising our own memory and creativity in order to determine what the lines mean, for they rarely mean simply what they say" ("Biblical Women in the *Merchant's Tale*," 389). Awareness of the multiple positive understandings of these biblical figures adds what R. E. Kaske called a "moral edge" to a bawdy tale.[1] In the *Merchant's Tale*, Emerson argued, this "'moral edge' is introduced allusively, indirectly; and capturing its essence puts a burden on the reader, for he must listen for the voice of love hidden beneath the words spoken in hatred" ("Biblical Women," 408). In his "Epicurus and Voluptas in Late Antiquity," Emerson asks why Martianus Capella places Epicurus in the Milky Way, heaven of the philosophers, in his *De nuptiis Philologiae et Mercurii*: "Martianus appears to have accepted the distortions of Epicurus' enemies and then, defiantly and exuberantly, deem *that* Epicurus worthy of immortality. Why?" (83). For possible answers, he again goes outside the text of *De nuptiis* itself, and discovers multiple and important allusions to the writings of (especially) Cicero and Prudentius, "texts which may constitute part of Martianus' own text, in that complex process historical criticism has long been concerned with, and which critical theorists are now calling 'intertextuality'" (88).

In his excellent close reading of the *Physician's Tale*, Emerson explored intertextuality not only between the tale and its sources, but also between this and other *Canterbury Tales*, arguing that though Pilgrim Chaucer praises the Physician in the *General Prologue* for his ability to discern causes of disease, a comparison of his telling of the tale of Virginia with the versions in Livy and Jean de Meun makes it evident that the Physician cannot discern clearly the cause of Virginia's tragedy. For Livy and Jean the cause was, unambiguously, judicial corruption. By contrast, in his tale the Physician introduces Nature, nurses, fathers, mothers, "the feend" and those who fail to forsake sin, muddying the moral waters and clouding the clear cause of disaster. Emerson connects the *Physician's Tale* to the *Franklin's Tale* which precedes it in the Ellesmere order. Both are (temporarily) concerned with causes, but fail to follow through. Dorigen asks the cause of the rocks, but drops the question as unanswerable. In the end it doesn't matter, and "as the rising tide hides the 'rokkes blake' so the rising tides of 'gentillesse' hide the dangers of death, adultery, dishonor and financial ruin" (142). By contrast, the Physician introduces so many competing causes for evil that no logical moral understanding is possible. The *Pardoner's Tale* concludes the sequence of tales seeking causes of evil. In his tale the Franklin optimistically minimizes evil, the Physician finds its causes everywhere and nowhere, while the Pardoner knows that it resides in his own heart.

If the first methodological thread I see in Emerson's work might be called intertextual, the second is textual, manifesting itself most visibly in those writings which concern the editing of medieval texts. While the textual thus might appear at first glance to be radically different from the intertextual, it is perhaps not. In such essays as "Guilt by Punctuation," "The Poet's Last Words,"

---

[1] "The *Canticum Canticorum* in the *Miller's Tale*," *Studies in Philology* 59 (1962), 497.

"Thoughts on the Variorum Chaucer," and "Thoughts on Editing Chaucer," Emerson demonstrated again, though in a very different way, a willingness to question the inviolability of the texts. Whereas in his work on allusion he showed the text reaching for its full meaning beyond its apparent boundaries, in his work on the editing of texts Emerson argued again that in taking at face value the integrity and unproblematic self-presence of the (especially modern edition of a) medieval text, readers may cut themselves off from important ambiguity of poetic meaning. In his 1986 article "*The Knight's Tale*, 2639: Guilt by Punctuation," for example, he demonstrated that our understanding of who struck whom in that tale's climactic battle has been skewed by modern insistence on adding punctuation to a medieval text which was written with virtually none. In "The Poet's Last Words," Emerson disputes the rationale for Manly's emendation of the final 8 lines of the *Parson's Prologue*, an emendation followed by Robinson, Donaldon, Baugh and Pratt (and the *Riverside*). Chaucer's confirmed syntactic pattern of reporting speech—"And with that/this word" + Pronoun + Verb—is never ambiguous, "nearly always refers to the speaker whose words have just been reported" (238), and confirms the manuscripts' line order. Left as found, the final lines, "Beth fructuous and that in little space, / And to do wel God sende yow his grace," reveal the host is anxious that the Parson not go on too long; it is an afterthought seeking to take back some of the license offered in "Sey what yow list, and we wol gladly heere." While the Parson's prose treatise is focused resolutely on sin, Chaucer's last lines of poetry for the *Canterbury Tales*, restored to original order, conclude by asking for God's grace. On the one hand, then, Emerson's work questions where the text's borders lie, and on the other hand it often questions whether the "text" before us is what the poet wrote or rather a limiting and limited version of the medieval text imposed upon us by modern editorial practices which habitually seek to eliminate uncertainty and ambiguity.

Which brings me to the third thread. As I re-read Emerson's work I am struck forcibly by his work's openness to poetic ambiguities, complexities, and variabilities; the erudition he brought to bear on literary texts was never used to settle a text's meaning, to "impose a limit on that text, to furnish it with a final signified, to close the writing," in Barthes' words, but rather to open it to further richness. In his "What's Wrong With Being Worthy? *General Prologue* line 68 and Chaucer's Knight," for example, Emerson examined the vexed case of Chaucer's attitude towards his Knight, especially focusing on the notoriously difficult line "And though that he were worthy he was wys" (I 68). He argued against both the widely held position that the Knight was an unambiguously positive character and the position that he is presented as deeply flawed, even corrupt. Rather, pointing to the way the word "worthy" subtly changes values as it passes through the length of the Knight's portrait, Emerson argued that "the subtle darkening of 'worthy' from its first appearance in the Knight's portrait to its last reflects the darkening and complicating of not only the ideals of chivalry but of much else in the troubled century that separated Chaucer from Aquinas

and Bonaventure" ("Chaucer's Knight," 192). The very idea of chivalric wor-
thiness, the semantic worth of "worthy," had suffered in the actual practices of
late medieval chivalry a pejoration: "The fate of 'worthy' shows what happens
when language undergoes what Bakhtin calls 'dialogization,' that process that
occurs when language 'becomes relativized, de-privileged, aware of competing
definitions for the same things'" (192).[2] The 1971 *Dante Studies* essay "Proserpina, Matelda, and the Pilgrim," similarly brings Emerson's learning to bear
on a moment in *Purgatorio* in such a way as to open the passage to greater richness and complexity than had been seen. Whereas commentators on the scene
in canto 28 in which Pilgrim Dante sees Matelda and tells her that she reminds
him of Proserpina just before her ravishment by Pluto[3] have been unanimous in
assuming that Dante was thinking of Ovid's *Metamorphoses* 5.390–96, wherein
he describes her abduction, an equally plausible and potentially more complex
allusion may be operating towards Claudian's *De Raptu Proserpinae*, a poem
widely read as part of a standard medieval textbook, the *Liber Catonianus*. In
Claudian's as in Ovid's telling of the story, Proserpina is an innocent victim of
Pluto's lust, but "in Claudian the case is more complicated and more human"
(35). Claudian asks the gods to help him tell the story, "with what torch Love
made Pluto bend; how high-spirited (*ferox*) Proserpina was stolen away and
came to possess Chaos as her dowry" (1.26–28).[4] Shortly thereafter, Claudian
describes Proserpina as on the brink of sexual awareness: "Her maidenhood had
matured with the fullness of years so that she was now ripe for marriage, now
the wedding-torch stirred her delicate modesty and she trembled at the vow
with a mingling of fear" (1.130–32; Gruzelier, 11–13).

In this version of the story it is Venus herself who has begun to instill desire
within the young girl which will lead her to the fields where she will be abducted.
Thus though no less a victim than Ovid's heroine, Claudian's Prosperpina is
not wholly ignorant of sexual feelings, and when Dante tells Matelda that she
reminds him of Proserpina "he is saying to Matelda not only that she reminds
him of a lovely and innocent maiden in a scene of perpetual spring, but also, and
most emphatically, that she reminds him of one of the participants in an action"
(36). Dante's comparison, if it is to (or includes) Claudian's version of the story
would thus be unsettlingly erotically charged; one could say that he is looking
at Matelda as Pluto looked at Proserpina. The potential for (inappropriate)
eroticism in Dante's gaze is corroborated a few lines later by two further classical allusions: "In the first he compares the look on Matelda's face as she raises
her eyes to him with the look of Venus at the moment she became enamored
of Adonis. In the second he compares his hatred for the stream separating him
from Matelda with Leander's hatred of the Hellespont, which separated him

---

[2]The reference to Bakhtin is to the Glossary to M. M. Bakhtin, *The Dialogic Imagination*,
ed. Michael Holquist and trans. Caryl Emerson and Michael Holquist (Austin: University of
Texas Press, 1981), s.v. "dialogue" (p. 427).

[3]"Tu mi fai rimembrar dove e qual era / Proserpina nel tempo che perdette / la madre lei,
ed ella primavera" (*Purg.* 27.49–51).

[4]The translation is by Claire Gruzelier, *Claudian* De Raptu Proserpinae (Oxford: Clarendon Press, 1993), 5.

from his beloved (xxviii, 61–75)" (40). One way to understand Dante's desire
for Matelda is allegorical: in her eternal innocence she might represent a glimpse
of Dante's own prelapsarian state. "He senses this, but cannot recognize that
innocence without at the same time realizing that it is forever lost" (41), and
"his inability to describe this innocence in terms other than those applicable to
the perishable innocence of fallen man reflects his, and our, irreducible limitations. Yet at the same instant we realize this, we are forced to a dim awareness
that the full magnificence of original innocence surpasses all human powers of
comprehension. The obvious and calculated failure fully to understand Matelda
succeeds better at communicating her essence to us than could any approximate
success" (45).

The methodological and temperamental threads detected in this sampling
of Emerson's work are of course the product of my own reading, but I hope
they may serve as an introduction to this body of scholarship to those not yet
familiar with it, and a provocation to revisit it for those who are. Emerson's
interest in and knowledge of late antique and medieval Epicureanism makes
it appropriate to conclude with one of the philosopher's "Vatican Sayings,"
epitomizing as it does the joy Emerson took in study and teaching: "The benefits
of other activities come only to those who have already become, with great
difficulty, complete masters of such pursuits, but in the study of philosophy
pleasure accompanies growing knowledge; for pleasure does not follow learning;
rather, learning and pleasure advance side by side."

The Publications of Emerson Brown, Jr.

"*The Merchant's Tale*: Why is May Called 'Mayus'?" *Chaucer Review* 2 (1967–68): 273–77.

"*Hortus Inconclusus*: The Significance of Priapus and Pyramus and Thisbe in the *Merchant's Tale*," *Chaucer Review* 4 (1969–70): 31–40.

"*The Merchant's Tale*: Why Was Januarie Born 'Of Pavye'?" *Neuphilologische Mitteilungen*, 71 (1970): 654–58.

"Proserpina, Matelda, and the Pilgrim," *Dante Studies* 89 (1971): 33–48

"*The Merchant's Tale*: Januarie's 'Unlikely Elde,'" *Neuphilologische Mitteilungen* 74 (1973): 92–106.

A Student's Edition of *The Owl and the Nightingale*, reproduced by photo-offset. Stanford, California, 1973.

"Biblical Women in the *Merchant's Tale*: Feminism, Antifeminism, and Beyond," *Viator* 5 (1974): 387–412.

"Priapus and the *Parlement of Foulys*," *Studies in Philology* 72 (1975): 258–74.

"Chaucer and the European Literary Tradition," in *Geoffrey Chaucer: A Collection of Original Articles*, ed. George D. Economou (New York: McGraw-Hill, 1975), 37–54.

"The Poet's Last Words: Text and Meaning at the End of the *Parson's Prologue*," *Chaucer Review* 10 (1975–76): 236–42.

"William Carlos Williams' 'Full Moon' and the Medieval Dawn Song," Norman Britten *Festschrift* issue, *Southern Humanities Review* 11 (1977): 175–83.

"Chaucer, the Merchant, and Their Tale: Getting Beyond Old Controversies," Part I, *Chaucer Review* 13 (1978–79): 141–56; Part II, 13 (1978–79): 247–62.

"Thoughts on the Variorum Chaucer: Editorial Intervention in the Explanatory Notes," *Chaucer Newsletter* 2.1 (1980): 4–6.

Review of *J. R. R. Tolkien, Scholar and Story Teller: Essays* in Memoriam, ed. Mary Salu and Robert T. Farrell, *Studies in the Age of Chaucer* 2 (1980): 204–7.

"Thoughts on Editing Chaucer: The 'Electronic Information Revolution' and a Proposal for the Future," *Chaucer Newsletter* 2.2 (1980): 2–3.

"Word Play in the Prologue to the *Manciple's Tale*, 98: 'T'acord and love and many a wrong apese,'" *Chaucer Newsletter* 2.2 (1980): 11–12.

"Diverse Folk Diversely They Teach," in *Approaches to Teaching Chaucer's Canterbury Tales*, ed. Joseph Gibaldi (New York: Modern Language Association, 1980), 63–75.

Review (with Suzanne Fleischmann) of *Love and Marriage in the Age of Chaucer*, by Henry Ansgar Kelly, *Romance Philology* 34 (1981): 496–502.

"What is Chaucer Doing With the Physician and His Tale?" *Philological Quarterly*, 60 (1981): 129–49.

"A Note on Henri-Augustin Gomont's Chaucer," *Chaucer Newsletter* 4.2 (1982): 1, 3.

Review of *A Distinction of Stories: The Medieval Unity of Chaucer's Fair Chain of Narratives for Canterbury*, by Judson Boyce Allen and Theresa Anne Moritz, *JEGP* 81 (1982): 554–56.

"Epicurus and Voluptas in Late Antiquity: The Curious Testimony of Martianus Capella," *Traditio*, 38 (1982): 75–106.

"Chaucer and a Proper Name: Januarie in the *Merchant's Tale*," *Names* 31 (1983): 79–87.

Review (with Eren Hostetter Branch) of *Chaucer's Knight: Portrait of a Medieval Mercenary*, by Terry Jones, *Anglia* 102 (1984): 525–32.

Editor, with others, *Magister Regis: Studies in Honor of Robert Earl Kaske* (New York: Fordham University Press, 1986).

"R. E. Kaske: *Magister Regis*," biographical essay in *Magister Regis*, 1–8.

"Epicurean Secularism in Dante and Boccaccio: Athenian Roots and Florentine Revival," in *Magister Regis*, 179–93.

Review of *Metaformations: Soundplay and Wordplay in Ovid and Other Classical Poets*, by Frederick Ahl, *Studies in the Age of Chaucer* 8 (1986): 157–60.

"Of Mice and Women: Thoughts on Chaucerian Allusion," in *Chaucer and the Craft of Fiction*, ed. Leigh A. Arrathoon (Rochester, Michigan: Solaris Press, 1986), 63–84.

"*The Knight's Tale*, 2639: Guilt by Punctuation," Judson Boyce Allen Memorial Issue, *Chaucer Review* 21 (1986): 133–41.

Review of *Boethius and Dialogue: Literary Method in The Consolation of Philosophy*, by Seth Lerer, *Studies in the Age of Chaucer* 9 (1987): 226–29.

Review of *Geoffrey Chaucer*, by Robert O. Payne, *Speculum* 63 (1988): 210–12.

Review of *Chaucer: The Earlier Poetry*, by Derek Traversi, *English Language Notes* 26 (1988): 77–80.

Review of *Chaucer Name Dictionary*, by Jacqueline de Weever, *Studies in the Age of Chaucer* 11 (1989): 204–8.

"Fragment VII of Chaucer's *Canterbury Tales* and the 'Mental Climate of the Fourteenth Century,'" in *Traditions and Innovations: Essays on British Literature of the Middle Ages and the Renaissance*, ed. David G. Allen and Robert A. White (Newark, Delaware: University of Delaware Press, 1990), 50–58.

"The Merchant's Damyan and Chaucer's Kent," *Chaucer Newsletter* 13.1 (1991): 5.

Review of *The "Consultation" of Boethius: An Analytical Inquiry into His Intellectual Processes and Goals*, by Steven Varvis, *Carmina Philosophiae* 1 (1992): 97–101.

"What's Wrong with Being Worthy? General Prologue Line 68 and Chaucer's Knight," *Mediaevalia* 15 (1993 [for 1989]): 182–205.

"The Ruthless Artistry of Hardy's 'Convergence of the Twain,'" *Sewanee Review* 101.2 (Spring 1994): 233–43.

Review of *Studies in the Vernon Manuscript*, ed. Derek Pearsall, *Studies in the Age of Chaucer* 16 (1994): 241–45.

"Shakespeare, Zeffirelli, Monty Python, and the Medieval Dawn Song," *Medieval Perspectives* 10 (1995): 1–26.

"The Joy of Chaucer's Lydgate Lines," in *Essays on the Art of Chaucer's Verse*, ed. Alan T. Gaylord (New York and London: Routledge, 2001), 267–79.

The Canterbury Tales

"And I seyde his opinion was good"
How Irony Works in the Monk's Portrait

HOWELL CHICKERING

A MONK ther was, a fair for the maistrie,   165
An outridere, that lovede venerie,
A manly man, to been an abbot able.
Ful many a deyntee hors hadde he in stable,
And whan he rood, men myghte his brydel heere
Gynglen in a whistlynge wynd als cleere   170
And eek as loude as dooth the chapel belle
Ther as this lord was kepere of the celle.
The reule of Seint Maure or of Seint Beneit—
By cause that it was old and somdel streit
This ilke Monk leet olde thynges pace,   175
And heeld after the newe world the space.
He yaf nat of that text a pulled hen,
That seith that hunters ben nat hooly men,
Ne that a monk, whan he is recchelees,
Is likned til a fissh that is waterlees—   180
This is to seyn, a monk out of his cloystre.
But thilke text heeld he nat worth an oystre;
And I seyde his opinion was good.
What sholde he studie and make hymselven wood,
Upon a book in cloystre alwey to poure,   185
Or swynken with his handes, and laboure,
As Austyn bit? How shal the world be served?
Lat Austyn have his swynk to hym reserved!
Grehoundes he hadde as swift as fowel in flight;   190
Of prikyng and of huntyng for the hare
Was al his lust, for no cost wolde he spare.
I seigh his sleves purfiled at the hond
With grys, and that the fyneste of a lond;
And for to festne his hood under his chyn,   195
He hadde of gold ywroght a ful curious pyn;
A love-knotte in the gretter ende ther was.
His heed was balled, that shoon as any glas,

3

And eek his face, as he hadde been enoynt.
He was a lord ful fat and in good poynt;   200
His eyen stepe, and rollynge in his heed,
That stemed as a forneys of a leed;
His bootes souple, his hors in greet estaat.
Now certeinly he was a fair prelaat;
He was nat pale as a forpyned goost.   205
A fat swan loved he best of any roost.
His palfrey was as broun as is a berye.

Among Emerson Brown's many exemplary qualities as a Chaucerian, I always particularly cherished his acute critical sense, his good ear (and voice), and his persistent commitment to "getting it right"—but not ever completely right: As he wrote in 1980, it is our obligation as Chaucerians "to refrain from confusing the conclusions of a single critic with a satisfactory, comprehensive interpretation of the poetry. Exercising such restraint should not be too difficult. Surely we all recognize that a truly comprehensive interpretation of a literary work is simply beyond the capacities of any critic or critical approach."[1]

It is in the spirit of these words that I offer this essay in Emerson's memory. I want to challenge the widely held view that in the *General Prologue* Chaucer's satiric irony arises chiefly from his deployment of a wide-eyed observer, "the pilgrim Chaucer," and to urge critics instead to adopt a model that explains irony as generated by a complex interaction of the reader with Chaucer's text. I will show how this model works using the portrait of the Monk as my main illustration because it is one of the most complex portraits, exhibiting several kinds of ironies, including the most characteristic type of "pilgrim" irony.[2] However, it is not a comprehensive exemplar for all the ironies in the entire *General Prologue*. Overall, Chaucer's invitations to see irony are more various than those found in any one portrait, an important point to which I will return.

The notion that the poet manipulates his own pilgrim character to create irony seems inherently reasonable. Although this critical formulation was

---

[1] Emerson Brown, Jr., "Diverse Folk Diversely They Teach," *Approaches to Teaching Chaucer's* Canterbury Tales, ed. Joseph Gibaldi (New York: Modern Language Association of America, 1980), 71.

[2] Over a fifty-year period at least six major interpreters of how Chaucer's irony and persona are related in the *General Prologue* have chosen the Monk's portrait as an explanatory illustration of their claims. It is a distinguished roster of critics: E. Talbot Donaldson, "Chaucer the Pilgrim," *PMLA* 69 (1954): 928–36, repr. in *Chaucer Criticism: The Canterbury Tales*, ed. Richard J. Schoeck and Jerome Taylor (Notre Dame: University of Notre Dame Press, 1960), 1–13 [citations from this reprint], discussion of the Monk at 5; Wayne C. Booth, *A Rhetoric of Irony* (Chicago: University of Chicago Press, 1974), 235; H. Marshall Leicester, Jr., "The Art of Impersonation: A General Prologue to the *Canterbury Tales*," *PMLA* 95 (1980): 213–24, where the Monk is discussed at 219–20, and again in his *The Disenchanted Self: Representing the Subject in the Canterbury Tales* (Berkeley: University of California Press, 1990), 387–89; Douglas C. Muecke, *Irony and the Ironic* (London and New York: Methuen, 1982), 56–57; Jesse M. Gellrich, *The Idea of the Book in the Middle Ages* (Ithaca and London: Cornell University Press, 1985), 232–34; and David Lawton, *Chaucer's Narrators* (Cambridge: D. S. Brewer, 1985), 99–101. The portrait remains a touchstone passage for whether Chaucer's irony arises from his manipulation of the pilgrim persona or from his direct authorial speech.

challenged sharply soon after E. Talbot Donaldson put it forth in 1954, it has remained irresistibly attractive to many readers, and has tended to creep back into
the arguments of its recent critics when they substitute such terms as "voice"
for "character" (Leicester, Gellrich, Edwards).[3] Even David Lawton, who sees
Chaucer's narrators as often no more than rhetorical devices, ends up regarding
the pilgrim Chaucer as a stable character in a past-tense fiction.[4] On the other

---

[3]The first, and perhaps most pungent, challenges were by Bertrand H. Bronson, *In Search
of Chaucer* (Toronto: University of Toronto Press, 1960), 28–30, and John M. Major, "The
Personality of Chaucer the Pilgrim," *PMLA* 75 (1960): 160–62. Rosemary Woolf offered
a view that complements Donaldson's in "Chaucer as Satirist in the *General Prologue* to
the *Canterbury Tales*," *Critical Quarterly* 1 (1959): 150–57. For discussions of Donaldson's
influence see Joseph A. Dane, *The Critical Mythology of Irony* (Athens and London: University
of Georgia Press, 1991), 143–45, and his *Who is Buried in Chaucer's Tomb? Studies in the
Reception of Chaucer's Book* (East Lansing: Michigan State University Press, 1998), 165–71.
A. C. Spearing offers a skeptical review of persona criticism, rejecting even "an unreliable
narrator" in favor of "an unstable first person" pronoun, in "A Ricardian 'I': The Narrator of
Troilus and Criseyde," in *Essays on Ricardian Literature in Honour of J. A. Burrow*, ed. A.
J. Minnis, Charlotte C. Morse, and Thorlac Turville-Petre (Oxford: Clarendon Press, 1997),
1–7. Similar views about the instability or multiplicity of "voice" in Chaucer's poetry are
held by Barbara Nolan, "'A Poet Ther Was': Chaucer's Voices in the General Prologue to
The Cantebury Tales," *PMLA* 101 (1986): 154–69; Robert R. Edwards, *The Dream of Chaucer:
Representation and Reflection in the Early Narratives* (Durham and London: Duke University
Press, 1989), 42–46; Burt Kimmelman, *The Poetics of Authorship in the Later Middle Ages:
The Emergence of the Medieval Literary Persona* (New York: Peter Lang, 1996, 1999), 2–3;
and Helen Phillips, *An Introduction to the* Canterbury Tales*: Reading, Fiction, Context* (New
York: St. Martin's Press, 2000), 2–3, 42–45. The Donaldsonian view remains alive and well in
Edward Wheatley's account of satire in the Monk's portrait in "Modes of Representation," *A
Companion to Chaucer*, ed. Peter Brown (Oxford: Blackwell, 2000), 305–7.

[4]Lawton is very good at historicizing the heteroglossic sources of various narratorial tones
in Chaucer's earlier works, but he is rather cursory in his treatment of the *Canterbury Tales*.
When he comes to describe the narratorial voice in the *General Prologue*, he shifts his terminology from "voice" as a rhetorical construction back to "persona" and, in effect, re-introduces
Donaldson's dichotomous model of Chaucer the pilgrim and the poet.

> By placing an earlier self in the company, Chaucer achieves the distance of the
> dream-vision poet in a naturalistic context, and brings to the presentation of
> a verse *novelle* collection the full range of tone made possible by the temporal
> interaction of his two ages.... The pilgrim vouches for the veracity of the poet's
> description; and the narratorial first-person pronoun appears most often in the
> more complex portraits, confirming the strong interest felt by both poet and
> pilgrim. The portrait of the Monk contains what might be called a signed
> opinion: ... 'And I seyde his opinion was good' (183). The past tense, 'I seyde,'
> controls the irony of this line. It would still be possible to have irony with a line
> like 'I seye his opinion is good,' but it would be a different kind of irony which
> would involve the poet directly; as the line stands, it is the younger self whose
> folly is implicated and from whom the poet keeps a discreet distance." (p. 99)

It was truly a stroke of insight to see that the present-tense version of line 183 creates a
different kind of irony than the past-tense version. However, as I will show, the irony of
Chaucer's text is actually controlled by other factors than "the temporal interaction of his
two ages." In addition, the notion of an older and younger Chaucer has scant textual support.
While the text clearly establishes the fiction of a pilgrim Chaucer, his account of the pilgrimage
is nowhere modified by adverbial phrases that put it in the deep past. The pilgrimage can
even be imagined to take place only shortly before the present-tense narration. And how much
"younger" would the pilgrim have had to be in order to commit "folly"? This "younger" and
therefore foolish "self" is only another version of Donaldson's naïve pilgrim. Lawton has
mistakenly fastened on the difference in tenses in order to conceptualize the ironies he hears.

side of this long argument, Bertrand Bronson heard no pilgrim character being manipulated, only Chaucer's own sophisticated voice continuously present in the text: "In perhaps no other poetry ever written has an author established between himself and his audience a bond so immediate, so personal, so amusing, so teasingly full of nuance, so deceptively transparent, so delicately elusive—in a word, so highly civilized" (30). Noble words, and all true, but they do not acknowledge the fact that there *is* an "I" character who comes to us from the past-tense fiction even while he speaks to us in the present tense.

This is an indisputable point, but it is also one we must not apply wholesale. When we construct the character of the pilgrim Chaucer, we risk overstabilizing the volatility and irregularity of the full ironic effects available in the text. Lawton is surely right in characterizing the *General Prologue* as having a "generous and unpredictable tonal range" (100). Not only are its tones variable; its types of irony are variable, even within a single portrait, often leading to multiple or indeterminate perspectives. I don't dispute that there is an "I" character from the past who speaks to us in the present tense, but it is also true that we don't hear the pilgrim at every moment in the text. For instance, the first eighteen lines are in the poet's own voice, or the voice of poetry. We need a conceptual model that will more fully account for the fluidity and instability of "the play of voices" that Gellrich hears within the text (234). Once Chaucer tells us that he is a character in his own fiction, readers often accept his claim at face value and then attribute all the observations in the text to that character's eye and mind. We may, if we like, imagine this character as continually present throughout the poem—most modern critics seem to have done so—even though "I" or "me" statements are only intermittent throughout more than six hundred lines of portraiture.[5] The illusion is further maintained by most sentences in the text being past-tense report, sometimes without discernible irony or false naïveté. However, when critics go on to treat lines 30–32,

> And shortly, whan the sonne was to reste,
> So hadde I spoken with hem everichon
> That I was of hir felaweship anon,

as if it were "realistic" representation, they extend the fictional premise into imaginative territory uncontrolled by the text. Critics then imagine that the

---

[5]The pilgrim character is cued seventeen times throughout the anatomizing descriptions of the *General Prologue*, often only in brief phrases such as "as I gesse" (117), "for aught I woot" (389), "of which I telle" (619). He is always available to the poet on demand, and Chaucer clearly wants to invoke him periodically (on average once every thirty lines or so) to keep alive our sense that there was, in some indefinite recent past, an observable and describable company of pilgrims at the Tabard. However, this past is only a pretext, a relatively undeveloped reference point, and not a credible resource for what the poet puts forth about each portrait. That one night in the Tabard broadens out into an indefinitely large area from which Chaucer can appear to draw anything he wants to say about any of his characters. They were never really "there" in the past fiction. Nor is Lawton's "rumour" in fact how the poet, or even the pilgrim character, knows about each character in the portrait gallery. Chaucer knows them from his prior reading, as he individualizes estates satire types, softening and ambiguating them, as Jill Mann has shown in her invaluable *Chaucer and Medieval Estates Satire* (Cambridge: Cambridge University Press, 1973).

pilgrim Chaucer somehow had to gather up all the information "reported" in the portraits. Lawton, for instance, asserts that his information must have come to him from "rumour" (100). Once this process of extrapolation is under way in a reader's mind independently of the text, there is no check upon it and it can lead to wild critical excesses.[6] Even so, this freehanded constructional process encounters no interpretive difficulties until critics see an irony. At that point, if they wish to explain how the irony works, they either echo Donaldson and say that the fallible first-person narrator does not understand the full import of what he says, or else they manipulate the slippery terms "speaker" and "voice"—with increasing sophistication as the decades pass, but with no confident resolution of the question of how the persona and Chaucer's irony are related.

This question has remained unresolved because of our persistent disregard for what Lawton has insightfully identified as the elastic function of the "narrator" as a rhetorical device in the poem. "He" is not always present in the text, and indeed is a far less consistent presence than Donaldson claimed. For instance, we do not need to posit the pilgrim character as a narrator to hear the potential for irony concerning the Doctor of Physic in "His studie was but litel on the Bible" (438), even though it may be difficult to decide what the irony is.[7] In the Prioress's portrait, if we are to see the irony of "And al was conscience and tendre herte" (150), especially the irony of "al," we cannot, in fact, posit a naïve speaker.[8] At those points when we think we do hear a narrator, it is really only a *pose* that the reader constructs from the text, and that pose goes in and out of the reader's mind as the text varies. Marshall Leicester saw this very clearly, except that he reified the text as "the speaker of the poem," as itself the impersonator who assumes this pose. In point of fact, it is *the reader* who voices the text and tries out its various poses. How else to explain the sharp difference between Donaldson's and Bronson's reading of the same text? They were doing two different voicings or, in Leicester's terms, two different impersonations.

We also assume that the poet's ironies are generated through his pilgrim persona because we try to read the portraits as if they arise from his presumed narrative experience. In fact many of the ironies in the *General Prologue* do not depend upon narration at all. There is a frame-narrative before and after the portraits, to be sure, and occasionally there are implied narratives within individual portraits, but mainly the portraits are static, describing typical traits and behavior. From line 42, "And at a knyght than wol I first bigynne," until lines 720–21, "But now is tyme to yow for to telle / How that we baren us that ilke nyght," the genre of the poem is *anatomy*, not narration. Then from line

---

[6] For a discussion of the unlimited "inferential capacity" of the audience of any narrative act, see Seymour Chatman, "Towards a Theory of Narrative," *New Literary History* 6 (1975): 303–5.

[7] Interpretations of this line have varied greatly, with no final consensus. For a digest of commentary, see Malcolm Andrew, *A Variorum Edition of the Works of Geoffrey Chaucer*, Vol II, *The Canterbury Tales, The General Prologue*, Part One B, *Explanatory Notes* (Norman and London: University of Oklahoma Press, 1993), 388–90.

[8] It is worth noting that Donaldson does not discuss this line in his account of the Prioress. See Schoeck and Taylor, 8.

720 onward there is a series of new maneuvers: the vigorous reinstatement of the frame-narrative; the introduction of the storytelling contest; the re-presentation of "Chaucer" as now both the present-time narrator and also the pilgrim character; and, not least, his teasing ironical claim in lines 725–46 that he must tell the truth about his own fiction, be it "never so rudeliche and large." These framing features have combined to lead the majority of critics to treat the portrait descriptions as narration by the pilgrim character. We tend to do this even when the lines clearly do *not* cue a naïve speaker, as in the sharply witty line about the Summoner, "And also war hym of a *Significavit*" (662). To explain the ironies in the portraits, then, critics have continued to read the narrative framework back into the portraits, using whatever conceptions of narration and voice they may espouse.

To get out of this difficulty, let us turn to a more fundamental explanation of how irony works, one that has been available to criticism for over thirty years, formulated by the Australian critic Douglas C. Muecke. His model, followed by Wayne Booth in *The Rhetoric of Irony* (1974), sees ironic meanings as generated and circulated through a communication system that has only two basic parts, the text and the reader.[9] If we apply this explanation to the open-endedness of Chaucer's text, his habit of laying before us a do-it-yourself kit for assembling meanings, we will see that the ironies of the *General Prologue* portraits do not arise initially or essentially from the poet's manipulation of the pilgrim persona, although he often uses the persona to complicate his ironic effects.

We are concerned here only with the verbal irony we see in the text, which Muecke calls Instrumental Irony (because it operates through the instrumentality of words). However, as both Muecke and Booth argue, the same basic definition holds true for any kind of irony: someone must observe a discrepancy between appearance and reality.[10] The discrepancy will be observed not as a simple unlikeness but as "a contrast (or an opposition, contradiction, contrariety, incongruity or incompatibility)."[11] This explanatory model puts the burden

---

[9]Douglas C. Muecke produced his initial taxonomy of irony in *The Compass of Irony* (London: Methuen, 1969), which was soon followed in 1974 by Wayne C. Booth's equally hefty *A Rhetoric of Irony* (n. 2 above) in which Muecke's influence is generously acknowledged. Booth wrote at the time that Muecke "has done about all that we can expect to see done" in sorting out different kinds of irony and that "his help is evident everywhere" in Booth's own book (xiii). However, because of Booth's "exclusive rhetorical focus," which has close affinities with his earlier and better known *The Rhetoric of Fiction* (Chicago: University of Chicago Press, 1961), the two books on irony are finally very different. In 1970 Muecke also produced *Irony*, a précis of his thinking about the subject for the Methuen Critical Idiom series. He went on thinking about irony and in 1982 produced a second edition with a changed title, *Irony and the Ironic* (n. 2 above), to indicate that it was "less a revision of my earlier work ... than a complete rewriting" (Preface, n.p.) In the present essay I rely on this last book because it is the most satisfactory analysis of the operation of different types of irony that I have yet found. It contains an annotated bibliography of major critical and theoretical works on irony. For medieval theories of irony, see Donald A. Monson, "Andreas Capellanus and the Problem of Irony," *Speculum* 63 (1988): 539–72.

[10]Some ironies do not depend on words, only on events: She was killed by her airbag. The lifeguard drowned. The mugger was robbed. This large class of ironies has been labeled the Irony of Events, or Objective Irony, or, better yet, Observable Irony.

[11]Muecke, 35.

of creating irony squarely upon the reader, which is where it belongs. Verbal irony states a literal meaning to which *we* apply a discrepant understanding. It does not necessarily come into being from the author's intention. The actual headlines "Cow Injures Farmer With Axe" and "Plane Too Close to Ground, Crash Probe Told" were not intended to be ironic.[12] They only become so when their words are understood discrepantly by readers. Usually, and especially in literature, verbal irony has two further basic features, an ironist and an ironic pretense. "And I seyde his opinion was good" (183): the ironist said then, and appears to aver now, that the Monk's opinion was good, but in fact he means something else. Readers understand this almost immediately, whether or not they imagine their understanding to proceed from a naïve pilgrim or a sophisticated poet. The ironist *means* them to see through his pretense.

Muecke explains: "Until an ironic message is interpreted as intended it has only the sound of one hand clapping.... The ironist ... proffers a text but in such a way or in such a context as will stimulate the reader to reject its expressed literal meaning in favour of an unexpressed 'transliteral' meaning of contrasting import. This may sometimes be fully expressible; 'What a nice clean face!', for example, offers no serious challenge. But generally ... the transliteral meaning is better thought of as a 'latent semantic sphere' ... 'The act of reconstruction ... cannot really be *said*, it must be *performed*.' ... The game is played out when there is, to use Aristotle's terms, not only a peripeteia or reversal in the reader's understanding but also an 'anagnorisis' or recognition of the ironist and his real intent behind the pretense.... The ironist conveys his real [i.e., transliteral] message to his audience only in the sense that he provides them with the means for arriving at it" (39, 40–41).

Muecke regards the complicated process by which ironies are generated and interpreted as a "dramatic structure." This metaphor underscores the fact that we must *hear* verbal ironies before we can grasp them cognitively, but the "dramatic" metaphor works best when there is an actual ironic speaker and a live listener, or else when they are contemporaries. We need to make two changes to Muecke's model to account for the historical distance between Chaucer's text and the reader. I therefore would add two features to his explanation. First, let us locate "the ironist" as a construction entirely in our own minds, generated by our interpretations of the literal text. It exists only as a text, after all, without clarifying gestures or facial expressions, even though many critics like to imagine the historical Chaucer performing his poetry orally with such signals. Necessarily, modern readers must also construct "the real intent," or transliteral meaning, from the text alone. We do so as we "perform" the text, mentally or orally, while imagining we are hearing an ironist. This complicated transaction of Muecke's "dramatic structure" takes place entirely in our own minds.

My second change to Muecke's model concerns our assumption that the ironist is playing with the received expectations and values of his medieval audience. What *are* those, precisely? We think we know, but we cannot be absolutely sure. This text is six hundred years old, and culture changes over the

---

[12] Cited from http://lims.mech.nwu.edu/ brokow/humor/headlines.html

centuries. We need to acknowledge frankly that "the historical author's socio-cultural context" *also* exists only as an imagined construct inside each reader's mind. Of necessity, this construct varies as readers' knowledge of fourteenth-century England and their preferences for different historical perspectives vary. To assign a specific degree of fault to a fourteenth-century monk who is "out of his cloystre," readers first must decide what the historical reality of an un-cloistered monk meant to Chaucer and his contemporaries. Only then can they assess the precise degree of ironic discrepancy between that reality and the bland appearance of the literal text. However, different modern scholars have constructed significantly different fourteenth-century historical realities, as the notes to the Variorum amply demonstrate.[13] Thus we need to accept that one's own version of "the socio-cultural context of 1300–1400" is part of each reader's mental furniture, and varies from reader to reader as each constructs the ironic meanings of the text. Some versions are, of course, more complete and satisfying than others, but the critical community cannot prevent inaccurate or tenden-tious historical contexts from being applied to the Monk's portrait. Indeed, it is hard to reach a consensus even about the most likely contexts, and, for the Prioress, it is well nigh impossible.[14]

Not only do the historical contexts in which we set the text vary with each reader's knowledge and judgment: the text itself offers many different ways for readers to construct its verbal ironies. It requires considerable readerly agility to follow the sudden shifts of tone and viewpoint within the *General Prologue* portraits, which may explain why some readers prefer to view them only through the lens of the fictional pilgrim Chaucer. That naïve pose, however, is only one way we are invited to interact with the text. Muecke's model of complex verbal irony includes two traditional roles: the *eiron*, after the clever dissembler of Greek comedy who exercises conscious ironic pretense; and his counterpart, the *alazon*, the confident boaster who is unaware that he is the butt of irony. The *alazon* need not be just the swaggering braggart of Greek comedy; the ever-dull Mr. Collins in *Pride and Prejudice* delightfully illustrates how widely the state of *alazony* varies in its species of unawareness. In practice, the ironist can play the *alazon* as he pretends unawareness and apparent sincerity. Or he can play the falsely self-deprecating trickster, the *eiron*. Can he, perhaps, on occasion play both roles at once? Could this be the case with "And I seyde his opinion was good" (183)? I would answer with a resounding Yes.[15]

We can hear the speaker of line 183 as an unknowing *alazon* whom we know better than—i.e., the pilgrim character—or as a bland and transparently decep-tive *eiron* sharing his knowingness with us. In fact I would argue that we hear

---

[13] See Andrew, *Variorum*, 176–82 for an overview, and 182–217 for widely varying readings of different details.

[14] See Andrew, *Variorum*, 117–70.

[15] In "On The Communication of Verbal Irony," *Journal of Literary Semantics* 2 (1973): 36, Muecke muses on the difficulty of distinguishing author from persona in the description of the Manciple in lines 573–75 of the *General Prologue*, and concludes by saying "This sort of difficulty, I am happy to say, ... falls outside the scope of this paper." It is the direct focus of the present article, however; I hope a more chameleon conception of Chaucer's ironic performance may resolve the difficulty.

them both, one after another, in a lightning instant. Either role, interestingly enough, *must* posit an imperceptive audience who won't "get" the transliteral message. There is no joke, no satisfaction, for readers who are the perceptive audience unless the literal text has posited an imaginary audience who agrees that to "studie" will indeed "make himselven wood." We need something to see through, something which fools accept. We are free to think that it is the fictional past-tense Chaucer who doesn't see the fault in what he approves so enthusiastically, and we should seize the opportunity do so, because such imagined obtuseness adds to the comical effect.

Both Muecke and Booth single out this passage from the Monk's portrait as a defining example of Stable Irony. Muecke cites lines 183–87 as "probably the best known instance of ironic agreement in English literature" and an example of "high-relief" verbal irony (56). Booth cites lines 177–83 as a prime example of "Stable-Covert-Local" irony, aligning them with Jane Austen's famous opening sentence, "It is a truth universally acknowledged, that a single man in possession of a good fortune, must be in want of a wife" (235). Both critics claim that line 183 creates a stable reversal of meaning. This claim is true to some extent, but it, too, needs considerable modification. First, because of the historical distance, we are not sure exactly how far to reverse the meaning: is this a "hard" or "soft" ironic jibe at the Monk? Secondly, the intrusion of the pilgrim *alazon* complicates our reading. Ordinarily, such a mock-pose mimicking the Monk's opinion would encourage readers to discount the *alazon* position entirely, but, because the *alazon* has been posited as a fictional character reporting on a past encounter, the total effect is more than simple reversal. We see a sharp irony in the Monk's disdain for labor and learning even as we laugh indulgently at the silly pilgrim's indignant concurrence with that disdain. During the time that we entertain the premise that the naïvely admiring pilgrim is speaking lines 183 and following, we credit him as a character as well as a mimicker of the Monk. This duality leads to yet further possibilities. Incautious readers may even share some of his enthusiasm for shaking off Saint Augustine's commands. More speculative readers, lingering on the sense of the passage alone, may see an enduring quandary beneath the question "How shal the world be served?" (187), which begins to float free of its immediate monastic context.

Thus the full effect of Chaucer's ironic agreement with the Monk in line 183 is multiple, a complex instance of what Muecke sees as one possible outcome of Instrumental Irony: our perception of "a double contradictory reality" in which we take in *both* the literal meaning and the transliteral meaning. Even though we "see through" the literal meaning, it is still there as a statement, not entirely reversed or negated, and it thus contributes to "that curious special feeling of paradox, of the ambivalent and the ambiguous" that distinguishes irony from sarcasm.[16] To quote Judith Anderson about this moment in the *General Prologue*, "the irreducible doubleness of the passage [183–89] implies

---

[16] Muecke, 45–46, who approvingly quotes Allen Rodman's photographic metaphor for irony: it is not so much "seeing a 'true' meaning beneath a 'false,'" but of seeing a double exposure . . . on one plate."

criticism of the Monk but also denies it." The degree of mockery and the degree of approval are "left utterly and deftly unclear."[17]

We can see this doubleness or, better said, this opacity of judgment, throughout the Monk's portrait. Its sequence of different kinds of ironic discrepancies leads us to a variety of possible judgements which play against each other. When we take them all together and stand back a bit, we can confidently identify the portrait as basically satiric, but when we read it more closely and allow Chaucer's different strokes of irony to jostle each other, the exact nature and degree of criticism expected from us seems indeterminate, and throws us back on our own subjective perceptions (and on our own subjective notions of the portrait's historical context). We are left, as Virgina Woolf said of Chaucer more largely, "to stray and stare and make out a meaning for ourselves."[18]

Even the opening three lines, which are usually treated as a stable irony turning on the incongruous association of "manliness and spiritual responsibility," to quote Derek Pearsall, lead us into complexities:

> A MONK ther was, a fair for the maistrie,
> An outridere, that lovede venerie,
> A manly man, to been an abbot able.   (165–67)

Pearsall, following Booth, again associates Chaucer's irony in line 167 with Jane Austen's famous sentence by claiming that both rest "on a community of shared values."[19] This concept is a shibboleth of satire criticism that holds true in many cases, but Chaucer's portrait is more than simply satiric. All readers agree that it is, at the very least, incongruous to think that hyper-masculinity qualifies a man to be an abbot. The degree of satire that readers assign to that incongruity may sharpen or soften as the portrait develops, but at this initial moment it remains an unexplored potentiality. The irony is set up by only three short phrases: the Monk is superlatively handsome (165), an outrider who loves hunting, and someone who is "all man"—these are the characteristics that qualify the Monk "to been an abbot able."

We are not sure that a transliteral meaning is intended until the third line comes to us in its entirety: "A manly man, to been an abbot able." Here the irony turns mainly upon the poetic play of sound and meaning. The palpability of the double alliteration keeps the literal meaning a reality even as we instantly see the incongruity of associating "manly man" and "abbot able." The two quick and exact repetitions of "man-" and "ab-" give a jaunty insouciance to the implicit claim that virility is a qualification for abbothood. The structure

---

[17] Judith H. Anderson, "Narrative Reflections: Re-envisaging the Poet in *The Canterbury Tales* and *The Faerie Queene*," in *Refiguring Chaucer in the Renaissance*, ed. Theresa M. Krier (Gainesville: University Press of Florida, 1998), 95.

[18] Virginia Woolf, "The Pastons and Chaucer," *The Common Reader* (New York: Harcourt, Brace, 1925), 32–33. My reading of the different strokes of irony depends heavily on the subtle and comprehensive interpretation of the Monk's portrait by Mann, 17–37.

[19] Derek Pearsall, "Epidemic Irony in Modern Approaches to Chaucer's *Canterbury Tales*," in *Medieval and Pseudo-Medieval Literature: The J. A. W. Bennett Memorial Lectures, Perugia, 1982–83*, ed. Piero Boitani and Anna Torti (Tübingen: Gunter Narr Verlag, 1984), 84.

of the line is so firm that it remains fixed in the reader's eye and ear. No matter how blandly or how tartly a reader voices the line, its two halves clash with such vocal energy that we almost feel that a manly abbot *would* be an able abbot. Almost. At the same time as we see the transliteral meaning overturning the literal sense, the heavy caesura acts as an equals sign in a self-cancelling equation: $X = $ not X. In short, we hear both the literal and transliteral at once.

This poetic play results in a feeling of verbal liberation that is so strong that it doesn't really matter whether we hear the line spoken by an *eiron* or an *alazon*. We are delighted by the line itself, as poetry.[20] And this liberating verbal delight leads to the sensation—so frequent in irony—that there is more to be said. We might, for instance, entertain the fleeting notion, no sooner thought of than dismissed, that perhaps there might be circumstances that would require an abbot to reform unruly monks with a strong and manly hand. We can't know that this would ever be true, but as readers of irony we enjoy *entertaining* contrarieties and possibilities even as we dismiss them.

Another way of saying this is that our construction of Chaucer's irony must remain incomplete, or at least open-ended to some degree. A precise understanding of even just this one single line's complete transliteral meaning lies beyond the reader's grasp. Jill Mann, after reading the Monk's portrait against traditional estates satire, expresses her own quandary thus:

> And what exactly does this line mean? Is the narrator saying that manly authority is desirable for anyone in a position of superiority? Or that the Monk was capable of being an abbot because in these degenerate days worldliness is a better qualification than holiness? Is he even, perhaps, implying only that it is the Monk's own opinion that he is fit to be an abbot, as it is later clearly the Guildsmen's own opinion that they are fit to be aldermen? We find that we cannot pinpoint with exactness the target of Chaucer's satire. Previous tradition raises the expectation that we shall be called on to make a moral judgement on the holder of, or aspirant to monastic office, but we are not, in this case, given enough information to do so.
>
> A similar ambivalence characterizes Chaucer's use of the word "manly" in this line.... while Chaucer makes us aware that the word is susceptible of both favourable and unfavourable interpretations, he gives us no help in deciding which to choose.... It would not be easy to agree in what sense the Monk is "manly" or how far this quality is to be admired in him.[21]

Thus even in the context of its determining literary genre, the line will not settle down. It keeps vibrating with possible meanings.

---

[20] And we hear immediate echoes of these playful features as the next line closes the couplet with a brilliant rhyme: "Ful many a deyntee hors hadde he in stable." The initial iambic stress again falls on "man-" while the Monk's favorite kind of "able" is to be found inside a "stable." See further Charles A. Owen, Jr., "Thy Drasty Rhyming ..." *Studies in Philology* 63 (1966): 557.

[21] Mann, 33, 34, 36.

This is not always the case, however. Occasionally in the *General Prologue* we make definite moral judgments with confidence and authority. There is very little play of mind in the text or in the reader when we encounter the line about the Summoner, "Of his visage children were aferd" (628), especially coming as it does after the most violent and disgusting images of his face. Nonetheless, "Variability carried to the point of contrariety" seems to be Chaucer's guiding artistic principle in the *General Prologue* as a whole. It stands to reason, then, that Chaucer's ironies should also be of different kinds, even within this one portrait. The next ironic stroke depends both on poetic sonorities and on the reader's making a silent comparison. Chaucer is both sly and open-handed in applying the simile of the chapel bell to the sound of the Monk's bridle jingling in the wind. Once we see it, the implication is obvious: he should be *in* the chapel instead of out riding. But there is a lingering emphasis on the sound of the bridle: "Gynglen in a whistlynge wynd als cleere / And eek as loude" ("eek" is a lovely touch because it is so unnecessary). This keeps the focus on auditory sensation with a sort of mock seriousness. Then the full criticism implicit in the simile announces itself with Chaucer's jingling his own rhyme, matching "belle" with "celle." This clear liquid closing-off of the simile keeps the tone balanced between the sensory music of the lines and something else: a sneering laugh up the sleeve? a disbelieving shake of the head? a disappointed sigh of acceptance? The degree of distaste is hard to specify when the simile has such a sweet sound. The important point for my argument is that this opaque irony is created by the interplay of the satiric concept with these poetic effects. It does not require, or even invite, our imagining a pilgrim speaker.

Then Chaucer changes his mode of irony yet again and we hear the Monk's speech filtered through free indirect discourse. The very nature of this mode of discourse allows us to hear 177–82 both as the pilgrim *alazon* reporting what the Monk said in the past and as the slap direct (in slapstick rhyme) of standard estates satire. Initially it creates a droll effect to say, with a straight face, that the Benedictine Rule is something to let pass because it is "old and somdel streit." Next, the irony twists a little more sharply: the Monk is heedless of the text that says that heedless, disobedient monks are like fish out of water. Chaucer then turns the waterless fish back into the monk in an aside ("This is to seyn, a monk out of his cloystre," line 181) that makes this simile much more overt than the bridle-and-bell simile. After he has thrust in his own comical rhyme-word "cloystre" (what on earth could rhyme with that?), he finds an equitone in which to close the couplet: "But thilke text heeld he nat worth an oystre." By "equitone" I mean that it is almost impossible to tell whether Chaucer wishes us to imagine the Monk having said it, or whether he is interrupting his own mimicry of the Monk's opinions in order to explode them by the comic rhyme. This alternation between mimicry and the boldly silly rhyming is, again, an instance where the ironic effects do not rely on our positing a pilgrim character, although we will want to hear some degree of pretense in order to appreciate the full humor of the passage.

These different kinds of ironic strokes create a prior context, variable in its viewpoint and containing as much verbal fun as implied criticism, for the introduction of the famous *antiphrasis* of line 183: "And I seyde his opinioun was good. / What sholde he studie and make hymselven wood," and so on. Even more hilarious than the idea that studying will drive a manly man crazy is Chaucer's tone of either bland or mock-earnest agreement with the Monk's opinion. The falsity of Chaucer's approval is so apparent that both Donaldson and Lawton felt it necessary to hear two voices in this passage. However, I think it makes more sense simply to hear a single voice of asseveration, in head-bobbing and overly serious agreement, that engages both the *eiron* and the *alazon* roles at once. By the very firmness of this tone of agreement, we know that the writer thinks something like the opposite, but not necessarily the direct opposite. Does he himself value holy texts more than all the oysters in Lent? The indefinite distance between what is said and what is not said does not allow us to answer that question. We may locate the Monk's opinion wherever we like in the gray area between the apparent literal approval and the disapproval that remains unspoken. Mockery by false agreement does not specify the degree of disagreement, and, unless continued with consistency, it does not permanently establish a stable naïve observer.

After this falsely approving line, Chaucer throws his voice into a cascade of comic questions and exclamations. Now the *alazon* approves of the Monk's opinions even more hotly, and asserts them as though they were his own. While this should be seen, delightfully, as the pilgrim character's own agreement with the Monk's words, it also silently mocks, even more sharply, the Monk's self-justifying attempts to dismiss St. Augustine's advice. This is one of the moments in the text where Donaldson's account of Chaucer's *alazon* works best. But then there is an even sharper jab in the next causative adverb: "*Therfore* he was a prikasour aright" (189). Some readers will plausibly imagine that the pilgrim speaker has now been persuaded, as if by logic, that the Monk's hunting is justified, but "Therfore" is such a *non sequitur* that I am inclined to hear it said by a blandly scornful *eiron* who has already taken the measure of the Monk's delinquency.

The pose of the pilgrim as only an observer has faded in and out of the portrait thus far, and will do so again toward the end of the portrait, but at this point the "realistic" observations are quite deadpan, and they alternate with *eironic* generalizations both subtle and broad. "Of prikyng and of huntyng for the hare / Was al his lust" (191–92) has potential sexual connotations if we recall the *double-entendre* of "venerie" (166), meaning both "hunting" and "amorous pursuit,"[22] or line 11, "So pricketh hem nature in hir corages." The ironic nuances of "prikyng" and "lust" are decidedly not the product of naïve observation, and clearly "for no cost wolde he spare" (192) is a broad satiric stroke. However, the next details of the portrait are direct ocular report:

> I seigh his sleves purfiled at the hond
> With grys, and that the fyneste of a lond;
> And for to festne his hood under his chyn,

---

[22]See Andrew, *Variorum*, 185, for further discussion.

> He hadde of gold ywroght a ful curious pyn;
> A love-knotte in the gretter ende ther was.   (193–97)

We may presume that the expensive gray squirrel fur edging of his sleeves is an excess, but we cannot be sure whether it is usual and expected (along the lines of "Monsignor's Cadillac") or whether it should be seen as directly flaunting an earlier papal prohibition,[23] an example of the Monk's holding "after the newe world the space." On the other hand, once we see the similarity between his "love-knotte" and the Prioress's "brooch of gold ful shene" with its ambiguous Latin legend, the two objects do more than speak for themselves: we understand that Chaucer as the silent ironist—indeed as the composer of the entire *General Prologue*—is not only suggesting another aspect of the Monk's "lust" but also is inviting us to make an open-ended comparison between the unspiritual desires of the two cloistered ecclesiastics. Of course, the Monk's ornament is only a hood-pin, and sometimes a cigar is only a cigar. Yet the text stimulates the reader's mind to play actively and ironically with the possible meanings of such a comparison. This play of mind arrives at no clear or necessary resolution, but we do feel that we know something more about the proclivities of this handsome hunter of a Monk.

Were we as naïve as Donaldson would make the observing eye, we might almost feel we know the Monk as an individual whom the pilgrim reporter has recreated for us. However, the deadpan ocular report now warps into broad exaggeration:

> His heed was balled, that shoon as any glas,
> And eek his face, as he hadde been enoynt.
> He was a lord ful fat and in good poynt;
> His eyen stepe, and rollynge in his heed,
> That stemed as a forneys of a leed.   (198–202)

We immediately assign metaphorical value to these clever pseudo-realistic details. His bald head and oily face appear to be more basted than anointed, leading the reader to reflect on the discrepancy between the two similar actions. "In good poynt" literally means "in good condition," but following "ful fat" it also connotes "well-nourished,"[24] and the comic rhyme of "enoynt"/"poynt" sonically increases the Monk's girth. "Stepe" eyes are either "bright" or "prominent," and, in a fat man, might even seem to bulge. Their rolling in his head, a comical image in itself, may connote a roving eye. That his eyes "gleamed like a furnace under a cauldron" (F. N. Robinson's generally accepted gloss) leads to Jill Mann's happy perception that it is "as if kitchen terms spontaneously came to mind when Chaucer thought of him."[25] The firm rhyme of "heed"/"leed"

---

[23] Andrew, *Variorum*, 208.

[24] Chaucer's phrase appears to derive from Fr. *en bon point* 'in a good state,' 'in a state of well being,' a phrase attested by a 1377 citation in Oscar Bloch and W. von Wartburg, *Dictionnaire étymologique de la language française* (Paris: Presses Universitaires de France, 1950), 471. I owe this reference and English translation to Paul V. Rockwell, French Department, Amherst College. Various other interpretations about the nature of the Monk's "good state" have been advanced: see Andrew, *Variorum*, 211.

[25] Andrew, *Variorum*, 212–13; Mann, 20.

clinches this effect, and allows us to associate the lead cauldron with the earlier comparisons of "pulled hen" (177) and "oystre" (182) and the deluxe delicacy of "a fat swan" (206), which the "ful fat" Monk comes to resemble by adjectival association.

Then, from these metaphoric associations, more hinted at than stated, the text turns back to uninflected ocular report: "His bootes souple, his hors in greet estaat" (203). The suppleness of his boots occasions nearly an entire page of commentary in the Variorum without reaching any conclusion about an intended ironic meaning. The tonal muteness of this detail contributes to our sense that the Monk is really "there"[26] while at the same time deliberately interrupting the build-up of metaphorical descriptions. One would certainly hope that the horse of an enthusiastic hunter would be "in greet estaat," ("in excellent condition," according to Riverside 3) and this detail, too, might be taken as an un-ironic observation, were it not for its similarity to the phrase "in good poynt"; if there is an ironic nuance here, it may be that a horse whose "estaat" is "greet" is of higher rank than the sort a monk should ride.

But the main poetic utility of "in greet estaat" is to set up the lovely ironic rhyme: "Now certeinly he was a fair prelaat" (204). With this couplet-closing line, the text modulates into an equitone in the voice of the *eiron*, both firm and indefinite in asserting its satiric intention. The knowing and savoring words "Now certeinly" are a momentary present-tense address to the audience of the poem. This posture creates a warm, almost affectionate, tonal envelope for "fair prelaat." The phrase repeats the very first adjective of the portrait, where "fair" meant "handsome," but, after the many intervening details and attitudes, the word has gained a new twist. Now he is "a fair prelaat" in that he is as fat, and perhaps as edible or at least as readily basted as the "fat swan" he loved "best of any roost." The degree and type of judgment that we make about this line remain indeterminate. He certainly is some picture of a prelaat—he is as tangible as lard—and yet that is somehow laudable; at the very least, we are grateful for the comic grossness of his corporeality. At the same time, most readers sense that to some unstated degree "fair" is meant as scorn, and some would say as equivocal scorn. Perhaps he is a verray parfit picture of a Monk, as monks go these days. Isn't a "prelaat" supposed to be of "greet estaat"? (Does "greet" also suggest "fat"?)

We may entertain such questions without resolution but we are also encouraged to answer them satirically and confidently by the rhythm of this and the following couplet, and by the latter's open swipe at the Monk's unspirituality:

> His bootes souple, his hors in greet estaat.
> Now certeinly he was a fair prelaat;
> He was nat pale as a forpyned goost.
> A fat swan loved he best of any roost. (203–6)

The "goost"/"roost" rhyme pushes the spirit and flesh together with such clanging incongruity that we can only think of how far apart they have become as

---

[26]The gratuitousness of the detail also contributes to this sense, as Mann, 198, points out, citing Rosemary Woolf (n. 3 above).

the portrait has developed. The rhythm of the end-stopped couplets, each line a sentence complete in itself, implies that each assertion is of equal weight, which is itself a comical idea that is further punctuated by the two rhymes. But then the portrait ends with "His palfrey was as broun as is a berye" (207), the first line of a couplet that is closed by the opening line of the Friar's portrait. The incomplete, hanging quality of the last line about the Monk matches Chaucer's deployment of open-ended and indeterminate details elsewhere in the portrait. As usual when he ends a *General Prologue* portrait with a hanging line, it seems an apparently casual and unjudging observation that emphasizes the portrait's status as observed past reality.[27] Here it validates as true observations the sweaty, fattened images of the previous ten lines. At the same time, the matter-of-fact tone in which the final five lines are said makes the Monk not only more palpable, but also less the butt of mocking tonal play as in "Lat Austyn have his swynk to hym reserved!"

What is most impressive about Chaucer's art in this portrait is the ease and deftness of his sudden shifts of tone and ironic mode, his *modulations*. How delightful it is when "And I seyde his opinion was good" surges forth unexpectedly from its context! The portrait is a richly varied sequence of ironic invitations to make satiric judgments, yet the ironic meanings of the text remain, as I think Chaucer intended, in the hands of (or better said, in the mental voicings performed by) his readers. It is worth re-emphasizing that our constructions of his irony are subjective and, to a noticeable extent, uncontrollable, even when we perceive limiting contexts. To measure any given stroke of irony within the portrait, for instance, a reader can choose to set it in various contexts made up of other lines in the portrait. Beyond that, there is the context of all the other *General Prologue* portraits, into which we may set the picture of the Monk in whatever way we will. While I believe that what holds true for the Monk's portrait—disparate details, conveyed by disparate strokes of irony, jostling against each other as they create mutual (and sometimes contradictory) contexts for each other—also holds true for the *General Prologue* as a whole, it would take an entire book to demonstrate this thesis convincingly. In the present article, by delineating the major strategies of the Monk's portrait, I hope to have proven two narrower but important points: that we can account for all the different kinds of irony in the Monk's portrait by using only the text-reader model of Muecke and Booth, and that we should regard the reader's construction of the "naïve pilgrim" pose as only one strategic maneuver among many.

---

[27] As with the Yeoman (117–18), Friar (269–70), and Plowman (341–42). But this is not true for the hanging couplet that closes the portrait of the Cook (387–88), because the edibility of his "blankmanger" resonates nauseatingly against his "mormel" in the preceding line. For an overview of Chaucer's manipulation of details throughout the *General Prologue*—indeed, of many aspects of his literary art—, see Mann, 187–202.

Chaucer's *Knight's Tale*

Were Arcite and Emelye Really Married?
Why It Matters

Paul R. Thomas

A fact of the history of criticism of Chaucer's *Knight's Tale* for more than the past 50 years is that much of the fuller interpretation of the tale continues to be colored by two seminal essays published in 1949 and 1950 respectively. In this essay, after reviewing William Frost's and Charles Muscatine's opposing views of the three young people at the center of Chaucer's romance, I will extend Muscatine's balanced view of the blood brother cousins, Arcite and Palamon, showing both of them were eventually married to Emelye, embodying therein both spiritual and physical ideals of medieval *fin amor* within marriage in the *Knight's Tale*. A broader reading of Chaucer's works involving *fin amor* will show the *Knight's Tale* as important evidence of the poet's repeated emphasis that the ideals of *fin amor* worked only within an acknowledged and public marriage. To put it another way, *fin amor* was a possibility for the ruling classes and their arranged marriages.

William Frost's "An Interpretation of Chaucer's *Knight's Tale*" was first published in the *Review of English Studies* in 1949. Of the *Knight's Tale* Frost says in his opening section, "But whether classical, realistic, or chivalric, the atmosphere of the Tale has three abiding attributes: it is predominantly noble, predominantly tragic, and deeply infused with a sense of significance transcending both human beings and their material environment." Like Muscatine, Frost believes that Chaucer presents Palamon and Arcite in a "systematic and delicately balanced parallelism. . . ." But Frost sees only Theseus as "the man who unites in his person successes in war and love alike."[1] Arcite only triumphs in war and Palamon only triumphs in love. I will argue below that both Palamon and Arcite are notable—even equivalent—warriors and lovers. In the third section of his essay, Frost sums up his view of why Palamon was essentially more worthy to love Emelye than his cousin Arcite:

---

[1] William Frost, "An Interpretation of Chaucer's *Knight's Tale*," *Review of English Studies* 25 (1949): 289–304. I have used the version of this essay reprinted in *Chaucer Criticism*: The Canterbury Tales, ed. Richard J. Schoeck and Jerome Taylor (Notre Dame: University of Notre Dame Press, 1960), 98–116. The first two quotations are found on page 100 and the third on page 102 of this reprinted version. All further citations of Frost's essay will come from this reprinted version.

We are also presented, in the minds of Palamon and Arcite, with
two views of the same situation, Palamon being the spokesman of the
greater idealism. The contrast comes first in the way each regards
Emelye. In Boccaccio both saw her as Venus; in Chaucer Palamon
alone, in the following metaphor charged with religious overtones,
makes that identification:

> Venus, if it be thy wil
> Yow in this gardyn thus to transfigure,
> Bifore me, sorweful, wrecched creature. . . .   (1104–6)

Arcite emphatically differs, and seeks to use the difference as an
argument for his own priority; he says to Palamon,

> Thyn is affeccioun of hoolynesse,
> And myn is love, as to creature [sic]. . . .   (1158–9)

.... It is a conflict, not between love and love, but between devotion
and desire. (p. 104)

Again, I will show a rather different reading of the text in my argument below.

In 1950 Charles Muscatine's counter-proposal entitled "Form, Texture, and
Meaning in Chaucer's *Knight's Tale*" appeared in *PMLA*.[2] At the end of the
second section of his essay, Muscatine says that the *Knight's Tale* as he reads it
is "of a kind having a much closer affinity to the mediæval tradition of conven-
tionalism than to realism" (p. 68). Earlier he had explained some of the details
of this "conventionialism" in these words:

> The symmetry of scene, action and character-grouping, the slow pace
> of the narrative and large proportion of concrete description, the
> predominantly lyric and philosophic kind of discourse—along with
> a lack of subtle discrimination in the stage business—all indicate
> that the tale is not the best kind in which to look for either delicate
> characterization or the peculiar fascination of an exciting plot.

Muscatine suggested that Chaucer had composed his *Knight's Tale* to show
the characters of Palamon and Arcite to be "symmetrical" and that, therefore,
neither is more worthy of the love of Emelye than the other. In his changes to
Boccaccio's *Teseida*, Chaucer's "crowning modification ... is the equalization
of Palamon and Arcite" (p. 68).

Muscatine's reading of Palamon and Arcite in the *Knight's Tale* as part of
the manifestation of the "symmetrical 'poetic pageant' which reveals the conflict
between the ordered character of the noble life and the forces of chaos"[3] certainly

---

[2] Charles Muscatine, "Form, Texture, and Meaning in Chaucer's *Knight's Tale*," *PMLA* 65
(1950): 911–29, reprinted in *Chaucer: Modern Essays in Criticism*, ed. Edward Wagenknecht
(New York: Oxford University Press, 1959), 60–82. Again, my citations are from the reprinted
version.

[3] The article is summarized in these words by John Leyerle in John Leyerle and Anne
Quick, *Chaucer: A Bibliographical Introduction*, Toronto Medieval Bibliographies 10 (Toronto:
University of Toronto Press, 1986), 136.

fits the evidence of the descriptive passages in the tale. Chaucer determines that there will be little to choose between the two cousins. Here are some of the evidences that we read in the tale, some of which are mentioned by Muscatine and some of which are the sorts of discoveries of longtime readers of the *Knight's Tale*.

The symmetrical presentation of Palamon and Arcite

For those students and readers who are convinced that Palamon is the superior courtly lover of Emelye, clearly a lot of attention—as in Frost's essay—must center on the initial reaction of the blood brothers/cousins when they look at Emelye with their eyes and are smitten with Eros's arrows, more or less simultaneously. This is such a key passage in the *Knight's Tale* to Frost and his followers that I will set it out fully and then interpret it in detail.

Let me briefly set the scene first. Palamon and Arcite have been on the losing Theban side in the fight against the formidable duke of Athens, Theseus. As princes of that impious realm ruled by the willful Creon, who has failed to bury the bodies of his dead enemies, Palamon and Arcite are given the unusual medieval punishment of perpetual imprisonment, rather than the more lucrative ransom (I 983–1024). Years and days pass, and finally one May day Emelye appears in a garden adjoining the chief dungeon where Palamon and Arcite are imprisoned (1033–61). We can see clearly the chance or Fortune that figures in the following scene.

> Bright was the sonne and cleer that morwenynge,
> And Palamoun, this woful prisoner,
> As was his wone, by leve of his gayler,
> Was risen and *romed* in a chambre an heigh,

[See the discussion of the verb *romen* starting three pages below.]

> In which he al the noble citee seigh,
> And eek the gardyn, ful of braunches grene,
> There as this fresshe Emelye the shene
> Was in hire walk, and *romed* up and doun.
> This sorweful prisoner, this Palamoun,
> Goth in the chambre *romynge* to and fro
> And to hymself compleynynge of his wo.
> That he was born, ful ofte he seyde, "allas!"
> *And so bifel, by aventure or cas,*

[We are not meant to think of this initial sighting of Emelye as destiny, just as chance.]

> That thurgh a wyndow, thikke of many a barre
> Of iren greet and square as any sparre,
> He cast his eye upon Emelya,
> And therwithal he bleynte and cride, "A!"
> As though he stongen were unto the herte.

[And here his blood brother steps in to offer comfort.]

And with that cry Arcite anon up sterte
And seyde, "Cosyn myn, what eyleth thee,
That art so pale and deedly on to see?
Why cridestow? Who hath thee doon offence?
For Goddes love, taak al in pacience
Oure prisoun, for it may noon oother be.
Fortune hath yeven us this adversitee.

[Then Arcite speaks words full of tragic irony in relation to his momentary tournament triumph later in the tale.]

Som wikke aspect or disposicioun
Of Saturne, by some constellacioun,
Hath yeven us this, although we hadde it sworn;
So stood the hevene whan that we were born.

[The evidence of the tale is that these sons born of two sisters were born at the same time with the same confluence of heavenly/planetary influences.]

We moste endure it; this is the short and playn."
   This Palamon answerde and seyde agayn,
"Cosyn, for sothe, of this opinioun
Thow hast a veyn ymaginacioun.
This prison caused me nat for to crye,
But I was hurt right now thurghout myn ye
Into myn herte, that wol my bane be.
The fairnesse of that lady that I see
Yond in the gardyn *romen* to and fro
Is cause of al my criyng and my wo.
I noot wher she be womman or goddesse,
But Venus is it soothly, as I gesse."   (1062–1102; emphasis added)

At this point, Palamon, thinking he has seen Venus, falls to his knees and prays to his favored goddess, asking that she will help the two cousins escape from prison rather than die there, and further requesting that she will have some compassion on their lineage brought so low by Theseus's tyranny (1103–11).

   Palamon's prayer provokes Arcite's curiosity to see the beautiful lady/goddess Palamon describes.

And with that word Arcite gan espye
Wher as this lady *romed* to and fro,
And with that sighte hir beautee hurte hym so,
That, if that Palamon was wounded sore,
Arcite is hurt as muche as he, or moore.
And with a sigh he seyde pitously,
"The fresshe beautee sleeth me sodeynly
Of hire that *rometh* in the yonder place;
And but I have hir mercy and hir grace,

That I may seen hire atte leeste weye,
I nam but deed; ther nis namoore to seye."

(1112–22; emphasis added)

Muscatine's idea of symmetry in these two princes is very evident throughout this passage. Just as the two first cousins are described initially in the tale as both being wounded with multiple grievous wounds, being dressed alike with the same heraldic devices on their coats of armor, and lying side by side after the battle's end like two peas in a pod, Chaucer does not strive to differentiate the two here either (see 1009–19 for their initial description). Chaucer purposely delays any differentiating *effictiones* or head-to-toe delineations of the two warriors, though an *effictio* idealizing Emelye in her May garden setting for twenty-one lines (1035–55) closely precedes the disjointed dialogue in which each man is falling in love with Emelye, more or less simultaneously. In a way, each man is speaking distractedly almost in soliloquy as he is falling in love at first sight with Emelye. Admittedly, here these two "soliloquies" are overheard by the blood brother standing by, perhaps proving the paralleling of each man as almost a part of the other—rather like two soliloquies aloud from attached twins—two who are one.

Though Frost makes a major point out of Palamon's ambiguity about knowing whether Emelye is "womman or goddesse" (1101), let it be noted Palamon first sees a "lady" (1098) according to his own words, just as Arcite is described by the narrator as seeing a "lady" (1112–13). The comparison of Palamon's lady to the goddess Venus is only the first of many hyperbolic comparisons of the beauty of their beloved poetically imagined by these courtly lovers—a part of the lyrical side of *fin amor* revealed in this romance. How can we take seriously Palamon's anger that his blood brother will not support him in his love affair that has a precedence of only a few seconds any more than we should regard Arcite's superior claim as the first lover in that he always knew that Emelye was a woman, whereas Palamon loved her as a goddess mistakenly?

The central dilemma that both fell in love with the same woman at the same time suddenly casts doubt on all the previous relationships between the two cousins/blood brothers. From that moment of complication, the rest of their contending is spurious legalese. Following Palamon's reasoning that as a blood brother, Arcite must help Palamon in his love affair, surely it must also follow that Palamon as blood brother must help Arcite succeed in his love affair. This is a logical impossibility based on the "trouthe" of blood brothers and cousins (see 1129–51 and 1153–71). A far better response for us as readers to pursue at this moment of conflict is to ask why Chaucer has allowed/forced both of the "twins" to fall in love with the same woman at the same time. What is the point of these two princes falling in love with the same princess instantly? How can such a dilemma be resolved? Analogous to this query is the ending of Part I of the tale with the famous court of love *demande d'amour* or question of love asking us as the lovers/members/jury of that *fin amor* court which of the lovers has the worse fate: Palamon, who can see Emelye daily but is perpetually imprisoned, or Arcite, who may walk or ride as a knight where he will outside

Athens but is banished on pain of death from returning to Athens where his lady lives (1347–54). A shorter version of this *demande d'amour* might be, which of these lovers is truly freer? Similarly, a shorter model for the earlier dilemma might be, which of these two princes of equal rank, born at the same time into the homes of sisters has the greater claim for the love of Emelye? Unlike Frost, who sides with Palamon for seeing Emelye as a goddess, many readers may see equal claim in both young men, accepting this *demande d'amour* for the impossibility it seems under these circumstances imposed by Theseus. Both blood brothers must, of necessity, part and be false to the other if, as Arcite suggests, "Love is a gretter lawe, by my pan, / Than may be yeve to any erthely man" (1165–66).

A further interesting parallelism, as Frost would call it, in the language of both of these knights and the narrator throughout these symmetrical passages where the two cousins fall in love with Emelye is the frequent use of *romen*, the noble verb for walking. Chaucer (or Chaucer's Knight, if you prefer) describes Palamon's daily routine of having "risen and *romed* in a chambre an heigh" (1065), and Emelye too has "*romed* up and doun" (1069; here and in all occurrences above and below, the emphasis is added). Clearly this verb has different connotations in the broad garden of Emelye versus the narrow chamber in the tower—perhaps with typical Chaucerian ironic effect. In refuting Arcite's well-meant consolation for him, Palamon says,

> The fairnesse of that lady that I see
> Yond in the gardyn *romen* to and fro
> Is cause of al my criyng and my wo.   (1098-1100)

The parallelism and symmetry is completed when Arcite says, "The fresshe beautee sleeth me sodeynly / Of hire that *rometh* in the yonder place" (1118–19).

Chaucer uses this gentle verb in other tales of nobles such as the *Merchant's Tale*, when January wants to cavort with May in his enclosed garden, and says to her, "Now kys me, wyf, and lat us *rome* aboute" (IV 2184). Here this unexpected verb takes on fabliau-like connotations. Perhaps even more amusingly the same gentle verb for wandering lovers is used in that other enclosed garden better known as a chicken-yard in the mock-heroic *Nun's Priest's Tale*, just after Chauntecleer has defied his dream in order to make love to Pertelote:

> And with that word he fley doun fro the beem,
> For it was day, and eke his hennes alle,
> And with a chuk he gan hem for to calle,
> For he hadde founde a corn, lay in the yerd.
> Real he was, he was namoore aferd.
> He fethered Pertelote twenty tyme,
> And trad hire eke as ofte, er it was pryme.
> He looketh as it were a grym leoun,
> And on his toos he *rometh* up and doun;
> Hym deigned nat to sette his foot to grounde.   (VII 3172–81)

Of course, chickens do roam that way quite naturally and amusingly, while it appears that the noble Palamon, Arcite, and Emelye always pursue their gentle walks with the verb *romen*.

Perhaps one issue raised in the parallel falling-in-love-at-first-sight descriptions of Palamon and Arcite may tend to undercut for some readers the equality of the degree of the love of the two knights. This idea stems from Arcite's argument describing how he truly fell in love with Emelye first: "Thyn is affeccioun of hoolynesse, / And myn is love as to a creature" (1158–59). First of all, we must remember that this is a spontaneous argument between the blood brothers, fueled by their mutual love of Emelye and their attendant irrational jealousy— one of the faults of these two resolved by the end of the story.[4] If on the other hand, we are to take all the words of these two lovers quite seriously—a view I do not agree with—it is at least true that these words of Arcite will bear the fruit of tragic irony at the end of his life. Whereas he has won the right to marry Emelye first by winning the battle, it turns out that his shortlived marriage is truly Platonic love or "affeccioun of hoolynesse." This sort of verbal irony is another way Chaucer balances the love of these two princes for Emelye.

After Emelye and the Greeks complete the extended mourning rites for Arcite lasting "certeyn yeres" (2967), Theseus arranges to "maken vertu of necessitee" (3042) and marry Palamon to Emelye, securing the alliance of the royal house of Thebes with the royal house of Athens and negotiating permanent peace between the two cities by gaining "fully of Thebans obeisaunce" (2970–74). By this marriage, Palamon will in fact achieve the "love as to a creature" that Arcite earlier claimed. In other words, both princes loved Emelye as a goddess in a Platonic sense, and both have felt the strokes of loving her as a creature: for Arcite notably through his two years' experience of the lover's malady of Hereos and mania and for Palamon in his protracted courtship of an indeterminate number of years after Arcite's death.[5] Rather than trusting the hot-headed argument of the jealous young lovers shortly after the arrows of blind Cupid have hit them each in the eye, I would trust the words of the even-handed narrator of the *Knight's Tale*, who clearly says that Cupid has wounded them more or less equally (see 1115–16).

There is also a hint of further equality between the two cousins in the consoling words of Arcite after he hears Palamon cry "A!" The clear implication of Arcite's consolation is that these two cousins were born the same day and time and are subject to the same heavenly, planetary influences, especially of Saturn,

---

[4]See Arcite's final speech at 2783–97 when he re-establishes his *amitie* with Palamon that had been broken by his love for Emelye and his jealousy for Palamon's love of her. Further, to show he has conquered jealousy, despite his mortal injury, he urges his wife Emelye to marry Palamon if ever she has the desire to marry again. See also the narrator's comments at story's end in 3101–6 where the married Palamon and Emelye are in love without signs of jealousy.

[5]See the beginning of Part Two of the tale at 1361–1413 for Arcite's love sickness and the command by Mercury that he should return to Athens where "is thee shapen of thy wo an ende"—an enigmatic prophecy with a double meaning, as the tale develops (1391–92). See also 2967–3093 for Palamon's patient progress in his love for Emelye the woman—along with Theseus's counsel and the advice of his parliament in overcoming Emelye's maidenly reluctance to marry.

because "So stood the hevene *whan that we were born*" (1086–90; emphasis
added). This heavenly patterning would be far more important to Chaucer's
audience than it is in our day,[6] but it does further strengthen the likelihood
of an equal destiny for these cousins *born at the same time*. Though much is
made of the differences in the prayers before the tournament of Palamon and
Arcite, could it be argued that the favorable answers of both Mars and Venus
represent an equivalency for these knights born simultaneously? For both will
marry Emelye before the story ends.

The balanced experiences of Arcite and Palamon while they are parted

Given the equality of experience and background and, potentially, physical nature of these two cousins, let us further the argument about the balancing of
their experiences, especially after they are separated. The role of *amitie*, of
deep, ideal friendship between two men, is an oft-treated idea in the writings of
Chaucer and Shakespeare. The unholy trinity of rioters in the *Pardoner's Tale*
illustrate blood brotherhood gone amok as the two guarding the deathly gold
begin to unravel their earlier pledge of unity:

> Herkneth, felawes, we thre been al ones;
> Lat ech of us holde up his hand til oother,
> And *ech of us bicomen otheres brother*,
> And we wol sleen this false traytour Deeth.
>
> (VI 696–99; emphasis added)

After the youngest heads off to town to buy bread and wine for his fellow
gluttons, the blood brotherhood is broken by the oldest of the rioters as he
suggests:

> Thow knowest wel *thou art my sworen brother*;
> Thy profit wol I telle thee anon.
> Thou woost wel that oure felawe is agon.
> And heere is gold, and that ful greet plentee,
> That shal departed been among us thre.
> But nathelees, if I kan shape it so
> That it departed were among us two,
> Hadde I nat doon a freendes torn to thee?
>
> (VI 808–15; emphasis added)

And as they plot the youngest rioter's death, the youngest is prompted by "the
feend" to buy poison to murder his two friends. He thinks he covers his lie
about what he needs from the apothecary as a poison for the "vermyn that
destroyed hym by nyghte" (VI 844–67), but this clause contains appropriate

---

[6] See Curry's chapter on the *Knight's Tale*, especially pages 120–26, where he is suggesting
that planetary influence takes over in this tale. "By the beginning of Part Three, then, there is
felt behind the action of the story a mysterious, impelling power, the force of the planets in the
affairs of men; perhaps the fortunes of Palamon and Arcite were written at birth among the
stars." Walter Clyde Curry, *Chaucer and the Mediaeval Sciences*, rev. ed. (London: George
Allen & Unwin, 1960), 121.

double meaning and irony more truly than he knows of his equally treacherous "blood brothers."

The importance of this idea of blood brotherhood extends to the mature model for these two Theban princes, Theseus. As Palamon and Arcite have been blood brothers in their *amitie*, so have Theseus and Perotheus: "For in this world he [Perotheus] loved no man so, / And he [Theseus] loved hym als tendrely agayn" (1196–97). Like Theseus, Perotheus is also a duke (1202), further setting up the hierarchical symmetry between this other set of blood brothers in the tale. So great is the love between Perotheus and Theseus that like Odysseus and Aeneas, who also visited family and friends in the underworld, Theseus "wente and soughte hym doun in helle" after Perotheus died (1198–1201). It seems as if Chaucer is intervening here as the narrator when he states, "But of that storie list me nat to *write*" (1201; emphasis added).

As it turns out, Arcite and Perotheus are also good friends, and Perotheus secures Arcite's release from prison. This linking of the two friends Perotheus and Arcite from the two pairs of sworn brothers links the two who die early. Palamon and Theseus are similarly linked by years together after Arcite's death, becoming friends, even relatives, by the marriage at the end of the tale. In the *Knight's Tale*, of course, the blood brotherhood of the "twin cousins" is renewed in the dying words of Arcite, showing part of the resolution of the jealous break between the two blood brothers who loved the same woman. This helps also to reinforce Muscatine's overall view of the order and concord belonging to the noble classes who conform to the wise leadership of the great ruler Theseus.

The equality of the suffering and fighting of Palamon and Arcite

So far in this essay, I have mostly been outlining the balancing of experiences of the "twin" princes: though Palamon spends far longer in prison, Arcite suffers love sickness and mania severely and does not dare to reveal his true identity as he serves Emelye and Theseus, even though changed in appearance by the lover's malady. Theseus has threatened Arcite with decapitation by sword if he ever appears again in Athenian territory (1209–15). Though their suffering differs, the blood brothers continue to suffer equivalently over the seven years. Perhaps the best evidence of this equality is our inability as a court of reading lovers to differentiate between their two states in the *demande d'amour* ending Part One of the *Knight's Tale*:

> Yow loveres axe I now this questioun:
> Who hath the worse, Arcite or Palamoun?
> That oon may seen his lady day by day,
> But in prison he moot dwelle alway;
> That oother wher hym list may ride or go,
> But seen his lady shal he nevere mo. (1347–52)

Though this *demande d'amour* describes only the first two years of Palamon and Arcite's separation, since the transformed Arcite as Filostrato dares to re-enter Athens at Mercury's urging, the equality of their mutual decision to defy Theseus's perpetual banishment or imprisonment of them unites them in the clearing as jealous Maytime lovers. They arm one another like Arthurian knights, fighting up to their ankles in blood in that field where Theseus will soon build his tournament bowl to settle this jealous love (see 1542–1660 and 1862). There is no question that Palamon and Arcite fight more or less equally in this first fight, Palamon being described as a mad lion and Arcite as a cruel tiger, and both are likened to wild boars (1656–58 and 1699). Even in the subsequent tournament where Arcite and his knights barely prevail, there really is little to separate the two princes: both are able to unhorse the other in the lists (2625); they are compared again to tiger and lion in epic similes (2626 and 2630); and, though Palamon is seized by King Emetreus as he fights Arcite, he very nearly escapes before he is taken to the stake in defeat (2647–48)—virtual symmetry even in battle.

When Theseus proposes the tournament as the test of whose destiny will prevail in their mutual love of Emelye, the right to have Emelye as his wife will fall to whoever wins the battle. In Frost's view of the character of the blood brothers, Palamon's prayer to Venus that he will win Emelye as opposed to Arcite's prayer for "victory in arms" shows that Palamon "puts his love for Emelye above life itself" (p. 105). But just as the two princes have the destiny of twins, so the effect of their prayers to the planets/gods of Mars and Venus have an equalizing effect: both men will win Emelye as their wife. The order of winning Emelye as wife is reversed from the initial order of falling in love with her, as a further sign of the balance in the *Knight's Tale* between the two blood brothers, reunited as blood brothers in Arcite's suggestion in his dying speech that Emelye love Palamon, "That serveth yow, and wol doon al his lyf" (2795). I should admit at once that the next two lines (2796–97), "And if that evere ye shul ben a wyf, / Foryet nat Palamon, the gentil man," may seem to imply that Emelye has not been a wife to Arcite before his death. Although Chaucer, in speaking of Emelye's being a wife, has not included words like "eft" or "eftsone(s)" ('again, another time'—see the Glossary in *Riverside*, p. 1242), it is clear in Arcite's own language as well as in the language of Theseus and in the mourning that Emelye dutifully pursues that she has been a true if Platonic wife to Arcite for a period of years—for her desire in her prayer to Diana had been to remain a maiden—and this marriage and mourning period is followed immediately (as in the falling in love of Palamon and Arcite in the beginning of the tale) by her politic and physical marriage to Palamon for the rest of their lives together. In his speech before parliament and Palamon and Emelye, Theseus says the following about the premature death of Arcite:

> Why grucchen we, why have we hevynesse,
> That goode Arcite, of chivalrie flour,
> Departed is with duetee and honour
> Out of this foule prisoun of this lyf?
> Why grucchen heere his cosyn *and his wyf*
> Of his welfare, that loved hem so weel?
> . . . .

> I rede that we make of sorwes two
> O parfit joye, lastynge everemo.
>
> (3058–63, 3071–72; emphasis added)

Though we should beware either the hyperbole or the political ring of this last line—can there be perfect joy in this world, lasting evermore?—clearly Theseus is working towards the peace and joy of this mourning couple, the wife and the blood brother/cousin. The mourning over Arcite, "By processe and by lengthe of certeyn yeres" (2967), has affected Theseus's whole people. The desire to bring joy and alliance through this marriage would ring true to its medieval audience and to Chaucer from his own experience as a diplomat negotiating for the marriage of Richard II, for example, to a French princess.[7]

In his notes to the *Knight's Tale* in the *Riverside Chaucer*, Vincent DiMarco shows his agreement with Frost when he says in his note to the line, "Allas, myn hertes queene! Allas, my wyf" (2775), "In Tes. 9.83 Arcita and Emilia are wed in a formal ceremony. Chaucer here and in I.3062 is no doubt using **wyf** merely as a term of endearment, as in Tr 3.106, 1296."[8] If lines 3062–63 above introduce Emelye as Arcite's wife, merely as a term of endearment in Theseus's formal presentation to parliament, it seems a careless public and legal slip before such a large group of distinguished citizens. I would argue that Theseus has held to his "trouthe" as a knight in the rules of the tournament as he established them at the end of Part Two of the tale:

> Ye woot yourself she may nat wedden two
> Atones, though ye fighten everemo,
> That oon of you, al be hym looth or lief,
> He moot go pipen in an yvy leef;
> This is to seyn, she may not *now* han bothe
> ⋯⋯⋯⋯⋯⋯⋯⋯⋯⋯⋯⋯⋯⋯⋯⋯
> And forthy I yow putte in this degree,
> That *ech of yow shal have his destynee*
> *As hym is shape.* . . .
> ⋯⋯⋯⋯⋯⋯⋯⋯⋯⋯⋯⋯⋯⋯⋯⋯
> Thanne shal I yeve Emelya to wyve
> To whom that Fortune yeveth so fair a grace.
>
> (1835–39, 1841–43, 1860–61; emphasis added)

The phrase "to wyve" (1860) is glossed in the *Riverside* text as "as a wife." By winning the tournament, Arcite has Emelye "as a wife." Further, Theseus's words here about each knight's having "his destynee" reminds us again of their

---

[7] Derek Pearsall, *The Life of Geoffrey Chaucer: A Critical Biography* (Oxford: Blackwell, 1992), 105–6.

[8] Vincent J. DiMarco, Explanatory Notes to *The Knight's Tale*, *The Riverside Chaucer*, 840. Professor Kelly brings up again in his recent book "that Chaucer described the union of Troilus and Criseyde in their first night together at Pandarus's house in terms suggestive of a valid and binding marriage." Not all readers would dismiss, as DiMarco does, the notion of Criseyde's leaving Troilus as his "derne love" [secret love] wife. Henry Ansgar Kelly, *Chaucerian Tragedy* (Cambridge: D. S. Brewer, 1997), 248.

having been born more or less simultaneously and having fallen in love almost simultaneously too (1842). Both will quite literally have Emelye as wife.

In his summary heading Part Four of the *Knight's Tale* (*Riverside*, p. 838), DiMarco remarks that Chaucer "greatly compresses the material of Tes. 7–12," leaving out the marriage ceremony of Emilia and Arcita as well as her pledge to remain a widow. That does not mean that such a marriage is not implied by Arcite's tournament victory. If Emelye does not think she is truly Arcite's wife, why does she not demur from the years of mourning for him described in Part Four? Palamon never objects to these devotions and proves himself worthy of Arcite's dying recommendation to Emelye by such devotion to his blood brother. Let me conclude by saying that it really does matter that all the devotions of the Platonic wife Emelye are sincerely offered to her husband. In his dying words, Arcite asks Emelye to fulfill all the service to properly honor his soul in the obsequies of the Greeks (2768–69), the obsequies Creon earlier mistakenly denied his enemies in this tale. These are not slight formalities as the conclusion to them in the text makes clear. Like the formel eagle in the *Parlement of Foules*, Emelye has had her wish that she remain a virgin for a time, but in her behavior, she is Arcite's wife, as if they had lived happily together in marriage for years—and she has at least known him as her personal servant for a year or two before he became Theseus's chief squire (1426–41, 1730). With the parliament, the balance between the twin cousins whose destiny has actually been the same since the time of their birth achieves its final stasis; the virgin widow can prepare to fulfill her dying husband's will that she love Palamon and become a wife again. The symmetry of the blood brothers is fulfilled; in a way, Emelye has been wife to both cousins, as Theseus's enigmatic words before the tournament had suggested. Stated like the narrator's *demande d'amour* ending Part One but now directed to the general audience of lovers first and then to Palamon and Arcite, and arising from Theseus's rules for the tournament, this second *demande d'amour* might read as follows:

> Yow loveres axe I now this questioun:
> Who hath the worse, Arcite or Palamoun?
> . . . .
> Ech of you bothe is worthy, doutelees,
> To wedden whan tyme is; but nathelees—
> . . . .
> Ye woot yourself she may nat wedden two
> Atones, though ye fighten everemo.   (1347–48, 1831–32, 1835–36)

In this speech about rules for the tournament, Theseus goes on to say that Arcite and Palamon will each "have his destynee" (1842).

Whether we look at Theseus's speech as an enigma or as a *demande d'amour*, the answer in either case is that the "twin" cousins will marry Emelye "whan tyme is," not "Atones," and according to their "destynee." This fits all the prayers and their answers given in the temples at Theseus's theatre, with the bonus for Emelye of living as a married woman in virginity for a number of years before entering her second marriage. See the gods'/planets' answers at

2432–33 for Arcite's answer of "Victorie" from Mars (the last prayer answered, though he will have Emelye as his wife first), 2348–53 for Emelye's ambiguous answer from Diana that fits the idea of being married to one prince at a time, and 2265–69 for the first answer that is fulfilled last for Palamon since Venus's favorable answer also "shewed a delay" (2268).

As we reflect on the love triangle of the *Knight's Tale*, other *demandes d'amour* for the audience of lovers emerge. Can two equal princes who have fallen in love with the same princess both marry her? The prayers in Theseus's theatre and their answers lead to the unraveling of this enigma by the end of the tale, as does the argument over the powers of the various gods/planets. Corollary questions at least for Emelye are, first, can a woman who is a devotee of Diana remain a chaste virgin after her marriage, and, second, when two men have won the right to marry her, can she love them both? The *Knight's Tale* answers all of these difficult *demandes d'amour* through a sophisticated narrative set within an epic scale of time. Though Arcite wins the right to claim Emelye as his wife by his victory in the theatre of battle, Palamon, after substantial delay, can win Emelye's hand through political intervention by the presiding genius of the tale, Theseus, as well as through Palamon's sincere devotion to Emelye and the obsequies due his blood brother Arcite. With Arcite's victory, Emelye soon shows that she can become a lover as well as a devotee of Diana (see 2678–83). Moreover, the planetary influences of Mars, Venus, and Saturn bring the happy answers for lovers in the audience as both Arcite "hath al his boone" (2669) and Palamon, like his goddess Venus, "sha[l] ben esed soone" (2670). In an epic setting, Venus's "soone" is an indeterminate time of patient suffering for Palamon, rather like the scriptural injunction of John throughout Revelation that Christ's second coming to judge the world will "come quickly," in spite of thousands of years in the epic eternal life of Christ having passed (Revelation 22:20, for example). When the moment comes for Palamon, too, the sorrow of waiting soon passes: "For now is Palamon in alle wele, / Lyvynge in blisse, in richesse, and in heele" (3101–2).

In the lore of *fin amor*, Arcite has won his lady through prowess at a tournament and yet has a Platonic relationship with his wife who will continue to honor him through years of death rites as one who worships him from afar, a virgin devotee of the goddess Diana. Palamon, who has worshipped Emelye from afar for years and who joins her in her lengthy obsequies for Arcite, finally is granted his *fin amor* beloved in marriage through the act of Duke Theseus and the advice of the parliament, reinforcing the notion put forward in Chaucer's *Franklin's Tale* that *fin amor* can endure with open communication, freedom, and public, patient marriage. The long test of love with liberty, freedom, and patience on both sides of the relationship is mirrored in both the *Knight's Tale* and the *Franklin's Tale*. The words of the narrator of the *Franklin's Tale* indicate that this higher love between those of high degree is possible:

> Thus been they bothe in quiete and in reste.
> For o thyng, sires, saufly dar I seye,
> That freendes everych oother moot obeye,

If they wol longe holden compaignye.
Love wol nat been constreyned by maistrye.
Whan maistrie comth, the God of Love anon
Beteth his wynges, and farewel, he is gon!
Love is a thyng as any spirit free.
Wommen, of kynde, desiren libertee,
And nat to been constreyned as a thral;
And so doon men, if I sooth seyen shal.
Looke who that is moost pacient in love,
He is at his avantage al above.
Pacience is an heigh vertu, certeyn,
For it venquysseth, as thise clerkes seyn,
Thynges that rigour sholde nevere atteyne.
For every word men may nat chide or pleyne.
Lerneth to suffre, or elles, so moot I goon,
Ye shul it lerne, wher so ye wole or noon.
                                (V 760–78; emphasis added)

Such a speech would fit very well near the end of the *Knight's Tale* as it does near the beginning of the *Franklin's Tale*, for all the sets of lovers in these two tales have been tested, have occasionally been found wanting, and have survived through patience and suffering.

   Kathleen Tillotson was perhaps the first person to query the definition of *fin amor* in C. S. Lewis's famous study of the idea, *The Allegory of Love: A Study in Medieval Tradition* (New York: Oxford University Press, 1936).[9] Lewis includes adultery ("Humility, Courtesy, Adultery, and the Religion of Love") as one of the four features of all *fin amor* (p. 2). It has always seemed strange to me that Lewis, who studied and taught Chaucer throughout his career, should insist that *fin amor* should always be adulterous. In Chaucer's works, a successful *fin amor* needs to be brought into a public marriage of noble folk. The adulterous loves imitating *fin amor* are typically satirized in Chaucer. I believe all the fabliaux of Chaucer, with the exception of the unfinished *Cook's Tale*, cast a parodic eye on the notions of *fin amor*. Because of the upward mobility of his day and of Chaucer himself, we should not be surprised, perhaps, at the satire of religious, middle class, and lower class people who aspire to the heights of noble *fin amor* in the fabliaux. But even the "noble" January parodies this religion of love in his lechery for May in the *Merchant's Tale*. As such a repeated theme throughout Chaucer's works, *fin amor* appears in all forms from ideal to grotesque, with many levels in between.

   This theme of *fin amor* succeeding within a nobleman's marriage is found early and late in Chaucer. While I do not have space here to review all the works in which Chaucer promulgates *fin amor*, it is notable in the early *Book of the Duchess* honoring Blanche of Lancaster and John of Gaunt's love for her that *fin amor* within marriage is presented as the higher sort of relationship that

---

[9]See Tillotson's review of *The Allegory of Love* in *The Review of English Studies* 13 (1937): 477–79.

is available for the nobility. The noble Criseyde, who proves faithless late in *Troilus and Criseyde*, finds her male counterpart in the false Arcite of *Anelida and Arcite*, whose queenly wife Anelida of Armenia shows the higher fidelity that *fin amor* should illustrate. As I hint above, the *Parlement of Foules* may have been the first stage in the development of the idea in the *Knight's Tale* of satisfying both of the princes/tercelets with the love of Emelye/the formel eagle through marriage. In a way, the *Knight's Tale* is the *Parlement of Foules*, Part Two.

Though both *Troilus and Criseyde* and the *Knight's Tale* fit into epic time schemes, there is always the sense in the former that time is running out for the Trojans, which no doubt has its influence on the hurried love affair of Troilus and Criseyde. The long-term devotion shown in the *Knight's Tale* contrasts with the lack of openly affirmed marriage and public commitment in the love affair, even "marriage," of Troilus and Criseyde. Had their love been brought within a publicly acknowledged marriage, their *fin amor* might have survived the rigors of war, and certainly Criseyde would not have become a pawn in prisoner exchange had she and Prince Troilus been openly married. Perhaps too Criseyde and Troilus might have chosen a slower path to love than Pandarus envisioned. The strength of the epic length of time for *fin amor* to develop in the *Knight's Tale* is that it both shows the enduring power of the two cousins in their love for Emelye and brings the love of both Arcite and Palamon within the interests of the state and its reasonable ruler, Theseus. Arcite as Theseus's chief squire has proven his worth in his service to the ruler (1437–48); Palamon has been observed over the long run to become the friend that Theseus had had him swear to be when he and Arcite were found fighting in the clearing (1815–25, the friendship line being 1824). In the "Firste Moevere" speech in which Theseus finally grants Palamon the privilege of marrying his sister-in-law Princess Emelye, Theseus stresses the importance of Palamon's service to Emelye over the long years and the adversity that he has suffered because of his love for her as meriting her "grace," the *fin amor* euphemism for the granting of her physical being to him—here within the bond of matrimony (3077–96). The end result is that Emelye loves him tenderly and he continues to serve her gently without any words of jealousy or grief between them (3103–06). *Amitie* and devotion between the two blood brothers has been restored before Arcite's death, Arcite has died nobly and been remembered by his wife in the rites denied by Creon to the worthy dead that brings Theseus to Thebes at the beginning of the epic romance, and Palamon's *fin amor* has been brought to its destined conclusion in another marriage to the fair Emelye. God's providence has been shown to work out all the seeming problems of Emelye's being granted to both Arcite (by Mars) and Palamon (by Venus), and *fin amor* has achieved each prince both a physical and a Platonic victory in winning the love of their wife Emelye. The symmetry and equality that this paper has argued is achieved by both Arcite and Palamon in their mutual physical and Platonic conquest of the fair Emelye, their mutual wife and princess.

The *Vita Sancte Alicie Bathoniensis*

Transgressions of Hagiographic Rhetoric in the *Wife of Bath's Prologue* and *Tale*

JOSEPHINE A. KOSTER

In a discussion of medieval genre, transgression, parody, and artistry, there is no better place to start than with the great modern theorist of parody, Alfred Matthew Yankovic, better known as Weird Al. For those who don't know his inspired work, Yankovic is the acknowledged master of contemporary music parodies, and his genre-bending send-ups, such as "Like a Surgeon," "It's All About the Pentiums," "(Living in an) Amish Paradise," and "The Saga Begins" have garnered numerous Grammys as well as MTV Video Award nominations. The genius of Yankovic's art is that it works on many levels: first of all, as better-than-average pop-song writing and musicianship, secondly as humorous send-ups of successful songs, but above all as transgressions of the genre expectations of contemporary music videos. And the more the audience knows about music and videos, the better Yankovic's parodies get, since it catches casual references to nuances in the originals being parodied. For instance, knowledgeable viewers quickly recognized that Yankovic's video for "Smells Like Nirvana" used the same high school gym, the same cheerleaders and rented costumes, and many of the same extras as in Nirvana's "Smells Like Teen Spirit," while *Star Wars* addicts and Don MacLean fans alike saw many familiar references in Yankovic's *The Saga Begins*. Every camera shot modern video watchers expect in the contempory folk rock ballad is included in Yankovic's work—it's just that the lyrics fit the tune of MacLean's classic rock anthem "American Pie," and the action takes place in one of the cantinas of George Lucas's Tattooine as Yankovic, costumed as Ewan MacGregor's young Obi Wan Kenobi, sings to a rhythmic guitar accompaniment, "My, my, this here Anakin guy, Maybe Vader someday later, now he's just a small fry."[1]

Why do I start a paper on Chaucer with this rehearsal of contemporary culture? Because I believe that in *The Wife of Bath's Prologue* and *Tale* we see similar genre-transgression taking place, and that the more familiar we are with the genre being manipulated, the more we can appreciate Chaucer's artistry and achievement. Many scholars seeking the sources and analogues of Chaucer's

---

[1] Videos, lyrics, and details of many of Yankovic's works are available at http://www.weirdal.com/

most noteworthy female creation have pointed to La Vieille, estates satire, anti-feminist tracts in Latin and French, and astrological and physiognomical lore as the genres from which the Wife of Bath's richly-drawn portrait draws. But they usually neglect another, and closer genre: hagiography. Saints' lives were one of the most popular kinds of narrative in Middle English literature, if we judge from surviving manuscripts; Chaucer's audience, especially his female audience, would have known the genre and its standard twists and turns well. By using the conventions of the female saint's life in subtly perverted ways, Chaucer adds a richness and depth to Alice's story—what I would call the *Vita Sancte Alicie Bathoniensis*—that we as modern readers may miss if we aren't alerted to its presence.

It is no longer necessary to point out how many books of pious devotion were produced for or owned by female readers in the late middle ages. As Larissa Tracy points out, "Saints' lives served a twofold purpose: while elevating the subject they also provided a clearer picture of what role women were expected to play and how they played it, very often in their own terms with their own voice [sic]."[2] It's clear that tales of pious women held particular interest for the female readership of late medieval England. Collections as early as the three saints' legends in the *Katherine* group and as extensive as those in the *South English Legendary* or *Northern Homily Cycle* show how pervasive such stories were: by the fifteenth century, when Capgrave, Bokenham, and others were writing, the saint's life was an accepted female genre, much as the romance novel is for today's reader. It was considered culturally appropriate for women to "rede on holy seyntes lyves," as Chaucer's Criseyde wryly points out (2.118).

The similarities between romance and hagiographic narrative are many. Julia Boffey notes that "Like romances saints' lives usually involve a sequence of episodes which pit the central figure against some opposition, so generating action and response, and in both genres the contests can generate accumulations of graphic and sometimes lurid detail."[3] The conventional rhetorical structure of a female saint's life consists of a recognized succession of episodes. The saint's geographic and family backgrounds are established, as are her piety and general "passivity." She is exposed to a number of increasingly dangerous physical and spiritual perils, which she surmounts triumphantly, either exacting appropriate revenge on her persecutors and rejoicing at their deaths or converting them and mass numbers of their followers to her way, all while preserving control of her

---

[2] Larissa Tracy, *Women of the* Gilte Legende: *A Selection of Middle English Saints' Lives* (Cambridge: D. S. Brewer, 2003), 1.

[3] Julia Boffey, "Middle English Lives," in *The Cambridge History of Middle English Literature*, ed. David Wallace (Cambridge: Cambridge University Press, 1999), 620. For further examination of the genre, see Jocelyn Wogan-Browne, "The Virgin's Tale," in *Feminist Readings in Middle English Literature: The Wife of Bath and All Her Sect*, ed. Ruth Evans and Lesley Johnson (London: Routledge, 1994), 165–94, and John Scahill, *Middle English Saints' Legends*, Annotated Bibliographies of Old and Middle English Literature 7 (Cambridge: D. S. Brewer, 2005), 1–4. For the literary terms used to name the many varieties of hagiographic narratives in the Middle Ages, see Paul Strohm, "*Passioun, Lyf, Miracle, Legende*: Some Generic Terms in Middle English Hagiographical Narrative," *Chaucer Review* 10 (1975): 62–75 and 154–71.

virginity. In her final test, the saint is usually martyred, but only after offering a last oration or sermon on her own conduct and on her beliefs that inspires mass conversions and sets the stage for divine retribution against her persecutors. Quantity is an all-important feature: there must be a sequence of perils, each greater in duration and degree than the ones before; and massive numbers of unbelievers must be converted through the saint's agency. As Thomas Heffernan points out,

> In this narrative frame, action becomes ritual, and specific action becomes specific ritual. For sacred biographers, there existed a veritable thesaurus of established approved actions which they could employ in their texts.... Within this cultural setting, the saint's life, with its emphasis on right action, served as a catechetical tool much like the stained glass which surrounded and instructed the faithful in their participation at the liturgy.[4]

Unlike the male saints, in whose narratives physical action on the saint's part often figures largely, the female saints most often work their ends through verbal action—either orations or *orationes*, that is, prayers. Tracy identifies that female voice as a key element of the genre:

> Male ecclesiastical authors, though they may have been concerned with the lasting obedience and silence of women, gave their female saints a vocal presence in their legends. While it may be the voice of Christian doctrine providing examples of sanctity for general edification, the women saints are allowed to speak for themselves.... The women are largely historical inventions constructed as representations of sanctity, but the fact that they speak clearly and loudly for themselves, instead of having their message conveyed by a male narrator, shows the female voice is an integral part of hagiography.
>
> (108)

Such voices, of course, are characteristic of Chaucer's artistry, and may indeed be one of the elements that drew him to work in the genre of the saint's life. Another attraction may have been the intrinsically transgressive nature of the woman saint's life as a genre: in showing women triumphing consistently over men, controlling their own sexuality and even using it as a weapon, in ridiculing father figures, suitors, husbands, prefects, and other patriarchal figures of authority, the woman saint's life allows its writer to challenge many of the accepted norms of the culture—a stance with which Chaucer apparently had considerable sympathy.

Among the numerous Chaucerian characters drawing from the hagiographic tradition, Virginia in the *Physician's Tale,* Constance in the *Man of Law's Tale*, Griselda in the *Clerk's Tale*, and Cecilia in the *Second Nun's Tale* are the most notable, but Chaucer frequently uses the rhetorical and structural details that characterize medieval female saints' lives in other works as well. In

---

[4]Thomas J. Heffernan, *Sacred Biography: Saints and their Biographers in the Middle Ages* (Oxford: Oxford University Press, 1988), 6.

the *Physician's Tale*, Virginia, though described in a typical hagiographic blazon (VI 30–66), actually speaks only twice: to ask her father if there is "no
grace ... no remedye" for her death sentence, and then to praise God "that
I shal dye a mayde" and to ask for a quick death "er that I have a shame"
(236, 248–49). As a virgin martyr, she is present so briefly that she is actually a
negligible character in her own *passio*. In the *Clerk's Tale* of Griselda, however,
the female voice is heard more clearly.[5] The blazon of the saint's geography and
genealogy is conducted rather quickly: the second fitt of the tale tells us that

> Noght fer fro thilke paleys honurable,
> Wher as this markys shoop his mariage,
> There stood a throop, of site delitable,
> In which that povre folk of that village
> Hadden hir beestes and hir herbergage.
> ....
> Amonges thise povre folk ther dwelte a man
> Which that was holden povrest of hem alle;
> But hye God somtyme senden kan
> His grace into a litel oxes stalle.
> Janicula men of that throop hym calle;
> A doghter hadde he, fair ynogh to sighte,
> And Grisildis this yonge mayden highte.   (IV 197–210)

Griselda, the daughter of the poorest of the poor, is yet at the same time of
high heritage, for she is compared to the grace God sent into the stable at
Bethlehem: she is a figure of Christ. Griselda is repeatedly described with
adjectives common to hagiographic discourse that delineate her saintly status:
patient, stedefast, and *benign.* She promises total obedience to the decrees of
father and husband, thus marking her as a figure of the Church's obedience to
Christ and the average Christian's obedience to the Church.

Now come her perils, each increasingly stressful. She is separated first from
her daughter, then her son, and finally believes herself to be divorced by her
husband—and called back to prepare her ex-husband's second wedding. To each
new torment she responds with an approximation of "Thy will be done," the
saint's true response to any test of her faith. In so doing she achieves numerous
conversions: more and more of the courtiers who rejected her for her low birth
are won over by her pious *gentilesse*, until, when she is ordered to return to
her father's home, she does so followed by hordes of weeping converts. Finally,
even Walter relents: the chief torturer is won by her demonstration of patient
temporal suffering, and he restores to Griselda at least some of what she has
lost. Her patient piety, then, has not been passivity but non-violent resistance,
and has given her the power to endure and finally change her situation.

---

[5]I would agree with many of the observations about this tale made by Kate McKinley
in "The *Clerk's Tale*: Hagiography and the Problematics of Lay Sanctity," *Chaucer Review*
33 (1998): 90–111, but not with her contention that Griselda is so perfect a figure that her
actions as a saint are unconvincing (105–06).

Griselda's rhetoric is also strongly reminiscent of hagiography. Most of her direct speeches are, in fact, Chaucerian additions to Petrarch's story, and Griselda's speeches move strongly toward the pious oration so common in stories of saints. When she is ordered to leave Walter's house, she responds with a theme-and-variations take on "Thy will be done" that lasts 76 lines (IV 500 ff). Many of her added speeches are prayers—or, as in the case of her speech after reuniting with her children, prayers punctuated with culturally-appropriate swoons. As an exemplary female figure, Griselda is drawn in terms with which Chaucer's audience would have been not only familiar but comfortable; she offers them reification of their beliefs, not challenges to them.

Constance in the *Man of Law's Tale* is a more complex figure. Her tale again begins with her genealogy and history: she is the extraordinarily beautiful daughter of the Emperor of Rome, and her piety and beauty are so renowned that the Sultan of Syria comes from afar to marry her and convert his entire kingdom to Christianity. (This is powerful piety, even in a saint's life.) Her first oration, a Chaucerian addition to the story, is two rhyme royal stanzas (II 274–87) on the "Thy will be done" theme, stressing the speaker's strong beliefs that such is woman's fate. She becomes immediately popular with everyone in Syria except her mother-in-law's faction, and the Soudaness immediately arranges the massacre of her son and the newly-converted Christians. Only Constance survives, to face greater tortures in being put to sea in a rudderless ship. Her subsequent prayer, another Chaucerian addition, is short again, just under two stanzas (451–62); however, Chaucer also adds, in the narrator's voice, six more stanzas reminding readers that such things happen all the time in biblical stories, rebuking them for finding her long survival difficult to believe. (Petrarch, too, faced similar disbelief in his audience, who found the actions of female saints implausible, and reacted similarly to Chaucer; apparently such resistance in the audience was not unprecedented; see McKinley, 97.)

Constance, of course, is swept up on the beach in Britain, where she is befriended by the constable and converts his wife, is falsely accused of murder, is cleared by divine intervention, and marries King Alla and bears him a son, while in the process converting large numbers of heathens to Christianity. Once again this brings her into conflict with a jealous mother-in-law, in the pattern of repetition so common to hagiographic narrative. The mother-in-law so contrives that Constance is put to sea again, with her son, in the same ship in which she had arrived. She lands in heathen territory again, where she is menaced by a lustful steward but through divine intervention avoids rape, and is swept out once more through the straits of Gibraltar into the Mediterranean, to be rescued by a Roman senator who takes her and the baby home to his wife. For reasons never explored she does not reveal her identity to her father until her husband Alla comes to Rome on pilgrimage and she is reunited with him; then she is also reunited with her father; and all seems set for a pious happy ending. But such cannot be, for to live in marital congress is to engage in sin, and Constance, after all, is a saintly woman. So Alla conveniently dies a year later, allowing Constance to finish out her life in prayer, chastity, and good works among the poor—the true saintly ending when martyrdom is not required.

In the *Second Nun's Tale* of St. Cecilia, we see Chaucer more explicitly begin to highlight the heroine's voice for his readers. As Priscilla Martin so succinctly puts it, "Like Constance, Cecilia is a paradigm of the Christian witness and missionary activity of the early Church, but while Constance is swept away and sent passively on her epoch-making journeys, Cecilia is a militantly active heroine."[6] She inspires action through her rhetoric: her impulsive power is verbal, not physical. To mirror this difference, Chaucer tells us less about her temporal and more about her spiritual genealogy. We are told that she comes "of Romayns, and of noble kynde," but more importantly that she is determined on Christian virginity. When she is married to Valerian, a fairly innocuous fellow, Chaucer sets the readers up for her entry into wifehood conventionally:

> The nyght cam, and to bedde moste she gon
> With hire housbonde, as ofte is the manere.   (VIII 141–42)

But Cecilia is not about to leave any of her holiness aside, and skillfully uses her rhetorical talents to achieve her ends. First she convinces Valerian that she is loved by an angel who will kill Valerian if he touches his wife. Valerian, of course, wants to see the angel, and Cecilia sends him away from her bed to Pope Urban at the catacombs for baptism, for only the baptised can see the angel. Valerian is confronted with a vision of a man holding a book of gold, which immediately convinces him to convert. He is baptized, returns home to find Cecilia and the angel, and requests that his brother Tiburce be converted, which the angel promptly achieves, with Cecilia preaching the catechism. The three take up proselytizing, are captured, and tortured. They convert one of their torturers, Maximus, who begins to witness his Christianity to great effect and is arrested and beaten to death. Finally, the prefect Almachias decides to put a stop to all this conversion and orders Cecilia arrested. She whips him handily at debate; he has her tortured, and even orders her beheading. But the torturer is unable to complete the job; the sword won't cut her neck, and for three days and nights (a significant number, of course) she addresses the crowd, inspiring mass conversions and the building of a church by the pope, before finally dying.

Nowhere in this tale does Chaucer give Cecilia freedom to act: he constructs her as a collection of provocative speeches rather than a physically realized character. She is, truly, a saint: a collection of idealized virtues. Unlike Constance, Cecilia never rails against her fate or accepts it as divine will, but instead embraces it enthusiastically, even using it as the opportunity for some judicious fund-raising. Unlike most of the female saints in tales Chaucer's audience knew, here is one who is pious without being passive. Like Griselda she strikes modern readers as rather inhuman in her eager dismissal of Valerian and Tiburce and her rather callous approach to her own martyrdom. (One senses that a modern Cecilia would have had her execution televised on *Oprah*, if she'd had the chance.)

---

[6]Priscilla Martin, *Chaucer's Women: Nuns, Wives, and Amazons* (Iowa City: University of Iowa Press, 1990), 150.

In such conventional adaptations of hagiography, Chaucer manipulates the voices of his female protragonists to address disbelief and thoughtless imitation, reality and divine unreality, and the whole concept of modeling behavior, as he confronts his audience with the question of right conduct for Christians facing challenges to their faith. Strohm notes that

> The reader's expectations about the movement of the narrative help
> to highlight and to explain any deviations from the pattern common
> to narratives of other martyred saints.... The audience still finds its
> satisfaction in anticipation and fulfillment of a design, rather than
> in suspense and surprise and other responses less well suited to a
> devotional work written for the purpose of confirming belief. (167)

It's noteworthy that these are some of Chaucer's longest tales, for the necessary cycles of repetition needed to create the picture of pious resignation demand space for the *amplificatio* and *elaboration* his readers anticipated in an exemplary life. Chaucer's Virginia, Griselda, Constance and even Cecilia raise and meet his audience's expectations of what becomes a *legende* most.

So, when Chaucer comes to write his most famous *Lyf*, that of the hetero-dox Wife of Bath, he has command of a wide range of conventions for female exemplary biography at his command—and ready for exploitation in the *Wife's Prologue* and *Tale*. We know from the promises of the drunken Miller to tell "a legende and a lyf" (I 3141) and of the merchant's wife in the *Shipman's Tale* to "telle a legende of my lyf" (VII 145), and indeed from the entire project of the *Legend of Good Women*, that Chaucer understood the potential uses of hagiographic elements in parodic circumstances. Here, in his creation of Alys of Bath and her life story, he takes the elements of occasional parody to a higher, more sustained level. If one accepts that the belief structure he inverts is that of conventional Christianity, where female submissiveness and passivity are valued, we can see that Alice is, in a funhouse-mirror way, a saint and martyr—that she wears the costumes and occupies the settings of the saint's life genre, but in unexpected ways. Indeed Alice is the exact opposite of the physical 'type' of the saintly heroine—unlike the beautiful, barely pubescent heroines of most saints' lives, she is older, wiser, and no longer virginally lovely. Where the typi-cal heroine of a saint's life is from a noble family, the Wife is "barly-breed" and proud of it (III 144). And where the saint espouses, usually at great length, the virtues of virginity, the Wife spends even more time celebrating the necessity for active sexuality when virginity is no longer an option. Unlike the squeamish but well-mannered Virginia, who feigns sickness to avoid the kind of people found at "feestes, revels, and at daunces, / That been occasions of daliaunces" (VI 65–66), the Goodwife of Bath seeks out such occasions, where she can put her convictions to the test. Unlike the saintly Cecilia, who wears a hair shirt un-der her wedding garments and retreats in maidenly modesty from public gaze at church, the Wife insists on first place in the offertory procession, wearing her ten pounds' weight of coverchiefs and her scarlet hose (I 449–56). Brigitte Cazelles states that, "Indifferent to her own appearance, eager not to provoke unchaste gazing, the female [saint] seeks to become invisible."[7] Chaucer's transgressing Saint Alys seeks just the opposite.

The Wife's *vita* begins with her biography and genealogy: she was married first at age twelve, and was widowed twice at a young age. She follows a consistent pattern (in her first three marriages) of marrying men who are old, jealous, and miserly, but she triumphs over them by manifesting her "virtues" of sexuality, quarreling skill, and counter-argument. Where the traditional female saint is silent and lacks initiative, the Wife, like St. Cecilia, claims that she "baar [her] proprely" (III 224), as does a wise woman, by turning men's traditional weapons of sexual desire and speech against them. Whereas in typical saints' lives, a disregard for property, material goods, and inheritances is the hallmark of the virgin martyr, Chaucer's Saint Alys positively glories in the wealth she accumulates through her successive marriages—a wealth that empowers her to face more effective temptation.

Her tests against masculine persecution grow more serious when she is matched against her fourth husband, the "revelour" who provides her belief system with a stronger challenge by being "daungerous" to her (514).[8] This is temptation to fall, indeed, for the fourth husband matches her in sexual desire and licentiousness, and the Wife must call on all her acquired knowledge and faith in her beliefs to overcome him and "in his owene grece ... ma[k]e hym frye" (487). Whereas in the typical hagiographic narrative the heroine figures as a new Eve, resisting the sexual temptations of a Satanic prefect or other suitor, the Wife defends herself not with the excellence of her virginity but with the achievements of her mature carnality. Using the language of pious discourse, she boasts that "in erthe I was his purgatorie, / For which I hope his soule be in glorie" (489–90)—wishing on the fourth husband the salvific result of a very unsaintly conversion.

The arch-torturer of Saint Alys, of course, is fifth husband Jankyn, the wily clerk of Oxford. Like Almachius and the other noteworthy torturers of the saint's life tradition, he starts with verbal assaults on her beliefs, reading to her from his book "of olde Romayn geestes" (642) and turning to physical assault when she counter-attacks by tearing a page from his book. His blow leaves her deaf in one ear, literally unable to take in his point of view. As is typical of the female saint, she is undaunted by the physical abuse heaped on her, and gives back as good as she gets. Jankyn extends and increases Alys's torture by reading to her every day out of his "book of wikked wyves" (685), attempting to shake her faith by reading from Theophrastus and Jerome. The Wife must draw on all her strength to remain "stubborn as a lioness" and to ask "who painted the lion?" (and one of the great Chaucerian parodic notes is, of course, that St. Jerome was frequently depicted in medieval portraiture as having a lion nestled tamely at his feet).

---

[7] *The Lady as Saint: A Collection of French Hagiographic Romances of the Thirteenth Century* (Philadelphia: University of Pennsylvania Press, 1991), 50.

[8] On the possible meanings of the word *daungerous* in this passage see T. L. Burton, "The Wife of Bath's Fourth and Fifth Husbands and Her Ideal Sixth: The Growth of a Marital Philosophy," *Chaucer Review* 13 (1978): 34–50, p. 42.

Finally, in a physical confrontation, Jankyn strikes the Wife down so that she lies as one dead—but when he goes to raise up her corpse, she finds the strength to proclaim him a murderer, kiss him one last time, strike him in the face, and begin preaching her 'last sermon.' That, of course, is the heretical *Wife of Bath's Tale*, in which the triumphant heroine demonstrates to her own satisfaction that men can successfully deal with women only by converting to women's belief system, accepting that *gentilesse* depends on conduct rather than rank, and granting women *maistrye* in intersex dealings. As both Heffernan and McKinley point out, a major feature of female saints' lives was an argument that virtue was not dependent on the saint's political, economic, or social class (Heffernan, 270 ff.; McKinley, 94 ff.). But here, Chaucer totally inverts his audience's expectations, by using an argument usually proffered to support a saint's right to preserve her virginity to campaign, instead, for a woman's right to be free of patriarchal domination.

Saint Alys's torturer, Jankyn, converts in the face of his wife's strong beliefs, burns his book of wicked wives, and grants her the 'soverayntee' she so desires. He dies, she tells us, in the state of grace appropriate to such a convert, and she prays for God's blessing on her one-time torturer's soul, as well as for God's vengeance against all men who do not convert when faced with such incontrovertible evidence of female moral superiority. Thus, like the female saints whose lives Chaucer's audience knew, the final note of the *vita* of this very unorthodox saint is that of salvation, conversion, and redemption—but totally different salvations, ones which would both amuse and confound Chaucer's audience as contrary to their doctrinal and narrative expectations.

Generically, all the conventions of the saint's life are present in the Wife of Bath's *Prologue* and *Tale*, just as the expected conventions are present in one of Yankovic's videos. Similarly, it is the superb reversal and exploitation of expected elements that enriches the joke for an audience familiar with the conventions being transgressed, as Chaucer's audience was with those of hagiographic narrative. And with the linguistic artistry that is his hallmark, Chaucer even plays with the language the Wife uses to reinforce the identification of the parody in his listeners' minds. As one instance, consider the last four lines of the Wife's *Tale*, where the narrator prays,

> And eek I praye Jhesu shorte hir lyves
> That noght wol be governed by hir wyves;
> And olde and angry nygardes of dispence,
> God sende hem soone verray pestilence!　　　　　　　(1261–64)

If readers substitute "save" for "shorte" and "penitence" for "pestilence," they will see how close the parody is; just inserting those two traditional words from Middle English prayer would change Alys's speech to a totally orthodox statement. But Chaucer, by changing just two words, makes it a closing oration that challenges the entire basis of that orthodoxy, that women should be submissive to their husbands. The close verbal parallels to what his audience would have expected to hear at the close of a "standard" hagiographic narrative heighten the disruptive effect of the comic close to Alys's *lyf*.

What effects does Chaucer achieve by incorporating the most common elements of exemplary biography into this *vita* of a very unsaintly teller? This question applies in fact to the entire genre of female saints' lives: As Heffernan argues,

> What would women, married or single or widowed, make of tales
> which subjected women who defended principle to an encyclopedia
> of violent sexual abuse, ending in death?... The positive reception
> which greeted these vernacular narratives of the saints suggests
> some degree of sophistication on the part of its audience, an audience
> whose attitudes are not easily categorized despite the hegemony of
> orthodoxy, an audience in which men and women were aware of gender problems, and [sic] audience familiar with sexually explicit and
> deviant behavior, an audience who enjoyed stories which exploited
> class conflict, and an audience who believed that authority figures,
> whether clerical or political, often had feet of clay.   (264–65)

Familiarity with the genre of the female saint's life shows us that some of the elements we see today as most revolutionary and "proto-feminist" in Chaucer would have been recognized by his own audience as variations on the given conventions of a common genre. Thus, the audiences whose expectations are disrupted by the Wife of Bath's *Prologue* and *Tale* are as likely to be modern as medieval.

Modern critics, not attuned to these echoes, often find the Wife a very confusing character. As the *Riverside Chaucer*'s notes point out, the Wife is either a vehicle for critiquing marriage, or "a sympathetic figure, one of the great comic characters in our literature," who is "all the more human for her frailties and inconsistencies," or a character who "has no personality of her own, but is a universalized representation of some aspect of womankind," and who even seems to some "a monster—androgynous, spiritually corrupt in both sexes"—and all those comments come within the course of two paragraphs summarizing critical reaction to her portrait (865, column 1). When modern readers familiarize themselves with the rhetorical and generic conventions of medieval hagiography, her contradictions become less threatening. While the Wife is joyous and stalwart in her beliefs that patriarchal dominance and female continence are outcomes to be challenged and that sexual temptation and abuse are best trumped by female wiles and the rampant exercise of carnality, those beliefs are founded on her ignorance and misreading of the conventional pious texts and tenets of her times—just the kinds of ignorance that were supposed to be rectified by subjecting women to a literary diet of hagiography and that an audience should recognize when they hear her expound on them. Indeed, one of the greatest achievements Chaucer reaches in *The Wife of Bath's Prologue* and *Tale* is that it is a saint's life told by a female character who has obviously not absorbed any of the lessons of the saints' lives she *has* read. Thus, she is governed by morally fallible *experience* rather than the morally defensible *auctoritee* that a sequence of men have labored to expose her to. Unlike the Pardoner, she's unaware of her own shortcomings—and therein lies her failure as a "saint." The message that

Chaucer's transgressive *vita* relays, then, is a critique of those in his audience who agree with her beliefs as well as of the genre itself.

The comic possibilities of Chaucer's transgressions of genre are likewise tremendous: Alys's *vita* is a parody of the exemplary lives held up to late fourteenth-century women, the kind of exemplary lives that underlie the tale of Saints Cecilia and Virginia and to a lesser extent the tales of Griselda and Constance. In creating a woman who acts in *precisely* the opposite way to an orthodox saint and in making her live out the adventures—the increasingly difficult tests and torments, the steadfast opposition to "heathen" beliefs, the ability to convert the most hardened tyrant, the "miraculous" revival of the dead "saint"—Chaucer effectively lampoons an entire genre of approved textual consumption in his time, much as he skewers romance on the lance of Sir Thopas or as the modern Yankovic deconstructs music videos through parodic imitation. But more significantly, by having Alys espouse her anti-misogynist sentiments in the context of a genre aimed chiefly at female readers, Chaucer forces his readers to confront a real issue, for his time and for ours: what sort of examples ought the female reader to follow? Should she be a patient pushover, like Griselda and Constance? What kind of life did that earn her? The out-and-out attack Alice mounts on misogynist teaching, while first and foremost humorous, also requires readers to ask not only "What do women most desire?" but "What should women be allowed to desire?" At the same time, if Boffey is correct that the aim of narratives of holy lives is "less to warn, more to hearten and encourage" (618), we also see the inherent dangers in Chaucer's transgressive creation, for the appeal of this lively and engaging character's arguments could indeed cause the unaware to "sownen into synne" (X 1085), in Chaucer's time or our own.

Recognizing the elements of the saint's life in the Wife of Bath's *Prologue* and *Tale* does not, of course, "solve" the problem that Alys and her beliefs presents for the modern reader, but complicates it even further, reminding us that Chaucer may possibly have envisioned this creation, in part, as a critique of the impossibility of the exemplary life his world demanded that women live. By incorporating the structural and rhetorical features of the saint's life with the other sources and elements that make up the Wife of Bath's portrait, Chaucer turns the genre and the expectations of his audience inside out with her performance. The humor comes in hearing the echoes of the saint's life in such an unsaintly setting, the *sentence* in reflecting on the implications such juxtapositions raise. Like those who watch a Yankovic video, Chaucer's readers, knowing what a saint's life should and should not contain, and how a saint should and should not face her tests and tortures, can find in the *Vita Sancte Alicie Bathoniensis* a richness and depth hitherto unnoticed.

Chaucer on the Couch

The Pardoner's Performance
and the Case for Psychoanalytic Criticism

BRITTON HARWOOD

My title alludes, of course, to the several slight strictures on the use of Freud in medieval studies that Lee Patterson published not long ago.[1] Patterson makes a distinction reminiscent of the one Fredric Jameson made in *The Political Unconscious*. Jameson pointed to "the paradoxical situation of Freudian criticism today, about which we may affirm that the only people still seriously interested in it are the Freudians themselves, at the same time that the prestige and influence of ... psychoanalysis as a method and a model has never been so immense at any moment of its history."[2] So Patterson takes no position on psychoanalysis in literary studies generally, where the interest has been, he says, in "a kind of hermeneutics, as a model for doing interpretation." Rather, Patterson taxes medieval literary studies for having rushed backwards to "Freud's beliefs about human sexuality and its dominance as a force in character formation and pathology" (643). Freud's theories were bereft of evidence, Patterson maintains, and actually resisted empirical procedures. The Freudian mode of argument was typically a machine for absorbing all counter-evidence, a good deal of which Freud himself dishonestly suppressed (647–56).

That Patterson nonetheless may leave room for a "political unconscious" is cold comfort for the psychoanalytic critic, since the political unconscious developed by Jameson is just descriptively, not dynamically, unconscious. It "is *one* unconscious," as Lacan might say, "but is it enough to accommodate the unconscious as such? And if it is able to do so, does it accommodate the Freudian unconscious?"[3] Psychoanalytic criticism heuristically assumes that the dynamic unconscious exists. Patterson's test case for such criticism, which scandalously "has the reputation of being cutting edge in literary criticism even

---

[1] "Chaucer's Pardoner on the Couch: Psyche and Clio in Medieval Literary Studies," *Speculum* 76 (2001): 638–80.

[2] *The Political Unconscious: Narrative As a Socially Symbolic Act* (Ithaca: Cornell University Press, 1981), 65.

[3] Jacques Lacan, *The Four Fundamental Concepts of Psycho-Analysis* (1973), ed. J.-A. Miller, trans. Alan Sheridan (New York: Norton, 1978), 13. Lacan asks these questions of Jameson's source, Lévi-Strauss's *Pensée sauvage*. On the difference between the descriptively unconscious (the preconscious) and the dynamically unconscious, see my "Psychoanalytic Politics: Chaucer and Two Peasants," *ELH* 68 (2001): 18, n.3.

as it has disappeared from those fields for which it was designed" (656), is "the thoroughly psychoanalytic interpretation [of the Pardoner] offered by Carolyn Dinshaw in *Chaucer's Sexual Poetics*" (658).

Actually, the cutting edge of Pardoner criticism when Patterson's article appeared was not the fetishism that Dinshaw investigated in the 1980s or, in a similarly Lacanian vein, the horror of bodily fragmentation and the related desire for the maternal that Robert Sturges has pointed to more recently.[4] Rather, Dinshaw was drawing fresh attention with an argument for performativity: "the queer, *always* playing a role (and thereby revealing that others do), eliminating any idea of essence, obviates all question of originality, sincerity, even truth."[5] Similarly in the '90s, Glenn Burger was holding that "[t]he extent to which we can embrace as our own the Pardoner's inversions or perversions of apparently stable binaries may thus mark the extent to which we can affirm different or alternative kinds of cultural re-formation."[6] The Pardoner destabilizes binaries, so the argument goes, by queering one of the terms—for instance, queering the gender role of husband when he camps for the Wife of Bath the prospect of his getting married.

But to queer this or queer that is a matter of tactic, choice—although the Foucauldian tradition in which Dinshaw and Burger write does not often make a theme of agency. Everything that would disturb individual tactic and control, namely, the dynamically unconscious, seems to disappear from queer theory as thoroughly as it does for Jameson and presumably for Patterson.

What constitutes proof in psychoanalysis as a discipline no doubt continues to make an interesting debate, but it is not one I am qualified to contribute to.[7] About literary criticism, however, I shall venture two points, one of them, actually, a psychoanalytic one. The psychoanalysis of literary characters seems to me risky in principle. Clinicians might well hold up literary characters for illustrative purposes as if they exhibited the signs of a particular psychological organization. Some creative writers, copying a character from real life, might copy enough of it so that psychoanalytic questions about it might make sense. Some—I've thought of William Styron here—have surely read Freud and apparently tried to make their characters coherent in Freudian terms. But if psychoanalysis implies the existence of a dynamic unconscious, then there is, of course, only one unconscious that exists (leaving the reader's out of account for the time being). And that, obviously, is the author's.

---

[4] Dinshaw, *Chaucer's Sexual Poetics* (Madison: University of Wisconsin Press, 1989); Sturges, *Chaucer's Pardoner and Gender Theory: Bodies of Discourse* (New York: St. Martin's Press, 2000).

[5] Dinshaw, *Getting Medieval: Sexualities and Communities, Pre- and Postmodern* (Durham: Duke University Press, 1999), 135 (her emphasis).

[6] "Kissing the Pardoner," *PMLA* 107 (1992): 1152. Cf. his "Doing What Comes Naturally: The *Physician's Tale* and the Pardoner," in *Masculinities in Chaucer*, ed. Peter G. Beidler (Cambridge: D. S. Brewer, 1998), 117–30.

[7] For an illuminating discussion of what does constitute such proof (and thus for an analysis of criticism of Freud like Patterson's), see John Forrest, *Dispatches from the Freud Wars: Psychoanalysis and Its Passions* (Cambridge, Mass.: Harvard University Press, 1997), esp. 208–48.

What use is knowing that for the critic? Criticism, like other disciplines, has the ideal of elegance, explanations that minimize anomaly.[8] What Patterson considers the rubbish bin of psychoanalytic theory may inspire me to an explanation. Where the explanation comes from does not matter. What matters is its explanatory power with the loose ends of a text—the fractures, anomalies, all that New Criticism would reduce to a unity, details left out of other accounts or touched unconvincingly.

To let Patterson name the game, I shall take up the Pardoner's performance, but I am going to ignore the Pardoner himself for a while. He scandalizes and fascinates, but for the moment I shall think of him as a displacement, as if a single element of latent content had found its way into the manifest text and "expanded to a disproportionate extent"[9]—or expanded this way at least in criticism of the text. Instead I will begin with what it has been generally beneath criticism to notice, although students have not failed to notice it, since, if the Pardoner's performance is ever boring or hard to read, what I am going to start with accounts for at least some of that. I mean a certain recursiveness near the beginning of the performance.[10] It starts with the Pardoner's Prologue.

(a) First I pronounce whennes that I come,
And thanne my bulles shewe I, alle and some.

. . . .

And after that thanne telle I forth my tales.   (VI 335–41)

(a) Bulles of popes and of cardynales,
Of patriarkes and bishopes I shewe

. . . .

To saffron with my predicacioun.   (342–45)

(a) Thanne shewe I forth my longe cristal stones,
Ycrammed ful of cloutes and of bones—
Relikes been they, as wenen they echoon.

. . . .

And whan the lewed people is doun yset,
I preche so as ye han herd bifoore.   (347–93)

---

[8] See, for example, Alexander Nehamas: "To interpret a text is to place it in a context which accounts for as many of its features as possible" ("The Postulated Author: Critical Monism As a Regulative Ideal," *Critical Inquiry* 8 [1981]: 144); and Nelson Goodman: "Knowing cannot be exclusively or even primarily a matter of determining what is true. Discovery often amounts, as when I place a piece in a jigsaw puzzle, not to arrival at a proposition for declaration or defense, but to finding a fit" (*Ways of Worldmaking* [Indianapolis: Hackett, 1978], 21).

[9] Freud, *The Interpretation of Dreams*, The Standard Edition of the Complete Psychological Works (SE), trans. James Strachey, 24 vols. (London: Hogarth Press, 1966–74), 4: 305.

[10] For one, Lisa Kiser notices this, although she makes it part of the characterization of the Pardoner: "The narrative's effectiveness for an audience would surely be hindered by the Pardoner's early and digressive moralizing, which interrupts the story line, wandering from sin to sin and from exemplum to exemplum with the kind of agitated awkwardness that one might expect from the Squire" (*Truth and Textuality in Chaucer's Poetry* [Hanover, N.H.: University Press of New England, 1991], 143).

(b) Of avarice and of swich cursednesse
Is al my prechyng, for to make hem free
To yeven hir pens, and namely unto me.
For myn entente is nat but for to wynne.   (400–403)

(b) But shortly myn entente I wol devyse:
I preche of no thyng but for coveityse.
Therefore my theme is yet, and evere was,
Radix malorum est Cupiditas.   (423–26)

(b) Thanne telle I hem ensamples many oon
....
And wynne gold and silver for I teche.   (435–40)

When the Pardoner begins his tale, which is to say his sermon, at least some readers, I imagine, bog down in a comparable repetitiveness in the part that dwells on gluttony, a repetitiveness that distends that section to a length half again as long as the sections on dicing and swearing put together.[11] The gluttony section seems to me not entirely under control. There is, there, a certain compulsion to repeat. The Pardoner—which is to say, Chaucer—begins by denouncing drunkenness for some thirteen lines as something that causes people to do crazy things. Then, for another twenty-five lines or so he castigates eating too much as the original sin, the cause of disease, and the reason for unnecessary labor. Then he reverts to too much drinking—

Allas, a foul thyng is it, by my feith,
To seye this word, and fouler is the dede,
Whan man so drynketh of the white and rede
That of his throte he maketh his pryvee
Thurgh thilke cursed superfluitee   (524–28)

—and follows through with a reversion to eating: where earlier it had been "Mete unto wombe, and wombe eek unto mete" (522), here it is the belly as "stynkyng cod, / Fulfilled of dong and of corrupcioun!" (534–35) and again the wasted labor provoked by gluttons. Then Chaucer reverts again to the drunk, this time a disgusting as well as crazy one, foul of breath, snorting, falling down like a stuck pig. Curiously, it's *wine* that does this, not the cheaper ale that the Pardoner might be expected to mention with rural audiences. This return to wine gets forty lines all by itself, longer than either the section on dicing or the one on swearing. It includes its own recursion, a reprise of the snorting— "Sampsoun, Sampsoun!"—eighteen lines after the first mention. This return to wine includes also three references to the way people with power should stay away from wine. The first of these references, the one to Samson the judge, comes early. The last two, to Attila and Lemuel, close the whole section on gluttony (573–87).

---

[11] Cf. David Lawton, *Chaucer's Narrators* (Cambridge: D. S. Brewer, 1985), 22.

I know nothing like this degree of recursiveness—this compulsive going back—anywhere else in Chaucer's poetry. It tends to the parapractic. And before I try to explain it by looking at another parapraxis, I want to suggest what may have been the "exciting cause" of it all, a passage on the miseries of old age from Maximianus, a sixth-century Roman who appeared regularly in schoolbooks of Chaucer's day. The passage is the source for a large part of the speech that Chaucer gives the mysterious Old Man. Two things are to be noted here. In Chaucer, the father having disappeared, the Old Man wants to return, not to the mother's lap ("gremio ... tuo"), but to the mother's house. The paternal ground ("patrio ... solo") has become "the ground, which is my moodres gate" (729).[12]

The parapraxis I mentioned a moment ago occurs in the last large reproof of drunkenness.

> Now kepe yow fro the white and fro the rede,
> And namely fro the white wyn of Lepe
> That is to selle in Fysshstrete or in Chepe.
> This wyn of Spaigne crepeth subtilly
> In othere wynes, growynge faste by,
> Of which ther ryseth swich fumositee
> That whan a man hath dronken draughtes thre,
> And weneth that he be at hoom in Chepe,
> He is in Spaigne, right at the toune of Lepe—
> Nat at the Rochele, ne at Burdeux toun—
> And thanne wol he seye "Sampsoun, Sampsoun!"   (562–72)

Fish Street is important. In all Chaucer's existing work, he mentions only three streets. One is Watling Street, the Roman road running through London that has lent its name, as Chaucer reports in the *House of Fame*, to the Milky Way. The second is Cheap, or Cheapside, London's main artery, a street wide enough for tournaments to have been held in it and, with stalls in the middle, to have served as something of a country fair. Chaucer alludes to taverns in Cheapside in the *Cook's Tale* and the *Manciple's Prologue* as well as in the Pardoner's performance. This leaves Fish Street, which occurs only here, the only non-famous street in all of Chaucer—so non-famous that a great Chaucerian confused it with New Fish Street in East London, well removed from the Vintry, the ward dense with wine merchants, some of whom ran taverns on their premises, and some of whom unlawfully used strong wines like the Spanish ones to mix with weaker French wines that went to vinegar faster.[13] With this reference to Fish Street, Chaucer sets us down less than two hundred yards from what was likely

---

[12]See Mary Hamel, "The Pardoner's Prologue and Tale," in *Sources and Analogues of the Canterbury Tales*, ed. Robert M. Correale and Mary Hamel (Cambridge: D. S. Brewer, 2002), 267–319; quotations from Maximianus, *Elegy I*, p. 317.

[13]See André L. Simon, *The History of the Wine Trade in England*, 3 vols. (London: Wyman & Sons, 1906), 1: 237, 304–5.

his boyhood home on Thames Street, where he probably lived from at least 1345 until no later than 1357, when he would have been about seventeen.[14]

The strong Spanish wine for sale in Fish Street can intoxicate you fast:

> whan a man hath dronken draughtes thre,
> And weneth that he be at hoom in Chepe,
> He is in Spaigne.

But think about it. If he is hallucinating, he may suppose, imagine, *wenen* that he is somewhere foreign, Spain, for instance, all the while he has never left Cheapside. But he does not hallucinate he is in Cheapside. Cheapside is where he is. If "in Spaigne" means that the man is unconscious, dead to the world, then of course he is not supposing, *wenyng*, anything at all. That's what unconscious means. It's Chaucer who unconsciously wants to "be at hoom in Chepe." Why in Cheapside rather than Fish Street has to do perhaps with a counter-wish, the wish not to go home, the wish counter to all this recursiveness. He gets a street away from Thames Street, then turns back north.

Why the counter-wish? Why not just the wish to go back, but also the wish not to? In all Chaucer's work, happy relations between son and father are few indeed. A. C. Spearing observes that "Chaucer goes further than most of his contemporaries in the persistence with which he presents paternal authority as absent or cruel."[15] Three times Chaucer writes that men with authority should stay away from the retail purchase of wine. This preaching seems odd for the Pardoner's rural audience, who are unlikely to identify themselves with the judges of Israel. The unconscious inversion of this, however, is that men involved with the *sale* of wine—in fact, involved with the wholesaling of it—should be kept away from the exercise of power.

Freud writes in his case history of Dora about "unconscious processes of thought which are twined around a pre-existing structure of organic connections, much as festoons of flowers are twined around a wire."[16] This pre-existing structure can be a matter of narrative connections rather than organic ones. So this compulsion to go back twines itself around narrative elements that Chaucer takes up. There are many analogues to the story of the three men who discover death by discovering gold. Yet only in Chaucer's telling do they need to get home again if they are to succeed:

> myghte this gold be caried fro this place
> Hoom to myn hous, or elles unto youres—

[14] *The City of London from Prehistoric Times to c. 1520*, The British Atlas of Historic Towns, vol. 3, ed. W. H. Johns (Oxford: Oxford University Press, 1989), Map 3. See also V. B. and L. J. Redstone, "The Heyrons of London: A Study in the Social Origins of Geoffrey Chaucer," *Speculum* 12 (1937), sketch map following p. 184. See *Chaucer Life-Records*, ed. Martin M. Crow and Clair C. Olson (Oxford: Clarendon Press, 1966), 8–9.

[15] *Medieval to Renaissance in English Poetry* (Cambridge: Cambridge University Press, 1985), 95; cf. 92–103. And cf. Jill Mann, "Parents and Children in the *Canterbury Tales*," in *Literature in Fourteenth-Century England: The J. A. W. Bennett Lectures, Perugia, 1981–82*, ed. Piero Boitani and Anna Torti (Tübingen: Gunter Narr; Cambridge: D. S. Brewer, 1983), esp. 167, 169, 178.

[16] *Fragment of an Analysis of a Case of Hysteria*, SE 7: 84–85.

> For wel ye woot that al this gold is oures—
> Thanne were we in heigh felicitee. (784–87)

Only in Chaucer are these three poised between a boy who comes out from his mother and an Old Man who wants to go back to his mother.

I should like to move now from repetition to a transference by asking Freud's question: where in the Pardoner's performance is "His Majesty the Ego, the hero alike of every day-dream and of every story"?[17] In all of Chaucer, the only two characters who tell stories as a way of life are the Pardoner, who says that "lewed peple loven tales olde," and Chaucer himself, who, the Man of Law complains, has used up all the available tales. I am suggesting an identification here, but one kept unconscious by its being generally inverted. Chaucer describes himself in the *House of Fame* as reclusive. The Pardoner is obviously audacious, in your face. The Pardoner has protuberant eyes, "glarynge eyen," like a hare. In an inversion of that, one of the Canterbury pilgrims tells Chaucer, "Thou lookest as thou woldest fynde a hare, / For evere upon the ground I se thee stare" (VII 697). Chaucer won't meet your eye. The Pardoner insists on filling it. This identification and inversion are worth arguing for, it seems to me, not least because they would offer a solution to an ongoing problem for critics, the way in which Chaucer imputes to the Pardoner an overload in his sexual life. Does he lack facial hair because he is a eunuch or because he has become feminized through an excess of copulation? Is he a homosexual, passive to the Summoner's "stif burdoun" (I 673), or, in insisting on "a joly wenche in every toun" (VI 453), bisexual or even heterosexual? This sexual surplus seems redundant with the Pardoner's insistence on a multiplicity of object choices:

> I wol have moneie, wolle, chese, and whete,
> Al were it yeven of the povereste page,
> Or of the povereste wydwe in a village,
> Al sholde hir children sterve for famyne.
> Nay, I wol drynke licour of the vyne
> And have a joly wenche in every toun. (448–53)

This profusion of object choices, all precisely named, inverts the "certeyn thing" that Chaucer the narrator of the early poems wanted, did not get, and could not even name. To this inversion I shall return at the conclusion of the essay. Inversions notwithstanding, however, Chaucer's identification with the Pardoner depends crucially on recursiveness, a feature that the two share and that can be represented directly since it is drained of sexual or any other strong interest.

Chaucer describes the Pardoner as succeeding in his viciousness by doing certain things over and over again. The first of these is the sermon that he has down to a science, efficiently terrifying, as we see from its effect on Harry Bailly. Another instance of perfected technique is his "gaude," a 'trick' that has been good for a hundred marks a year ever since the Pardoner was a pardoner (VI 389–90). I shall shortly come back to it. What is thus represented as serviceable

---

[17] "Creative Writers and Day-Dreaming," SE 9: 150.

in story time has its source in what had been dysfunctional, parapractic in narrative time—the recursiveness in narration that led Kiser to think that Chaucer was characterizing the Pardoner as incompetent. In other words, Chaucer misrecognizes his own recursivenessness in repetitions that are functional for the Pardoner.

Meanwhile, repetitions permeate what David Lawton has called the Pardoner's "final bizarre essay in salesmanship" (*Chaucer's Narrators*, 18). We approach it through the exordium of his rote sermon:

> Now, goode men, God foryeve yow youre trepas,
> And ware yow fro the synne of avarice!
> Myn hooly pardoun may yow all warice,
> So that ye offre nobles or sterlynges,
> Or elles silver broches, spoones, rynges.
> Boweth youre heed under this hooly bulle!
> . . . .
> I yow assoille, by myn heigh power,
> Yow that wol offre, as clene and eek as cleer
> As ye were born.—And lo, sires, thus I preche.
> And Jhesu Crist, that is oure soules leche,
> So graunte yow his pardoun to receyve,
> For that is best; I wol yow not deceyve.
> But, sires, o word forgat I in my tale:
> I have relikes and pardoun in my male,
> As faire as any man in Engelond.   (904–21)

Except the Pardoner has not forgotten it. He just said it—said it four times actually (904–5, 906–8, 910–12, 913–15): I can cure you all, he had said, just as long as you offer. And now we have to ask, is this repetition like the Pardoner's preaching the same sermon repeatedly? Is Chaucer characterizing the Pardoner as doing this purposefully, serviceably? What does Chaucer intend the ending of this poem to be about? Surely Patterson is right to maintain that critics may not efface authorial intent entirely. Some time ago, I did inquire "what Chaucer might plausibly be thought to have meant [here]" (Patterson, 679), and I began with the fact that on this occasion the Pardoner is not preaching his sermon, he is quoting it—a change which means, I think, that Chaucer apprehends that the Pardoner is getting to hear it himself for the first time.[18] Warning and quoting are different speech acts and place different conditions upon the speaker. But if you assume the existence of the unconscious, then you believe that our conscious acts serve unconscious purposes. And so all the while Chaucer is conscious of something going on here—first of all the repetition of the quotation of an invitation ("I yow assoille, . . . / Yow that wol offre") in the form of an invitation *tout court* ("Com forth anon, and kneleth heere adoun")— repetition in itself is going on for Chaucer, going back, going back towards home, never quite getting there, a little lullaby on the same thing over and over again:

---

[18]See "Chaucer's Pardoner: The Dialectics of Inside and Outside," *Philological Quarterly* 67 (1988): 414–16.

Or elles taketh pardoun as ye wende,
Al newe and fressh at every miles ende,
So that ye offren, alwey newe and newe.   (927–29)

And then something changes—a kicking of the habit, so to speak. Lévi-Strauss writes of "The Story of Asdiwal" that later sequences of the story "are organized in schemata which are at the same time *homologous* to those which have been described and more *explicit* than them. Everything seems to suggest that, as it draws to its close, the obvious narrative ... tends to approach the latent content of the myth."[19] Thus, with enough repetitions, what is at stake in the return that is never completed and thus never abandoned becomes clear in a transference.[20] In what appears to be a new parapraxis, the identificatory figure seems to forget what works. Actually, he stands it on its head. Year by year the Pardoner succeeds by letting people imply that they are not the worst sinners imaginable. This has been his perennial *gaude*. Now he turns to the Host, this taverner signifying vintner, and says, you are the "moost envoluped in synne." You're the worst. You start it off.

Where the identificatory figure, like most of the other pilgrims, had begun by deferring to "oure governour" (I 813), now he turns upon the father the terror of his story—a poor thing, but his own. The father for his part, in his fear and hatred, first infantilizes his son by alleging painted breeches. And then, "though noon auctoritee" were in no book of rat men or wolf men, he goes for the boy's testicles.

This is not, of course, the end. The *Wife of Bath's Tale* (III 1258–64) and the *Clerk's Tale* (IV 1177–212) each finish with a sort of abscission layer—a reductive restatement of what has gone before, a self-cancellation that protects the Tale by sealing it up. The Pardoner's performance ends by the Knight's breaking up a fight. In another of Chaucer's abscission layers, patently inadequate to all that has happened, a "governour" is substituted from the class of (for all we have been told) non-incompetent fathers. The Squire carved before his father at the table. He was not carved.

The Pardoner, who desires everything, is the unconscious inversion of the poet for whom the object of desire is not only missing but always unnamed. I wish to conclude by reverting to that narrator of the earlier poems and saying why I think the Pardoner is an unconscious inversion of him.

The narrator of the *Parliament of Fowls* has done a great deal of reading but finally reports, "I hadde thyng which that I nolde, / And ek I ne hadde that thyng that I wolde" (90–91). Does Chaucer know what these are? Does he have any idea what this "thyng" might be? A. C. Spearing observes that the *Parliament* "is framed by references to something missing that cannot even be named, precisely because it is missing."[21] The unnamed, perhaps unnamable "thing" that Chaucer reads to find, the "thyng" he doesn't get from reading,

---

[19] "The Story of Asdiwal" (1958–59), in *The Structural Study of Myth and Totemism*, ed. Edmund Leach (London: Tavistock Publications, 1967), 21; Lévi-Strauss's emphasis.
[20] I owe this point to Dr. Joanne Lindy.
[21] "Al This Mene I By Love," *Studies in the Age of Chaucer*, Proceedings no. 2 (1987): 175.

the "thyng" that may someday make him "fare / The bet" strikingly recalls the
"Thing" that Julia Kristeva posits in her study of depression and melancholia—
"the real that does not lend itself to signification, the center of attraction and
repulsion, seat of the sexuality from which the object of desire will become separated."[22] Lacan had called "*das Ding*" (which he had found in the 1925 paper
on "Negation" and elsewhere in Freud) "the beyond-of-the-signified," "*fremde*,
strange and even hostile on occasion, or in any case the first outside," "the absolute Other of the subject, that one is supposed to find again. It is to be found
at the most as something missed."[23]

    Kristeva's study originates in one sense with "Mourning and Melancholia,"
where Freud claims for melancholia a special mode of retention of a lost object.
Among objects we must sometimes abandon are narcissistic ones that we feel
about ambivalently. A father can be a pre-oedipal object for a little boy: the
boy can identify himself with him narcissistically (find himself as boy in his
father), and he may also desire him.[24] This attraction to the father is ambivalent
from the first, since it falls under the prohibition upon same-sex love. The
ensuing abandonment of the father as erotic object is accomplished through a
"narcissistic identification with the object," an identification that "then becomes
a substitute for the erotic cathexis." This means of abandonment splits the ego:
the narcissistic identification exists as an unconscious witness to a guilty love,
but one never relinquished like other lost loves when a substitute object in the
external world comes to be desired. Split off from this identification, on which
"the shadow of the object" has fallen, "the critical activity of the ego" punishes
the ego for a guilty love that never reaches consciousness.[25]

    Judith Butler has pressed the implications of these same-sex gender identi-
fications consequential for melancholia. When, on the one hand, for one reason
or another, I lose an other-sex object, desire can be displaced on to a substitute
object because a "heterosexual aim" has been retained. "On the other hand,
the loss of the homosexual object requires the loss of the aim *and* the object. In
other words, the object is not only lost, but the desire fully denied."[26] Because
aim as well as object must be repressed, identification with the lost same-sex
object bars all signification. Freud's *Ding*, Kristeva's *Chose*, the narrator's lost
object cannot be represented except as "thyng," an unnamable object for which

---

[22] *Black Sun: Depression and Melancholia*, trans. L. S. Roudiez (New York: Columbia University Press, 1989), 13. I owe this suggestion to Laura Mandell. "Le dépressif narcissique
est en deuil non pas d'un Objet mais de la Chose" (*Soleil Noir* [Paris: Gallimard, 1987], 22).
('The depressed narcissist mourns not an Object but the Thing.')

[23] Lacan, *The Seminar*, ed. J.-A. Miller, 4 vols. to date (New York: Norton, 1988–), vol.
7, *The Ethics of Psychoanalysis*, trans. Dennis Porter (1959–60), 54, 52. Kristeva makes a
distinction between her own conception of *la Chose* and Lacan's if not Freud's: see *Black Sun*,
262–63, n. 10.

[24] The mutual exclusiveness of identification and desire does not seem to hold for pre-oedipal
objects. See Freud, "Group Psychology" (1921), SE 4: 105.

[25] "Mourning and Melancholia" 249, 245. On this "clivage" in the ego, see esp. Jean Florence,
"Les Identifications," in *Les Identifications: Confrontation de la clinique et de la théorie de
Freud à Lacan*, ed. Patrick Guyomard and Maud Mannoni (Paris: Denoël, 1987), 168–69.

[26] *Gender Trouble: Feminism and the Subversion of Identity* (New York and London: Routledge, 1990), 69; Butler's emphasis.

even the unconscious content of the *Parliament*, if it became conscious, would remain a screen.

Because archaic aim and object have been lost together, any particular pleasure can "shield from the pain of pre-oedipal separation" without yet reproducing the first attraction. A host of sexual pleasures, like the plethora imputed to the Pardoner, all of them separated, in Kristeva's phrase, from "the seat of the[ir] sexuality," saves the subject from destruction in the process of seeking blindly "to *refind*" the "thing."[27] I suggest that Chaucer unconsciously identifies himself with the Pardoner in part because the Pardoner's insistent, conflicting, perverse hungers would shield from the loss of an archaic aim and object in Chaucer's unconscious.

Only nine lines in the General Prologue concern the Pardoner's physiognomy, as Lawton has pointed out, and yet there is now a large literature on his gender and sexuality (*Chaucer's Narrators*, 27). Obviously, I have contributed nothing to that. By contrast, virtually nothing has been written on Chaucer's sexuality, although we have, so to speak, the *corpus*. If some knowledge of E. M. Forster's sexuality helps us to understand *A Passage to India*, or some knowledge of Virginia Woolf's helps us read a passage to a certain lighthouse, then some knowledge of Chaucer's sexuality might improve our understanding of, say, the *Troilus*. Here I've said little about his sexuality, of course; but his wouldn't be the first that had something to do with his father. Like all texts, his keeps silent before our question. It doesn't rise up from the couch and begin snarling at us. But poems speak in the first place, and psychoanalysis is a heuristic for hearing them.

* * *

Emerson Brown was a 1956 graduate of Hamilton College, where I followed him a couple of years later. Amiable, visible, admired, he played jazz at reunions year after year, bicycling from Nashville to do so at least once, youthful even when his health was no longer good. Not least for his courage, the alumni learned of his death with affectionate grief; and as perhaps the only alumnus contributing to this volume, I would like to represent that here.

---

[27] Kristeva, *Black Sun*, 49, 48; Freud, "Negation" (1925), SE 19: 237; Freud's emphasis. Cf. Lacan, *The Seminar* 7: 53.

Wifely Eye for the Manly Guy

Trading the Masculine Image in the *Shipman's Tale*

HOLLY A. CROCKER

"An ounce of image is worth a pound of performance"
—political maxim, *Roll Call*, 11 September 1988

The explicit connection between sex and money in Chaucer's *Shipman's Tale*, for all the critical attention devoted to it, has not yielded very plain insights into the tale's meaning. It is true, as critics including William F. Woods, Thomas Hahn, and R. H. Winnick suggest, that the sex that goes into marriage is commodified by the tale's transactional dynamic.[1] But that does not mean that sex *is* money in this tale, even if criticism of the tale lately has presumed that such is the case.[2] In what follows I argue that we should *get back to the sex* in this story, because like getting sex, making money depends upon the valuations of desire.[3] Like making money, getting sex requires careful management of visibility, of making others see one's image as one wishes. As the merchant in this story knows well, cultivating an image of manly generosity is a crucial element in his successful financial dealings. Daun John, too, despite his façade of celibacy, is quick to assume a pose of virile potency as soon as the wife complains of her husband's faulty performance. As if on command, each man seeks to associate himself with an image of masculinity that secures parity between his financial and sexual abilities.

In order to achieve this comprehensive fantasy of masculinity, the merchant and the monk attempt to use the wife's (in)visibility to authenticate their performances. But the wife does not fit the receptive yet complicit model of feminine

---

[1] William F. Woods, "A Professional Thyng: The Wife as Merchant's Apprentice in the *Shipman's Tale*," *Chaucer Review* 24 (1989): 139–49; Thomas Hahn, "Money, Sexuality, Wordplay and Context in the *Shipman's Tale*," in *Chaucer in the Eighties*, ed. Julian N. Wasserman and Robert J. Blanch (Syracuse: Syracuse University Press, 1986), 235–49; R. H. Winnick, "Luke 12 and Chaucer's *Shipman's Tale*," *Chaucer Review* 30 (1995): 164–90.

[2] John M. Ganim, "Double Entry in Chaucer's *Shipman's Tale*: Chaucer and Bookkeeping before Pacioli," *Chaucer Review* 30 (1996): 294–305; Helen Fulton, "Mercantile Ideology in Chaucer's *Shipman's Tale*," *Chaucer Review* 36 (2002): 311–28; W. E. Rogers and P. Dower, "Thinking About Money in Chaucer's *Shipman's Tale*," in *New Readings of Chaucer's Poetry*, ed. Robert G. Benson, Susan J. Ridyard, and Derek Brewer (Cambridge: D. S. Brewer, 2003), 199–238.

[3] See Janet Thormann, "The Circulation of Desire in the 'Shipman's Tale,'" *Literature and Psychology* 39 (1993): 1–15.

passivity needed to fulfill these desires. While the wife is perfectly willing to benefit from her husband's financial acumen and Daun John's sexual savvy, she does not allow either man to use her image as a means to gain comprehensive masculine dominance. Instead, the wife herself becomes an active player in this tale, as Woods suggests, by using her body as currency to gain the money she needs to satisfy her taste for "array" (VII 14; see Woods, 146–47). While I too will suggest that the wife becomes a trader in the economy of this tale, I submit that her currency is masculinity itself. Because these men read their success *as men* according to the wife's satisfaction, their masculine credit depends on giving her "ynough" (money or sex) to gain her allegiance.[4]

As a result, we might say that Daun John is a better masculine player in this tale, since he compels the wife's complicity even after he cheats her out of the cash her husband fails to provide her in their daily affairs. Such would be true, I submit, if the stakes of manliness in this tale were tied to the wife's *actual* fidelity. They are not. As I shall argue, securing the image of masculine plenitude in this tale depends on the wife's *appearance* of loyalty. Intersecting with what Michael Camille calls "the increasing emphasis on sight" in the late Middle Ages, I suggest that characters in the *Shipman's Tale* know that a man's *image* of potency is more important than his performance.[5] And, in a concluding scene that illustrates for many the tale's amorality, the tale suggests that performance of an image actually gives substance to the appearance it situates.

"You're So Money"

The merchant's introduction suggests that his ability to succeed in the financial world depends on the way that others see him. As Helen Fulton points out, merchants were associated with a particular public image, a careful masculinity that equates self-discipline and financial control.[6] While the tale's equation

---

[4]The word "ynough" is used five times in the tale, (lines 100, 219, 245, 287, 380), and itself seems to connect sex and finance. See Vern L. Bullough, "On Being a Male in the Middle Ages," in *Medieval Masculinities: Regarding Men in the Middle Ages*, ed. Clare Lees (Minneapolis: University of Minnesota Press, 1994), 31–45. Bullough states that for a man to maintain his image in the community, he must satisfy women: "It was part of his duty to keep his female partners happy and satisfied, and unless he did so, he had failed as a man" (41). Masculinity, we might say, is connected to giving a woman "ynough."

[5]Michael Camille, "The Image and the Self: Unwriting Late Medieval Bodies," in *Framing Medieval Bodies*, ed. Sarah Kay and Miri Rubin (New York: Manchester University Press, 1994), 62–99 (77).

[6]For information on merchants' changing social position in the late fourteenth century, see the foundational work, Sylvia Thrupp, *The Merchant Class of Medieval London* (Chicago: University of Chaicago Press, 1948; reprint, Ann Arbor Paperback, 1962). See also D. Vance Smith, *Arts of Possession: The Middle English Household Imaginary* (Minneapolis: University of Minnesota Press, 2003) especially 23–43; 126–36. Smith also suggests that the problematic account of their exchange of money in the medieval imaginary made merchants conceal their identities more carefully in the public eye. While Fulton, 311-28, agrees that merchants did not mark their social identities through ostentatious displays, she also points out that "By the late fourteenth century, merchants were too powerful, too visible, too integral to the urban economy, especially in London, to be marginalized through the odd satirical portrait or unflattering anecdote based on the conventional stereotype of the greedy materialistic merchant" (312).

of wealth and wisdom is perhaps a mocking jab that nevertheless admits the inevitability of commercial culture, this conjunction, "That riche was, for which men helde hym wys" (VII 2), underscores the power of public perception in this emerging social milieu.[7] People believe the merchant is wise because they know that he is rich. This surplus-value is all very nice for the merchant, assuming that his wealth is money in the bank. But as we know from the *General Prologue's* description of the pilgrim Merchant, and as we find out during this tale's unfolding events, a merchant's wealth is a fluctuating variable. So, it seems that being rich also involves a performative aspect. Now, acting wise is perhaps one way of creating the impression that one is rich; but since acting wise is not a conspicuous mode of conduct, this association threatens to become soft. As we see with the merchant, a surer way to let on that one is rich, and thus to prove that one is wise, is to make people think one has money. The simplest way to make people think that one has money is through a program of financial "largesse" (22).

Although it might seem a simple enough task to gain a reputation for generosity, if one also seeks to preserve a reputation for careful management of wealth, this balancing act becomes tricky. Here's where a wife comes in handy, especially a beautiful one who is known to be "compaignable and revelous" (4). Not only does an attractive wife imply that one's financial prowess and sexual capacity are interconnected; she may also act the part of sociable hostess that a man's regard for his own reserved figure might preclude. My description here admittedly casts this type of marriage in its most reductively bourgeois light. Nevertheless, I believe the merchant's marital arrangement shares with our current "trophy wife" model a preoccupation with public image. Making money, even from the tale's outset, is about managing visibility. The wife's initial concern with "array," then (14), far from making her a threat to the merchant's cultivation of wealth, makes her one of his most important assets in his pursuit of money. Her taste in finery suggests that she too takes great care to present a refined public image. While the wife may not fulfill biblical or moral prescriptions for a model wife, she shows through her attention to appearance that she is a perfect wife for her mercantile husband.[8] She is part of his "worthy hous" (20), consolidating through her sociable habits her husband's "riche" manly estate (2).

Leaving the issue of the tale's teller aside, it remains true that the feminine pronouns in the opening lines, especially in light of the events that follow, undercut the image of masculine continence that the merchant seeks to construct for himself.[9] But the feminine agency introduced here is not part of a satire, either

---

[7]Lee Patterson, *Chaucer and the Subject of History* (Madison: University of Wisconsin Press, 1991) 352; 365, suggests that the tale nods to the legitimate inevitability of the bourgeois life. Rogers and Dower, 199–238, give a helpful reading of Patterson's argument as it relates to criticism of the tale.

[8]Theresa Coletti, in "The *Mulier Fortis* and Chaucer's *Shipman's Tale*," *Chaucer Review* 15 (1980–81): 236–49, argues that Chaucer's initial description of the wife suggests that she is an inversion of the "good wife" from Biblical prescription.

[9]See Richard F. Jones, "A Conjecture on the Wife of Bath's Prologue," *Journal of English and Germanic Philology* 24 (1925): 512–47; Robert A. Pratt, "The Development of

of insatiable women or of materialistic merchants.[10]   Instead, the tale allows
a woman's voice to over-write the image of manly control that the merchant
desires, admitting right from the beginning that a husband's status depends on
the way his wife's agency becomes visible in the public eye. Even if this voice
is ominous, threatening possible infidelity as punishment for a miserly husband,
what I would like to acknowledge is that the transactional cast that this wom-
anly voice gives marriage only illustrates the suitability of the merchant and his
wife *as partners* in their conjugal union. If the merchant is married to a wife who
expects to be rewarded for the good face she puts forward to the public, she is
a perfect match for her "superficial" husband, who gains substantial profit from
his creative ability to pass off value through market exchange. Furthermore,
the tale's characterization of their bond as a contractual arrangement between
parties who exert equally limiting agency literally makes true the doctrine of
conjugality upon which marriage's sacramental status was based.[11]   Instead of
looking at this marriage as commodified, somehow corrupted by the taint of
money, I suggest that we view it from the outset as an arrangement that gives
equal play to women's power to exercise agency in the marital economy figured
through the household.[12]

The merchant's problem, therefore, is his refusal to see his wife as a partner
in this visible arena of exchange. Instead, he views her as a passive ornament
decorating the estate he builds for both of them. Because he makes his wife
invisible by assuming that she is a fully incorporated part of his character, he
does not recognize that *because* marriage makes her part of his estate, she is able

---

the Wife of Bath," in *Studies in Medieval Literature*, ed. MacEdward Leach (Philadelphia:
University of Pennsylvania Press, 1961), 45–79; William W. Lawrence, "Chaucer's *Shipman's
Tale*," *Speculum* 33 (1958): 56–68; and William W. Lawrence, "The Wife of Bath and the
Shipman," *Modern Language Notes* 72 (1957): 87–88. There have been several readings of
the tale that seek to establish the Shipman's appropriateness for this story by claiming that
he mocks a feminine perspective by speaking with feminine pronouns. See, for example, Fred-
erick Tupper, "The Bearings of the Shipman's Prologue," *Journal of English and Germanic
Philology* 33 (1934): 352–72; Robert L. Chapman, "The *Shipman's Tale* Was Meant for the
Shipman," *Modern Language Notes* 71 (1956): 4–5; and Hazel Sullivan, "A Chaucerian Puzzle," *A Chaucerian Puzzle and Other Medieval Essays*, ed. Natalie Grimes Lawrence and Jack
A. Reynolds (Coral Gables: University of Miami Press, 1961): 1–46.

[10]See V. J. Scattergood, "The Originality of the *Shipman's Tale*," *Chaucer Review* 11
(1977): 210–31; Robert Adams, "The Concept of Debt in the *Shipman's Tale*," *Studies in the
Age of Chaucer* 6 (1984): 85–102.

[11]See Glenn Burger's chapter, "Medieval Conjugality and the *Canterbury Tales*," in his
Chaucer's Queer Nation (Minneapolis: University of Minnesota Press, 2003), 37–77; Burger
discusses the opportunities and pressures that an emerging emphasis on conjugal affection
placed on lay gender roles in the late Middle Ages. As he states, "What I am interested in
here is how the married estate ... nonetheless comes to be redefined in a way that allows it
to structure an empowering identity for individuals and groups not previously given represen-
tational force. At the private level, it allows individual men and women to assert their right
of choice, although clearly family and economic factors still worked to constrain individual
choice" (70–71).

[12]While I am much influenced by Peter G. Beidler's essay, "Contrasting Masculinities in
the *Shipman's Tale*: Monk, Merchant, and Wife," in *Masculinities in Chaucer*, ed. Peter G.
Beidler (Cambridge: D. S. Brewer, 1998): 131–42, because his argument acknowledges both
the presence and legitimacy of the wife's agency, I disagree with his initial assumption that the
wife's self-control would ever be viewed as "masculine," even in a medieval gender economy.

to exercise even greater influence over the ways that others see him. In plainest terms, if the wife is part of the husband, what she does affects the husband's identity. Whether or not he likes it, the merchant already contains the wife's character, so her actions already affect his image. Structures of conjugality and laws of coverture, then, make the husband's dependence on his wife's behavior more visible. Although the men in the *Shipman's Tale* perhaps wish that they could inhabit a cloistered community immune to feminine influence, when the monk comes to exploit the largesse of the friend with whom he claims a bond of "cosynage" (36), it becomes apparent that women exercise control over the kinds of masculinities that men are able to take up. Unlike other fabliaux, the *Shipman's Tale* admits that women have agency, and it suggests that such control is legitimate in this transactional world of manly exchange. As the feminine voice at the tale's beginning reveals, through their dealings women can make or break men's images in their communities.

First Movers

The wife's skill in manipulating appearances has its initial impact during her garden-encounter with Daun John. Although it is unclear exactly who begins the seduction that leads to their adulterous compact, John C. McGalliard points out that they both show themselves to be opportunists waiting to capitalize on any opening that might confer advantage.[13] If we look at the events leading up to the garden scene, however, it is clear that the monk *thinks* he is in control because he already believes he masters the domain of his friend the merchant. While the tale suggests that the merchant and his wife have many guests, "For his largesse, and for his wyf was fair" (22), the monk is a regular visitor whose company the merchant obviously values. Treating the monk like his sworn brother, the merchant invites Daun John "That he sholde come to Seint-Denys to pleye / With hym and with his wyf a day or tweye" (59–60). After Daun John arrives bearing the gifts that give him his reputation for generosity among the members of the merchant's household, the two friends take a couple of days to enjoy each other's company. Now, in all likelihood the wife is involved in their festivities, but the tale is nevertheless careful to underscore the masculine community that their society fosters: "And thus I lete hem ete and drynke and pleye, / This marchant and this monk, a day or tweye" (73–74). It is only on the third day, after they have affirmed the affection that causes "ech of hem ... [the] oother for t'assure / Of bretherhede whil that hir lyf may dure" (41–42), that the merchant withdraws from his friend to attend to his business accounts.

My point in rehearsing the bonds of friendship that connect these men is that the wife, for all her presence earlier and later in the story, is hardly worthy of mention in the lines that set out the history and affection that exist between merchant and monk. Even if the wife is party to the fun these men share, by all appearances this is a relationship between *men*. They do not consider her presence important because they do not think her activity has significant impact on their affairs. Assuming she indeed helps her husband entertain his guests,

---

[13] John C. McGalliard, "Characterization in Chaucer's *Shipman's Tale*," *Philological Quarterly* 54 (1975): 1–18.

she is the unseen mover in this episode. When the wife appears in the garden, the monk is already installed in an environment where he feels comfortable in his assumption of control. While I do not think that the monk has cultivated his friendship with the merchant in order to seduce his wife, his close ties to the merchant give him a sense of intimacy with the wife that exceeds normal bounds of propriety. As in the Old French fabliau *des ii. Changeors*, the wife becomes the monk's object of desire *because* of his friendship with her husband.[14] While in the Old French tale the wife serves as conduit of desire between the two men (albeit without the husband's knowledge), in Chaucer's story the wife's agency short-circuits this flow of homosocial desire.[15] When the monk makes a joke that is potentially off-color, responding to the wife's social pleasantries with a comment that asserts his sexual potency in relation to "thise wedded men, that lye and dare" (103), his jesting indicates the assured dominance he believes he wields.

Teasing his friend's wife about her husband's sexual potency, "I trowe, certes, that oure goode man / Hath yow laboured sith the nyght bigan" (107–8), the monk assumes a posture of familiarity that indicates his sexual control over the wife. In other words, because he is so close to her husband, he already assumes that she is his to "pley" (59) with, because he already assumes that the merchant's "chaffare" (285) is equally his own. While Daun John certainly steps over the line with his verbal sport, his inappropriateness simply illustrates the presumption that accompanies relations that men assume are only between themselves. There is no harm in joking with the merchant's wife, his comment suggests, because as his friend's possession there is no danger that she can take the initiative, even to take offense at his comments. Because both men assume that she is a passive player in their relations, a conduit through whom their masculine good cheer is circulated, he acts as if he can tease her in the same way that he would her husband. But he could not be more wrong. As the wife's reaction illustrates, what may have begun as an unfitting joke quickly misfires. Showing the rippling productivity of misfire in language, it is not just that his joke here doesn't do what he intends; rather, it does something else, producing a completely different set of possibilities than those he perhaps imagined.[16]

More Than He Bargained For

When Daun John teases the wife about her husband's sexual prowess, she unleashes an emotive complaint that suggests her sexual despair is so serious that

---

[14] *des ii. Changeors*, edited and translated by N. E. Dubin. © N. E. Dubin 2003. Warmest thanks to Professor Dubin for allowing me to read and use his unpublished verse translation of this fabliau.

[15] See "Verses Concerning the Pepper-Mill," in *The Literary Context of Chaucer's Fabliaux*, ed. Larry D. Benson and Theodore M. Andersson (New York: Bobbs-Merrill, 1971), 280–81; "The Priest and the Lady," in *Literary Context*, 328–37. For analysis of the circulations of homosocial desire that "trafficking" women can facilitate between men see Gayle Rubin, "The Traffic in Women: Notes on the Political Economy of Sex," in *Towards an Anthropology of Women*, ed. Rayna R. Reiter (New York: Monthly Review Press, 1975), 157–210, and Eve Kosofsky Sedgwick, *Between Men: English Literature and Male Homosocial Desire* (New York: Columbia University Press, 1985), 1–27.

[16] Shoshana Felman, *The Literary Speech Act* (Ithaca: Cornell University Press, 1983), 84.

it might even lead to suicide: "In al the reawme of France is ther no wyf / That lasse lust hath to that sory pley.... Wherfore I thynke ... of myself to make an ende" (116–17; 121–23). Now, in Daun John's line of work it is certainly possible that a misplaced joke can trigger a revealing response. But since the tale works hard to emphasize the social relationship that this monk has with the merchant's "meynee" (48), theirs is no regular confessional bond. And, considering that the topic of conversation is the wife's sexual satisfaction with her husband, when she takes the monk's joke seriously, Daun John's kidding quickly elicits personal information that a man's friend just might not want to hear. It is no wonder, then, that the monk "bigan upon this wyf to stare" (124). If he is shocked by the wife's response, the monk does not shut down this line of conversation. He invites further disclosure, perhaps even invoking the power of his office to secure the wife's trust. When Daun John swears on his "portehors" to keep the wife's secrets (135), he makes a play to see what he may gain out of this situation. But that does not mean that he is particularly after sex at this point. Given the bent of the conversation, sex is a possibility; however, the monk might just as easily gain embarrassing details about his friend that would reinforce his sense of superiority over the merchant. Since the wife exercises a type of independent agency that he does not expect, the monk is not in control of what happens next. Instead, Daun John must wait for the wife to tip her hand before he knows how to play the game that is unfolding.

While the two certainly play each other move for move, the wife works to convince Daun John to fit himself into a model of manhood that she desires. As she worries about the masculine bonds her disclosure might break, she gives the monk the opportunity to become the type of man for whom such loyalties are superficial. Telling Daun John that she will unfold her woe with her husband, although he is the monk's "cosyn" (147), the wife sounds the depths of masculine loyalty that the monk is willing to profess. As if on cue, the monk takes up the position she offers, telling her that his friendship with the merchant has always served a different purpose, "To have the moore cause of aqueyntaunce / Of yow, which I have loved specially / Aboven alle wommen, sikerly" (152–54). The monk may be telling the truth, but since he claims for himself the identity of a deceptive opportunist, his affection for the wife is impossible to authenticate and is really unimportant to her anyway. The wife goes on to tell the monk that what she really needs is a man who is not like her husband, a man who will satisfy her sexual and financial demands in the barest of transactional arrangements. In fact, when she tells him that she will "doon to yow what plesance and service / That I may doon, right as yow list devise" (191–92), she leaves affection completely out of the bargain. While the wife promises to give herself over in payment to the monk, what she wants is a man who is willing to take her body, give her money, then be on his way. She does not want a lover, a man who expects her submission to him to last for more than the single meeting to which she agrees.

The wife's chiding rebuke of her husband after her return from the garden illustrates the difference between the role she expects for him and the one that she has just negotiated with the monk. As Derek Pearsall points out, "The ease and speed with which she converts her own offence into a cause of complaint against her husband is nicely observed."[17] But the merchant's behavior, we also should admit, provides a sharp contrast to the kind of masculinity the wife claims to want, and perhaps validates the complaints that she makes to the monk. Having shut himself away to attend to his wealth, the merchant is the picture of husbandly respectability. But paired with his sententious speech outlining the responsibilities that attend their financial security, it is perhaps understandable that the wife is a bit bored with her husband. I am not suggesting that the merchant has been neglectful of his domestic duties or that he is a bad husband.[18] On the contrary, when the merchant explains to his wife the complexities of his trade and instructs her concerning how to run the household during his absence, he performs the role of husband to perfection. In his display of responsibility he fulfils five of the six expectations that the wife tells the monk all women have for their husbands: "Hardy and wise, and riche, and therto free, / And buxom unto his wyf and fressh abedde" (176–77). It seems the only thing the merchant lacks, or the only charge that he does not disprove in this short scene, is the ability to satisfy his wife sexually. The wife, her reaction suggests, wants to exercise agency in her relationship, but she also wants her partner to show some manly "get up." She does not want a henpecked husband whose only defense against her abuse is a cultivated space of isolation that excludes her from household dealings.

How To Spice Things Up ...

If this were a modern couple, we might see them on *Dr. Phil.*, *Oprah*, or even *Queer Eye*, talking about their problems, looking to remake their lives in order to improve their relationship. Even if we don't buy the wife's complaints, it seems true that *something is missing* in their marriage, that *they've lost that special spark* that made them the envy of all their friends and neighbors. While our contemporary patience for such rot is thankfully confined to afternoon and cable TV, the fabliaux have even less tolerance for the sort of precious sanctimony that fits neatly between commercial breaks. According to the relentless typologies traditionally associated with fabliaux, the wife is unsatisfied because she is a wife. As an unmitigated site of desire, as a locus of fleshly appetite, a woman *wants*. "Pity the fool" whose husbandly mandate requires him to contain, regulate, or satisfy such a creature. Yet this version of the fabliau's sex/gender system holds only if we assume that women's lack of agency in marriage is both descriptive and normative. While some fabliaux suggest the dangers of feminine agency, those are fewer in number than we might initially suspect, especially since women's unruly conduct is often represented as a justified response to "unreasonable" masculine domination.[19] And even though the

---

[17] Derek Pearsall, *The Canterbury Tales* (London: George Allen and Unwin, 1985), 214.

[18] Many critics do see the merchant's neglect as reason for the wife's infidelity. See David H. Abraham, "Cosyn and Cosynage: Pun and Structure in the *Shipman's Tale*," *Chaucer Review* 11 (1976–77): 319–27; Paul Stephen Schneider, "'Taillynge Ynough': The Function of Money in the *Shipman's Tale*," *Chaucer Review* 11 (1977): 201–209.

[19] Some Old French tales show wives acting outrageously in order to teach a moral lesson

wife of Chaucer's *Shipman's Tale* is an adulteress, I do not think this story is designed to show the ills of feminine agency itself. From the tale's outset the wife's agency is apparent, even if the men in the tale refuse to acknowledge its presence or potential. It is this willing masculine blindness, the attempt to make feminine agency invisible, that this tale takes apart. In other words, because the merchant refuses to see his wife as a partner with equal influence over the goings-on in the household, she directs her energies to other activities. As the first portion of the tale shows, a wife's ability to use the invisibility imposed upon her can damage the fantasy of masculine control it is supposedly designed to consolidate.

But the same goes for what we might call the tale's second part, after the monk sets up his deal with the wife in the garden. As I have been arguing, the monk views the wife's agency from the same perspective as the merchant. Because he believes in the myth of his own masculine potency, he refuses to recognize that the wife has influence over his performance of manliness. Daun John's confidence in his self-direction is apparent when he cheats the wife, designing a scheme that will allow him to get sex without giving money. While his clever trick allies this tale with other "lover's gift regained" plots, Chaucer's description of the way in which the monk gains the needed money from the merchant underscores the shared belief that important negotiations take place between men. In order to have sex with the wife, the monk goes to her husband, suggesting a need for contact that reveals the actual stakes of his game. Sexual gratification is not Daun John's primary goal; rather, he principally wants to confirm his masculine superiority over his friend. Now, if sleeping with a friend's wife is not enough to confirm one's manly dominance, then getting the money to facilitate this adulterous liaison from that same friend will surely illustrate the comprehensive scope of one's masculine control. Because he sees the wife as a passive possession of the merchant, the monk is primarily interested in cuckolding his friend, and in a way that will allow him to make his masculine power visible. The monk's second trick, then, is designed to ensure exposure. Even if the merchant never finds out about his friend's free use of his "chaffare" (285), Daun John's deception will show *the wife* that he has been in control of their negotiation all along.

When the monk claims he has paid back the money he owes the merchant, he leaves the player who has hitherto been his interactive accomplice to shift for

(just as they show priests, husbands, jongleurs, etc.); other fabliaux show that moral and social prescriptions are rules that all men and women break, if for no other reason than their very imposition. For the view that most fabliaux offer at least a lesson to their readers, see Mary Jane Stearns Schenck, *The Fabliaux, Tales of Wit and Deception*, Purdue University Monographs in Romance Languages 24 (Philadelphia: John Benjamins, 1987), 20; 30–32. Lesley Johnson, "Women on Top: Antifeminism in the Fabliaux?" *Modern Language Review* 78 (1983): 298–307, counters this reading, claiming instead that the Old French fabliaux illustrate women's superior wit and agency. Examples of fabliaux that use moral and social prescriptions as a means to open up sexual pleasure for men and women include *Ci commance de la grue, De la damoisel[le] qui vost voler*, and *De l'escureul*. Other fabliaux, including *De Freire Denise le cordelier* and *Dou maunier de Aleus* illustrate the dangers of women who do not exert agency over themselves.

herself. Illustrating Karma Lochrie's claim that cuckoldry depends on exposure, Daun John's "repayment plan" is designed to display his dominance over himself and the merchant.[20] If the wife does not cover for him, she will be exposed as an unfaithful wife who exploits her husband's largesse to suit her unreasonable demands for finery. Failing to keep the monk's deception under wraps, then, has the consequence of making the wife's agency visible only in its negative aspect. Any positive effect her influence may have had will be effaced by the deed that the monk uncovers through his trick. But if the wife keeps the monk's secret, she also illustrates his power. Like the Old French fabliau *Des ii. Changeors*, the monk seeks to make the wife's agency into a sign of his control. In the Old French story, as I mentioned earlier, a currency trader develops a passion for his best friend's wife, who, after much pursuit, finally agrees to take him as her lover. Their secret relationship gives both much pleasure until, one day, the lover decides to use the power of exposure to make his dominance visible. Showing his friend (her husband) the naked body of his beloved, he uses the lady's fear to show her how much power he wields over her and her duped husband. As the lady struggles to keep her face hidden from her husband's perusal, her lover (her husband's friend) brags about the beauty of his lady. The husband of course does not recognize the body in the bed as his wife's, and even shows his foolishness by wishing that his wife were as beautiful as the female figure put before him: "Au tesmoing que j'en ai veü, / aucun pechié m'avoit neü / que j'ai si tost fame espousé" "[The testimony I have seen, / shows that for some sin I have been / punished, in that too soon I wed]" (Dubin, 167–69). The lover's trick is similar to Daun John's because it simultaneously makes the wife and husband passive in the face of the lover's potency.

The Man Show

If the wife covers for the monk—and of course she must do so if she can—it signals that she is under his control as a result of this game. Her agency becomes a product of his management, making Daun John look like the superior player in this battle of wits and wills. In similar fabliau plots, such as those from Boccaccio's *Decameron*, the wife's answer simply serves to confirm this conclusion. For example, in story VIII, 1 the wife is forced to admit that she received the lover's money and so must hand it over to her husband to conceal what is characterized as *her* guilt. In a variation on this motif, in VIII, 2 the wife can only register her frustration with the priest who dupes her by sending him a pointed message: "Belcolore says that she swears to God you won't be grinding any more of your sauces in her mortar, after the shabby way you've treated her over this one."[21] The clever Belcolore is clearly fooled by the priest's

[20] Karma Lochrie, "Women's 'Pryvetees' and Fabliau Politics in the *Miller's Tale*," *Exemplaria* 6 (1994): 287–304; Lochrie pursues the broader implications of this argument in her *Covert Operations: The Medieval uses of Secrecy* (Philadelphia: University of Pennsylvania Press, 1999).

[21] Giovanni Boccaccio, *The Decameron*, trans. G. H. McWilliam (London: Penguin, 1972), VIII, 2 (p. 560). See John Finlayson, "Chaucer's *Shipman's Tale*, Boccaccio, and the 'Civilizing' of Fabliau," *Chaucer Review* 36 (2002): 336–51; and Carol F. Heffernan, "Chaucer's *Shipman's Tale* and Boccaccio's *Decameron*, VIII, i: Retelling a Story," in *Courtly Litera-*

ploy, but despite her quick answer, she cannot redirect the situation to reassert her autonomy. In this story, as in VIII, 1, it seems that the wife will think twice before making such bargains in the future.[22] These tales, like many others, are not specifically designed to punish a wife's adultery; however, other "lover's gift regained" plots contain feminine agency by making masculine regulation visibly superior through this double trick. The feminine agency these stories admit, then, becomes subject to masculine control and part of the savviest man's ability to figure his own identity. Women may have agency in Boccaccio's fabliaux, but only when it defines and confirms the superior masculine player in the tale's economy.

When Daun John exploits his friendship with the merchant to acquire the money he needs to sleep with his friend's wife, he sets out to gain this kind of manly authority by harnessing the wife's agency. If he can compel her to act in his defense, to shift the blame so that he gets away with cheating her, then the monk can affirm the control that he believes he has had all along. Like the merchant, the monk seeks to build a public image of masculine control for himself, and like the merchant, he similarly refuses to acknowledge the wife's part in this enterprise. The only moment when he is not able to assert his self-determination happens in the garden, when the monk must measure the wife's intentions in order to get the most out of the situation she offers. By pulling his double-deception, Daun John attempts to recast his meeting with the wife as part of his design and thus to affirm his position as superior man in this setting. The only problem with this plan, it seems, is the wife's answer itself. The quick-witted turn of her reply is similar to those of other wives in similar situations. The wife's comeback parts ways with other answers, however, because it illustrates that masculine potency is itself a show over which she exerts influence.

When the wife tells her husband that she will repay the debt the monk owed using the very terms of conjugality that were meant to affirm marital affection, she consolidates the merchant's image of masculine potency even as she thwarts Daun John's attempt to assert manly dominance. In preventing her husband from looking like a cuckold, she keeps intact the guise of manly potency with which she has hitherto invested him. Despite her actual infidelity, throughout the tale the wife acts the part of a good wife. As others have pointed out, this couple's marriage is strikingly tender compared to that of other fabliau

---

ture: *Culture and Context*, ed. Keith Busby and Erik Kooper (Amsterdam: Benjamins, 1990), 261–70, for a more developed discussion of connections between these stories and Chaucer's tale.

[22] Ibid., VIII, 1 and VIII, 2. While VIII, 1 is a story designed to punish a woman's greed, VIII, 2 is supposed to illustrate the deceptive nature of priests. It is clear that the woman in VIII, 1 is punished, but in VIII, 2 Belcolore comes to a reconciliation with the priest— yet only, as the tale points out, because he uses the authority of his office to frighten her: "But Belcolore was infuriated with the priest for having made such a fool of her, and refused to speak to him for the rest of the summer until the grape-harvest, by which time he had scared the life out of her so successfully by threatening to see that she was consigned to the very centre of Hell, that she made her peace with him over a bottle of must and some roast chestnuts" (560).

couples.[23] Although the wife complains of her husband's lack of sexual prowess, when he returns from his business trip we see a scene of marital affection that looks as genuine as any other in Chaucer's canon. And, even though Hahn is right to point out that the merchant's sexual potency is connected to his fiscal prosperity, this linkage does not cheapen the loving portrait of marriage we see near the tale's conclusion (p. 235). The wife's quick welcome for her husband, "ful redy [she] mette hym atte gate" (373), is not an index of his success in this particular business venture. As the tale points out, the wife's conduct is a standing habit: "As she was wont of oold usage algate" (374). The only conclusion we can really draw about the connection between the merchant's sexual and financial abilities, it seems, is to acknowledge that since the merchant is good at what he does, he often comes home from a trip ready to spend "al that nyght in myrthe" (375). And, since the wife is glad that her husband is good at what he does, his financial success *is* a sign of his ability to satisfy her wants, including her sexual desires.

Bobos in Paradise

To claim that this couple's values are mercantile, that they act according to the vexed materialism associated with the rising merchant-class in the late Middle Ages, then, is a trivially true observation. Furthermore, to read this tale as a satire of such values, as a condemnation of the admixture of money and sex in marriage, is a diagnostic overlay of moral tenets that the tale does not appear to share. As we see from the wife's ability to cover her adultery, the tale is quite frank about the ways people negotiate identities by managing visibility. So it is not just that this tale shows that the commercial view of the world was inevitable in Chaucer's day; rather, it demonstrates that the commercial outlook was inevitably visible as a constitutive factor in the lives of everyday people. By taking up visibility's power to transform perceptions of identity, the wife keeps her husband's image as fully empowered husband and savvy businessman from falling apart. She does so, moreover, by casting herself as an obedient spouse who nevertheless exercises legitimate agency in her marriage. The wife does not promise to change from unruly adulteress to obedient wife; indeed, her husband has no idea that such a transformation is warranted. Instead, when she proffers her body as payment for the spent franks, she freely offers that which she, as a loving wife, is supposed to give freely anyway. By taking up the position she is already expected to assume, the wife gains room to display the shaping influence she exerts over her husband's masculinity.

When she promises to be the obedient spouse, and thus to bear out the appearance she has worn all along, to the merchant her offer does not look like a real payment. And, indeed, as loving husband, he does not expect her body to become an actual register of the owed money. Because he is flush with cash due to his savvy dealing, the merchant does not need the money that has gone to pay for the wife's outfitting. Thus his concern in his mild rebuke of the wife is not with the money itself; once again, he worries about his manly appearance:

---

[23]Woods, 147; Schneider, 207, argues that the wife's display of affection for her husband indicates that she will not be involved in similar adulterous exchanges in the future.

> Ye sholde han warned me, er I had gon,
> That he yow hadde an hundred frankes payed
> By redy token; and heeld hym yvele apayed,
> For that I to hym spak of chevyssaunce;
> Me semed so, as by his contenaunce. (388–92)

He is afraid that he will look like a greedy broker to a man he considers to be a close friend. When the merchant scolds his wife, then, it is so that she will take better caution in her accounting of the debts owed. As the merchant explains, if a man pays her in his absence, she must inform the merchant so that he does not embarrass himself by asking for what has already been given. Without realizing it, the merchant here identifies the problem that leads the wife to form her adulterous agreement with the monk. As the complaint that situates her contract with the monk suggests, the wife does not properly credit the debts paid to her. Her fault, I suggest, arises from her lack of visible power in the household. Indeed, because the merchant has until this moment viewed his wife as part of his chaffare, she has had no productive way to exercise her agency. As the tale makes clear, when women are denied visible means to express self-direction, they take up the power that invisibility offers. The wife's unseen means of exerting her autonomy, however, puts the merchant's image of continent masculinity at risk.

When the merchant advises the wife to take better care in future dealings, he gives her legitimate space to act as a partner in their union. Although the merchant has no knowledge of the sexual valence his instructions carry, when he tells the wife to "Keep bet thy good, this yeve I thee in charge" (432), he gives her the power to make distinctions between proper and improper uses of assets, including her body. In other words, when the merchant admits that the wife will continue to have opportunities to influence his dealings with other men, he acknowledges her agency and gives her space to take responsibility for her own conduct in those situations. Now, the merchant does not suggest that the wife may act in any way that she sees fit; on the contrary, he depends upon the marital bond to limit the wife's agency so that it promotes his empowered status. She has power to conduct herself, but only insofar as her behavior remains within the boundaries permissible for a faithful wife. The merchant is able to assert the manly authority that marriage confers upon him, however, only because the wife gives him leave to do so. When she curses the monk, she follows her invective with a justification of her agency that outlines the way she will conduct herself in the *future*. Her disgust with Daun John, "I kepe nat of his tokenes never a deel" (403), suggests that she now prefers her husband's staid respectability to the monk's aggressive opportunism. The cleverness of her answer, then, derives not just from its ability to hide her infidelity; it too is a double-scheme, outlining her future commitment to a type of femininity that exercises agency for her husband's benefit.

In the Money

If it were not already clear to the wife that her husband is cut from completely different cloth than the monk, the way that he provides space for her exercise of indivdual autonomy shows that his masculinity offers her more than financial or sexual satisfaction. When she protests against the monk's deception, she identifies the bonds of masculine friendship Daun John breaks through his double-cross: "I wende, withouten doute, / That he hadde yeve it me bycause of yow / To doon therwith myn honour and my prow" (406–8). Realizing that the monk acts the part of philandering schemer in earnest, the wife turns away from this model of masculinity and reasserts her husband's superiority through her promise of submission. By pledging the obedience that she owes her husband according to a hierarchical version of marriage, "I am youre wyf; score it upon my taille" (416), she promises him that which, by all appearances, he believes he already has. Her suggestion, however, that she "bistowed [the money] so weel / for youre honour" (420–21), takes on new import in the context of her prior behavior. She gives her husband permission to exercise the authority his position is meant to confer. Her acts, including her prior bad acts, affect the appearance of the position that he secures. The wife takes responsibility for the way that her actions shape her husband's manly image in the public eye and, by so doing, converts what could have been a moment that exposes his frailty into an instance that confirms his power.

So, instead of a confessional about-face from a penitent adulteress, we see a clever wife turn the fallout from her deception to her husband's good. In giving her body as payment to her husband, she defines the parameters of her agency in a way that prevents her from trading sexual favors with *other* men. Granting her agency a place of visible legitimacy, I am suggesting, curtails her power to direct herself. But this is not to say that the merchant finally gains the type of comprehensive dominance that early in the tale he assumes is his by virtue of his position as husband. On the contrary, he must respect the influence that his wife exercises by admitting that she too dispenses their goods and thus influences the image of their collective "hous" (20). Furthermore, he must become the kind of man she desires; as we see from her dealings in this tale, the wife's ideal of masculinity falls somewhere between the scheming monk and the respectable husband. The merchant comes close to meeting her standard but, as I argued earlier, his deficiency stems from the sexual limitations that ignoring her agency produces. What we see when he comes home from his meeting with Daun John, therefore, is a sexual performance expanded by the realization that his wife can manage herself. When he seeks to satisfy the wife, which requires him to recognize her as a player with autonomous desires, he allows her to shape the masculinity that he performs.

At different junctures in this tale, therefore, the monk and the merchant must recognize the wife's agency. While the merchant gives the wife's autonomy legitimacy and allows it to mold his manhood, the monk takes the wife's control and tries to pass it off as a product of his masculinity. The merchant's response to the emergence of the wife's agency, I suggest, makes him a better man because it enables him to perform a better masculinity more persuasively. If we read this conclusion from the perspective of the monk, who can only see feminine autonomy as a destabilization of masculine authority, the wife's performance of submission is simply further evidence of the merchant's defeat. But the merchant does not look like a fool or a cuckold at the end of this tale, and that is because he is neither. The wife effectively manages visibility in order to cover her adultery, but the merchant cleverly uses visibility to negotiate his wife's fidelity. And, when the wife keeps her husband from looking like a cuckold, there is no way for him to look like a fool. Her submissive pose satisfies him, even as it reinstitutes the appearance of marital hierarchy designed to promote an image of masculine control in the Middle Ages. Some may object that the wife's obedience is *merely* a pose, a show she stages in order to hide her guilt. But as we see with her aggression, too, the performances a person puts on are constitutive of identity. As this tale illustrates, it is the way that certain performances of selfhood gain legitimate visibility that give them lasting impact. As we see with the wife and the merchant, when a pair collaborates to negotiate relational gender positions that are limited by one another, neither partner can use the visibility of the other to extend his or her image. By giving her husband's masculinity a place of visible legitimacy, the wife keeps herself from being used as a tally of his financial success.[24]

[24]I would like to thank the Charles Phelps Taft Memorial Fund, the University Research Council, and the Department of English and Comparative Literature at the University of Cincinnati for providing the funds and leave that allowed me to conduct the research and writing for this essay.

Sir Gawain and the Green Hag

The *Real* Meaning of the *Wife of Bath's Tale*

T. L. BURTON

Literary criticism in the last half century or so has shown a wonderful ability to accommodate itself to prevailing fashions in thought. The New Criticism of the 60s, which allowed us to analyse the words on the page without troubling about their historical or cultural circumstances, gave way to Exegetical Criticism, which encouraged us to find the fruit of scriptural doctrine in even the bawdiest of seeming chaff. The obliging Death of the Author at the hands of Roland Barthes freed us all to interpret texts in whatever way we pleased (though some were unsporting enough to suggest that whereas all interpretations might theoretically be equal, some are more equal than others). Psychoanalysis revealed the hidden phobias of every character—and even (sometimes) of the author (though never, of course, those of the critic). Marxism taught us to ask whose interests the text served (and inevitably answered that it was a tool by which the haves oppressed the have-nots). Feminism gave us two Chaucers, one a man with an astounding ability to think and feel like a woman, the other a male chauvinistic pig whose reputation for rape sprang not from some legal technicality but from the ugly thing itself. Textual Criticism gave up its search for what the author actually wrote, declaring that all variants had a validity of their own; and Deconstruction had us believing that the hidden meaning of every text was the incapacity of language to mean anything at all. Is it any wonder that we have reached a point at which many critics now pay more attention to the circumstances of a text's production than to anything that text might conceivably mean?[1]

The problem with all these enterprising approaches is that critics tend to get so wedded to their own point of view that they can't see any others. I take as an example a Jungian interpretation of the *Wife of Bath's Tale*, published some years ago by a critic who has since gone on to achieve widespread acclaim with his award-winning book, *The Secret Marriage of Sherlock Holmes*.[2] There are

---

[1]Scholarly convention calls here for a footnote documenting these claims in detail. Since, however, such a note would be longer than this brief essay itself, and since I am confident of my learned readers' familiarity with all these fashions (as well as others not mentioned), I pass over this formality in the interests of brevity and the preservation of our forests.

[2]Michael Atkinson, "Soul's Time and Transformations: The Wife of Bath's Tale," *Southern Review* 13 (1980): 72–78; since the article is short, page references are omitted in my discussion. Atkinson's *The Secret Marriage of Sherlock Holmes, And Other Eccentric Readings* (Ann

several reasons why I select this article from numerous other possible candidates: it is short and to the point; it appeared in a journal that has only a small circulation and consequently (to judge from the paucity of references to it in the literature) it is not well known; it cries out for a wider audience. I begin, accordingly, with a brief summary of this article (though no such summary can do justice to the subtlety of its argument) before proceeding to a consideration of how it might be refined by combining other approaches with the psychoanalytic perspective adopted.

Atkinson's interpretation is based on Jung's concept of the anima, according to which every man has within him an image or presence of the feminine, which is "projected out onto women in the world"; the various female figures in the tale symbolize the young knight's soul at various stages of its growth, representing "a development of femininity" within his experience. At the outset of the tale the knight (whom everyone knows to be Gawain, though Chaucer doesn't name him) is "unindividuated", i.e., "divided, fragmented.... set against himself." His task is to become "individuated, undivided, whole, at one." The rape is both *symptomatic* of his uncontrolled unconscious and *symbolic* of it; it is, in effect, a rape of his own soul. The subsequent events are designed to correct his "lack of self-knowledge." The court's sentence of beheading is "an outward manifestation of an inner remorse so intense it longs for self-annihilation." The "stern but compassionate" queen (the soul, the inner feminine) is the helpless maiden transformed; she transforms Gawain's careless life to a quest for understanding.

The knight's approach to his task is "intellectual, not soulful." He attacks the problem by conducting an opinion poll. His year's questing reflects the "unincremental round of habitual behaviour and unexamined living" until the meeting on the last day with the twenty-four and more ladies dancing "at the margin of the woods." These "maidens" are "the next transformation of the anima," their plurality signifying "a collective aspect of the unconscious to balance the collective consciousness of the opinion poll." They are dancing (Atkinson assumes) in a circle. He suggests that they are the elf-queen's company of line 860, dancing in a ring (as fairies are known to do), their circle symbolizing wholeness. The "and mo" of line 992 indicates the magnitude of the dance, but the twenty-four maidens themselves represent two for each month of the year, each month showing "a double face of hope and disappointment" for the questing knight.

The transformation of maidens into hag echoes that of raped anima into queen and mirrors in reverse that of hag into beautiful maiden. The connection between the hag and the queen is obvious. The hag is determined to be Gawain's "love" (1066)—to make him get the inner aspect, not just the outer action; but he sees her as his "dampnacioun" (1067): her foulness is an image of "the disorder and distortion of his neglected soul." The point of the pillow lecture is that "it is the inner experience that counts for everything: outer forms ... are worth naught." The reconciliation the knight needs is not a matter of reason but

---

Arbor: University of Michigan press, 1996) won a 1997 Edgar Allan Poe Award as Best Critical Book of the Year.

"must penetrate his entire being." He must "utterly surrender control" to his feminine side. The answer he needs has to come from an internal transformation within his psyche; and his words "My lady and my love, and wyf so deere,/ I put me in youre wise governance" (1230–31) show that he has achieved this inner transformation, which is immediately reflected in the outer transformation of old hag into beautiful young woman. He can now see her beauty because he has acknowledged "the reality, the power, and the worth of psyche"—which will now serve him since he serves her. He has achieved his atonement.

Attractive though such interpretations may be, they lose something in being restricted so severely to the one angle of approach. What happens if the insights from this approach are combined with others from such angles as palaeography and textual criticism, intertextuality, colour symbolism, numerology, etc.? What follows is a tentative exploration of the possibilities opened up by a truly multidisciplinary approach: it should appeal to all who chafe against the shackles of the old disciplines.

It is well known that Sir Gawain (the hero of the tale, whom Chaucer "allows," as Atkinson puts it, "to remain anonymous") had red hair and a fiery moustache, to match the bright gules and red gold of his peerless pentangle—so well known, indeed, as to make proof superfluous; and doubtless this redness contributed to his later reputation for philandering, as in Malory and Tennyson—cf. Chaucer's lecherous Summoner, with his "fyr-reed cherubynnes face" (I 624–26)—as well as explaining the fury of his assault on the hapless maid at the outset of *WBT* (III 885–88; cf. the description of "The crueel Ire, reed as any gleede" in *The Knight's Tale* I 1997). There used to be some uncertainty as to whether or not Chaucer knew the contemporaneous *Sir Gawain and the Green Knight*; and the old orthodoxy was that in his Parson's contempt for alliterative verse—"I am a Southren man,/ I kan nat geeste 'rum, ram, ruf,' by lettre" (X 42–43)—he gave voice to his own opinion. The many parodic allusions to this text in *WBT* should, however, put the matter beyond doubt.

"To understand this fully" (if I may borrow both a phrase and a strategy from Atkinson), "we need" Susan Brownmiller's concept of rape by warriors: "It's funny about *man's* attitude toward rape in war. *Unquestionably* there shall be some raping.... War provides men with the perfect psychologic backdrop to give vent to their contempt for women."[3] It is true, of course, that the Wife of Bath's Gawain was not *actually* at war (so far as we know); nevertheless he must have been armed at the time of the rape (which comes to the same thing)—who ever heard of a knight going riding without that potent phallic symbol, his sword? And his overcoming of the hapless maiden by "verray force" (III 888) must surely imply something other than the words say, something more than *mere* brute strength?

Now Gawain in *SGGK* was faced with certain beheading at the hands of the Green Knight, and "beheading and castration," as Atkinson reminds us, "are equivalent symbolically"—which is of course the reason (though no one,

---

[3] Susan Brownmiller, *Against Our Will* (London: Secker & Warburg, 1975), 31–32. The italics are Brownmiller's.

so far as I know, has previously noticed it) why Sir Gawain is unable to satisfy his importunate hostess, the Green Knight's gorgeous wife. In *WBT* Chaucer echoes this situation parodically: whereas the earlier Gawain beheads a supernatural enemy and thus as good as cuts his own head off, Chaucer's knight deflowers a maiden and thus, like some sado-masochistic earthworm, rapes himself (as Atkinson has shown us).

The key character in the salvation of Chaucer's Gawain is the mysterious "wyf" whom he encounters at the margin of the woods, one of those "uncharted areas" where anything can happen. And (to follow Atkinson's fearless lead, albeit in a different direction) "I would venture, without proof," that this "olde wyf" is of a colour in keeping with her background on the forest's edge: viridescent, verdant, emerald, enker-green. (Why settle for one adjective when you can fit in four?) Lines 997–1001 in the *Riverside Chaucer* read as follows:

> No creature saugh he that bar lyf,
> Save on the grene he saugh sittynge a wyf—
> A fouler wight ther may no man devyse.   999
> Agayn the knyght this olde wyf gan ryse,
> And seyde, "Sir knyght, heer forth ne lith no wey."

Line 999 (that most potent of numbers symbolically) declares that it would be impossible to imagine a "fouler wight"; the line preceding and the line following this crucially placed comment suggest one powerful reason for her foulness. The "wyf" is sitting on "the grene" in line 998; the first two words after "this olde wyf" in line 1000 are "gan ryse," the initial letters of which give us the first two letters of "grene": the savvy reader cannot miss the suggestion that the old hag is of the same colour as "the grene" on which she sits. And this, I think, must be sufficient proof that the last four of the five non-Hengwrt passages in *WBP* printed in *Riverside* and most other editions, and included in the numbering (575–84, 609–12, 619–26, 717–20), are authorial, it being only the first of the passages—the one excluded from the sequential numbering (44a–44f)—that is spurious.

As for the "ladyes foure and twenty, and yet mo" of line 992 whose dancing delays the appearance of the green hag, I must beg leave to differ from Atkinson as to their number and significance. There is no doubt in my mind that the number intended is *twenty-five*, "yet" being a scribal error for "one". This is not difficult palaeographically: numbers are frequently written as small Roman numerals in the manuscripts, a *j* being used for the number one or as the last in a series of minims; thus j = one, iij = three, vj = six, etc. Moreover, the letter i and minims standing for the digit *one* in numerals were sometimes given a stroke to distinguish them from u, n, etc., so that the number *one* was sometimes written as j with a superscript stroke. The stroke is easily mistaken for a superscript t and the j for a y, giving y^t, which in turn is easily (albeit incorrectly) expanded to *yet*. That none of the surviving witnesses has such a reading need not concern us: this merely indicates that the error y^t for y occurred early enough in the transmission of the text to contaminate all subsequent witnesses.

Clearly, then, we have to do with "ladyes foure and twenty, and one mo," the "one mo" being the hag herself in her pre- and post-hag form of beautiful maiden. This gives us a total of twenty-five ladies dancing; but the careful wording (twenty-four plus one) gives Chaucer double mileage numerologically, since it enables him to play with the associations of both twenty-four and twenty-five. That twenty-four is unusually rich symbolically is shown by other commentators besides Atkinson;[4] it needs no further comment. As for twenty-five, it is the square of the number of the Wife of Bath's husbands, thus giving fivefold significance to that number;[5] at the same time it constitutes an artfully concealed allusion to the five ways in which Gawain was perfect in each of the five points of his pentangle (*SGGK* 631–65)—thus providing further evidence of Chaucer's acquaintance with that work.

Sir Gawain *was* perfect, that is, until he got carried away when "ridynge fro ryver" (*WBT* 884). This returns us to the hag, the bedroom, and Gawain's particular predicament. Evidently what Gawain has to do to atone for his rape, in which he forced himself violently on a woman who didn't want him, is to make love to a woman *he* doesn't want: he has not merely to submit graciously to the overtures of a woman he finds repulsive and fearful, but to return her advances lovingly. (This scene is strongly reminiscent of the payback episode in *The Hotel New Hampshire*, in which Chipper Dove the rapist is made to believe that he is himself about to be raped—not, indeed, by a woman, but by a bear—a bear in heat. It is curious that, whereas the influence of T. S. Eliot on Shakespeare is now widely recognized, thanks to the pioneering work of Persse McGarrigal, no attention has hitherto been given to John Irving's influence on Chaucer.)[6] Gawain's task is confirmed by the hag's comment, "I nolde for al the metal, ne for oore / That under erthe is grave, or lith above, / But if thy wyf I were, *and eek thy love*" (1064–66, my italics). Or (to put it another way), he must learn to put his rapacious weapon to pacific purposes, like the sword of the "strange knyght" in *The Squire's Tale*:

> This naked swerd, that hangeth by my syde,
> Swich vertu hath that what man so ye smyte,
> Thurghout his armure it wole kerve and byte,
> Were it as thikke as is a branched ook;
> And what man that is wounded with the strook
> Shal never be hool til that yow list, of grace,
> To stroke hym with the plat in thilke place
> Ther he is hurt; this is as muche to seyn,

---

[4]See Carole Koepke Brown, "Episodic Patterns and the Perpetrator: The Structure and Meaning of Chaucer's *Wife of Bath's Tale*," *Chaucer Review* 31 (1996): 18–35, especially p. 26 and note 16.

[5]On the numerological significance of the number five see D. W. Robertson, *A Preface to Chaucer: Studies in Medieval Perspectives* (Princeton, NJ: Princeton University Press, 1962), 318–22, and Robert F. Fleissner, "The Wife of Bath's Five," *Chaucer Review* 8 (1973): 128–32.

[6]See John Irving, *The Hotel New Hampshire* (New York: Dutton, 1981), chapter 11. For McGarrigal's thesis on Eliot and Shakespeare see David Lodge, *Small World: An Academic Romance* (London: Secker & Warburg, 1984), 51–52.

> Ye moote with the platte swerd ageyn
> Stroke hym in the wounde, and it wol close.   (V 156–65)

But this the knight is impotent to do: he is castrated by his partner's colour, her "filthe" and her "eelde" (III 1215) as cleanly as if he *had* been beheaded (a further parodic echo of the "defence" of Sir Gawain in *SGGK* 1282). And perhaps it is just as well, for the conjunction of his red with the green of her present transformation could lead only to melancholic *brown*, the colour, it is said, of "renunciation, monasticism penitence sorrow, barrenness"[7] (though our dedicatee might have had a thing or two to say about that).

What then remains? Having forfeited his masculine initiative, he has become "wedded to, and in the power of, his feminine side" and "must utterly surrender conscious control" (as Atkinson says)—hand over his sword, as it were—to the lady. In so doing he brings about her final transformation from green hag to beautiful maiden (III 1251), thus enabling the lovers (his red self and his lily-white soul) to bathe forever in their narcissistic bath of pink—a colour that, according to de Vries (s.v. *pink*, 3 & 4) represents "sensuality, emotions, joy, [and] youth" and that just happens to be "associated with [the] number Five."[8]

* * *

Amongst Emerson Brown's most delightful characteristics were his exuberant sense of humour, his delight in the ridiculous, his unfailing joie de vivre. "Joy" was one of his favourite words. Where Emerson went, fun followed (as well as the meticulous scholarship and care for people that other contributors have spoken of). This essay is offered as a small token of gratitude for the joy and laughter his life brought to all who knew him.

---

[7] Ad de Vries, *Dictionary of Symbols and Imagery*, 3rd rev. ed. (Amsterdam: North-Holland Publishing, 1981), s.v. *brown*, 4 & 5.

[8] My debt to Charles Kaplan's *The Overwrought Urn: a potpourri of parodies of critics who triumphantly present the* real *meaning of authors from Jane Austen to J. D. Salinger* (New York: Pegasus, 1969) will, I trust, be obvious throughout this essay, from the subtitle onwards.

Early Poems

"My first matere I wil yow telle"

Losing (And Finding) Your Place in Chaucer's *The Book of the Duchess*

Michael Kensak

Emerson Brown once compared his Dante seminar to a meaningful digression. The class had reached the second canto of the *Purgatorio* where Dante rests before beginning the arduous climb up Mount Purgatory. There Dante, Virgil, and other newly arrived souls gather to hear a song, "Amor che ne la mente mi ragiona" ("Love which discourses to me in my mind") (2.112). The group is still rapt when severe Cato recalls them to their task: "Correte al monte" ("Haste to the mountain!") (2.122). With ages of suffering ahead, these souls had found in poetry a final diversion from Purgatory's unrelenting teleology. Emerson lingered over this passage, pleased, I believe, that his classroom might provide a similar space for reflection and pleasure. Here, like Dante, students could pause, "come gente che pensa a suo cammino.... come colui che nove cose assaggia" ("like those that ponder on their road.... like those that make trial of things new") before harsher voices recalled them to their respective mountains (2.11, 54).[1]

In the spirit of Emerson's fondness for meaningful diversions, this essay considers moments when Chaucerian narratives get side-tracked. It is a distinctive feature of Chaucer's poetry that his narrators frequently express anxiety over how their tales are progressing. A surprising number of them realize at some point that what they have been saying is irrelevant. The preceding material must be dismissed, excused, or labeled immaterial before tellers can find their tales again. In *The Canterbury Tales*, the Man of Law interrupts his own bemoaning of Custance's cruel fate:

> And forth I lete hire saille in this manere,
> And turne I wole agayn to my matere.   (II 321–22)

The Physician, similarly, gets carried away railing against betrayers of childhood innocence when he remembers he was telling of one such child:

> Suffiseth oon ensample now as heere,
> For I moot turne agayn to my matere.   (VI 103–4)

---

[1] Quotations of Dante's poetry are from John D. Sinclair, ed. and trans., *The Divine Comedy* (New York: Oxford University Press, 1961). For some of Emerson's students, Dante has become more than a diversion and his *Commedia* a mountain purgatory all its own.

83

Among Chaucer's narrators, however, none is so anxious or distractible as the speaker of *The Book of the Duchess*.[2]

The dreamer–narrator in *The Book of the Duchess* presents himself as an enigma even to himself. For eight years he has suffered from insomnia, making him question his very existence:

> I have gret wonder, be this lyght,
> How that I lyve, for day ne nyght
> I may nat slepe wel nygh noght.   (1–3)

The speaker knows his condition will provoke curiosity—"men myght axe me why"—but he declares all such inquiry futile—"who aske this / Leseth his asking trewely" (32–33). For readers of *The Canterbury Tales*, this uninterpretability is frustrating: in framed narratives we are accustomed to examining the tale in light of the teller. For readers of medieval dream lore it is equally distressing: the dreamer's character is an important criterion in interpreting a dream vision.[3] Neither of these hermeneutic operations, it appears, will be possible in *The Book of the Duchess*.

After protesting ignorance about his condition, the speaker suddenly changes tack and reveals something of his story:

> Myselven can not telle why
> The sothe; but trewly, as I gesse,
> I holde hit be a sicknesse
> That I have suffred this eight yeer;
> And yet my boote is never the ner,
> For there is phisicien but oon
> That may me hele.   (34–40)

This passage, which purports to explain the speaker's insomnia, only further confuses an already muddled situation. Does the narrator know the cause of his malady or not? Does this sudden revelation reflect the speaker's addled mind, or does it impugn his veracity?[4] The narrator teases us with words like "sothe"

---

[2] In what follows I treat the dreamer–narrator as a character rather than a rhetorical function. What others have seen as fragmented narrative perspective, I take as Chaucer's characterization of his speaker. David Lawton, similarly, finds him a narrator "whose psychological state and growth is vital to the meaning of the poem" (*Chaucer's Narrators* [Cambridge: D. S. Brewer, 1985], 53). William Calin argues that Machaut provided Chaucer the model of the obtuse poet–narrator: "For the Machaldian and Chaucerian 'I' is the center of consciousness and single focus in the narrative. The world of the text is his world, filtered through him" ("Machaut's Legacy: The Chaucerian Inheritance Reconsidered," in Barton Palmer, ed., *Chaucer's French Contemporaries: The Poetry/Poetics of Self and Tradition* [New York: AMS Press, 1999], 36).

[3] According to Macrobius, Cicero's virtue guarantees the veracity of his dream. Macrobius assumes that Cicero's vision of Scipio was "public and universal" because Cicero "excelled as much in philosophy as in deeds of courage" (William Harris Stahl, trans., *Macrobius: Commentary on the Dream of Scipio* [New York: Columbia University Press, 1952], 91).

[4] Rosemarie McGerr points out another reason to distrust the speaker's judgment: "contrary to his earlier account [of not sleeping for eight years], he has slept recently, while having the vision he goes on to recount, and he has felt sympathy for someone else after all"

and "trewly," but then, as if frightened by his brush with clarity, retreats to the murky rhetoric of uncertainty: "as I gesse" and "I holde hit be."

The speaker's references to an eight-year sickness and a single physician have occasioned a prodigious amount of commentary and a minuscule amount of certainty. The speaker's condition has been interpreted as unrequited love, Boethian error, grief over Duchess Blanche's death, melancholy, and simple insomnia. His one physician has been interpreted as a love interest, Christ, philosophy, and sleep.[5] Most critics, though, have assumed that the dreamer is an unsuccessful lover. In the *Roman de la Rose* and the derivative *dits* of Guillaume de Machaut and Jean Froissart, a stricken, often insomniac lover pines for a lady he often terms his physician.[6] Chaucer's cryptic references become clear if *The Book of the Duchess* belongs to the genre of amatory dream visions developed by Machaut and Froissart. This temptation to closure should be resisted, however. While Chaucer's poem owes much to the French tradition, the resounding ambiguities of its opening complicate any straightforward generic classification. Contrasting *The Book of the Duchess* with Froissart's *Paradys d'amour* (from which much of it derives), Arthur Bahr finds Froissart's opening lines "remarkably coherent in both meaning and sound" and Chaucer's "noteworthy for how little they tell us, and how little closure, semantic or otherwise, they provide."[7] If the sleepless narrator is no more than a hapless lover, then Chaucer has wasted a great deal of effort interweaving his text with complex strands of uncertainty. In a poem which foregrounds the difficulty of its own interpretation—"no man had the wyt / To konne wel my sweven rede" (278–79)—the narrator himself remains a mystery.

(*Chaucer's Open Books: Resistance to Closure in Medieval Discourse* [Gainesville: University Press of Florida, 1998], 47).

[5] John M. Hill interprets the speaker's malady as melancholy and his physician as sleep in "*The Book of the Duchess*, Melancholy, and that Eight-Year Sickness," *The Chaucer Review* 9 (1974): 35–50. Edward Condren, noting the connection between the dreamer's grief and the Black Knight's, infers that "the narrator was deprived of [his lady's] favor because she had died" ("The Historical Context of *The Book of the Duchess*: A New Hypothesis," *The Chaucer Review* 5 [1971]: 198). Michael Herzog argues against this interpretation, citing the narrator's "lack of real interest ... in the courtly love elements of the Black Knight's story" ("*The Book of the Duchess*: The Vision of the Artist as a Young Dreamer," *The Chaucer Review* 22 [1988]: 272). Berhard Huppé and D. W. Robertson conclude that "the poet is suffering because Blanche the Duchess has died; his comfort must come from Christ, who died and was resurrected" (*Fruyt and Chaf: Studies in Chaucer's Allegories* [Princeton: Princeton University Press, 1963], 45). Sherron Knopp sees a Boethian malady: "his senses no longer respond to the world outside him" because he has "overdosed on the images of poetry" ("Augustinian Poetic Theory and the Chaucerian Imagination," in James M. Dean and Howard K. Zacher, eds., *The Idea of Medieval Literature: New Essays on Chaucer and Medieval Culture in Honor of Donald R. Howard* [Newark: University of Delaware Press, 1992], 97. James Wimsatt points out that all interpretations of the physician passage are "genre-bound" and depend on extra-textual material ("*The Book of the Duchess*: Secular Elegy or Religious Vision?" in John P. Hermann and John J. Burke, Jr., eds., *Signs and Symbols in Chaucer's Poetry* [University, Alabama: University of Alabama Press, 1981], 112).

[6] For a representative example, see lines 1467–69 of Guillaume de Machaut's *Remede de fortune* in James I. Wimsatt, ed., *Le jugement du roy de Bahaigne; and, Remede de fortune* (Athens: University of Georgia Press, 1988).

[7] Arthur W. Bahr, "The Rhetorical Construction of Narrator and Narrative in Chaucer's *The Book of the Duchess*," *The Chaucer Review* 35 (2000): 44.

If the speaker tells us little about the cause of his insomnia, he does reveal
a great deal about its effect. Whatever its origin, the narrator's sleeplessness
has deranged his three intellectual faculties. Bartholomaeus Anglicus describes
these faculties in his *De proprietatibus rerum*:

> The innere witte is departid aþre by þre regiouns of þe brayn, for in
> þe brayn beþ þre smale celles. þe formest hatte *ymaginatiua*, þerin
> þingis þat þe vttir witte apprehendiþ withoute beþ i-ordeyned and
> iput togedres withinne, *vt dicitur Iohannicio i.* þe middil chambre
> hatte *logica* þerin þe vertu estimatiue is maister. þe þridde and þe
> laste is *memoratiua*, þe vertu of mynde. þat vertu holdiþ and kepiþ
> in þe tresour of mynde þingis þat beþ apprehendid and iknowe bi þe
> ymaginatif and *racio*.[8]

The imagination, or *virtus imaginatiua*, governs the construction of images in
the mind. The reason, or *virtus aestimatiua*, governs the processing of sensory
images through comparison and abstraction. The memory, or *virtus memoratiua*, governs the retention of sense images and rational processes.

In describing the effects of his insomnia, the narrator reveals the impairment
of all three virtues. First, his imagination is oppressed by "many an ydel thoght"
and "sorwful ymagynacioun" (4, 14). The images which enter his mind, the
narrator claims, are "ydel"—"of no effect or significance, futile, vain, worthless;
also, false, sinful."[9] Second, the speaker has lost his ability to reason. He lacks
even elemental powers of discernment, including whether something is coming
or going, pleasing or displeasing:

> by my trouthe, I take no kep
> Of nothing, how hyt cometh or gooth,
> Ne me nys nothyng leef nor looth.
> Al is ylyche good to me—
> Joye or sorowe, wherso hyt be—
> For I have felynge in nothyng.   (6–11)

Finally, we may infer that the speaker's memory is also impaired. Perhaps he
does not reveal the cause of his insomnia because, in his present state of mind,
he cannot remember it. When the narrator describes his malady as an eight-year
illness—"as I gesse"—perhaps he is only guessing. In light of this possibility,
his statement "I take no kep / Of nothing" may mean both "I don't care about

---

[8] Middle English quotations of Bartholomaeus are from John of Trevisa's fourteenth-century
translation: M. C. Seymour, ed., *On the Properties of Things: John Trevisa's Translation of
Bartholomaeus Anglicus' De Proprietatibus Rerum: A Critical Text*, 2 vols. (Oxford: Claren-
don Press, 1975), 2.98. Subsequent Latin quotations are from Bartholomaeus Anglicus, *On the
Properties of Soul and Body*, ed. R. James Long (Toronto: Centre for Medieval Studies, 1979),
3.10. For a discussion of Chaucer and medieval cognitive theory, see Robert R. Edwards, *The
Dream of Chaucer: Representation and Reflection in the Early Narratives* (Durham: Duke
University Press, 1989), 4–11.

[9] *Middle English Dictionary* (Ann Arbor: University of Michigan Press, 1952–), "ydel,"
definition 1a.

anything" (*virtus aestimatiua*) and "I do not take and keep anything" (*virtus memoratiua*).

This mental derangement has implications for the speaker's narrative art. The imaginative, rational, and mnemonic impairments resulting from his insomnia manifest themselves as a tendency to wander off course. Robert Jordan, in his rhetorical analysis of *The Book of the Duchess*, generously characterizes "the aesthetic principle" that holds the divers elements of the poem together as "one of accommodation."[10] Laura Howes describes the poem as full of "thwarted narratives, whole scenes that are seemingly insignificant, peripheral figures who become central, and central figures who become peripheral."[11] Unable to distinguish relevant from irrelevant, important from unimportant, the speaker repeatedly loses track of his original subject matter.

There is, of course, no infallible heuristic for identifying a literary tangent or defining narrative irrelevance, especially in Chaucer where chaff and fruit so thoroughly intertwine. We must rely, therefore, on the speaker's own announcements that he is returning from a digression to matters more germane.[12] The first digression–return in *The Book of the Duchess* occurs after the speaker introduces his insomnia. After teasing us with inconclusive hints about its etiology, the narrator revokes the entire subject:

> Passe we over untill eft;
> That wil not be mot nede be left;
> Our first mater is good to kepe.
> So whan I saw I might not sleep.... (41–44)[13]

Forty-three lines into the poem, the speaker labels the preceding material immaterial and announces his (first) return to our "first mater." But what exactly was our first matter? How far back does the judgment of irrelevance extend? Since the narrator has spoken of nothing other than his insomnia, his announcement appears to retract everything that has gone before. Perhaps, though, the speaker merely refers to "his insomnia [*per se*], as opposed to the underlying cause thereof about which he has just digressed."[14] Alistair Minnis's interpretation makes sense, but it hardly irons out the narrative's wrinkles. Taking

---

[10] Robert Jordan, "The Compositional Structure of *The Book of the Duchess*," *The Chaucer Review* 9 (1974): 111. Jordan describes a "mode of indirectness" in the poem which "employs a devious, roundabout approach to its thematic center via the Ceyx and Alcione story and other diversions" (102).

[11] Laura Howes, *Chaucer's Gardens and the Language of Convention* (Gainesville: University Press of Florida, 1997), 39.

[12] The Middle Ages appears to have had no rhetorical term for the announcement of a return from a digression. The Greek *epanodos* would later take on this meaning, but it does not yet exist in Horace's *Ars poetica*. Bahr and other critics have adopted the term *abbrevatio* "to describe instances of Chaucer's characteristic moves to close off a given subject and move to another" ("Rhetorical Construction," 57).

[13] Any attempt to explicate this passage runs into a referential brick wall. What exactly is the "that" which is "don"—the sickness, the healing, the possibility of healing, the hope for healing, the relationship if the physician is indeed a love interest? When will "eft" be? The narrator claims he will return to this subject at a later time, but he never does.

[14] A. J. Minnis, V. J. Scattergood, and J. J. Smith, *The Shorter Poems: Oxford Guides to Chaucer* (New York: Oxford University Press, 1995), 104.

our "first mater" as the dreamer's insomnia divorced from any consideration of
its cause or meaning leaves us with little understanding of the narrator and no
basis for interpreting his dream.

The narrator's second digression–return occurs as he retells the story of Seys
and Alcyone. In order to drive the night away, the speaker takes up "a book, /
A romaunce" in which are written

> fables
> That clerkes had in olde tyme,
> And other poetes, put in rime
> To rede and for to be in minde,
> While men loved the lawe of kinde.   (52–56)

The disjunctive syntax of this sentence reflects the narrator's muddled mind
and suggests he is not in control of his text. The speaker's *that*-clause begins
with a single subject ("clerks") and proceeds through an auxiliary verb and an
adverbial phrase ("had in olde tyme") before he doubles back and adds a second
subject ("and other poetes"). The final line ("while men loved the lawe of kind")
is likewise misplaced. At first glance, the adverbial phrase appears to modify
the verbs of the preceding line ("rede" and "be"), when in fact it modifies an
earlier verb ("put"), in apposition with "in olde tyme" four lines earlier. On
the syntactic as well as the narrative level, the speaker fails to govern the linear
unfolding of his text.[15]

The "romaunce" he reads is the story of Seys and Alcyone, though most of
it appears to make little impression. In recounting the tale, the narrator hurries
"shortly" over Seys's marriage to Alcyone, his departure on a sea voyage, and
his subsequent death (unbeknownst to his wife) in a tempest. The speaker does
seem interested, however, in Alcyone's reaction—sorrow and uncertainty—for
these are his own defining characteristics. Distraught at her husband's unex-
plained absence, Alcyone prays to Juno asking, oddly, not to have her husband
back but only to *know* his present condition: "yeve me grace my lord to se
/ Soone or wite wher-so he be, / Or how he fareth" (112–14). In particular,
Alcyone requests "som *certeyn* sweven / Wherthourgh that [she] may *knowen*"
if Seys is alive (119–20, my emphasis).[16]

---

[15] J. J. Anderson describes another digression: "Some details smack of the kind of narrative
ineptitude which characterizes the retelling of the story of Ceyx and Alcione. The reference
to Argus the great mathematician is meant to convey another superlative, but it seems to lose
its way. The narrator starts off as though he wants to say that there are so many animals in
the wood that even Argus would be unable to count them (434–37). But the sentence, and
the thought, are not completed. The narrator cannot resist diverting into an explanation of
the practical value of the system of Arabic numerals (438–40)" ("The Narrators in *The Book
of the Duchess* and *The Parlement of Foules*," *The Chaucer Review* 26 [1992]: 226–27).

[16] As readers of Macrobius' *Commentary on the Dream of Scipio* know, "swevens" are
anything but "certeyn." The foremost medieval authority on dream lore identifies five species
of dream, of which three are true and two are false. In classifying a given dream as an
oraculum, visio, somnium, insomnium, or *visum,* however, Macrobius offers no help at all.
In fact, he classifies the dream of Scipio as belonging to *all five* categories (see *Macrobius,*
1.3.12). Medieval dream lore was so convoluted, Chaucer elsewhere suggests, that people who
attempt to apply it end up sounding like chickens.

Despite medieval skepticism about nocturnal revelations, Alcyone's dream vision is unmistakably clear and unimpeachably authentic. Hearing Alcyone's prayer, Juno summons Mercury, who finds Morpheus, who locates "the dreynte body" of Seys and bears it to Alcyone's bedroom (195). Then, in a grotesque puppet show, Morpheus has Seys's corpse announce to his sleeping widow,

> Awake! Let be your sorwful lyf,
> For in your sorwe there lyth no red;
> For, certes, swete, I am but ded.   (202–4)

Readers have long noted the inept handling of Seys's appearance to Alcyone. Ridiculous as it is, though, the dream gives Alcyone exactly what she asked for, "grace [her] lord to se." In other versions, Morpheus counterfeits the appearance of Ceyx, introducing an element of representation and uncertainty.[17] In the narrator's retelling, however, Seys unambiguously resolves Alcyone's uncertainty: "Certes," her sea-bloated husband mouths, "I am but ded."

Once Alcyone's uncertainty has been resolved, the narrator loses interest in her story. As Alcyone wastes away from grief, the speaker returns to *abbrevatio* and issues his second digression–return:

> "Allas!" quod she for sorwe,
> And deyede within the thridde morwe.
> But what she sayede more in that swow
> I may not telle yow as now;
> Hyt were to longe for to dwelle.
> My first matere I wil yow telle
> Wherfore I have told this thyng
> Of Alcione and Seys the kyng.   (213–20)

The narrator only tells "this thyng," he claims, to explain how he finally fell asleep: after closing the book, he prays to Morpheus. We should not be quick, however, to accept the speaker's identification of his "first mater" as insomnia. If the narrator cared only about falling asleep, he would have lost interest in Alcyone's tale once she nodded off. On the contrary, he spends one hundred lines detailing her dream vision. Judging by his use of *abbrevatio* and *amplificatio*, the narrator does not tell *The Tale of Alcyone Falling Asleep*. He tells *The Tale of Alcyone Gaining Certainty Through a Dream Vision*. It is this certainty that the dreamer really seeks. Had he wanted sleep alone, the narrator would have prayed to Juno, "throgh" whom sleep came to Alcyone. Subconsciously intrigued by the clarity of Alcyone's dream, the speaker prays instead to Morpheus, conveyer of nocturnal truth. The narrator may believe that his "first mater" is insomnia, but this misprision carries him away from his real first matter, a vexing inability to make sense of the world around him.

The speaker's digressive tendency is strongly condemned by medieval literary theory. Geoffrey of Vinsauf's *Poetria nova*, the most popular *ars poetica* in the

---

[17] In Ovid's *Metamorphoses*, Morpheus sheds his wings to take on the appearance of Ceyx. See Frank Justus Miller, ed., *Ovid: Metamorphoses* (New York: G. P. Heineman's Sons, 1916), 11.650 ff.

fourteenth century, emphasizes forethought, planning, and fidelity to a poem's initial conception:

> Si quis habet fundare domum, non currit ad actum
> Impetuosa manus: intrinseca linea cordis
> Praemetitur opus, seriemque sub ordine certo
> Interior praescribit homo, totamque figurat
> Ante manus cordis quam corporis; et status ejus
> Est prius archetypus quam sensilis.

> (If anyone is to lay the foundation of a house, his impetuous hand does not leap into action: the inner design of the heart measures out the work beforehand, the inner man determines the stages ahead of time in a certain order; and the hand of the heart, rather than the bodily hand, forms the whole in advance, so that the work exists first as a mental model rather than as a tangible thing.)[18]

Geoffrey's insistence on narrative coherence would mortify our dreamer–narrator:

> Circinus interior mentis praecircinet omne
> Materiae spatium. Certus praelimitet ordo
> Unde praearripiat cursum stylus, at ubi Gades
> Figat. Opus totum prudens in pectoris arcem
> Contrahe, sitque prius in pectore quam sit in ore.
> Mentis in arcano cum rem digesserit ordo,
> Materiam verbis veniat vestire poesis.

> (Let the inner compasses of the mind lay out the entire range of material. Let a certain order predetermine from what point the pen should start off its course and where the outermost limits shall be fixed. Prudently ponder the entire work within the breast, and let it be in the breast before it is in the mouth. When, in the recesses of the mind, order has arranged the matter, let the art of poetry come to clothe the matter with words.)

Describing the very facets of literary composition that frustrate Chaucer's speaker, Geoffrey claims that composition should proceed linearly from initial conception to poetic expression, "seriemque sub ordine certo." A string of time indicators reveals the importance of planning, of putting first matters first: "praemetitur," "praescribit," "praecircinet," "praelimitet," "prearripiat," "ante," "prius." Images of wholeness abound: the maker's heart "totamque figurat"; his mind lays out "omne materiae spatium"; he ponders "opus totum." Central to the poet's job, furthermore, is the patrolling of literary boundaries: the author must determine beforehand "ubi Gades figat" —where, in Geoffrey's geographical metaphor, the port city of Cadiz marks the end of the Mediterranean Sea

---

[18]Quotations of Geoffrey of Vinsauf are from Margaret F. Nims, trans., *Poetria nova* (Toronto: Pontifical Institute of Mediaeval Studies, 1967), section 1.A., lines 43–48 and 55–61.

and the beginning of the wide-open sea. Poets, in other words, must avoid sailing beyond the boundary stones of their poem's subject matter.[19]

Geoffrey of Vinsauf associates the shape of a literary text with the mental state of its author. He emphasizes that poetic forms originate in the mind: "in pectoris arcem," "mentis in arcano," in the "intrinseca linea cordis." Horace, whose *Ars poetica* was widely read in the Middle Ages, also associates a disunified text with a disturbed mind. He imagines a painted figure with the neck of horse, the head of a woman, the tail of a fish, and colored feathers, and asks,

> spectatum admissi risum teneatis, amici?
> credite, Pisones, isti tabulae fore librum
> persimilem, cuius, velut aegri somnia, vanae
> fingentur species.

> [Could you, my friend, if favoured with a private view, refrain from laughing? Believe me, dear Pisos, quite like such pictures would be a book, whose idle fancies shall be shaped like a sick man's dreams.][20]

Like Horace's sick man, Chaucer's narrator forms his idle fancies and dreams into a chimerical poem, which, like the woman-horse-bird-fish in Horace's analogy, violates medieval standards of artistic propriety.

When Chaucer's distracted narrator finally falls asleep, he dreams of meeting a knight "clothed al in blak" alone in a beautiful glade (457). Lost in grief, the Black Knight tells of losing his "fers" (queen) in a chess game with Fortune. His lady, we understand—though the obtuse dreamer does not—has died. The Black Knight unfolds his tale of love and loss until the speaker breaks in to ask about the couple's first meeting. In his distraction, the dreamer has not understood how the knight first approached his lady and how he first made her understand what he was saying:

>   wolde ye tel me the manere
> To hire which was your firste speche—
> Therof I wolde yow beseche—
> And how she knewe first your thoght,
> Whether ye loved hir or noght?   (1130–34)

The dreamer's interest in the couple's first meeting arises from his preoccupation with first matters. The same bumbling narrator who labors to express himself—the same narrator who does not understand the Black Knight is lamenting his

---

[19] Rose Zimbardo's account of the poem suggests its violation of Geoffrey of Vinsauf's standards: "Lines of demarcation are set, confused, reset. Boundaries are unreliable. Attention is given to the book, or tale, only to be sharply and abruptly withdrawn and redirected to the narrator's 'first matere,' his state of mind" (*"The Book of the Duchess* and the Dream of Folly," *The Chaucer Review* 18 [1984]: 330–31).

[20] H. Rushton Fairclough, ed. and trans., *Horace: Satires, Epistles and Ars Poetica* (Cambridge: Harvard University Press, 1966), 450–51, lines 5–8. This passage is cited by Geoffrey of Vinsauf in his *Documentum de modo et arte dictandi et versificandi,* trans. Roger P. Parr (Milwaukee: Marquette University Press, 1968), 90, sections 154–55.

wife's death—cannot imagine how, at their first meeting, "she knewe first [his] thought."

Having been warned of the speaker's deranged *mens*, we are not surprised at his disordered *materia*. What is surprising, however, is that the Black Knight shares the dreamer's problem with narrative organization. Describing his first contact with his lady, the Black Knight, too, gets distracted and wanders off course:

> Trewly I dide my besynesse
> To make songes, as I best koude,
> And ofte tyme I song hem loude;
> And made songes thus a gret del,
> Althogh I koude not make so wel
> Songes, ne knewe the art al,
> As koude Lamekes sone Tubal,
> That found out first the art of songe;
> For as hys brothres hamers ronge
> Upon hys anvelt up and doun,
> Therof he took the firste soun—
> But Grekes seyn Pictagoras,
> That he the firste fynder was
> Of the art (Aurora telleth so);
> But therof no fors of hem two.
> Algates songes thus I made
> Of my felynge, myn herte to glade;
> And, lo, this was [the] altherferste—
> I not wher hyt were the werste.   (1156—74)

One can imagine the look on the dreamer's face. Having asked for the story of a first romantic encounter, he finds himself hearing about hammers ringing on Israelite anvils! Significantly, the Black Knight frustrates the dreamer's request for his first song with a tangent on humanity's first song.

The Black Knight's digression conveys his insecurity over communicating with his lady. It also conveys a deeper anxiety about the possibility of poetic expression. What the knight's early songs lacked in quality, he admits, they made up in quantity, repetition, and volume. Mankind's first practitioner, however, "knewe the art al." Who this "altherferste" poet was, though, is not so easy to say. In medieval culture, not one but two names were enshrined as the inventor of song: Pythagoras and *Jubal*—not, as the Black Knight claims, Tubal. F. N. Robinson points out that "In Genesis 4.21 it is Jubal, not Tubal, who is called the 'father of all such as handle the harp and the organ.'" Jubal was misspelled as Tubal, however, in several sources Chaucer might have consulted, including some copies of the *Aurora* of Petrus de Riga, a text mentioned in this passage. After examining the manuscripts, Peter Beichner concluded that Chaucer wrote Tubal "either because he was using one of the rare copies of the *Aurora* with this spelling, or because he changed 'iubal' to 'tubal' thinking it was right."[21]

There is a third possibility. Given the text's attention at several levels to the difficulties of poetic communication, perhaps Chaucer intentionally had the Black Knight get it wrong. Uncertainty, after all, pervades the passage: the dreamer is uncertain how the knight could communicate his feelings; the Black Knight is uncertain about the quality of his first songs; and medieval authorities were uncertain whether the first singer was Hebrew or Greek. One more level of ambiguity—uncertainty over the name of the Hebrew candidate—demonstrates even more clearly the elusiveness of the knight's fantasy of poetic first matters. The referential quagmire inscribed in the Black Knight's tangent suggests that he shares the speaker's narrative ineptitude.[22]

As with the narrator, the Black Knight's digressive tendency reflects his mental distraction. When we first see him, the Black Knight is half-dead from grief:

> Hit was gret wonder that Nature
> Myght suffre any creature
> To have such sorwe and be not ded.   (467–69)

Oblivious to the world around him, the Black Knight does not notice the speaker's approach: "he herde me noght; / For he had wel nygh lost hys mynde" (510–11).[23] James Winny associates this "dazed inertness" with the description of the narrator earlier: "The mental depression which paralyses the Man in Black is an aggravated form of the listless melancholy which weighs down the dreamer."[24] "Like the Narrator," Arthur Bahr observes, "the Black Knight takes a long time to convey little information; also like the narrator, he at times becomes suddenly chatty, promising enlightenment but delivering more riddles."[25] "Sorwe," the Black Knight confides in language we have heard before, "hath [his] understondynge lorn," and "no phisicien" can heal him (563–71).

---

[21] See *The Riverside Chaucer* explanatory notes to line 1162 of *The Book of the Duchess*, 975. The misspelling also occurs in Peter Comestor's *Historia scholastica* and Vincent of Beauvais's *Speculum doctrinale*.

[22] On another occasion the Black Knight gets sidetracked and launches into an extended declaration of love for his queen (lines 1115–25). To repent of loving her, he claims, would be an act of treason comparable to that of Achitofel, Antenor, or Ganelon. What was supposed to be an account of a first meeting with the White Lady instead turns into an academic discourse on political treachery.

[23] B. H. Bronson finds in the dreamer and the Black Knight "a kindred stupefaction" (*"The Book of the Duchess* Re-Opened," *PMLA* 67 [1952]: 871). Bronson's essay is reprinted *Chaucer: Modern Essays in Criticism*, ed. Edward Wagenknecht (New York: Oxford, 1959), 281–93.

[24] James Winny, *Chaucer's Dream-Poems* (London: Chatto and Windus, 1973), 59.

[25] Bahr, "Rhetorical Construction," 51. Referring to lines 597–601, Bahr compares the digressive narrative style of the Black Knight to that of the speaker: "The Black Knight's inconsistency in promising to explain the 'why' of his distress and instead providing a long and abstract catalogue of its effects, recalls the Narrator's earlier avowal that further discussion of Alcyone would be 'to longe for to dwelle' (217), followed by thirteen lines that offer a parodically expanded explanation of why he mentioned her at all" (52). Laura Howes also admits that the story told by the Black Knight is "not altogether coherent—he tells his story in more than one way, and he has a difficult time getting the narrator to understand him" (*Chaucer's Gardens*, 52).

Why would Chaucer afflict the Black Knight with the same stupefying sorrow
and digressive tendency as the dreamer? Perhaps, these remarkable coincidences
suggest, the dreaming narrator and the dreamed knight are not, in fact, separate
characters. In the Black Knight, the narrator confronts not another person but
his own anxieties projected onto an external figure. According to Macrobius,
this kind of nocturnal projection characterizes the *insomnium*:

> Nightmares may be caused by mental or physical distress, or anxiety
> about the future: the patient experiences in dreams vexations similar
> to those that disturb him during the day.... Anxiety about the
> future would cause a man to dream that he is gaining a prominent
> position or office as he hoped or that he is being deprived of it as he
> feared.[26]

Sad and confused, the speaker reads at bedtime of a sorrowful queen wondering
whether she has lost her husband. In his dream, this day-residue is projected
onto a sorrowful knight who wonders why he has lost his wife. For 830 lines the
dreamer struggles to figure out what every reader knows from the beginning—
that the White Lady is dead. The speaker's dream thus embodies a situation
that has come to define him—his confrontation with an implacable reality. *The
Book of the Duchess*, consequently, is not so much about what the Black Knight
has lost but what the dreamer himself has lost. As a reader of signs and a teller
of tales, he has lost his place.

It remains for us to consider why Chaucer adopted the persona of an inept
narrator in this particular text. Among Chaucer's poems, *The Book of the
Duchess* is the most closely associated with a historical event. It was almost
certainly written to commemorate Duchess Blanche, wife of John of Gaunt, who
died in 1368.[27] The names of both Gaunt and Blanche are woven cryptically into
the text, and Chaucer elsewhere refers to the poem as "The Deeth of Blaunche
the Duchesse" (*LGW*, line 418). Given the circumstances, Chaucer's rhetorical
strategy must have something to do with elegy and consolation. Offering solace
to John of Gaunt was complicated, however, by their enormous difference in
station, Chaucer the son of a London vintner and Gaunt the son of King Edward
III. Arthur Bahr summarizes Chaucer's predicament: "Faced with the task
of comforting her grieving husband, yet unable to assume the appearance of
superior emotional wisdom that would allow him to do so directly, Chaucer
must work obliquely" ("Rhetorical Construction," 43).

Despite the awkwardness Bahr describes, many critics see the poem as a *con-
solatio* in which the dreamer comforts or instructs the sorrowing nobleman.[28]

---

[26] *Macrobius*, 88–89, section 1.3.3. Macrobius claims that this kind of dream is "not worth
interpreting since [it has] no prophetic significance" (88).

[27] John of Gaunt held memorial ceremonies each year on the anniversary of Blanche's death
in 1368 until his own death in 1399. See Sydney Armitage-Smith, *John of Gaunt, King of
Castile and Leon, Duke of Aquitaine and Lancaster, Earl of Derby, Lincoln, and Leicester,
Seneschal of England* (London: Constable, 1964), 77. Phillipa Hardman interprets the poem
as a "poetic monument" to Blanche ("*The Book of the Duchess* as a Memorial Monument,"
The Chaucer Review 28 [1994]: 206).

[28] Helen Phillips summarizes the various means by which the dreamer is said to effect con-

The dreamer's bumbling manner and apparent obtuseness, they argue, are the clever contrivances of a masterful psychotherapist whose plan is to guide the knight through a nocturnal regimen of talk therapy. According to Charles Muscatine, the dreamer "tactfully and sympathetically pretends ignorance of the lady's death so that the other may find relief in pouring out his sorrow."[29] For Alistair Minnis, likewise, the dreamer's apparent confusion is a "successful ploy" to enable the Man in Black to "'telle ... al.'" (*The Shorter Poems*, 133). Appealing as the consolationist interpretation is, however, it fails to account for the tone and style of the dreamer's comments.

After an initial declaration of sympathy, the dreamer's responses to the Black Knight are at best insensitive and at worst downright mean. When the Black Knight claims his lady was the best of women, the speaker replies that the knight only "*thoghte* that she was the beste" (1049, my emphasis). Trampling the rules of tact, the dreamer casts aspersions, quite eagerly it seems, on the worth of everyone involved. In the lines that Minnis quotes, the dreamer even suggests that the Black Knight did something to get himself dumped:

> "What los ys that?" quod I thoo;
> "Nyl she not love yow? Ys hyt soo?
> Or have ye oght doon amys,
> That she hath left yow? Ys hyt this?
> For Goddes love, telle me al."
>
> (1139–43)

---

solation in "Structure and Consolation in *The Book of the Duchess*," *The Chaucer Review* 16 (1981): 107. Arguments for the consolatory effect of the poem often rely on tenuous assumptions or extra-textual material. M. Angela Carson argues that the dreamer's consolation succeeds based on an analogy between the "hart" pursued by Octoveyn at the beginning of the dream and the "heart" of the black knight: "when the hunters return home without having killed their game, we can conclude that the 'ese' provided by the narrator has been effective" ("Easing of the 'Hert' in *The Book of the Duchess*," *The Chaucer Review* 1 [1967]: 159). Wolfgang Clemen also finds evidence of consolation in an analogy: "Just as Halcyone was comforted by the reappearance of her husband in a dream, the knight was comforted by recalling his dead wife to mind as he told his own story" (*Chaucer's Early Poetry* [New York: Barnes & Noble, 1963], 31). (Alcyone, of course, dies of grief three days after her dream.) Kay Gilliland Stevenson finds evidence of the knight's consolation in his return home: "something wonderfully successful" has apparently happened if "the Man in Black is moving homeward in the last lines and the narrator is writing poetry again" ("Readers, Poets, and Poems within the Poem," *The Chaucer Review* 24 [1989]: 1). Dennis Walker's argument for consolation rests on gossamer *Affektkomplexe*: the birdsong in the speaker's dream "glances at the previously suppressed metamorphosis of the Ovidian Ceyx and Alcyone" ("Narrative Inconclusiveness and Consolatory Dialectic in *The Book of the Duchess*," *The Chaucer Review* 18 [1983]: 5). Bahr argues that consolation is achieved through "the chiastic pattern of contrasting rhetorical styles that links the tale of Alcyone with the denoument of the central dialogue" ("Rhetorical Construction," 43). F. H. Whitman finds evidence of consolation in its very absence: "Here, of course, is the consolation of the poem: though the man in black is not consoled, it is perfectly clear to any Christian that he ought to be" ("Exegesis and Chaucer's Dream Visions," *The Chaucer Review* 3 [1969]: 233). Rodney Delasanta passes judgment on all such "consolationist" theories: "final consolation can only be inferred at the end of the dreamer's dream" ("Christian Affirmation in *The Book of the Duchess*," *PMLA* 84 [1969]: 249).

[29] *Chaucer and the French Tradition: A Study in Style and Meaning* (Berkeley: University of California Press, 1964), 102.

The impertinent barrage of speculations and thudding Anglo-Saxon monosylla-
bles suggest a chattering busybody rather than a sensitive listener. The dreamer
asks three questions, the second and third doubled by breathless repetitions,
and then demands with a mild oath that the knight cough up the whole story.
How telling this tale will affect the Black Knight seems the farthest thing from
the speaker's mind. The tone, style, and content of this passage indicate that
the narrator's "mental and emotional numbness" have followed him into his
dream.[30]

If Chaucer does not console John of Gaunt through a comforting or edifying dream vision, how does the poem achieve its presumed rhetorical purpose?
Chaucer's strategy in *The Book of the Duchess*, we may conclude, operates on
two distinct levels. On one level, it is a poetic monument to Duchess Blanche.
Chaucer offers Gaunt a fictionalized version of himself praising his late wife in
fine French fashion. However distracted, the Black Knight pays touching tribute
to the White Lady's virtue and beauty. On a second level, however, the poem
is a monument to inexpressibility. On this level, there is only one character in
The Book of the Duchess, the melancholy narrator who fails to communicate
the cause of his grief, fails to read Alcyone's tale sympathetically, fails to understand the Black Knight's loss, fails to comfort the knight, and fails to tell
his own tale without distracting tangents and digressions.

Chaucer's inept dreamer–narrator is born out of the impossibility of the
author's rhetorical situation. Chaucer's first matter in this botched dream vision, in short, is his own inability to console his noble patron. *The Book of
the Duchess*, nevertheless, comprises Chaucer's deferential obeisance to John of
Gaunt. Through it Chaucer offers the satisfaction of knowing that lesser men
like himself cannot adequately express the depth of love or the degree of loss
Gaunt has experienced. For a poet of Chaucer's social status, this may be as
close to commiseration or consolation as one dare come.[31] Confronted with a
seemingly impossible bind, Chaucer hits upon the happy solution of a bumbling
narrative persona which would remain with him in various forms in *The House
of Fame*, *The Parliament of Fowls*, and *Troilus and Criseyde*, and even in the
chubby lack-wit who tells the two worst tales on the road to Canterbury.

---

[30] Dennis Walker, "Narrative Inconclusiveness," 11. It is difficult to imagine how this passage could be reconciled with Bertrand Bronson's judgment that "[the dreamer's] etiquette is
unimpeachable" (*"The Book of the Duchess* Reopened," 283).

[31] For a similar interpretation of this "odd, truant little poem," see J. Stephen Russell's *The
English Dream Vision: Anatomy of a Form* (Columbus: Ohio State University Press, 1988),
142–59. The central obstacle to consolation, Russell argues, is the "bankrupt conventionality"
of the "French school" of amatory verse (149).

"Peynted ... text and [visual] glose"

Primitivism, Ekphrasis, and Pictorial Intertextuality in the Dreamers' Bedrooms of *Roman de la Rose* and *Book of the Duchess*

In describing the walls of his "chamber," on which "Were peynted, bothe text and glose,/ Of al the Romaunce of the Rose,"[1] the narrator of Chaucer's first dream vision, the *Book of the Duchess* (hereafter *BD*) briefly but explicitly alludes to the thirteenth-century allegorical poem and seminal dream vision the *Roman de la Rose* (hereafter *RR*). This astonishing incorporation of the "text" of a twenty-thousand-line poem as well as its attendant commentary into the wall décor of the *BD*-dreamer's well-appointed bedroom has intrigued literary critics as well as art historians.[2] Despite this blatant clue about intertextuality between *RR* and *BD*, Chaucerian "source and analogue" critics have concentrated mainly on Chaucer's indebtedness to the works of Machaut and Froissart instead of exploring more deeply the relationship between *BD* and a text that Chaucer names by title, almost as if acknowledging *RR*'s preeminence as the paradigmatic French exemplar of the genre he practices in his first extant poem.[3]

---

[1]The *Book of the Duchess*, 333–34. References to the text of the *Roman de la Rose* are cited parenthetically from Guillaume de Lorris and Jean de Meun, *Le roman de la rose*, ed. Daniel Poirion (Paris: Garnier–Flammarion, 1974); translations are from Charles Dahlberg, *The Romance of the Rose by Guillaume De Lorris and Jean De Meun* (Hanover: University Press of New England, 1986). To conserve space, unless analysis of the original language is crucial to the argument, long passages from *RR* are from Dahlberg's translation.

[2]See the notes to lines 321–22, 322–27, and 332–34 in Helen Phillips, ed., *The Book of the Duchess*, (Durham: Durham and St. Andrews Medieval Texts, 1982). Art historians include Joan Evans, "Chaucer and Decorative Art," *Review of English Studies* 6 (1930): 408–12; June Osborne, *Stained Glass in England* (Dover, N.H.: Alan Sutton, 1993), 45–46; Richard Marks, *Stained Glass in England during the Middle Ages* (London: Routledge, 1993), 94.

[3]Barry Windeatt includes no excerpts from *RR* in his collection of sources for *BD* even though nearly a century ago Dean Fansler catalogued many verbal echoes of *RR* in *BD*. See Barry Windeatt, ed., *Chaucer's Dream Poetry: Sources and Analogues* (Cambridge and Totowa N.J.: Cambridge University Press, 1982), xiv; Dean Spruill Fansler, *Chaucer and the Roman De La Rose* (1914; repr. Gloucester, Mass.: Peter Smith, 1965), 123–33. Windeatt acknowledges *RR*'s effect on *BD* only in passing when he notes that Chaucer "conveys meaning through setting," as exemplified by the dreamer's bedchamber "with ... its walls decorated with the *Roman de la Rose*, [which] forms a room-interior itself expressive of the dreamer's inner disposition and cast of mind through the influences upon him." Fansler argues that

97

In the present essay I fill this critical lacuna, first by comparing how the respective authors of *RR* and *BD* use the rhetorical device of *ekphrasis* to depict the interior spaces inhabited respectively by *RR*'s Amant [the Lover] and *BD*'s narrator before they enter the more famous exterior landscape spaces where most of the "plot" of their dreams takes place: *RR*'s "bois" [woods] and cultivated "vergier" [garden]; and *BD*'s "forest" (363, 372), "floury grene" (398), and "woode" (414). Next, I reveal a complicated program of mixed media intertextuality between *RR* and *BD* wherein Chaucer's ekphrastic verbal "painting" of the dreamer's bedroom reflects his visual experience of several media of "painted" plastic arts—painted miniatures illustrating the *incipit* folios of *RR* manuscripts and painted glass windows and murals in buildings he had seen—a true illustration of Horace's definition of *ekphrasis*, "ut pictoria poesis" [as in pictures, so in poetry]. Finally, in the respective representations of the bedrooms of their narrators, I argue that the authors of *RR* and *BD* take opposing positions within the discourse of primitivism, with *RR* ultimately championing "Nature" and *BD* taking an anti-primitivist stance by valorizing "civilization."[4] Preceding my analysis of the visual/verbal intertextuality between *RR* and *BD*, I define the discourse of primitivism and the rhetorical device of *ekphrasis,* and outline the relation between *ekphrasis* and primitivism in *RR* and *BD*.

Primitivism defined

Primitivism is a discourse that promotes "nature" over "civilization"[5] by positing that a model "human condition" may be achieved through living in a "state of nature." Chronological primitivism locates the best time in the history of mankind in the very distant past, or the "first age" or "golden age,"[6] a time when the prevalent lifestyle was such a "state of nature." Cultural primitivism expresses the discontent of the civilized with civilization and the belief of people in a highly evolved and complex cultural condition that a simpler life, such as the "state of nature," is more desirable. Cultural primitivism often proclaims the lifestyle of a primal or "savage" race (such as the medieval Wild People) to be superior to that of the contemporary "civilized" population.[7] Although,

---

"Chaucer's extensive use of many different parts of the *Roman de la Rose* in the *Book of the Duchess* makes it clear that before 1369 the poet was familiar with the French poem as a whole" (22).

[4] On Chaucer's use of the "primitivistic myth" of the Golden Age" in *BD*, see John M. Fyler, "Irony and the Age of Gold in the *Book of the Duchess*," *Speculum* 52 (1977): 314–28, which is incorporated verbatim in John M. Fyler, *Chaucer and Ovid* (New Haven: Yale University Press, 1979), 65–81. Fyler does not treat the passages in *BD* I cover. In a larger study about the primitivist discourses employed respectively in *RR* and *BD*, I deal at length with the treatment of the exterior landscape spaces of *RR*'s "bois and "vergier" and *BD*'s "forest" and "woode." The present analysis focuses specifically on the *ekphrases* of the bedrooms.

[5] On the Western development of the concept of "Civilization," see Raymond Williams, *Keywords: A Vocabulary of Culture and Society* (New York: Oxford University Press, 1983), 57.

[6] On the concept of the Golden Age, see Harry Levin, *The Myth of the Golden Age in the Renaissance* (Bloomington: Indiana University Press, 1969).

[7] For the effects of civilization see Norbert Elias: *The Civilizing Process: The Development of Manners*, trans. Edmund Jephcott (New York: Urizen Books, 1978); Arthur O. Lovejoy and George Boas, *Primitivism and Related Ideas in Antiquity* (Baltimore: The Johns Hopkins

compared to the perquisites of civilized life, the primitives' simple lifestyle is
considered unrefined and "backward," its avoidance of the negative aspects of
"progress" that ironically accompany the "civilizing" process–technology, luxury
goods, commercial trade, private property, the profit motive, nationalism, and
wars—well compensates for the crudeness of this aboriginal group's existence.
Living the "blisful" (Chaucer, "Former Age," 1), if less convenient and comfortable life of the "Golden Age," the primitive literally embodies the exemplary
"state of nature."

Significantly, in his continuation of *RR*, Jean de Meun practices intertextuality with earlier primitivist texts, endorsing both chronological and cultural
primitivism.[8] Mirroring similar primitivist passages in Ovid's *Metamorphoses*
I: 89-112 and Boethius's *Consolation of Philosophy* II. Metrum 5, Jean de Meun
inserts into *RR* a cynical hundred-line-long address by Ami [Friend] to Amant
[the Lover], decrying the greed of contemporary women and contrasting their
acquisitive behavior with the ideal conduct of the inhabitants of the celebrated
"golden" past (*RR* 8355–8455). This group satisfied the basic human need for
sustenance without killing animals for protein, or procuring food artificially
through organized agriculture, or processing foodstuffs or drink; instead, they
relied on the bounty that the earth gave up freely. This mode of living fulfilled the need for clothing without wearing mass-produced, artificially-dyed,
woven-fabric "fashion"; utilizing the landscape for natural protection and sleeping space also satisfied the need for shelter without erecting complicated architectural edifices. The age was also "golden" for its lack of vertical social
hierarchies. All inhabitants lived democratically in a communal existence of
shared (naturally acquired) food and shelter without personal possessions.

In its immediate textual situation, Jean de Meun's borrowed primitivist
passage is intended to satirize the venal materialism of contemporary females.
However, in the *RR*'s larger context, the passage also serves as an antithesis
to and antidote for life in Deduit's [Pleasure's] garden as described by Guillaume de Lorris in the poem's opening. Interestingly, both the generic people of
the Golden Age and the inhabitants of Deduit's garden lead an enviably idyllic
and *idle* existence. Despite superficial similarities, the former group's inactiv-
ity definitely seems more innocent than the latter's. As in the Golden Age,
Deduit and his companions participate in or observe elaborately orchestrated
carol-dancing, music-making, and other entertainments (*RR* 727–77; 8439–44).
However, the gatekeeper to Deduit's garden is personified Idleness. When not

---

Press, 1935); Charles H. Long, "Primitive/Civilized: The Locus of a Problem," *History of
Religions* 20 (1980): 43–44.

   [8]For the medieval adoption of classical primitivism, see George Boas, *Essays on Primitivism and Related Ideas in the Middle Ages* (1948; New York: Octagon Books, 1966); for
medieval English chronological primitivism see James Dean, "The World Grown Old and Genesis in Middle English Historical Writings," *Speculum* 57 (1982): 548–68. On the related topic
of the Ages of Man, see John Burrow, *The Ages of Man* (Oxford: Clarendon Press, 1988);
Mary Dove, *The Perfect Age of Man's Life* (Cambridge: Cambridge University Press, 1987).
On primitivism in another thirteenth-century French text, see Lorraine K. Stock, "Civilization
and its Discontents: Cultural Primitivism and the Depiction of Merlin as a Wild Man in the
Roman de Silence," *Arthuriana* 12 (2002): 22–36.

performing the role of concierge to the exclusive society of Deduit, this rich, powerful female aristocrat adorns herself in splendid array and brandishes a mirror that reflects her dazzling "glamour."[9] The elaborately embellished appearance of Idleness and her companions and the elitist ideology governing membership in Deduit's exclusive order (largely dependent on criteria such as age, personal attractiveness, income, and social rank) contrast provocatively with the sheepskin-costumed inhabitants of the Golden Age, who practice no exclusionary class distinctions in their sharing of natural resources.

What qualitatively distinguishes one group from the other is its relation to Nature and the landscape, its valuing of artifice, and its vertical rather than horizontal social structure. Indeed, the praiseworthy lifestyle of the Golden Age, which relied on and was supplied—without human interference—by Nature's generosity differs in several significant respects from the rather decadent standard of living enjoyed by Idleness and the self-indulgent inhabitants of Deduit's walled garden in *RR*. In contrast to the retrograde rustics of the "former" age, the appearance, practices, and social ideologies of Deduit's compeers mirror the ideals of Guillaume de Lorris's and Jean de Meun's thirteenth-century aristocratic audience. Deduit's companions inhabit a "garden," a fabricated space superimposing artificial boundaries upon the natural landscape. Further, this architectural space is decorated with exterior mural art announcing, through symbolic pictorial images, the snobbish exclusion from the garden of social groups and human types practicing the "vices" of courtly society (hatred, felony, covetousness, avarice, envy, hypocrisy) or who are superficially unacceptable for membership in this elite group because of their advanced age, physical unattractiveness, or financial poverty (*RR* 129–462).

While Ovid's and Boethius's descriptions of the Golden Age provided Jean de Meun with a satirical foil for Deduit's "civilized" micro-culture in *RR*, they also supplied raw material for Chaucer to appropriate into his own writing throughout his career. The oft-repeated description of the Golden Age also contrasts provocatively with the lifestyle of *BD*'s dreamer, who for eight years has the leisure to pine in a state of almost psychotic paralysis, surrounded by books and games in a comfortable, well-appointed bedroom that is lavishly adorned with various media of the plastic arts (*BD* 45–51, 299–300, 321–43). The Golden Age *topos* also serves as a foil for the behavior of the "characters" inhabiting Chaucer's narrator's dream—Emperor Octavian, his hunters, Lady White, and the Man in Black—who respectively practice venery to acquire food, domesticate animals for hunting and transport (*BD* 344–86), participate in the artifice and vertical social structure of Courtly Love (*BD* 758–74, 1199–1257), and inhabit

---

[9] For how light-reflective, literally dazzling costume and cosmetic images are used to connote the "glamour" of the inhabitants of the garden of Deduit, see Sarah-Grace Heller, "Light as Glamour: The Luminescent Ideal of Beauty in the *Roman de la Rose*," *Speculum* 76 (2001): 934–59. In analyzing the light-reflective aspects of the descriptions of the costumes and physical beauty of characters in *RR*, Heller discusses them neither under the rubric of the rhetorical device of *ekphrasis* nor as examples of the dichotomy between primitivism and civilization; nevertheless, the set piece *effictios* of the characters constitute *ekphrases* and the glittering adorned costumes are potent signifiers of "civilization."

a tall white-walled castle, the architectural hallmark of medieval aristocratic "civilization" (*BD* 1318). In engaging with these familiar ideals of primitivist discourse, Chaucer and the authors of *RR* clearly employ conventions that had significant literary and rhetorical antecedents.

The rhetorical figure of *ekphrasis*

The detailed descriptions of life in the Golden Age by Ovid, Boethius, and Jean de Meun also exemplify *ekphrasis*,[10] a stylistic exercise that was recommended in classical and medieval rhetorical handbooks.[11] By consensus, modern rhetoricians[12] define *ekphrasis* as a separable segment of text using words instead of paint or any plastic medium to depict a *visual* representation of a time, event, person, place, building, or work of art[13] so that the reader would virtually see the verbal subject as if pictured "before his own eyes."[14] In current usage, *ekphrasis* denotes the incorporation of a description of an actual piece of graphic art, such as a Grecian urn or a painting by Breugel, into the framework of a work of verbal art.[15] This redefinition underscores the mutually influential interrelationship between verbal and visual media, between the written and plastic arts, reflecting Horace's dictum "ut pictura poesis" [as in painting, so in poetry]. Defined as the mutual interplay between a written text and a visual image, *ekphrasis* therefore also constitutes a form of mixed media "intertextuality."[16] Following Ernst Curtius, medievalists customarily refer to *ekphrasis* and

---

[10] James A. Heffernan, *Museum of Words: The Poetics of Ekphrasis from Homer to Ashbery* (Chicago and London: University of Chicago Press, 1993), 191, n. 2, discusses the etymology of the term *ekphrasis*, composed of the Greek *ek* (out) and *phrazein* (tell, declare, pronounce), literally meaning "to tell in full."

[11] See Frank J. D'Angelo, "The Rhetoric of Ekphrasis," *JAC: A Journal of Composition Theory* 18 (1998): 439–47. On *ekphrasis* in other medieval texts see Marianne Shapiro, "Ecphrasis in Virgil and Dante," *Comparative Literature* 42 (1990): 97–115, and Linda M. Clemente, *Literary objets d'art: Ekphrasis in Medieval French Romance 1150–1210* (New York: Peter Lang, 1992). Clemente does not discuss *RR*.

[12] Excellent historical surveys of the varied meanings attached to *ekphrasis* include John Hollander, "The Poetics of Ekphrasis," *Word & Image* 4 (1988): 209–17; Rodney Stenning Edgecombe, "A Typology of Ecphrases," *Classical and Modern Literature* 13 (1993): 103–16; Ruth Webb, "*Ekphrasis* Ancient and Modern: the Invention of a Genre," *Word & Image* 15 (1999): 7–18.

[13] Richard Lanham, *A Handlist of Rhetorical Terms* (Berkeley and Los Angeles: University of California Press, 1968), 39, defines *ekphrasis* as, "A self-contained description, often on a commonplace subject, which can be inserted in a fitting place in a discourse."

[14] Henry Maguire, *Art and Eloquence in Byzantium* (Princeton: Princeton University Press, 1981), 22.

[15] Leo Spitzer defines *ekphrasis* as "the reproduction, through the medium of words, of sensuously perceptible *objets d'art*" in "The 'Ode on a Grecian Urn,' or Content vs. Metagrammar," in *Essays on English and American Literature*, ed. Anna Hatcher (Princeton: Princeton University Press, 1962), 67–97, quoted material from p. 72. See also Jean Hagstrum, *The Sister Arts: The Tradition of Literary Pictorialism in English Poetry from Dryden to Gray* (Chicago: University of Chicago Press, 1958); Heffernan, *Museum of Words*.

[16] Ross Murfin and Supryia M. Kay, "Intertextuality," *The Bedford Glossary of Critical and Literary Terms* (Boston: Bedford/St. Martin's 2003), 220, suggest *New Yorker* covers (visual art that often contains clever literary subtexts or references) to exemplify the broad spectrum of intertextuality. By analogy, I see the form of *ekphrasis* involving interartistic, multi-media verbal-pictorial exchange as another kind of intertextuality.

descriptio interchangeably, for medieval writers employed every permutation of *ekphrasis* listed above in their literary *oeuvres*.[17]

The redefinition of *ekphrasis* as "intertextuality" between words and pictures supports the visual-verbal "intertextuality" I propose exists between *RR* and *BD*, which expands the notion of intertextuality beyond the term's usual definition, "a text that exhibits signs of influence" or whose "language inevitably contains common points of reference with other texts through ... allusion, quotation, genre, style, and even revisions" (Murfin and Kay, "Intertextuality" 219). Instead of a purely verbal relationship between a source text and its literary progeny, I propose intertextuality between the mixed media of visual images painted on book folios, architectural edifices, or statues and a text's verbal images which are "painted" with the "colors" of rhetoric, a phrase by which medieval rhetorical manuals commonly denote a writer's use of figures of speech and verbal ornamentation. Chaucer alludes to the "colors of rhetoric" in *House of Fame* (859), the Clerk's *Prologue* (16), and at length in the Franklin's *Prologue*, where this self-proclaimed "burel" [unlearned] (716) pilgrim protests that, never having learned "rethorik," (719), he is capable only of "rude speche" (718) or plain language:

> Colours ne knowe I none, withouten drede,
> But swiche colours as growen in the mede,
> Or elles swiche as men dye or peynte.
> Colours of rethoryk been to me queynte.   (723–26)

Here the Franklin lists the very kinds of "colors" Guillaume de Lorris and Chaucer employ in the intertextual play between *RR* and *BD*: the colors "painted" by Nature on the landscape (as described by Chaucer and Guillaume); colored pigments applied by artists to miniatures illustrating manuscripts[18] and to pictorial wall murals or polychromed statues; and the ornamental language used by writers in such rhetorical exercises as *ekphrasis* or *descriptio*. Moreover, the Black Knight's self-description of his vulnerability or openness to the experience of loving Blanche is couched in exactly such "painterly" terms:

> Paraunter *I was* therto most able,
> *As a whit wal* or a table,
> For hit ys *redy to cacche and take*

---

[17] Ernst Robert Curtius, *European Literature and the Latin Middle Ages* (New York: Harper & Row, 1963), defines his conflation of the Greek *ekphrasis* and the Latin *descriptio* as "the elaborate 'delineation' ... of people, places, buildings, works of art" (69); he also discusses *ekphrasis* and *descriptio* under the *topoi* of portraits of ideal physical beauty and ugliness (181–82) and of descriptions of idealized landscapes such as the *pleasance* or *locus amoenus* (193–200). See also Charles S. Baldwin, *Medieval Rhetoric and Poetic (to 1400): Interpreted from Representative Works* (New York: Macmillan, 1928), 19, defining *ekphrasis* as "an account in detail, visible as they say, bringing before one's eyes what is to be shown."

[18] Significantly, the term "miniature," refers not to the size of the painting, but to the application of color to a manuscript, from the etymological root *miniare*, meaning "to color with red," as books were originally decorated with red ink or *minium*. See Michelle P. Brown, *Understanding Illuminated Manuscripts: A Guide to Technical Terms* (Malibu, Calif.: The J. Paul Getty Museum, 1995), 86.

> *Al that men wil theryn make,*
> Whethir so men wil portreye or peynte,
> Be the werkes never so queynte.   (*BD* 779–84, emphasis added)

The Man in Black is thus a blank wall upon which "men [can] portreye or peynte" either a mural or a rhetorically ornamented text of his love story. In such an inter-artistic context, Chaucer's verbal portrayal of the *BD*-narrator's chamber, which features the "peynted" text and "peynted" gloss of "al the Romaunce of the Rose" on its walls, legitimizes expanding the definition of intertextuality to encompass the influence of painted manuscript miniatures of *RR* and other painted works of visual art upon Chaucer's creation of verbal art in *BD*.

Ekphrasis in Chaucer's works and the *Roman de la Rose*

Notwithstanding the Franklin's self-effacing disclaimer, Chaucer's portraits of Blanche in *BD*, Venus and Dame Nature in *Parliament of Fowls*, Lady Fame in *The House of Fame*, and the pilgrims in the *General Prologue* to the *Canterbury Tales* attest his skill at producing *ekphrasis*, employing the "colors" of rhetoric to paint verbal "pictures" of people. His descriptions of the Palace of Fame in *House of Fame*,[19] the wall decorations in his respective glass and brass temples of Venus in *House of Fame* and *Parliament of Fowls*, and the murals in Theseus's temples to the gods in the *Knight's Tale* demonstrate his practice of the modern definition of *ekphrasis* discussed above as "the imitation in literature of a work of plastic art." These Chaucerian practices of *ekphrasis* were anticipated and perhaps influenced by the *ekphrasis* in *RR* of "les images et les paintures" [the images and paintings] (*RR* 134) depicted on the exterior walls of Deduit's enclosed "vergier" [garden] (*RR* 129–463). Describing visual images of allegorical *person*ifications, these ekphrastic passages in *RR* combine the rhetorical figure's capacity to depict simultaneously both people and works of plastic art. Indeed, Guillaume de Lorris's descriptions of the exterior mural art of Deduit's Garden are so detailed and "lifelike," the reader could forget that these figures of Hatred, Avarice, Old Age and the other personified ignoble "vices" that are to be barred from the courtly micro-society inside the walls, are really images, paintings, and sculptures rather than real people.[20]

When Chaucer engages with the opening of *RR* in his creation of *BD*, he significantly alters his source's use of exterior and interior spaces. Indeed, a comparison of the verbal texts of *RR* and *BD* and the manuscript illuminations of this section of *RR* reveals that in his handling of the transition between the interior bedroom space of his dreamer–narrator and the landscape space into which the dreamer enters, Chaucer again departs from the text of his literary model, though not necessarily from artists' visualizations of that section of text in the manuscript tradition of *RR*.

---

[19]See Mary Flowers Braswell, "Architectural Portraiture in Chaucer's *House of Fame*," *Journal of Medieval and Renaissance Studies* 11 (1981): 101–12.

[20]For the power of *ekphrasis* to achieve this effect, see Murray Krieger, "Ekphrasis and the Still Movement of Poetry; or, Laokoön Revisited," in *The Poet as Critic*, ed. Frederick McDowell (Evanston, Ill: Northwestern University Press, 1967), 5.

The beginning of the dream in *RR*

Chaucer's "auctour" Guillaume de Lorris opens *RR* with an *ekphrasis* of the primeval "bois"—an authentically "primitive" landscape untouched by human intervention. De Lorris emphasizes that the woods' hedges and bushes adorn *themselves* with new foliage and the earth clothes *itself* in an elaborately colored "robe" of new flowers. Guillaume's "bois" requires no seed-sowing, tree-planting, or branch-pruning, as does a "vergier," which connotes an "orchard" or "garden," both landscape spaces shaped by human intervention (*RR* 47–66). If the flora of the woods in springtime attract the attention of the dreamer, so do the fauna, for he proceeds to catalogue the various birds (nightingales, parrots, larks, and others) whose singing both awakes him and irresistibly awakens *in* him the stirrings of love on this May morning (*RR* 67–87), prompting him to rise, dress, perform his ablutions, and leave his room. *RR*'s dreamer next walks through those same primeval woods past a river flowing down from a hill and a meadow that follows along the banks of the river (*RR* 103–28) until he encounters a "vergier grant et lé" (*RR* 130) [large and roomy garden]. This exterior space replaces the wild "bois" as the *mise-en-scène* of the remainder of the dreamer's "aventure," an erotic quest in which the narrative persona develops from dreamer to Amant [lover]. Guillaume also introduces this civilized landscape space with an elaborate *ekphrasis*:

> When I had gone ahead thus for a little while, I saw a large and roomy garden, entirely enclosed by a high crenelated wall, *sculptured outside* and laid out with many *fine inscriptions*. I willingly admired the *images and paintings*, and I shall recount to you and tell you the appearance of these images as they occur to my memory. In the middle I saw Hatred. ... Felony ... Villainy.... The wall itself was high and formed a perfect square; it *took the place of a hedge* in enclosing and shutting off a *garden where no shepherd had even entered*. This garden stood in a very beautiful place, and I would have been very grateful to anyone who had been willing to lead me inside. ... No place was ever so rich with trees or songbirds: there were three times as many birds as in the whole kingdom of France. ... I found a little door that was very narrow and tight ... [the *ekphrasis* of Idleness follows]. Then I entered into the garden and ... I thought I was truly in the earthly paradise.... There were many singing birds gathered together [a long catalogue of birds ensues followed by *ekphrases* of the inhabitants of the garden, including Deduit, the God of Love, and others]. (*RR* 129–56; 463 ff.; my emphasis).

Guillaume's juxtaposition of two distinct landscape spaces serves to emphasize the extent to which the "vergier"—complete with man-made walls, mural decoration, and an exclusionary door—is the "civilized" antithesis of the "primitive" wildwood of the "bois." Guillaume's foundational setting for the *aventure* that comprises the dream thus sets up an opposition between a space signifying "primitivism" and a space signifying "civilization." When Jean de Meun introduces the *ekphrasis* of the Golden Age much later in the poem's continuation, he merely capitalizes on the polarity between primitivism and civilization already established at the start of the poem in the dreamer's physical boundary crossing from the wild setting of the "bois" to the civilized space of the "vergier."

Intertextuality between *RR* and *BD*: evidence from *RR* manuscripts

As noted earlier, in his *ekphrasis* of the *BD*-dreamer's bedchamber Chaucer claims that "al" the walls of the room "with colours fine/ Were peynted, bothe text and glose" of "al" the *RR*. This odd wall treatment raises many questions. Does the reference to "colours" refer to the "colors of rhetoric," suggesting twenty thousand lines of artfully chosen language copied on the walls in columns, as in a book, or does it denote colored pigments, suggesting pictorial scenes from the plot of *RR* depicted on the walls, as in mural paintings, perhaps duplicating manuscript miniatures from books? Does the "gloss" consist of verbal elucidation of the text inscribed on the walls or some other kind of interpretation of the words of the *RR* (like a cartoon or the *Biblia Pauperum*) depicted as mural art? Does the fact that both text and gloss are "painted" indicate that *both* are graphic rather than verbal? Chaucer's insistence on both texts and glosses being "painted," yoking the visual to the verbal, authorizes me to propose an unusual but (under the circumstances) appropriate intertext for *BD*—the combined text and miniatures of illuminated *RR* manuscripts. Because the illustrator visually renders the plot according to his reading (or misreading) of the text, changing the details at his or a patron's whim, his illustrations or illuminations literally "illuminate" the text and constitute a form of pictorial "interpretation." Thus the miniatures illustrating the manuscripts of *RR* provide a visual "gloss" of Guillaume de Lorris's verbal text. Together, they could be said to comprise the "peynted ... text and glose,/ Of al the Romaunce of the Rose." These miniatures, constituting the artist's painted *ekphrasis* of Guillaume's verbal *ekphrasis*, also demonstrate Horace's dictum "ut pictura poesis."

From the late thirteenth century onwards, many illustrated copies of *RR* were produced, especially in northeastern French workshops. With increased demand for copies of what was the medieval equivalent of a bestseller, in the second half of the fourteenth century the center of production shifted to Paris, where lavishly illustrated copies were produced in large quantity, following the style of northeastern French prototypes. Even mediocre copies averaged between forty and sixty illustrations, while deluxe exemplars contained even more. Early in his career of civil service, Chaucer's official business in France afforded him the opportunity for exposure to one or more of these manuscripts.[21] Given the fact that he incompletely translated *RR* into Middle English as *Romaunt of the Rose*,[22] unquestionably borrowed from *RR* to create the portraits of the Prioress, the Wife of Bath, the Pardoner, and other characters, and mentioned

---

[21] For records of Chaucer's presence in France see Martin M. Crow and Clair C. Olson, ed. *Chaucer Life Records* (Austin: University of Texas Press, 1966), chapters 2–4.

[22] The issue of authorship of the *Romaunt* is vexed. For a summary of the arguments posited for and against the authenticity of the *Romaunt*'s place in the Chaucer canon, see Charles Dahlberg, ed., *A Variorum Edition of the Works of Geoffrey Chaucer Volume VII, The Romaunt of the Rose* (Norman, Okla.: University of Oklahoma Press, 1999), 3–24.

RR's title in his *ekphrasis* of the *BD*-dreamer's bedroom, it is reasonable to propose that Chaucer actually owned one of these manuscripts.

When Chaucer or another medieval reader perused these *RR* manuscripts, what did they "read"? As discussed earlier, the textual opening of *RR* comprises an extensive *ekphrasis* of the landscape of "li bois" [the woods] in May time, in which Guillaume "paints" with the "colors" of rhetoric a vivid verbal "picture" of the re-greening and re-blooming meadows, birdsong, and water source, standard elements of the *reverdie* and *locus amoenus topoi*. Perhaps inspired by the colorful new "robes" metaphorically put on by Nature, *RR*'s Amant arises from bed, dresses, and ventures forth into the woods, eventually encountering the walled garden that will be the setting for his pursuit of the Rose.

Whereas Guillaume De Lorris is generous in his *descriptio* of the exterior spaces of both woods and garden, he is miserly with details about the interior space in which *Amant* sleeps and has his dream. The dreamer says:

> [A]s I slept I became aware that it was full morning. I *got up from bed* straightaway, and *put on my stockings* and *washed my hands.* Then I drew a silver needle from a *dainty little needlecase* and threaded it. I had a desire to *go out of the town* ["hors de vile"] to hear the sound of birds who, in that new season, were singing among the trees. *I stitched up my sleeves in zigzag lacing* and set out, quite alone, to enjoy myself listening to the birds who were straining themselves because the gardens were bursting into bloom.
>
> (*RR* 88–102, emphasis added)

The only room appointment explicitly mentioned is a bed. How *Amant* dons his hose[23] and stitches up his sleeves—both costume allusions indicate that he is a slave to "fashion," a characteristic of a "civilized" rather than "primitive" lifestyle—is left to the imagination of the reader. However, a possible "gloss" of this absence may be gleaned in artists' pictorial interpretations of this passage in miniatures illustrating the *incipit* folio of many illuminated manuscripts of *RR*. This part of *RR* corresponds, not to the beginning of *BD*, but to the beginning of the dream itself 350 lines later. Chaucer unquestionably appropriated aspects of De Lorris's *ekphrasis* of "bois" and "vergier" in his own *ekphrasis* of the landscape space in which the *BD*-dreamer eventually encounters the Man in Black.[24] It is worthwhile to ponder what Chaucer or other fourteenth-century readers may have "seen" in the pictorial "glose" provided by the incipit miniature of *RR*'s text. To demonstrate the plausibility of Chaucer's having been influenced by such miniatures, I support my argument with manuscripts that Chaucer putatively could have seen, all dated before the end of the fourteenth century.

---

[23] According to George Fenwick Jones, "Sartorial Symbols in Mediaeval Literature," *Medium Aevum*, 25 (1956): 63–70, wearing a jerkin and hose (as opposed to the shirt and breeches of the peasant or the fool figure) was a costume sign that the wearer belonged to the nobility (63–64).

[24] For putative borrowings of material from *RR* in *BD* see Fansler, *Chaucer and the Roman*, 123–33; Laura L. Howes, *Chaucer's Gardens and the Language of Convention* (Gainesville: University Press of Florida, 1997), 15–16.

One common model for *RR*'s *incipit* miniature serially depicts Amant first asleep in his chamber, then embarking on the "plot" of his dream,[25] as exemplified by early fourteenth-century *RR* manuscripts such as Selden Supra 57, folio 1r and Walters 143, folio 1r.[26] This artistic paradigm is divided into four separate scenes, two upper and two lower, both pairs viewed from left to right. The upper left quadrant represents the dreamer asleep in his bed with either the character Dangiers (a Wild Man type) hovering over the bed brandishing a club, or a stylized rosebush arching over the bed from the right, or both. Upper right depicts the dreamer in his chamber seated across from a washbasin and towel on a pedestal; his getting dressed is represented not by donning hose or lacing his sleeves as specified in the verbal text, but by tying his shoe. Sometimes the handwashing is implied by the presence of a basin and towel in the bedroom. Lower left shows the dreamer embarking on his dream-quest into a landscape scene. Lower right depicts the dreamer approaching or entering the exterior structure of the Garden of Deduit. Depending on the particular manuscript painter's interpretation, the lower right miniature, a graphic *ekphrasis* of an extensive verbal *ekphrasis*, depicts not only the Garden's outside walls, but also the pictorial images, either statues or paintings, of allegorical characters representing the "vices" of courtly society.[27]

Other examples of fourteenth-century French *RR* incipit miniatures reproduce this basic paradigm with minor, interestingly subtle variations on the theme. For example, the quartered incipit miniature of MS Morgan 48, dated the second half of the fourteenth century, shows the rosebush arching over the sleeping dreamer; the dreamer's shoe-tying and the washbasin and towel; the dreamer flanked by a pair of bird-inhabited, stylized trees; and the dreamer against a diapered background (the absence of flora perhaps here signifies his transition from a "wild" to a "civilized" space) approaching the Garden's walls on which are statues in niches.[28] Greatly resembling MS M 48 is fol. 1r of

---

[25] For the classification of various scene types in *RR* manuscripts see Alfred Kuhn, "Die Illustration des *Rosenromans*," *Jahrbuch der Kunsthistorischen Sammlungen in Wien* 31, (1913): 1–66.

[26] Oxford, Bodleian MS Selden Supra 57, fol. 1r dates to the second quarter of the fourteenth century and is classified in Kuhn's group VI. Before being acquired by the Bodleian, it belonged to the collections of John Betts (1606) and Thomas Howard, Earl of Arundel, (d. 1646), placing it in England. For bibliographic descriptions see Kuhn, "Die Illustration des *Rosenromans*," 46. Baltimore, Walters Art Gallery, MS Walters 143, fol. 1r dates to the second quarter of the fourteenth century. For a bibliographic description see *Medieval and Renaissance Manuscripts in the Walters Art Gallery,* ed. Lillian M. C. Randall (Baltimore: Johns Hopkins University Press, 1989), 1:173–76. Digitized color representations of these miniatures, listed under their manuscript shelfmarks and folio numbers can be seen (after obtaining a password) at http://rose.mse.jhu.edu/. I thank the owners of the *RR* site at Johns Hopkins University for permission to direct readers of this essay to *RR* miniatures published on this site.

[27] Stephen G. Nichols, "Ekphrasis, Iconoclasm, and Desire," *Rethinking the Romance of the Rose: Text, Image, Reception,* ed. Kevin Brownlee and Sylvia Huot (Philadelphia: University of Pennsylvania Press, 1992), 133–66, discusses these *ekphrastic* passages as "portraits of social, physical, and psychic states inimical to love" (152).

[28] See New York, The Pierpont Morgan Library, MS M 48, fol. 1r. This manuscript, written and illuminated in *grisaille* in Paris in the second half of the fourteenth century, contains two half-page miniatures, including the incipit illumination, and thirty-one smaller miniatures.

Morgan's MS M 324, produced in Paris in the mid-fourteenth century, whose lower right miniature adds a stylized tree to the diapered background, the dreamer entering the Garden through an opened door, and statues on the wall. Very similar to both MS M 48 and MS M 324 is fol. 1r of MS M 185, also produced in France in the fourteenth century, whose lower left quarter differs only by having the dreamer approach a vermilion-colored turret, representing the Garden wall, out of which a rose tree grows. This painter also employed diapered backgrounds in panels two and three depicting the dreamer's chamber and the stylized landscape. Other slight variations occur in fol. 1r of Morgan MS M 132, produced in France c. 1380, whose upper right image omits the washbasin. Both lower images portray the dreamer in a sparely depicted landscape, gazing into a stream and finally standing to the left of a stream, listening to the songs of three birds perched in two stylized trees.

Notwithstanding such minor differences, these fourteenth-century examples are remarkably similar. All *incipit* miniatures employing the quartet of serial panels condense the text's florid *descriptio* of the exterior space—the May time woodland landscape and the fabled Garden of Deduit—with pictorial minimalism approaching *reductio ad absurdum*. Sometimes (as in Selden Supra 57) the landscape into which the dreamer ventures is indicated austerely by a pair of stylized trees; in other examples (Walters 143, Morgan 324, Morgan 48, and Morgan 132) the stylized trees support one or two birds, a visual shorthand representing the many birds described in the verbal text, and a body of water representing the river bed along which the dreamer walks (Morgan 132, Walters 143). The lower right image depicts either a bare Garden wall (Morgan 185, Selden Supra 57, Walters 143) or one adorned with statues or images (Morgan 48, Morgan 324) and the dreamer either approaching (Walters 143, Morgan 48, Morgan 185), entering (Morgan 324), or already inside the Garden space (Selden Supra 57). Morgan 132 omits the wall altogether.

Mirroring the absence of detail in Guillaume's text, the artists also depict the dreamer's bedroom so minimally that often the bed does not appear to be surrounded by walls or to be inside any architectural structure. The stylized rose bush arching over the bed even suggests that the bed is outdoors rather than indoors (Walters 143, M 48, M 132, M 185, M 324, Selden Supra 57). Occasionally, the dreamer's sleeping is overseen by Dangiers, the character who will be introduced much later in the text as the Wild-Man-like guardian of the Rose (Selden Supra 57, Walters 143). In the pictorial shorthand of M 132, and M 185, the functional appointments of the bedchamber are represented merely by the bed, chair, or stool on which he sits while fastening his shoes.

Chaucer's dreamer's "painted chamber"

For any reader of *RR*, including Chaucer, the four images on the *incipit* page adumbrate the trajectory of the *RR*-dreamer's quest, for they lead him from the decorative simplicity of the bedroom to the symbolically-fraught decorated walls of the enclosed Garden of Deduit. For readers of Chaucer's first dream vision, however, they also provide a revealing and ironic context for the quest of Chaucer's dreamer in *BD*. Having evoked, through this *ekphrastic* allusion, the

pictorial representation of the inception of the Lover's dream in *incipit* pages of
RR manuscripts, Chaucer's narrator's entrance into his own dream in *BD* takes
a different course. If De Lorris creates a detailed *descriptio* of the woodland
landscape into which the *RR*-dreamer advances *from* his sparely described bed
and chamber, Chaucer expends most of his descriptive powers on an *ekphrasis* of
the *BD*-dreamer's chamber, whose ornamental excess contrasts strikingly with
the simplicity of Amant's chamber in both the text and visual gloss of the incipit
miniature of *RR*. The *BD*-narrator describes his interior space:

> Me thoghte thus: that hyt was May,
> And in the dawenynge I lay
> (Me mette thus) *in my bed* al naked
> And loked forth, for I was waked
> With smale foules a gret hep
> That had affrayed me out of my slep
> Thorgh noyse and swetnesse of her song.
> And, as me mette, *they sate among*
> *Upon my chambre roof wythoute,*
> *Upon the tyles*, overal aboute,
> And songe, everych in hys wyse,
> The moste solempne servise   (*BD* 291–302, emphasis added)

The *BD*-narrator calls attention not only to his bed, in which he reclines "ful
naked," but also to the roof tiles on which a flock of birds sit serenading him to
rouse him out of sleep. After nineteen more lines describing the quality of their
singing, through which "al [his] chambre gan to rynge/ Thurgh syngynge of her
armonye" (*BD* 312–13), Chaucer's dreamer describes the appointments of this
"chambre" more fully:

> And sooth to seyn, my *chambre* was
> *Ful wel depeynted*, and *with glas*
> Were al the *wyndowes wel yglased*
> Ful clere, and nat an hoole ycrased,
> That to beholde hyt was gret joye.
> For *hooly al the story of Troye*
> Was *in the glasynge ywroght* thus,
> Of Ector and of kyng Priamus,
> Of Achilles and of kyng Lamedon,
> And eke of Medea and of Jason,
> Of Paris, Eleyne, and of Lavyne.
> And *alle the walles with colours fine*
> *Were peynted, bothe text and glose,*
> *Of al the Romaunce of the Rose.*
> My *wyndowes were shette* echon,
> And throgh the *glas* the sonne shon
> Upon my bed with bryghte bemes.   (*BD* 321–37)

Unlike his source, Chaucer emphasizes the domicile of his dreamer by repeating four times the word "chambre" (299, 312, 321, 358) and by describing the architectural details of the chamber minutely, including the "bed," the tiled "chambre roof" outside, the "Ful wel depeynted" walls, and the "wel yglased" and tightly "shette" windows. The chamber's decoration includes fenestration consisting of an ambitious program of painted glass windows, which pictorially narrate the entire, vast history of the Trojan War, and a mural program depicting the entire text and gloss of *RR*.

Chaucer's ekphrases of interior and exterior spaces in the text of *BD* deliberately invert and thus subvert the opening of the dream sequence in his source, *RR*. Members of Chaucer's reading audience familiar with *RR* would be aware that in the opening of his poem, Guillaume created a fulsome *descriptio* of his landscapes while offering a rather skimpy *ekphrasis* of the dreamer's bedroom. His illustrators, imposing their own visual "glose" upon Guillaume's unbalanced rhetorical "coloring" of outside and inside in the "text" of *RR*, allocated their illustrative *ekphrasis* of exterior and interior space in inverse proportion to Guillaume's text, reducing the elaborately detailed landscapes of *RR* to pictorial minimalism and inventing implied but textually unauthorized appointments for Amant's chamber—the bench, water basin and towel. The contrast between the textual handling of the respective dreamers' bedrooms could not be more extreme. Although both dream visions move their narrators from an interior structure through a series of landscapes, Chaucer expends much more artistic energy on the interior space of *BD* than his *auctour* Guillaume does. Earlier in *BD*, Chaucer anticipates the motif of an ornately decorated bedroom when the narrator conceives of sumptuously redecorating Morpheus's bedroom in return for granting him some much needed sleep:

> Of down of pure dowves white
> I wil yive hym a fether-bed,
> Rayed with gold and ryght wel cled
> In fyn blak satyn doutremer,
> And many a pilowe, and every ber
> Of cloth of Reynes, to slepe softe—
> Hym thar not nede to turnen ofte—
> And I wol yive hym al that falles
> To a chambre, and al hys halles
> I wol do peynte with pure gold
> And tapite hem ful many fold
> Of oo sute; this shal he have
> (Yf I wiste where were hys cave),
> Yf he kan make me slepe sone.   (*BD* 250–63)

The splendid appointments of dove-down, gold striped, black satin featherbed, imported linen pillow cases, complete tapestry suites, and gilded walls reveal the narrator's (and therefore also Chaucer's) familiarity with deluxe bedroom décor.

In his emphasis on creating elaborate *ekphrases* of interior spaces, Chaucer seems to be responding to and imitating the illustrations of *RR* rather than its words. Literary critics and art historians have puzzled over whether Chaucer based his *descriptio* of the dreamer's bedchamber on "actual reality" or his "imagination" (see Evans, "Chaucer and Decorative Art," 408). Various works of material culture have been suggested as period models or analogues for Chaucer's creation of the literary-themed bedroom of *BD*.[29] Art historians cite Chaucer's passage in *BD* to evaluate the likelihood of such elaborate programs of glass in secular domiciles, concluding ultimately that the Trojan-themed bedroom windows were products of Chaucer's fancy.[30]

J. A. W. Bennett, P. M. Kean, John Fleming, and Michael Salda have proposed, as paradigms of the dreamer's bedchamber, two historical interior spaces in the Westminster Palace complex: the opulently decorated royal bedroom, otherwise known as the "Painted Chamber" and the royal Chapel of St. Stephen, which was "meant to be the major architectural achievement of Edward's reign, a Sainte Chapelle of England."[31] These suggestions make a great deal of sense. From 1389–91, as Clerk of the King's Works under Richard II, Chaucer had direct responsibility for the upkeep of Westminster Palace. Already by 1366–67, as Esquire to the Royal Household of Edward III, Chaucer had ample opportunity to see the windows and painted walls of both rooms. It is thus possible that when he was writing *BD* in the late 1360s–early 1370s, these exemplars of "illuminated architecture," seen while serving the royal family, offered models for the highly wrought English Decorated Style of the dreamer's chamber in *BD*.[32]

---

[29] See Phillips, ed., *The Book of the Duchess*, notes to lines 321–22, 322–27, and 332–34; Margaret Bridges, "The Picture in the Text: Ecphrasis as Self-reflexivity in Chaucer's *Parliament of Fowls, Book of the Duchess*, and *House of Fame*," *Word & Image* 5 (1989): 151–58, argues the "pointless" (151) inconclusiveness of such identifications of putative models for Chaucer's bedroom *ekphrasis*.

[30] Osborne, *Stained Glass in England*, 41; Marks, *Stained Glass in England During the Middle Ages*, 94.

[31] John V. Fleming, "Chaucer and the Visual Arts of his Time," *New Perspectives in Chaucer Criticism*, ed. Donald M. Rose (Norman, Okla.: Pilgrim Books, 1981), 125.

[32] J. A. W. Bennett, *Chaucer's Book of Fame* (Oxford: Clarendon Press, 1968), 13–14; P. M. Kean, *Chaucer and the Making of English Poetry*, II (London: Routledge & Kegan Paul, 1972), 23; Michael Norman Salda, "Pages From History: The Medieval Palace of Westminster as a Source for the Dreamer's Chamber in *The Book of the Duchess*," *Chaucer Review* 27 (1992): 111–25. Jean Bony, *English Decorated Style: Gothic Architecture Transformed 1250–1350* (Ithaca: Cornell University Press, 1979), 23, claims the extent and types of ornamentation incorporated in the Chapel of St. Stephen introduced "the most radically novel" developments, marking a "second stage" in the English Decorated Style. The term "illuminated architecture," describing the effect of the Decorated Style, was coined by Geoffrey Webb, *Architecture in Britain: The Middle Ages*, Pelican History of Art, 2nd ed. (Harmondsworth: Penguin, 1965) and has been evoked and echoed by other art historians, such as Nicola Coldstream, *The Decorated Style: Architecture and Ornament 1240–1360* (Toronto: University of Toronto Press, 1994), 17. Chaucer's emphasis on the light streaming through the *BD*-dreamer's enameled glass windows also evokes this phrase. For the influence of these examples of the Decorated Style in the Westminster Palace complex on Chaucer's description of the façade of Fame's dwelling place in *The House of Fame*, see "The Decorated Style and the Figurative Arts," in *Age of Chivalry: Art in Plantagenet England 1200–1400,* ed. Jonathan Alexander and Paul Binski (London: Weidenfeld and Nicolson, 1987), 443–62; Braswell, "Architectural

The almost total embellishment of the Painted Chamber's surface with ornamental gilding and murals painted in a brilliant riot of colors caused it to enjoy an international reputation.[33] Eight window jambs were painted with large allegorical figures of the Virtues, over which were blue-and-gilt-gowned angels on a red ground. Between the windows were vivid polychromatic murals depicting Old Testament battle scenes, all of which were decorated with raised, gilded gesso-work.[34]

The ornamentation of St. Stephen's Chapel, which was intended to rival Louis IX's Sainte Chapelle, was even more luxe. Eighty paintings of religious subjects and a program of stained glass windows, of unknown subject matter, decorated the walls. Overall, nearly every available surface was painted, gilded, diapered, or stenciled. John Fleming summarizes: "One imagines a royal church that combined the ethereal verticality of Sainte Chapelle with the more flamboyant and uninhibited surface brilliance of the southern Gothic" (126). The possibility that in his *ekphrasis* of the dreamer's bedchamber in *BD* Chaucer was mirroring the "decorated gothic" style of two prominent royal interior spaces to which he had almost certain access is compelling. However, the textual subject matter of the murals and stained glass in these royal interior spaces is biblical and religious-themed, while the fenestration and mural art of *BD*'s bedroom are decidedly literary-themed. As provocative as these putative architectural "sources" for the lavishly decorated bedroom of *BD* are, I maintain that they must yield precedence to a literary/visual model that Chaucer's own text acknowledges by name, the ur-dream vision *RR* and its attending manuscript illustrations.

Allowing both the architectural models and the literary intertext as Chaucer's possible sources, let us now consider how these historical rooms and the manuscript illuminations of *RR* contribute to our sense of what the dreamer's bedroom signifies about its occupant, and what that suggests about Chaucer's attitude to primitivism. Neither the Painted Chamber, nor St. Stephen's Chapel, nor the dreamer's bedroom suggests a primitivist "state of nature." Rather, all interior spaces proclaim the height of civilized, almost decadent excess and conspicuous consumption. Indeed, in his *ekphrasis* of the dreamer's bedroom in *BD*, we see Chaucer not embracing and promoting the austerity and stylistic simplicity of primitivism, but conversely endorsing those very aspects of civilized life that primitivism deplores: technology, foreign trade, the fabrication of luxury artifacts, creature comforts, and the excessively elaborate decoration of human living quarters. On the other hand, notwithstanding the mere pair of references

---

Portraiture," 101–12.

[33] See *Symon Semeonis, Itinerium Symonis Semeonis an Hybernia ad Terram Sanctam*, ed. and trans. Mario Esposito, Scriptores Latini Hiberniae 4 (Dublin: The Dublin Institute for Advanced Studies, 1960) for the account of visiting friars from Ireland who saw the Painted Chamber in 1323.

[34] For illustrations of various aspects of the Painted Chamber see W. R. Lethaby, "English Primitives: The Painted Chamber and the Early Masters of the Westminster School," *The Burlington Magazine* 7 (1905): 257–69; Paul Binski, *The Painted Chamber at Westminster* (London: The Society of Antiquaries of London, Thames and Hudson, 1986); Salda, "Pages From History."

to Amant's donning clothing before departing, the *RR*-Dreamer's modest bed-room bespeaks almost monastic austerity. Indeed, in some manuscript minia-tures illustrating the opening of *RR*, Amant's bed is not even located in a walled room, but outdoors, with nary a hint of the tiled roof or hermetically sealed win-dows that insulate Chaucer's dreamer from Nature, even from the obligatory birds whose song awakens the narrator of both dream visions. Moreover, Guil-laume removes him from the bedroom quickly and permanently, dispatching him first though the primordial woods and then to the infinitely more civilized locale of Deduit's Garden, a landscape space fraught with temptation and literal Dangiers [danger].

Conclusion

I suggest that what Chaucer leaves out and adds to his exercise in visual/verbal intertextuality with *RR* reveals much about his early attitudes to Nature and his position on primitivism. Skittish at best about Nature, when given the choice, he always chooses the creature comforts of civilization over the salutary benefits of living in a primitivist "state of nature." It is no accident that when *BD*'s dream ends, what started as "h-a-r-t-hunting" has turned into "h-e-a-r-t-hunting" and the poem concludes with such icons of the civilized state as a white-walled, long castle on a rich hill, whose bell, signaling the artificial divi-sion of time into hours—another feature of the civilizing process—awakens the dreamer from his vision of a forest locale, bringing him back to his own comfort-able chamber, appointed with servants, books, games of chess and backgammon, and most important, a soft featherbed. As morally salutary as it might be to embrace the primitivist ideals of the Golden Age, the sticking point is always that it is far more *comfortable* to be civilized than primitive. In *BD*, at the start of his literary career, Chaucer engaged tentatively with the ideals of prim-itivism, acquiescing to the seductive creature comforts of a bed in preference to sleeping on hard ground in the grass. After time and with maturity, near the end of his writing career Chaucer produced an unquestionably primitivist text, "The Former Age."[35] This lyric poem, inspired ostensibly by Boethius's *Consolation* II. Metrum 5, its Ovidian antecedent, and perhaps also by Jean's evocation of both in *RR*, definitely valorizes the primitive "former" age over contemporary late fourteenth-century "civilization."[36] If the younger Chaucer

[35] On "The Former Age" as a primitivist poem, see Lorraine K. Stock, "Before and After in Chaucer's 'The Former Age': Boethian Translation or Late Medieval Primitivism?," *Carmina Philosophiae: Journal of the International Boethius Society* 2 (1994): 1–37.
[36] Chaucer's late medieval embrace of primitivism anticipated another flowering of primi-tivist discourse in the early modern encounter between Europe and the New World of the Americas. On the application of primitivist discourse in the New World, see Henri Baudet, *Paradise on Earth: Some Thoughts on European Images of Non-European Man*, trans. Eliz-abeth Wentholt (New Haven: Yale University Press, 1965); Ronald L. Meek, *Social Science and the Ignoble Savage* (Cambridge: Cambridge University Press, 1976); Lorraine K. Stock, "Wild People, Mythical, and New World Relations," *The Encyclopedia of Medieval Trade, Travel, and Exploration*, ed. J. B. Friedman and Kristen Figg (New York: Garland, 2000), 643–45. On how the primitivist appropriates and contains the primitive, see Marianna Torgov-nick, *Gone Primitive: Savage Intellects, Modern Lives* (Chicago: University of Chicago Press, 1990); Michael Taussig, *Shamanism, Colonialism, and the Wild Man* (Chicago: University of

rejected the minimalism of the exterior and interior spaces depicted by the illustrators of Guillaume de Lorris's opening of *RR*, the mature Chaucer embraced Jean de Meun's valorizing of the primitive state in his ekphrasis of the Golden Age.[37]

Chicago Press, 1987).

[37] I gratefully acknowledge the aid of a University of Houston Small Grant, which funded my research about *RR* manuscripts at the Pierpont Morgan Library. I thank Laura Hodges, who read a draft of this essay and contributed valuable suggestions for its improvement.

Troilus and Criseyde and Henryson's Testament of Cresseid

Tereus, Procne, and Her Sister
Chaucer's Representation of Criseyde as Victim[1]

JOSEPH S. WITTIG

At the beginning of the second book of Chaucer's *Troilus and Criseyde*, Pandarus is about to begin his wooing of Criseyde on Troilus's behalf. We're told that it happens to be May (May 3rd), and that Pandarus

> for al his wise speche,
> Felt ek his part of loves shotes keene,
> ....
> So shop it that hym fil that day a teene
> In love, for which in wo to bedde he wente,
> And made, er it was day, ful many a wente. (2.57–63)

Apparently he does achieve at least some troubled sleep, for we are next told what wakened him:

> The swalowe Proigne, with a sorowful lay,
> Whan morwen com, gan make hire waymentynge
> Whi she forshapen was; and evere lay
> Pandare abedde, half in a slomberynge,
> Til she so neigh hym made hire cheterynge
> How Tereus gan forth hire suster take,
> That with the noyse of hire he gan awake. (2.64–70)

This reference to the shocking tale of Tereus, Procne and Philomela reflects, as Barry Windeatt and others have argued,[2] the wording of Dante's *Purgatorio*:

> Ne l'ora che comincia i tristi lai
> la rondinella presso a la mattina,
> forse a memoria de' suo' primi guai.... (9.13–15)

---

[1] Earlier versions of this essay were read at the 2002 SEMA Conference and at the 2004 Sewanee Medieval Colloquium.

[2] *Oxford Guides to Chaucer: Troilus and Criseyde* (Oxford: Clarendon Press, 1992), 129–30: "The resemblance between the rhymes on *tristi lai* and *sorowful lay* and the common settings of a mortal sleeping in the morning and hearing the noise of the swallow's lamenting its transformation, are strong connections between Chaucer and Dante." He also finds Chaucer shares larger preoccupations of the *Purgatorio* (freedom of action, disordered and misdirected love); see 134.

(At the hour near morning when the swallow begins her sad lays,
perhaps in memory of her former woes....)[3]

But Chaucer's details, however few, go well beyond Dante's terse allusion, and
we have every reason to think Chaucer was familiar with the long version of
the story found in Ovid's *Metamorphoses* (6.412–674), a story which Chaucer
will retell in *LGW* (2228–2393), and which Gower retold in *Confessio Amantis*
(5.5551–6074).[4]

Readers have argued about how we should understand Chaucer's great love
story and the kinds of love it portrays, how we should interpret and react to its
characters, and how we should understand the conclusion of the poem. They
have also disagreed about how we should react to allusions like this one: a
flourish asserting learning, a quick atmospheric brush stroke, or an indication
of larger tone and meaning? In this essay I want to explore how, and in what
way, the allusion can serve as a gloss on Chaucer's representation of love.

Let us briefly recall the main outlines of Ovid's story. Tereus king of Thrace
has married Procne, daughter of king Pandion of Athens. After five apparently
happy years in Thrace, Procne longs to see her sister Philomela and coaxes
Tereus to go and fetch her. Tereus sets sail straight way, is utterly smitten with
Philomela the instant he sees her, is consumed by passionate desire for her, and,
even as he asks that she be allowed to visit Procne, resolves that he will possess
Philomela by whatever means. The instant they reach Thrace, he drags her to
a hut in the woods and rapes her. To keep her from revealing his deed he cuts
out her tongue and confines her in the woods, under guard. To Procne he lies
that Philomela has died. A year passes; Philomela contrives to weave the story
of the violence done to her into a fabric and sends it to Procne. Procne reads,
is consumed by rage, and resolves on vengeance. Under cover of the seasonal
Bacchanalia she goes to where her sister is lodged and brings her to Tereus's
house. Procne decides to make Itys, her son by Tereus, the instrument of her
revenge; she, with Philomela's help, kills the boy, cooks him, and serves him to
Tereus as a special feast. Tereus comes to suspect what has happened; Procne

---

[3]The passage continues (9.16–21):

> e che la mente nostra, peregrina
> più da la carne e men da' pensier presa,
> a le sue visïon quasi è divina,
> in sogno mi parea veder sospesa
> un'aguglia nel ciel con penne d'oro,
> con l'ali aperte e a calare intesa;

> (and when our mind, more a pilgrim from the flesh and less captive to thoughts,
> is in its visions almost divine, I seemed to see, in a dream, an eagle poised in the
> sky, with feathers of gold, its wings outspread, and prepared to swoop.)

All references to and quotations from the *Commedia* use the edition and translation of Charles
S. Singleton, *Dante Alighieri: The Divine Commedy* (Princeton: Princeton University Press,
1973). On the parallel in Petrarch's sonnet "Zefiro torna" see Appendix I.

[4]Windeatt, *Oxford Guides*, 42, notes in manuscript copies of *Troilus* marginal glosses
pointing to "the likely Ovidian sources of such allusions as those to Procne or Niobe ('Require
in Methamorphosios', 'Require in Ouidio')."

and Philomela gleefully confirm his worst fears. He pursues them to kill them, and all are metamorphosed into birds: in the Latin tradition, Philomela into the nightingale, Procne into the swallow, and Tereus into the hoopoe.[5] A chilling tale, indeed, and one which could suggest a variety of implications for what is to come in Chaucer's poem. Does Tereus cast shadows? On Pandarus? On Troilus? On both? Do Philomela and Procne suggest Criseyde's victimhood before these males' advances? And how should we gauge the allusion's impact on our understanding of Chaucer's poem?

Several readers have thought to explore the allusion in relation to Dante's *Purgatorio* more than to Ovid's account. Winthrop Wetherbee has suggested that "the effect of the allusion is ... to contrast Pandarus's mission with Vergil's and to make still more plain what had been implied by the narrator's hapless evocation of the opening lines of the *Purgatorio* at the beginning of the Proem to Book 2: this is not the world of the *Commedia*, and the quest on which we are embarked is not a spiritual one."[6] Jeannette Hume Lutton has offered an extended reading of Chaucer's Book II, day one, against the first day in Dante's *Purgatorio*.[7] I admire the subtlety but resist the conclusions of Lutton's argument; since I cannot do it justice here, and since it takes an entirely different direction than I intend to, I must leave it for another time.[8]

Most of those who pursue the effects of this allusion in Chaucer do so through Ovid's version of the tale. Barry Windeatt has argued that Chaucer's Ovidian allusions, in general, bring Chaucer's poem "into association with such Ovidian stories of pride, obsession, and betrayal" (*Oxford Guides*, 111), that is, with such large themes and motifs; he suggests further that figures like Procne and Philomela, through their alleged transmutations into swallow and nightingale, yoke classical "past" to Chaucer's present because these "birds" persist in, inhabit, Chaucer's natural world.[9] Of this allusion, in context, Windeatt has suggested that it "introduces an ominous note."[10] Katherine Heinrichs would take the Ovidian allusions in *Troilus*, including this one, a step further: such figures as Tereus, Procne and Philomela were very widely understood as *exempla* of foolish, irrational love.[11]

---

[5] In his version in *LGW*, Chaucer stops the tale after Procne finds Philomela in the woods; the ghastly revenge is left untold (in keeping with his theme there of wronged "good" women).

[6] *Chaucer and the Poets: An Essay on Troilus and Criseyde* (Ithaca: Cornell University Press, 1984), 155–56.

[7] "'Inviolable Voice': Philomela and Procne in Dante's *Purgatorio* and Chaucer's *Troilus and Criseyde*," in *Spectrum of the Fantastic: Selected Essays from the Sixth International Conference on the Fantastic in the Arts*, ed. Donald Paslumbo (New York: Greenwood, 1988), 3–19.

[8] Lutton's argument depends, in the first instance, on a "symmetry" of references: in Dante, to Philomela, an eagle, and Procne; in Chaucer to Procne, a nightingale and an eagle. As an initial question, one confronts the identification of the birds / sisters in Dante's allusions: see Appendix II below.

[9] Procne and Philomela "not only evoke a sense of past time but are manifest in the present through a process of metamorphosis which has made them a part of the natural world" (*Oxford Guides*, 256).

[10] Barry Windeatt, ed., *Troilus and Criseyde: A New Edition of 'The Book of Troilus'* (London: Longman, 1984), 155, note to lines 64–70.

[11] Katherine Heinrichs, "Mythological Lovers in Chaucer's *Troilus and Criseyde*," *Journal*

C. David Benson acknowledges that this allusion is "prominent" but judges "its precise significance ... uncertain." Myth contributes, he argues, to the "historical setting," and it functions to display the poem's learning and literary ambition. He acknowledges that this allusion might suggest that "Pandarus' involvement in the affair is wicked even to the point of incest"[12]—a view which John Fleming has also entertained, *en passant*, in another context.[13] But Benson goes on to say he does not think the text compels such a reading: "The poem frustrates any attempt to forge a direct and irrefutable connection between the two episodes"; that is, the gap between what literally happens in the myth and what literally happens in *Troilus* is too large: there is no rape, no murder, no cannibalism (*Chaucer's Troilus and Criseyde*, 66).

Henry Ansgar Kelly, who reads the opening of Book II as dispelling a heretofore tragic mood, doesn't know quite what to make of the allusion: "no one," he says, "would think of classifying Troilus with Tereus"; nor does he see any grounds for comparing Pandarus with Tereus.[14] Elizabeth Robertson, considering the nature of female consent in the poem, notes that "Critics as different as John Fleming and Carolyn Dinshaw have discussed Book II's strong focus on rape as a threatening subtext," and she views this allusion at the book's opening as pointing us in that direction.[15]

These are all the significant discussions of this passage, with its allusion, that I have been able to discover. Apart from Kelly's serene understanding of Pandarus's selfless and innocent instrumentality,[16] many of their suggestions seem to me generally on the right track. Wetherbee's observation that Pandarus is no Virgil (just as he is no Lady Philosophy) certainly rings true. One also agrees with the comments by Windeatt, Benson, and Heinrichs about the general effect of Ovidian allusion, and the suggestion that this particular one introduces an "ominous" tone. Benson is of course correct that the grisly details (rape, murder) are not literally present in Chaucer's poem; I think he and Fleming are right to sniff *some* whiff of incest. Robertson, despite her essay's appearing in a

---

of the Rocky Mountain Medieval and Renaissance Association 12 (1991): 13–39. For this allusion see esp. 20–24. Heinrichs discusses Ovid as viewed in the accessus tradition, this tale as glossed by Giovanni del Virgilio, the *Ovide Moralisé*, and Bersuire, and allusions to it in *Yder*, *Filocolo*, and the *De Casibus*.

[12] C. David Benson, *Chaucer's Troilus and Criseyde* (London: Unwin Hyman, 1990), 66.

[13] "Deiphoebus Betrayed: Virgilian Decorum, Chaucerian Feminism," *Chaucer Review* 21 (1986): 188. "The whiff of incest is everywhere in the poem...." He cites these lines, Troilus's "elaborate comparisons of his own situation with that of Oedipus," and what he takes to be "the insistent evocation" of the rape of Tamar by Amnon (2 Sam. 13) which he sees underlying the elaborate plot staged at Deiphoebus's house (see *ibid.* 186–7). Heinrichs simply comments that the allusion "hints at the underlying nature of Pandarus's 'erand'" (24).

[14] Henry Ansgar Kelly, *Chaucerian Tragedy* (Cambridge: Brewer, 1997), 97 and n. 10.

[15] "Public Bodies and Psychic Domains: Rape, Consent, and Female Subjectivity in Geoffry Chaucer's *Troilus and Criseyde*," in *Representing Rape in Medieval and Early Modern Literature*, ed. Elizabeth Robertson and Christine M. Rose (New York: Palgrave, 2001), 300–301. Cf. John Fleming, *Classical Imitation and Interpretation in Chaucer's Troilus* (Lincoln: University of Nebraska Press, 1990), 113–24.

[16] "Pandarus strikes me as loving and well-intentioned toward both his friend and his niece, while Tereus is one of the most brutal characters in all of classical literature" (*Chaucerian Tragedy*, 97, n. 10).

book entitled *Representing Rape*, is very nuanced in her conclusions: Chaucer's poem "provides a particularly complex, poetic exploration of the troubled status of female consent" (304). Yet I wonder if one cannot read this allusion as providing a more precise and identifiable gloss on the complex of motives and attitudes Chaucer's poem explores. Let me work my way there by first considering some of the possible parallels between Ovid's story and Chaucer's.

Exploring Parallels

We know the relationship between Troilus and Criseyde is doomed from Book I, line 1. So is the relationship at the core of Ovid's tale: Juno and Hymen absent themselves from the wedding of Tereus and Procne, Furies light the bridal procession with torches snatched from a funeral, screech owls brood on the roof of the bridal chamber, and under such omens is their son Itys conceived (428–34).[17]

That Troilus is smitten by love at first sight conforms to the pathology of "literary love" and with what is, after all, a tradition of love trauma that goes back to Ovid. But one cannot fail to notice how Tereus, when he returns to Athens for Philomela, is inflamed with passion for her at first sight. "The moment he saw the maiden Tereus was inflamed with love" ("non secus exarsit conspecta virgine Tereus," 455); "his own passionate nature pricked him on" ("et hunc innata libido / exstimulat," 458–59):[18] in a series of striking metaphors, like a field of ripe grain, like fallen and dried leaves, like a mound of hay, he is consumed instantly by fire.

I do not intend to suggest anything so crude as that "Troilus is Tereus"; I am suggesting rather that, as Windeatt has noted in general, and as this tale of Ovid reveals in particular, the sudden inflammation of male passion, of "innata libido," is a feature of both accounts and that, as the case of Tereus demonstrates, it can have dire effects.

Many readers of Chaucer's poem have been struck, and disturbed, by what seems to be the vicarious pleasure Pandarus takes in his role of go-between,

---

[17] Ovid reads:

> non pronuba Iuno,
> non Hymenaeus adest, non illi Gratia lecto:
> Eumenides tenuere faces de funere raptas,
> Eumenides stravere torum, tectoque profanus
> incubuit bubo thalamique in culmine sedit.
> hac ave coniuncti Procne Tereusque, parentes
> hac ave sunt facti. (428–34)

(But neither Juno, bridal goddess, nor Hymen, nor the Graces were present at that wedding. The Furies lighted them with torches stolen from a funeral; the Furies spread the couch, and the uncanny screech-owl brooded and sat on the roof of their chamber. Under this omen were Procne and Tereus wedded; under this omen was their child conceived.)

All citations of and quotations from Ovid's *Metamorphoses* use the Loeb edition (Cambridge, Mass.: Harvard University Press, 1916) checked against the edition by William S. Anderson (Leipzig: Teubner, 1988); the English translation is that by Frank Justus Miller in the Loeb edition. For this passage, cf. *LGW* 2249–54.

[18] The account in *LGW* is somewhat less vivid: see 2288–93, ("fyry herte" 2292 comes closest).

culminating in his romance-reading by the fire and his problematical appearance at Criseyde's bed the morning after. I find these scenes, especially the latter, troubling, though I remain, with John Fleming ("Deiphoebus," 188), an agnostic as to the details we are meant to imagine. But I wonder if Chaucer did not see in Ovid's tale a vivid, and unambiguously awful, instance of vicarious indulgence. Philomela, anxious to see her sister, joins in Tereus's pleading with her father, throwing her arms about his neck and kissing him. Tereus's passion is further inflamed by this, and the passage culminates with Ovid's remark: "And whenever she embraces her father, [Tereus] wishes that he were in the father's place—indeed if he were, his intent would be no less impious" ("et, quotiens amplectitur illa parentem, / esse parens vellet: neque enim minus inpius esset," 481–82). (*LGW* omits these details.)

Tereus thus indulges in a complex web of vicariousness: married to Procne, he falls in love with his wife's sister; and, watching this sister's affection for her father, he wishes himself her father. Pandarus's vicariousness is equally complex. He is in love with *someone*: he "Felt ek his part of loves shotes keene" (2.58). He rises and sets out to woo, presumably, another lady, on someone else's behalf. That lady is an especially close relative to him: his sister's daughter. And he will come to delight in (and even observe?) his best friend's lovemaking with the lady.

Throughout Chaucer's poem, Pandarus's advice to Troilus often seems crass, its baseness highlighted by the narrator's *apologiae* for it. Tereus's behavior once again can be seen to offer a stark and completely unambiguous analogue: he will have Philomela by whatever means he must employ:

> His impulse was to corrupt her attendants' care and her nurse's faithfulness, and even by rich gifts to tempt the girl herself, even at the cost of all his kingdom; or else to ravish her and to defend his act by bloody war.

> (impetus est illi comitum corrumpere curam
> nutricisque fidem nec non ingentibus ipsam
> sollicitare datis totumque inpendere regnum
> aut rapere et saevo raptam defendere bello. [461–64])

(In *LGW* this is reduced to one line, 2293.)

There is also the matter of Pandarus's motives. Troilus protests that Pandarus is no bawd: he acted for love and not for money. Again, without pressing simple equivalence between Pandarus and Tereus, we have Ovid's comments on the disjunction between Tereus's words and his deeds. Pleading, as it seems, Procne's case that Philomela be allowed to return with him,

> In the very act of pushing on his shameful plan, Tereus gets credit for a kind heart and wins praise from his wickedness.

> (ipso sceleris molimine Tereus
> creditur esse pius laudem que a crimine sumit. [73–74])

(This is not in *LGW*.)

What I have been trying to suggest is that Ovid's tale is one of desire, of passion, of obsession, in which women are the objects of male libido and the occasion of male fantasies and male machinations. Ardent pleadings for apparently honorable and generous ends disguise more primal, even base, desires and intentions. It is not necessary, to hear these thematic echoes, that we equate Ovid's characters simply and directly with Chaucer's.

It is possible to pursue further, perhaps incidental, correspondences of detail. When introducing Criseyde Chaucer says of her: "For bothe a widewe was she and allone" (1.97); might one hear an echo, *mutatis mutandis*, of Ovid's description of Philomela: "nefas *et virginem et unam* / vi superat" (524–25)? Might the eagle of whom Criseyde dreams (2.926–31) owe anything to the eagle to whom Ovid compares Tereus when, with Philomela securely on his ship, he is bound for Thrace and the fulfillment of his passion?

> The barbarous fellow triumphs, he can scarce postpone his joys, and never turns his eyes from her, as when the ravenous bird of Jove has dropped in his high eyrie some hare caught in his hooked talons; the captive has no chance to escape, the captor gloats over his prize.

> (exultatque et vix animo sua gaudia differt
> barbarus et nusquam lumen detorquet ab illa,
> non aliter, quam cum pedibus praedator obuncis
> deposuit nido leporem Iovis ales in alto:
> nulla fuga est capto, spectat sua praemia raptor. [514–18])

(In *LGW* these lines appear as a simile cast, from Philomela's point of view, at the scene of the rape in Thrace (2319–22).) The eagles are by no means simply interchangeable. Criseyde is neither frightened nor hurt in her dream; she receives a heart, as well as giving one.[19] The nightingale which she has heard sing immediately before this dream seems to be just a nightingale, singing in "its" (not "her") manner (2.921) a song that cheers Criseyde's heart.[20] But within the whole context of the siege of Criseyde, might some echo of Ovid's comparison remain? If it does, the exchange motif, introduced by Chaucer,

---

[19] Chaucer's text reads:

> And as she slep, anonright tho hire mette
> How that an egle, fethered whit as bon,
> Under hire brest his longe clawes sette,
> And out hire herte he rente, and that anon,
> And dide his herte into hire brest to gon—
> Of which she nought agroos, ne nothyng smerte—
> And forth he fleigh, with herte left for herte.   (2.925–31)

[20] The passage reads:

> A nyghtyngale, upon a cedre grene,
> Under the chambre wal ther as she ley,
> Ful loude song ayein the moone shene,
> Peraunter in his briddes wise a lay
> Of love, that made hire herte fressh and gay.   (2.918–22)

(*His* in 921 is, of course, the neuter pronoun, modern English "its.")

serves to implicate Criseyde in the life of desire. Chaucer's representation of Criseyde's first reaction to the sight of Troilus flushed with victory and becomingly modest—("Who yaf me drynke?" 2.651)—in combination with this dream of exchanged hearts suggests that she herself participates in the passion which infuses Ovid's tale.

To say that Criseyde is "raped" is, I think, to blur completely the meaning of that verb. But to say that she is "wooed" seems to distort another. Pandarus teases, badgers, taunts, shushes, manipulates and perhaps even (on day 2?) manhandles Criseyde. He takes advantage of his relationship to her and her trust in him. When I hear the allusion to Ovid's tale, and of how the swallow sings "How Tereus gan forth hire suster take" (2.69), I think most especially of Philomela's words to Tereus after he has violated her:

> "Oh what a horrible thing you have done, barbarous, cruel wretch! Do you care nothing for my father's injunctions, his affectionate tears, my sister's love, my own virginity, the bonds of wedlock? You have confused all natural relations."

> ("o diris barbare factis,
> o crudelis!" ait "nec te mandata parentis
> cum lacrimis movere piis nec cura sororis
> nec mea virginitas nec coniugialia iura?
> omnia turbasti." [533–37])

(This is much reduced in *LGW*: cf. 2328–29.) But as in the case of all the other resonances I have suggested, we cannot map this Ovid literally onto Chaucer. One cares little for Criseyde's father's histrionic tears, when they finally come in Book IV; Criseyde has no literal sister. But just as Tereus has *omnia turbasti* ("shattered all natural relations" as Frank J. Miller renders it, quite aptly, in context), so in his way will Pandarus.[21]

Assessing the Effects of this Allusion

In assessing the general implications of Chaucer's Ovidian allusions, Katherine Heinrichs used the allegorical moralizations so often devised to accompany, or to explain, Ovid's text. Consider, for example, Peter Bersuire's mid-fourteenth century comments on the Tereus–Procne–Philomela story. After sketching the bare outlines of the tale, he writes:

> [a] Historically, these things are held to be spoken against the incestuous, who under the guise of blood relationship abuse their

---

[21] Fleming, "Deiphoebus," has made a similar point in a slightly different connection. Commenting on Pandarus in Criseyde's bedroom the morning after, he says: "I must say that at moments it looks like what in Washington is known as a 'worst case scenario' in terms of the violation of the basic laws of kinship" (188). For other suggestions of familial obligations disrupted, see 1.860 (Pandarus would give Troilus his sister); 3.409 (Troilus would give any of his sisters to Pandarus); 2.1693, 3.207 (Troilus deceives his own brother and sister-in-law); 5.1227 (Troilus ignores his family).

blood relatives, and these are therefore said to consume their own son because they delight in their own flesh.

[b] They are said to cut out the tongue of such [abused people] in as much as, having committed a shameful deed and a crime, they attempt to conceal it: the woven cloth nevertheless reveals it, in as much as subsequent impregnation proves and brings forth the crime.

[c] But they are afterwards turned into birds when, in confusion, they are known to flee. They are said to become swallows and nightingales in as much as such bad women are said to be occupied by dancing and singing more than with anything else.

[d] But evil men become those hoopoes who indeed build their nests in manure piles for the reason that they perform and commit a vile and shameful act.

[e] The father [Pandion, father to Procne and Philomela] therefore dies in grief in as much as carnal friends are made sad by such things.

[f] Scripture speaks against people like these in Osee 4 when it says [4.2] "Cursing, and lying, and killing, and theft, and adultery have overflowed, and blood hath touched blood," where blood is said to touch blood when, because of unchastity of [a woman] closely related or very near, murder happens to arise.[22]

I think such allegorizations force us to realize what Chaucer is not doing. Bersuire's "historically" [a] is striking, for Ovid's actual *historia* has disappeared. In its place is a generic domestic situation in which incest, shame, illegitimate children, frustrated hushups, "befouled" households, and resulting domestic violence are the real subjects of concern; the Ovidian narrative, with its individual characters, motivations and circumstances, vanishes to re-emerge

---

[22]Petrus Berchorius, *Reductorium Morale, Liber XV, cap. ii–xv, "Ovidius Moralizatus" naar de Parijse druk van 1509.* Werkmateriaal (2), [ed. J. Engels] (Utrecht: Instituut voor Laat Latijn der Rijksunuversiteit, 1962), 106–7; the tranlation is my own and I have added the bracketed letters to facilitate references. The Latin reads:

[a] Ista habent historialiter allegari contra incestuosos qui, sub specie consanguinitatis, consanguineis abutuntur, qui ideo proprium filium dicuntur comedere, quia in carne propria delectantur.

[b] Linguam vero dicuntur talibus abscindere inquantum, facti [sic] turpitudinem et crimen, nituntur celare: illud tamen tela revelat: inquantum sequens impraegnatio crimen probat et prodit.

[c] Sed in aves postea mutantur inquantum quandoque per confusionem fugere noscuntur; hyrundines etiam et luscinae dicuntur fieri in quantum ad modulandum et cantandum solent tales malae mulieres prae caeteris occupari.

[d] Ipse vero mali hupupae quae scilicet in stercoribus nidificant fiunt pro eo quod rem foedam et ignominiosam faciunt et committunt.

[e] Pater vero prae dolore moritur inquantum amici carnales tristes pro talibus efficiuntur.

[f] Contra tales loquitur scriptura. Oseae.IIII. dicens Maledictus et mendacium: et homicidium: et furtum: et adulterium innundaverunt: et sanguis sanguinem tetigit: ubi dicitur sanguis sanguinem tangere quando propter incestum consanguineae vel proprinquae contingit homicidium provenire.

as flimsy *integumenta* with which a generic "meaning" can be covered. Consider the female victims: "bad women [section c] ... occupied by dancing and singing more than with anything else." Given any regard for Ovid's story, any criticism of the women in it should arise from the nature of the vengeance they exact, not from the clichéd, and here irrelevant, suggestion that women fall victim to sexual assault because they are frivolous, morally confused, perhaps even flirtatious.(Criseyde, whatever her faults, cannot justly be called flirtatious, particularly at the beginning of the story.) In Chaucer's handling of Ovid's stories in *LGW* one sees an interest in the details of plot and situation, in the motivations of characters, and in human pathos. The allegorists exhibit almost no interest in such things. I can imagine Chaucer reading such a moralization; but I cannot imagine him learning anything from it, or finding its clichés morally or ethically interesting.

But I do think Chaucer recalls Ovid's story to provide an ethical and moral gloss on his own story's characters, motivations, and plot. He is inviting us to observe both the similarities and the differences. Consider once more the last passage from Ovid we examined, Philomela's words to Tereus:

> "Oh what a horrible thing you have done, barbarous, cruel wretch! Do you care nothing for my father's injunctions, his affectionate tears, my sister's love, my own virginity, the bonds of wedlock? You have confused all natural relations."

> ("o diris barbare factis,
> o crudelis!" ait "nec te mandata parentis
> cum lacrimis movere piis nec cura sororis
> nec mea virginitas nec coniugialia iura?
> omnia turbasti." [533–37])

Chaucer has adapted this speech for Criseyde, her corresponding rebuke of Pandarus. Let us recall the context.

Pandarus arrives at Criseyde's house, interrupts her group reading of the *Thebaid,* urges her to put off heavy matters and her widow's veil, and *daunce* (2.111); her initial reaction is to voice what is appropriate for her widowhood: sobriety and restraint (2.113–20). Nevertheless he has soon talked her into verbal play, has piqued her curiosity about the "good news" he has for her, and has twice gestured at leaving without telling her what his news is (209, 220). When he has finally goaded her into asking outright, he begins both with protestations of his good intentions (235–37, 295–99) and generalities about her "good fortune" (280–94). What he finally perpetrates upon her is the announcement that Troilus "loves her" (316ff.) in a way which, he asserts, offers her no "dishonor" (351–57). Crude language occasionally peeps through, as for instance when he says "'What, who wol demen, though he se a man / To temple go, that he th' ymages eteth?'" (2.372–3); but what he urges on her is simply "'lat youre daunger sucred ben a lite'" (2.384). Criseyde, "which that herde hym in this wise, / Thoughte, 'I shal felen what he meneth, ywis'" (386–87). Pandarus says "love him in return" (391–92). The only violence directed at her is aimed at her imagination: the long *carpe diem* with which Pandarus concludes (393–406). It is at this point that Chaucer imitates, adaptively, Philomela's accusation of Tereus:

> With this he stynte, and caste adown the heed,
> And she began to breste a-wepe anoon,
> And seyde, "Allas, for wo! Why nere I deed?
> For of this world the feyth is al agoon.
> Allas, what sholden straunge to me doon,
> Whan he that for my beste frend I wende
> Ret me to love, and sholde it me defende?
>
> "Allas! I wolde han trusted, douteles,
> That if that I, thorugh my dysaventure,
> Hadde loved outher hym or Achilles,
> Ector, or any mannes creature,
> Ye nolde han had no mercy ne mesure
> On me, but alwey had me in repreve.
> This false world—allas!—who may it leve?
>
> "What, is this al the joye and al the feste?
> Is this youre reed? Is this my blisful cas?
> Is this the verray mede of youre byheeste?
> Is al this paynted proces seyd—allas!—
> Right for this fyn? O lady myn, Pallas!
> Thow in this dredful cas for me purveye,
> For so astoned am I that I deye."
>
> Wyth that she gan ful sorwfully to syke.   (2.407–428)

The allusion to Tereus, Procne and her sister invites us to consider the extent to which Chaucer's tale, like Ovid's, is fundamentally one about sexual passion. Troilus's sexual desire is as real as Tereus's. In Pandarus we can see vicarious sexual satisfaction and the abuse of a natural relationship. Criseyde can indeed be considered a victim of male desire, of male manipulation, even of male-dominated structures of exchange. But in Chaucer's scene, Criseyde's tears and her concluding sigh are not the desperately wretched weeping of the raped Philomela.

The differences between the two tales are indeed so striking that one is initially moved to consider whether Chaucer might intend some mock-heroic effect: a proposed parallel which, turning out to be absurdly exaggerated, finally produces a comedic result. But here I sense no such thing. Rather the parallel with Ovid's tale suggests a two-fold gloss on Chaucer's story. In Chaucer's telling, human passions are cloaked in the language, attitudes, and gestures of *fin amor* and the *dits amoureuses*; in Ovid they are raw and hyperbolically naked. Chaucer's allusion to Ovid, juxtaposing these two cultural worlds, reinforces those other aspects of Chaucer's poem which strip away the verbal sublimation of sexual desire: Tereus and Philomela hover in the background, incapable of being politely explained away. But, at the same time, Pandarus is not simply Tereus dressed up in *gris*. Neither, of course, is Troilus. Not even "sudden Diomede" acts as violently. Nor is Criseyde simply Philomela: Criseyde has her own curiosity, her own desires, her own self-awareness and concern for independent agency, and her own complicity in the decorum of "fyn lovynge."[23] If she is a victim, she is a victim of the Trojan war, of her own humanity, and—finally—of *fin amor*, whose "bokes" she predicts will ruin her (5.1060).

Chaucer, I would argue, also found such books problematical and he problematically intertwined them with Ovid throughout his writing career. Though he can write with feeling and sympathy about human sexual love, he refuses to "romanticize" it and will not allow his characters to romanticize it, either. Throughout this poem Chaucer has the major characters use the language of *fin amor* to idealize and elevate their sexual negotiations. Pandarus sees a friend passionately longing to possess a woman to whom he happens to have access, and, preserving all the surface niceties, works things out. Criseyde is for various reasons persuaded to respond to Troilus with genuine, but merely human, love, casting her compliance in the conventional, idealizing language which she takes to be appropriate for such things. Troilus sees a desirable woman, falls deeply in love with her, and would make her into the *summum bonum*. Allusions like this one to Tereus, Procne and Philomela allow the narrator to assimilate himself completely to the conventional attitudes of *fin amor* and still invite the reader to maintain a more detached perspective.

---

[23]This is obvious throughout the poem, but for her curiosity in this scene see 309–12; for her desire, 651–65; for her awareness of her own free agency, 694–763; and for her active complicity in dressing desire with polite convention, 589–95.

Appendix I: Petrarch's "Zephiro torna"

Barney's note to *T&C* 2.64–70 in *The Riverside Chaucer* calls attention to a gloss in MS R which refers to Ovid's account and to Chaucer's use of Ovid in *LGW* 2228–2393, but it also raises the question of Petrarch's "Zefiro torna" being a possible source.

If Dante supplies the swallow's sad song in the morning, might one argue that this sonnet supplies the theme of *reverdie* and accompanying love-sickness? The sonnet is a *reverdie* in its octave, a lament by a lover deprived of his beloved in its sestet: I use text and translation from Robert M. Durling, *Petrarch's Lyric Poems: The Rime Sparse and Other Lyrics* (Cambridge: Harvard University Press, 1976), No. 310, 488–89:

> Zefiro torna e'l bel tempo rimena
> e i fiori et l'erbe, sua dolce famiglia,
> et garrir Progne et pianger Filomena,
> et Primavera candida et vermiglia;
>
> ridono i prati e'l ciel si rasserena,
> Giove s'allegra di mirar sua figlia,
> l'aria et l'acqua et la terra è d'amore piena,
> ogni animal d'amar si riconsiglia.
>
> Ma per me, lasso, tornano i più gravi
> sospiri che del cor profondo tragge
> quella ch' al Ciel se ne portò le chiavi;
>
> et cantar augelletti, et fiorir piagge,
> e'n belle donne oneste atti soavi
> sono un deserto et fere aspre et selvagge.

> (Zephyrus returns and leads back the fine weather and the flowers and the grass, his sweet family, and chattering Procne and weeping Philomena, and Spring, all white and vermillion;
>
> the meadows laugh and the sky becomes clear again, Jupiter is gladdened looking at his daughter [Venus, in favorable astrological position], the air and the waters and the earth are full of love, every animal takes counsel again to love.
>
> But to me, alas, come back heavier sighs, which she draws from my deepest heart, she who carried off to Heaven the keys to it;
>
> and the singing of little birds, and the flowering of meadows, and virtuous gentle gestures in beautiful ladies are a wilderness and cruel, savage beasts.)

The last three lines could reflect aptly enough on Pandarus's situation, that of a lover who feels excluded. (One might launch an entirely different line of speculative intertextuality: lines 9–11 recall the situation of Dante who has lost Beatrice to heaven. What of Pandarus as an anti-Dante-the-pilgrim?) But Chaucer goes further, recalling in his line 69 "How Tereus gan forth hire suster take." This seems to me unmistakably to direct our attention to Ovid's version.

Appendix II: Are both Procne and Philomela in Dante's *Purgatorio*?

Lutton's argument is based on a symmetry she perceives between three elements in the two works: in Dante, the series swallow, eagle, nightingale; in Chaucer the series swallow, nightingale, eagle. That these three birds are in Chaucer's text is indisputable. That they are in Dante's, it seems to me, is not at all obvious.

That Dante portrays the swallow ("la rondinella" *Purg.* 9.14) is explicit. He does not identify whose metamorphosis and whose sad lays, Procne's or Philomela's, he means: ("presso a la mattina" 14, "i tristi lai" 13, "forse a memoria de' suo' primi guai" 15). Singleton's note to lines 13–14 quotes Albertus Magnus on the swallow's singing at morning (13–14): "Garrula est et diem praenuntiando praecinit" (*de Animalibus* 23.24.56). His note to line 15 begins: "Dante alludes here to the legend of Philomela and Procne...." and then retells Ovid's version of the story, concluding with the metamorphosis, "Procne becoming a nightingale, Philomela a swallow, and Tereus a hoopoe. According to some versions, Procne became a swallow, Philomela a nightingale, and Tereus a hawk. See *Metam.* VI)." Why does Singleton suggest first what is surely the least common association of sister with bird?

First, note that Ovid's version does not specify:

> quarum petit altera silvas,
> altera tecta subit, neque adhuc de pectore caedis
> excessere notae, signataque sanguine pluma est.   (668–70)

And is not the reason that Ovid fails to identify the bird into which each sister is changed simply this: that "Procne" meant "swallow" and "Philomela" meant "nightingale"? That is certainly the impression given by the entries in Charlton T. Lewis and Charles Short, *A Latin Dictionary* (Oxford: Clarendon Press, 1955), s.v. Progne and Philomela:

> Progne: I. *Daughter of Pandion, king of Athens, sister of Philomela, and wife of Tereus; she was changed into a swallow* [citing Ovid *Met.*VI and Plautus Rudens 3.1.12,—who has them both turned into "hirundines"]. II. Poet., transf., *a swallow* [citing *Georg.* 4.15, Ovid *Fast.* 2.855 and *Tris.* 5.1.60]
> [Cf. the entry at *hirundo*, "swallow," with numerous citations of Pliny, Virgil, and Ovid.]
> Philomela: I. Lit. *daughter of Pandion, king of Athens, sister of Procne; she was violated by her brother-in-law Tereus and changed into a nightingale* [citing Plautus Rudens as above, Hyginus *Fab.* 45, Ovid *Met.*, Virgil. *Ecl.* 6.79, Servius, and Martial 14.75.1]. Transf. *the nightingale* (poet.). [citing Virgil Georg. 4.511. But here there is one dissenting voice, as the entry continues]: B. *the swallow*: mortalium penatibus fiducialis nidos philomela suspendit, Cassiod. *Var.* 8.31.

Thus the predominant lexical evidence suggests that *Procne* and *Philomela* are swallow and nightingale, respectively. Interpreters of Dante are faced with another reference to this myth in *Purgatorio* 17. As the first image of wrath which "imaginativa" presents the pilgrim, we find:

> De l'empiezza di lei che mutò forma
> ne l'uccel ch'a cantar più si diletta,
> ne l'imagine mia apparve l'orma.   (17.19–21)

> (Of her impious deed who changed her form into the bird that most delights to sing, the impress appeared in my imagination.)

That this refers to Procne we should most probably infer from "l'empiezza"; it was Procne who instigated the killing of her own child in her rage against what Tereus had done. Singleton's note, for instance, says this image "is that of Procne, daughter of king Pandion ... wife of Tereus, and sister of Philomela" (with a reference to his fuller note at *Purg.* 9.15). Singleton does not identify the bird here. What evidence is there that this is the nightingale? "The bird that loves to sing"? Why not the garrulous swallow? Singleton's note at 9.15 follows what is apparently a traditional assumption: since there were two sisters, and since Dante makes two references to the story, one must be to Philomela, the other to Procne; one to the swallow, one to the nightingale. But is it not possible that we have, in fact, two references in *Purg.* to Procne, one as swallow, one as committer of "the impious deed"?

In his commentary on the *Purgatorio*, W. W. Vernon wrote: "Commentators have differed considerably as to which of the two sisters is here meant, Procne, whom Jupiter changed into a swallow, or Philomela, who became a nightingale" (*Readings of the Purgatorio of Dante, chiefly based on the Commentary of Benvenuto da Imola* [London: Macmillan, 1889], I, 444).

C. H. Grandgent's school edition of the *Commedia, La Divina Commedia di Dante Alighieri*, rev. ed. (Boston: Heath, 1933) obviously takes the position Singleton followed. His note at 9.13–15 says, "According to the version followed by Dante it was the outraged princess, Philomela, who was turned into a swallow: cf. XVII, 19–21." At 17.19 his note states: "According to Aristotle (*Rhetoric*, III, 3) and most of the Greeks, Progne became a nightingale and Philomela a swallow; the Latins, followed by modern poets, usually made Philomela the nightingale. But Ovid (*Met.*, VI, 424ff.), the Latin poet from whom Dante got the story, does not tell, and Virgil (*Eclogue* VI, 79) seems to follow the Greek version, which Dante also adopted.... See d'Ovidio [*Studii sulla Divina Commedia*, 1901], 579–81." But the evocation of Virgil is a desperate stretch. I quote the sixth Eclogue from J. P. Goold, ed. and trans. (Cambridge, Mass.: Harvard University Press, 1999):

> aut ut mutatos Terei narraverit artus,
> quas illi Philomela dapes, quae dona pararit,
> quo cursu deserta petiverit et quibus ante
> infelix sua tecta super volitaverit alis.   (78–81)

([As Silenius sings,] he told of Tereus' changed form, what feast, what gifts Philomela made ready for him, on what wise she sped to the desert, and with what wings, luckless one! she first hovered above her home.)

d'Ovidio's argument about line 79 must have been that it is Procne who killed Itys and fed him to Tereus (*quas illi Philomela dapes, quae dona pararit*); therefore Procne is "Philomela." But Ovid's account reflects a tradition in which Philomela participates actively in the revenge; in *Met.*, after Procne has stabbed Itys to death, Philomela cuts the boy's throat (643) and together they cut up the body and cook it (644–46). And when Tereus calls for his son, it is Philomela who leaps into the room and flings the boy's head into Tereus's face (658–9). In the light of this tradition, Virgil might in fact be speaking of the sister Philomela—and saying nothing at all about what bird she became.

To sum up, what we find in the *Purgatorio* is:

> 9.13–15: swallow, sad lays, former woes
> 17.19–20: the performer of an impious deed who changed her
> form into that of the bird who loves to sing

Put another way, we have

> 1) swallow (Procne or Philomela?)
> 2) "Procne" (nightingale or swallow?)

In the light of that uncertainty, establishing a tidy symmetry between Chaucer's birds and Dante's seems problematical, at best.

Cresseid vs. Troylus in Henryson's *Testament*

WINTHROP WETHERBEE

Emerson Brown knew the Merchant's Tale better than anybody; the results of his long, attentive listening to the tale are distilled in his "Chaucer, the Merchant, and Their Tale: Getting Beyond Old Controversies" (*Chaucer Review* 13 (1978–79): 141–56; 247–62). His good ear and unfailing ethical sense enabled him to fend off simplistic readings, cynical or jolly, of the Merchant's performance, and his own assessment provides solid backing for his claim that "no literary work ... comments more fully or more ethically on the role and responsibility of the artist than Chaucer's *Canterbury Tales*."

This little essay, dedicated to Emerson's memory, aims to emulate his own, and get beyond old controversies by listening attentively to what is really going on in Henryson's *Testament*. Without seeking to open out such large vistas as those to which Emerson's essay leads us, I hope I have honored his deep conviction that hearing Chaucerian poetry was the beginning of wisdom about its "entente."

* * *

> Hire face, lik of Paradys the ymage,
> Was al ychaunged in another kynde.
> The pleye, the laughter, men was wont to fynde
> On hire, and ek hire joies everichone,
> Ben fled: and thus lith now Criseyde allone.
>
> (*Troilus and Criseyde* 4.864–68)

Pandarus himself weeps at the spectacle of Criseyde, overcome by the realization that she must leave Troy and Troilus. Within a few lines he has regained his composure, and begins distracting Criseyde from her own sorrow by describing the suffering of Troilus, but for this one moment, unique in Chaucer's poem, she is for him, and for us, nothing more or less than an unhappy human being, red-eyed and unlovely, an object of compassion.

In a sense, though she can hardly appreciate it as such, this is a moment of triumph for Criseyde. It amounts to an assertion of her essential humanity in the face of the overwhelming pressure of the male fantasy which has sought only to idealize her beauty and reduce her social and physical status to that of an attractive object, a piece to be pursued and taken in the game of love. Though her destiny has been largely defined by her father, her principal function in the poem has been to provide a focal point for the *corage* of Troilus, whose life is a series of idealized male roles, martial, spiritual, sexual, and finally tragic. From the moment when, with Pandarus's glowing praises still echoing in her mind, she beheld Troilus returning from the battlefield, it has been Criseyde's mission to respond to these postures with admiration, trust, passion and—equally important—betrayal.

The consequences and implications of this betrayal are ruthlessly followed out in Robert Henryson's *Testament of Cresseid*, which reports an episode imagined as occurring in the course of Book V of *Troilus and Criseyde*, during the interval between Criseyde's acceptance of Diomede and the death of Troilus. Not only is Henryson's Cresseid severely punished for blaspheming Venus and Cupid, but she accepts her horrifying fate in utter humility, and her last words praise the constancy and generosity of Troylus. (I use "Cresseid" and "Troylus" throughout in speaking of Henryson's characters, "Criseyde" and "Troilus" in speaking of Chaucer's.) Troylus himself, still tormented by the fact of her infidelity, nonetheless accords her a seemly burial.

Taken at face value, such a conclusion to the story of Criseyde would seem to constitute the harshest of condemnations, in its powerful contrasting of an utterly debased Cresseid and a Troylus whose noble idealism remains intact, and so it appeared to critics until fairly recent times. Cresseid was seen as having been justly punished, and she was redeemable only insofar as she could be seen as truly repentant for her sins.[1] The old harsh reading of the poem is still around,[2] but the prevailing emphasis has shifted to the human tragedy of Cresseid. A. C. Spearing noted early on that the condemnation of Cresseid by the planetary gods "is presented not as justice but as an arbitrary vengeance," and he sees in the final position of Cresseid, not true repentance, but "a pathetic helplessness."[3] For John Ganim, Cresseid's relegation to the leper community is a telling comment on the life of one who "has always depended on the kindness of strangers," and whose final dignity obliges us to suspend moral judgment.[4]

One constant in the history of criticism of the *Testament* has been agreement as to the role of Troylus. He alone in the poem demonstrates pity for Cresseid, a pity which approaches Christian compassion.[5] To the extent that Cresseid is seen as embarking on the path of penitence, it is because of her encounter

---

[1] On this approach to the poem see Douglas Duncan, "Henryson's Testament of Cresseid," *Essays in Criticism* 11 (1961): 128–30; Lee Patterson, "Christian and Pagan in The Testament of Cresseid," *Philological Quarterly* 52 (1973): 696–714. Patterson's is certainly the most persuasive reading of the poem in terms of the process of Christian repentance.

[2] A recent, more subtle version of the hard-line treatment of Criseyde is that of William A. Quinn, "Henryson's 'ballet schort': A Virgin Reading of The Testament of Cresseid," *Studies in Scottish Literature* 31 (1999): 232–44. He suggests that the poem's primary audience were nuns (236), whose approval of the treatment of Cresseid would exonerate Henryson of the charge of having abused women in general (243).

[3] *Criticism and Medieval Poetry* (2nd ed., New York and London: Edward Arnold, 1972), 187–89, 192.

[4] *Style and Consciousness in Middle English Literature* (Princeton, N.J.: Princeton University Press, 1983), 131, 141.

[5] See Duncan, 133; Patterson, 710–11; Larry M. Sklute, "Phoebus Descending: Rhetoric and Moral Vision in Henryson's Testament of Cresseid," *ELH* 44 (1977): 197–98.

with Troylus, whose behavior toward her is seen as perfectly expressed in the iconic moment when, without recognizing Cresseid among the lepers, he treats her with noble charity; and again at the poem's close, when he creates and dedicates her tomb. In a sense the lovers are reunited by Troylus's generosity of spirit; his pity for Cresseid validates ours, "and we are left in mind at peace with her as with Troilus."[6]

This final scene is worth a little more attention, for on closer examination it can be seen to contain details which might lead us to question the boundlessness and purity of Troylus's charity at this critical moment. When in the poem's final scene he hears the story of Cresseid's sickness and death, he is indeed moved to sorrow, but his last speech, heard clearly, indicates at the least a deep ambivalence about the rite he is about to perform on her behalf. Hearing of her illness and pauper's death, he "swelt for wo," but the woe is finally for his own betrayal, rather than for Cresseid's miserable end: "I can no moir; / Scho was vntrew and wo is me thairfoir."[7] The inconspicuous but telling opening phrase, "I can no moir," echoing as it does the opening stanza of the *Parlement of Foules*,[8] expresses Troylus's sense of how powerfully love has afflicted him. Troylus's self-preoccupation here is a sign that his ability to feel true compassion is severely limited, and that what dominates his feelings is a continuing resentment of Cresseid's untruth. The epitaph he goes on to compose is grimly factual, reviewing her fall from beauty and high estate to disease and wretchedness in what William Quinn aptly calls Henryson's "brutally laconic" manner (235). The decent thing is done, but with a bare minimum of human sympathy.

What I aim to demonstrate in this brief essay is that the behavior of Troylus in this final scene is consistent with his characterization throughout the *Testament*, a role which is both more complicated than the virtually universal reading of the poem suggests, and by no means unvaryingly noble. This standard reading is grounded, moreover, in a reading of *Troilus and Criseyde* which is similarly oversimplified, and misleading in its idealization of Chaucer's "sely" hero. I will begin, therefore, by suggesting the alternate reading of the *Troilus* that seems to me the necessary preparative for engaging the complexities of Henryson's.

The story of Troilus as epic hero and spiritual pilgrim can be viewed as the "other" of a story in which it is Criseyde whose role defines the significant action of the poem, and Troilus who fails to live up to the challenge she embodies. If Criseyde is finally incapable of keeping faith with what is unique and valuable in Troilus and his love, it is for reasons that are almost entirely circumstantial. If she is finally "slydynge of corage" (5.825), she nonetheless exhibits throughout the poem a maturity, a capacity for taking life seriously and an appreciation of what is at stake in pursuing the pleasures it offers, which is lacking in Troilus and which he fails to appreciate in her. More than an amiable woman, Criseyde lives,

---

[6] Sir Herbert Grierson, "Robert Henryson," *Aberdeen University Review* 21 (1933–34): 211.

[7] *Testament of Cresseid*, line 601. Quotations are from *The Poems of Robert Henryson*, ed. Denton Fox (Oxford: Clarendon Press, 1981).

[8] I am grateful to an anonymous reader for the press who pointed out to me this striking echo.

in the real world, a life that is far more complex, and arguably more heroic than that of Troilus. Her situation is fraught with political, economic, and ethical dilemmas which ensure that she is constantly on guard, and make her, in the very intensity of her practicality, one of Chaucer's most Boethian characters. She understands the difficulty of moral choice and the tenuousness of human felicity, and she is candid in acknowledging the limits of her own prudential vision. Thus there is no more telling instantiation of the sober moralizing with which the love-story proper concludes than the fact that this woman, so circumspect and clear-sighted, should be so much at the mercy of love in charting her course. "Love" for Criseyde is neither the blinding rapture of Troilus nor the all-consuming preoccupation of Pandarus, and it is hard to say how large a place it occupies in her inner life. But she is inescapably a beautiful woman, and Chaucer makes plain both her attractiveness to lovers and her capacity for reciprocating their love. Hence, though she remains undeceived by Troilus's fantasies of Dantean transcendence, or the desperate pressure of Pandarus's "entente," she too is a victim of what the poem will finally identify as "the blynde lust, the which that may nat laste" (5.1824).

The mature seriousness of Criseyde's engagement with love and fortune appears plainly in comparison to that of Troilus. When Troilus is not borne aloft on the wings of mystified desire, his world view shrinks to a self-defeating Boethianism, a fatalism which allows him only so much self-awareness as is necessary to rationalize his inability to act in the face of misfortune. "Reality" consists precisely in the authenticity of his experience of love, and Chaucer conveys this experience almost wholly by means of convention. In contrast to the highly individualized postures of Criseyde, Troilus's behavior is almost mechanical in its ritual quality, perfectly aligned with the standard moralizing and courtly dogma of the narrator's comments. He is humorless, self-absorbed, wholly the prisoner of the code that defines him, and the spark of authentic virtue that illumines his experience for the narrator and for us does not bring him fully and sympathetically to life.

It is such a reading of *Troilus and Criseyde* that seems to me to inform the *Testament*, and as with Chaucer's poem, recognizing this depends on our resisting the strong nudgings of Henryson's narrator. The narrator of the *Testament* not only approves wholeheartedly the "knichtlie pietie" of Troylus, but shows none of the elaborately asserted reluctance of Chaucer's narrator to distance himself from Cresseid. As I will argue, he is at one with his hero in this, and their solidarity is an important feature of the poem. One of the most striking features of the conclusion of the *Testament*, as compared with the violent shifts of perspective and tone in Chaucer's final stanzas, is the absence of any hint of dissonance. Troylus's last words, his epitaph for Cresseid, and the narrator's concluding reflections are remarkably similar in tone; the cold consideration they bestow on Cresseid is more than she herself would have asked or expected; and the closure they impose on her story would seem to be absolute.

This very unanimity provides a clue to the complex strategy of the *Testament*. Henryson has deliberately created a poetic world from which any alternative to the perspective of Troylus and the narrator is excluded. The universe itself, as represented by the gods who pronounce judgment on Cresseid, is pervaded and controlled by male attitudes, and Troylus can fairly claim to be duly acknowledging the demands of nature and religion in his performance of Cresseid's last rites. Forgiveness and pity are finally as alien to the poem's world view as the parable of the one lost sheep or the legend of the harlot-turned-saint. Even the narrator's "pietie" is an expression, not of concern for the sufferings of Cresseid, but of horror at the spectacle of a fair and noble lady descending, "giglotlike," to pursue "foull plesance" (83–84). It is finally Cresseid alone who, as she discovers in herself the ability to accept her own guilt and frankly acknowledge the virtues of Troilus, displays an authentic generosity of spirit.

In its thoroughgoing irony the *Testament* can thus be seen as a profoundly Criseydan reading of Chaucer's poem, and shows Henryson clearly aware of the spiritual and ethical limitations of the world view that frames the experience of Chaucer's lovers. Henryson's narrator exhibits these same limitations. His perspective is that of Chaucer's narrator at the point when he is forced to the reluctant recognition that his love story has run its course. Both narrators are spiritually enervated at this point, burdened by a sense of betrayal and emotional impoverishment, and reduced to a fatalism and *contemptus mundi* wholly devoid of hope or human sympathy. Chaucer's narrator will soon find himself renewed in spite of himself, and will be irresistibly drawn forward by the imagining of Troilus's final *aristeia* toward the enlightened perspective on his "tragedy" that emerges in the final stanzas of the poem. But Henryson's remains fixed in the posture of tacit condemnation, immune to the appeal of Cresseid's humble suffering and the inchoate charity of her final wishes, a monument to the misogyny by which the story is cursed.

The *Testament* begins by confirming our worst fears. Chaucer's Criseyde, rejected by Diomede, has become Henryson's Cresseid, a social outcast and a prostitute. Embittered, she curses Cupid and Venus for having bestowed upon her the treacherous gift of beauty:

> "3e causit me alwayis vnderstand and trow
> The seid* of lufe† was sawin‡ in my face,   *seed †love ‡sown
> And ay grew grene throw 3our supplie* and grace.   *aid
> Bot now, allace, that seid with froist is slane,
> And I fra luifferis* left, and all forlane."   *lovers (136–40)

These lines encapsulate the fortune of Chaucer's Criseyde, and show Cresseid clearly aware of how her beauty has determined the course of her life. At the same time the oddly striking image of the "seed" of love "sown" in Cresseid's face—an image rendered horrible by the suggestion of smallpox in the account of her ensuing disfiguration—reinforces the irony of her situation. In the *Roman de la Rose*, Cupid is said to have "tainted" the fountain of Narcissus, by sowing there seeds of love which provoke raging desire.[9] The image thus provides confirmation for the many suggestions in Chaucer's poem that Cresseid is the

---

[9] *Roman de la Rose*, ed. Felix Lecoy, 3 vols. (Paris: Honoré Champion, 1965–70), 1569–97.

agent in spite of herself of a love which affects her only as it draws upon her the self-centered desire of men.

The self-knowledge Cresseid has gained from her experience as a goad to love proves a curse in itself. In a dream, she beholds the planetary gods in council, summoned by Cupid to punish her impiety, and hears her doom pronounced by Saturn and Cynthia, goddess of the moon. Saturn afflicts her with age, illness and poverty, the ravages of time. Cynthia decrees that her illness shall take the form of leprosy and destroy her beauty:

"Thy cristall ene* mingit with blude† I mak:	*eyes †blood
Thy voice sa cleir, vnplesand hoir and hace*;	*rough and hoarse
Thy lustie lyre* ouirspred with spottis blak,	*complexion
And lumpis haw* appeirand in thy face:	*livid
Quhair* thow cummis, ilk† man sall fle the place."	*where †each
(337–41)	

Cynthia's words confirm the sad prophecy of Chaucer's Criseyde that "wommen moost wol haten me of alle" (5.1063). For she is described in terms which invite us to see her role as a celestial counterpart to that of earthly women. The last and least of the planets, she is submissive, possessed of no clearly identifying form or aspect of her own, and visible only in the borrowed light of the sun, without which she is dull and colorless (254–59). She is thus an extreme instance of the dependence of female identity and function on male authority, and her punishment of Cresseid is in effect the revenge of conventional womanhood on one who has brought discredit on her sex by straying from her proper sphere.

Waking to discover that she has indeed become diseased, Cresseid joins a community of lepers. Having overcome her initial despair and learned to beg, she is seen by Troylus as he returns from battle. Without recognizing her, he is reminded of the Criseyde he had known. Henryson explains:

The idole* of ane thing in cace† may be	*image †sometimes
Sa deip imprentit in the fantasy	
That it deludis the wittis outwardly,	
And sa appeiris in forme and lyke estait*	*condition
Within the mynd as it was figurait.	(507–11)

Troylus immediately feels the stirring of his old love, trembles as if with fever, and then, "For knichtlie pietie and memoriall / Of fair Cresseid" (519–20), gives the unknown leper a purse of gold before riding away, overwhelmed by sorrow.

Henryson's account of the "idole" of Cresseid in Troylus's memory shows him fully alive to both the beauty and the limitations of Troilus's experience of love as delineated by Chaucer. On the one hand it suggests a Platonic purity of mind. Reinforced by the sonorous beauty of "knichtlie pietie and memoriall," it invites us to see Troylus in his noblest, most Dantean aspect, the strength of his devotion undiminished by time or Cresseid's perfidy. But that Troylus's "piety" is "knightly" suggests that it is precisely as an embellishment of Troylus himself, the perfect embodiment of this male institution, that this piety is most meaningful. The lines just quoted, moreover, quietly remind us that what Troylus is responding to is precisely the image of Cresseid which he himself had formed in the "mirror" of his mind on first beholding her, and which has existed there ever since, "as it was figurait," unaltered by experience or by any evolving appreciation of the real Cresseid. As Troylus's feverish reaction makes clear, this image is a projection of his own desire, and it is this same desire that elicits his giving of alms. He is "pious" and no doubt charitable—to the lepers he appears "gentill and fre"—, but he is generous only to the extent that he is still a victim of his original fantasy of love, and the idol that goads him bears no more relation to the actual person and situation of Henryson's heroine than to Chaucer's.

The limits of Troylus's self-deceiving humanity will become clear, but not before Cresseid, learning her benefactor's identity, utters a long lament, extolling Troylus's virtues and condemning herself:

"Thy lufe*, thy lawtie† and thy gentilnes	*love †loyalty
I countit small in my prosperitie,	
Sa efflated* I was in wantones	*puffed out
And clam* vpon the fickill quheill† sa hie.	*climbed †wheel
All faith and lufe I promissit to the	
Was in the self* fickill and friuolous:	*itself
O fals Cresseid and trew knicht Troilus!	
For lufe of me thow keipt continence,	
Honest and chaist in conuersatioun;	
Of al wemen protectour and defence	
Thou was, and helpit thair opinioun;*	*reputation
My mynd in fleschelie foull affectioun	
Was inclynit to lustis lecherous:	
Fy, fals Cresseid! O trew knicht Troylus!"	(547–60)

Cresseid's reading of the history of her relations with Troylus outmoralizes the harshest male reading of *Troilus and Criseyde* one could imagine. Her speech recalls the final speech of Chaucer's Criseyde, but here, utterly humbled and close to death, she makes no attempt to extenuate or dissemble the guilt she feels. Though she sees herself as only one embodiment of the fickleness of women generally, this does not become an argument for excusing herself, but rather a reason for accepting as just, indeed taking upon herself, the harshest verdict that the male world, in its self-interest, pronounces on the female. As she dies, rebuking her perfidy one last time in her final words, the victory of chivalric male self-projection seems complete.

But Henryson's poem, like Chaucer's, offers more than one last word on its narrative, and his final three stanzas provide three perspectives on Cresseid, though as I have said these three can in some respects be reduced to one. Informed of Cresseid's death and the wretchedness of her last days, Troylus gives expression to intense grief—a grief which, however, is not finally for her death, but for the pain he continues to feel at the ineradicable memory of her infidelity: "Scho was vntrew and wo is me thairfoir" (602). To the end, Cresseid, like Criseyde, remains for Troylus, not a suffering human being in her own right, but a character in the story of his unique and tragic love. Once his ideal expectations of her have been disappointed, he is locked irrevocably into the view of her that she herself had expressed so eloquently in her final speech, with the difference that his attitude has none of her tormented humility, or the compassion that coexists with condemnation in the narrator's final stanzas in Chaucer's poem. The bitterness of the disappointment of Troilus's impossible vision dominates his memory, and is audible in the epitaph he composes for Cresseid's tomb:

> "Lo, fair ladyis, Cresseid of Troy the toun,
> Sumtyme countit the flour of womanheid,
> Vnder this stane*, lait lipper†, lyis deid."   *stone †leper   (607–9)

The balancing of "flour" and "lipper" expresses the absolute demands of the polarizing male code by which Cresseid stands condemned. We have already been given, in Cresseid's final speech, an extensive gloss on the warning implicit in "Lo fair ladyis!" The lines show Troylus true to the end to the code of chivalric love and the view of women that informs it. It is in the same spirit that the narrator of *Troilus and Criseyde* attempts to exorcise his lingering attachment to his lovers and their story:

> Swych fyn hath, lo, this Troilus for love!
> Swich fyn hath al his grete worthynesse!
> Swich fyn hath his estat real above!
> Swich fyn his lust, swich fyn hath his noblesse!
> Swich fyn hath false worldes brotelnesse!   (5.1828–32)

Chaucer's narrator cannot maintain this posture of uncompromising *contemptus mundi*, and he will soon be drawn, as if involuntarily, into the extreme tenderness of his appeal to the spiritual intuition of those "yonge fresshe folkes," male as well as female, whose destiny it is to love. In contrast, Henryson's concluding stanzas are shocking in their failure to provide the slightest hint of an alternative to Troylus's fixation. The narrator of the *Testament* makes no attempt to free himself from his vicarious investment in the fortunes of Troylus. The main effect of his final stanza is to spell out the anti-feminist message implicit in Cresseid's epitaph, and his final rhyme echoes the somber clank of Troylus's last words:

> Beir in your mynd this sore conclusioun
> Of fair Cresseid, as I haue said befoir;
> Sen scho is deid, I speik of hir no moir.   (614–16)

Fair Cresseid proved "untrew," became a leper, and is now dead. The bringing together of the unforgivable betrayal, the harsh judgment and the ignominious death is as overwhelming in its finality as the sense of guilt expressed in Cresseid's own final words. They ensure that the story of the real woman, the story that surfaces in her soliloquies and in the glimpses both poets give us of her private world, will remain tentative and other, a series of unfunctional intervals in the story of Troilus and his love.

But the world from which Criseyde is banished is a barren place, a world where an embittered Troilus will live on only to court death. Finally it is the world of Henryson's poet–narrator, beset by age and the chill of winter, sustaining with whiskey and tales of love the desperate hope that Venus will yet quicken his "faidit hart" and renew his "curage." Love and spirituality can have no real place in such a world. We meet them instead in the leper community, where suffering breeds sympathy, and where Cresseid, shamed and humbled, seems to discover in Troylus a charity that is really her own.

Minor Poems

Adam, "The Firste Stocke," and the Political Context of Chaucer's "Gentilesse"

Thomas D. Hill

In this paper I wish to solve a crux in the first line of Chaucer's "Gentilesse" and then briefly discuss the implications of this new reading in the context of what one might loosely call Chaucer's politics. The first problem is a relatively straightforward one, while the second, which involves Chaucer's attitude towards status and class, is much more subtle and difficult. But before discussing these issues in due order, it is appropriate to quote "Gentilesse" in full for the convenience of the reader.[1]

> The firste stocke fadir of gentilesse
> What man desireth gentil for to be
> Must folowe his trace and alle his wittes dresse
> Vertue to love and vices for to fle
> For vnto vertue longeth dignite
> And nought the reuerse sauely dar I deme
> Al were he miter . Coroune or dyademe.
>
> The first stok was full of rightwisenesse
> Trewe of his worde sobre pitous and fre
> Clene of his goost and loved besynesse
> Ayenst the vyse of slouthe in honeste
> And but his heire love vertue as did he
> He is nought gentil though he riche seme
> Al were he myter Coroune or dyademe
>
> Vice may well be heire to olde richesse
> But there may no man as men may well se

[1] Text from Geoffrey Chaucer, *The Minor Poems*, ed. George B. Pace and Alfred David, *A Variorum Edition of the Works of Geoffrey Chaucer*, Vol. 5, Part 1 (Norman: University of Oklahoma Press, 1982), 73–77. For fuller discussion of the reception of this poem and the response to this crux by Chaucer's contemporaries (Scogan and Lydgate) see *Oxford Guides to Chaucer: The Shorter Poems*, ed. A. J. Minnis with V. J. Scattergood and J. J. Smith (Oxford: Oxford University Press, 1995), 484–85.

Biquethe his heire his vertues noblisse
That is aproprid vnto no degre
But to the first fader in mageste
That maketh his heires hem that hym queme
All were he myter Coroune or dyademe   Explicit

The crux occurs in the first line. To whom is Chaucer referring when he
speaks of "The firste stocke fadir of gentilesse?" The editors of the variorum
echo the opinion of the majority of editors and commentators in remarking:
"*The firste stocke*: 'the original ancestor, the "stock" of the family tree,' glossed
in Scogan's ballade as 'God'.... Chaucer uses a genealogical image to say that
'gentilesse' traces its lineage from God or Christ" (*The Minor Poems*, 73). But
this identification raises certain questions. Although it is conventional in medieval religious discourse to speak of God without respect to person as the Father
of mankind, and to speak of Christ as the Word by whom all things were made
as the "Father" of mankind in a more specialized sense, if we take "stocke" to
mean "the progenitor of a family or race" as the *OED* suggests in citing this
verse (*stock*, *n*.[1], 3a), this seems a curiously specific way in which to address the
"fatherhood" of God. These difficulties are compounded in stanza two, in which
the "firste stocke" is described as being righteous, "trewe of his word," sober,
compassionate, noble, spiritually pure, and industrious. These are all eminently
desirable virtues, but the stanza does not read like an enumeration of the attributes of God the Father. John H. Fisher implicitly concedes these difficulties
in glossing *firste stocke* as "clearly God in the first stanza, but shading over into
Christ or even Adam in the second and third."[2] Fisher's comment underscores
the difficulties implicit in identifying "the firste stocke" directly with God, but
in the absence of a plausible alternative, one must assume that Chaucer was
writing rather loosely here, and this seems to be the conclusion of Pace and
David, who do not explicitly comment on these problems.

But there is a clear-cut alternative. "The firste stocke" of the human race
was Adam, and the human virtues which are attributed to "the firste stocke" in
stanza two could apply to Adam much more readily than they could to Christ
or God the Father. This suggestion has been made (*The Minor Poems*, 73),
but it has been rejected by most editors and commentators and there are at
least two immediate reasons for their decision. In the first place, while medieval
Christians believed that Adam was eventually saved, one would not immediately
think of the man whose sin brought death into the world as a model of ethical
conduct. And even less would one think that the man who lived by the sweat
of his brow for most of his 930 years could be thought to be the source of
"gentilesse," aristocratic virtues.

But although it is not hard to understand the reluctance of the various editors and commentators to accept what the phrasing of "Gentilesse" would seem
to imply, I submit that the most immediate meaning of "the firste stocke"—a
reference to Adam—is the correct one. By way of illustration I would like to

---

[2] *The Complete Poetry and Prose of Geoffrey Chaucer*, ed. John H. Fisher (New York:
Holt, Rinehart and Winston, 1977), 699.

cite some Latin texts from various genres, including homilies, exegetical texts, riddles and proverbs, not as the source of Chaucer's poem but as succinct and concrete expressions of ideas that were widely current. I begin with a riddle from the *Altercatio Hadriani Augusti et Epicteti Philosophi* tradition:

> Quis creavit primum Nobilem?—Deus in paradiso.
> Quis fecit primum rusticum?—Diabolus, quando Adam projecit in peccatum.[3]
> Who created the first nobleman? God [created Adam] in paradise.
> Who made the first peasant? The Devil when he cast Adam into sin.

These riddles are, in effect, a biblical gloss. Adam's punishment for his sin was, as God tells him, "in *laboribus* comedes eam cunctis diebus vitae tuae / spinas et tribulos germinabit tibi et comedes herbas terrae / *in sudore vultus tui* / vesceris pane / donec revertaris in terra de qua sumptus es" (italics mine; Genesis 3:17–19). Adam must support himself with hard physical work, and the earth will yield its fruit grudgingly. Thus Adam is reduced to a kind of servitude in that after the Fall he must work the earth; and of course the concept of the servitude of sin is a common biblical metaphor, specially prominent in the Pauline epistles (see for example Romans 1:17–18). Thus the Bible provides both a literal and metaphorical basis for the conception that Adam fell into a state of servitude. But before the Fall, as the riddle-master reminds us, Adam was noble indeed, both in the sense that he was not obligated to do hard physical work and that he was free from sin. The glory of Adam's prelapsarian condition was a favorite theme of the commentators and theologians,[4] and a number of medieval commentators comment on the "social" and political implications of the Fall. Thus for example Aelredus Rieuallensis (Ailred of Rievaulx) comments on the contrast between the modesty of John the Baptist, who specifically denied that he was the Christ, and the presumption of Adam, who wanted to achieve a higher social role than the one which God had appointed him.[5]

> O quam infelix Adam fuit, qui noluit in illo gradu manere in quo eum Dominus posuerat, sed uoluit uolare et esse sicut Deus! Noluit esse amicus, sed par; ideo de amico factus est uilis seruus. Amicus autem stat et audit eum (John 3:29). Felix qui potest audire sponsum! Hoc potest tantum facere illa anima quae est sponsa. Alii audiunt eum quasi regem, alii quasi iudicem, alii quasi magistrum. Sed amicus

---

[3] *Altercatio Hadriani Augusti et Epicteti Philosophi*, ed. William Lloyd Daly and Walther Suchier, Illinois Studies in Language and Literature 24 nos. 1–2 (Urbana: University of Illinois Press, 1939), 131. These riddles are nos. 12–13 in Text M, from an early-16th-century manuscript (Munich Staatsbibliothek 4424). For discussion of the filiations of this riddle collection with earlier medieval riddle collections, see Daly–Suchier, pp. 129–30. Note also Text M, no. 21 "Que est vera nobilitas? Que non nascendo, sed virtuose vivendo aquiretur" (p. 131).

[4] For a convenient summary of patristic and later authorities see the commentary of Cornelius a Lapide on Gen. 1:26 *et passim*. The edition I have consulted is that of Vives (Paris, 1868).

[5] Aelredus Rievallensis, *Sermones I–XLVI*, ed. Gaetano Raciti CCCM IIA (Turnhout: Brepols, 1989) "Sermo xliv, 11," pp. 347–48.

sponsi, cuius anima amica est sponsi et sponsa sponsi, audit eum
quasi sponsum.
(O how unfortunate Adam was who did not wish to remain in that
rank in which God placed him, but wished to ascend [fly] and to be
like God. He did not wish to be an amicus [friend] but the equal—
therefore from a friend he was transformed into a low slave. "The
friend, however, stands and hears him" (John 3:29). Some hear him
as if he is a king, others [hear him] as if he is a judge, others as if
he is a teacher. But the friend of the bridegroom—whose soul is the
beloved of the bridegroom and the bride of the bridegroom, hears
him as if he is a bridegroom.)

This is a dense and highly charged metaphorical passage—John the Baptist
is at the same time the friend of the bridegroom and the bride—but ignoring for
the moment the sexual metaphors and the allusions to John 3 and the Canticum
Canticorum which Ailred is elaborating, the implications of the social metaphors
in this passage require some comment. Adam before the Fall is the "amicus"
of God but when he falls into sin he becomes the "uilis servus." In the context
of medieval courtly society the term *amicus* does not simply denote personal
affection—to illustrate from the vernacular language of the country in which
Ailred of Rievaulx was writing and of which he was a native speaker, to be a
nobleman is to be of "siþcund" rank—that is to be the "kind" of person who
can be the companion ("gesið") of the king. To be in the king's favor, to be
the "amicus" of the king, is to be of high rank indeed, and to be cast down
from that rank to that of a "uilis servus," a "þeow," is a profound social change
indeed.

    Another text which illustrates the social implications of the Fall is a comment
by the twelfth-century homilist Godefridus Admontensis in which he plays with
various genealogical metaphors in discussing the consequences of the Fall.

Stamen nostrum Adam et Eva erant, qui nobile stamen erant, cum in
statu suo manserunt, et in deliciis paradisi deliciabantur. Putamen
autem, quod est sectio hujus staminis, totum est genus humanum,
quod abscissum et propagatum est ex illis primis parentibus nostris.
Hoc stamen, Adam scilicet et Eva, versum est in stuppam, quando
peccando degeneraverunt, nobilitatem que illam, in qua creati sunt,
a paradisi gaudiis exclusi amiserunt. Ex illa massa, ex illa ignobili
stuppa tractum est nobile illud filum, Filius Dei, qui rupit vincula
originalis et actualis peccati.[6]
(Our lineage [line] were Adam and Eve who were a noble lineage
while they remained in their [proper] place and rejoiced in the de-
lights of paradise. A clipping, however, which is the cut-off portion
of this lineage, is the whole human race, which [was] cut off and
grown from these first parents of ours. This lineage/line, Adam

    [6]Godefridus Admontensis, *Homiliae dominicales*, "Homilia 42. De Samsone et Dalila,"
Patrologia Latina 174, 277.

and Eve, was turned into flax when they un-nobled themselves [de-generaverunt] by sinning and they lost that nobility in which they were created, cut off from the joys of paradise. And from this mass, from this ignoble flax was drawn that noble thread [filus], the Son [filius] of God, who broke the [vincula] chain of original and actual sin.)

Here again, the homilist elaborates in richly metaphorical language the idea that Adam fell from nobility into servitude and that the nobility of the human condition was restored by Jesus. The line of descent from Adam and Eve to their descendants, which was a noble line, degenerated into flax, but from this "stuppa" was drawn that noble "thread" which broke the "chain" of sin which bound mankind. I cite these homiletic and exegetical texts, not because Chaucer necessarily would have known these particular texts, but because they illustrate a traditional understanding of the social consequences of Adam's fall into sin and illustrate the richly poetic quality of the medieval exegetical imagination. Negative arguments are always tentative and the Fall of Adam is such a common theme that it would be very difficult to survey the theme in Christian–Latin literature as a whole, but my impression, at least, is that while medieval authors talk fairly often about the Fall of Adam as a fall from "noble" to "servile" status, the great patristic authorities of the late Roman world are less interested in the social consequences of the Fall. That sin involves a kind of servitude is common enough, but in patristic texts the notion that the prelapsarian Adam was "noble" is relatively rare.

To return to *Gentilisse*, then, I would argue that the "firste stocke" in lines one and eight refers to Adam before he fell, who was the "primus nobilis," the source and the origin of all true nobility. Given the conventions of genealogical discourse, one claim to genealogical distinction is accounted better than another because one family can claim to be "older" than another. But the ultimate root of all genealogy is our first parent, Adam, whom Chaucer describes as "the first fader in mageste," perhaps playing on the double meaning of "mageste," a Latin/French borrowing which literally means "oldest" as well as "greatest" (cf. the late Middle English and later use of the terms "minority"/"majority" to denote periods of age). As a Latin proverb preserved in the fifteenth-century English MS Harley 3362 says, "Adam formosus factus et generosus / Excepto nullo nullus generosius illo. (Adam [was] made beautiful and noble/ With no exception no one was more noble than he.)"[7]

Part of the meaning of *Gentilesse* is that a "gentil" man, one who is free from the necessity of physical work, is free from some, at least, of the consequences of the Fall. Like Adam before the Fall, he need not work at servile labour, but he will only truly be "gentil" if he imitates the moral qualities of the prelapsarian Adam as well. Given the question, who is the "firste stocke fadir of gentilesse," the response "Adam before the Fall," seems to me to accord with the argument

[7] Hans Walther, *Proverbia sententaeque latinitatis medii aevi* (Gottingen: Vandenhoek and Ruprecht, 1963–69) no. 513. This proverb is drawn from Harley 3362, a fifteenth-century manuscript.

of the poem as a whole better than any of the proposed alternatives; and since this solution seems plausible I would like to explore briefly its implications.

The first point to emphasize is that with the possible exception of symbolic expressions of sexuality, few literary topics are more emotionally charged or complex than a given author's attitude towards class, status, and authority both in the real world which his fiction must to some degree "reflect," and in the imagined world of his fiction. Secondly, the critical assumption that Chaucer accepted the (presumed) viewpoint of the *haute noblesse* in sneering at any presumption to *gentilesse* by a commoner—an assumption articulated in Pace and David's notes—is uncritical and largely without foundation.[8] To cite an example from a later continental text composed in a social context in which the distinction between "gentleman" and commoner mattered profoundly, Dorante, who is a *comte*, both admires and respects Cléonte, the young bourgeois hero of *Le Bourgeois Gentilhomme*, and he admires him as a young man of real worth and dignity despite the fact that Cléonte makes no pretense to gentility in the strict sense. Members of the nobility, especially in England, where only the greatest nobles could provide titles for all their children, could and indeed would have had to accept certain commoners as their social peers and men like Chaucer and Gower were not themselves noble. But if Chaucer was not a nobleman and can hardly be presumed to have been a spokesman for the high nobility without more evidence than is usually offered, he was, nonetheless, a *gentil*—in the real world, at least, if not in the imagined world of the *Canterbury Tales*. And the social status of Adam was hardly a recondite theological abstraction in England after the rising of 1381. One of the slogans of the revolutionaries had been the famous metrical proverb "when Adam delved and Eve span, who was then the gentilman?"[9] This proverb expresses succinctly one of the latent ideological tensions of medieval Europe, the contrast between the implicitly egalitarian ideology of the biblical account of the origins of the nations, and the actualities of the hierarchical medieval social world. Defining Chaucer's "real" attitude towards the social world of which he was part is, as I have said, a complex problem. But it is unlikely that he would have been sympathetic to the radically egalitarian claims of the revolutionaries; and while we cannot date "Gentilesse" with any precision, it is tempting to see it as a measured response to the radical claim implicit in the metrical proverb. Adam was compelled to delve, according to the implicit argument of "Gentilesse," because Adam had sinned. Before he sinned he was *generosus* and those who are truly *gentil* will emulate his prelapsarian virtues as well as enjoying some at least of his privileges.

---

[8]The treatment of 'gentilesse' in *The Canterbury Tales* is far more complex.... Whether or not Chaucer shares [his characters'] views, there is surely a trace of amusement at the naiveté and innocent pretentiousness of middle-class pilgrims like the Wife and the Franklin who venture to teach the meaning of 'gentilesse'" (*The Minor Poems*, 67–68). Whatever the merits of this view, a variorum edition is hardly the place to assert it without qualification.

[9]For Middle English instances see *Proverbs, Sentences, and Proverbial Phrases from English Writings Mainly before 1500*, ed. Bartlett Jere Whiting (Cambridge: Harvard University Press, 1968), A38. See also Albert B. Friedman, "'When Adam Delved...': Contexts of an Historic Proverb," in *The Learned and the Lewed: Studies in Chaucer and Medieval Literature*, Harvard English Studies 5 (Cambridge: Harvard University Press, 1974), 213–30.

"Saving the Appearances" II

Another Look at Chaucer's
"Complaint to His Empty Purse"

R. F. YEAGER

To yow, my purse, and to noon other wight
Complayne I, for ye be my lady dere.
I am so sory, now that ye been lyght;
For certes but yf ye make me hevy chere,
Me were as leef be layd upon my bere;   5
For which unto your mercy thus I crye,
Beth hevy ageyn, or elles mot I dye.

Now voucheth sauf this day or hyt be nyght
That I of yow the blisful soun may here
Or see your colour lyk the sonne bryght   10
That of yelownesse hadde never pere.
Ye be my lyf, ye be myn hertes stere.
Quene of comfort and of good companye,
Beth hevy ageyn, or elles moot I dye.

Now purse that ben to me my lyves lyght   15
And saveour as doun in this world here,
Out of this toune helpe me thurgh your myght,
Syn that ye wole nat ben my tresorere;
For I am shave as nye as any frere.
But yet I pray unto your curtesye,   20
Beth hevy agen, or elles moot I dye.

Lenvoy de Chaucer

O conquerour of Brutes Albyon,
Which that by lyne and free eleccion
Been verray kyng, this song to yow I sende,
And ye, that mowen alle oure harmes amende,   25
Have mynde upon my supplicacion.

Paul Strohm, in a recent consideration of Chaucer's "Complaint to His Empty
Purse," has remarked that the five lines of its envoy contain "nothing wholly
original—that is, no single element not otherwise available within the broad
tradition of Lancastrian argumentation."[1] The chief text expressive of this "argumentation" is the so-called "Record and Process" statement of Henry IV's
"chalenge," or claim, to the throne of England presented at Westminster before
a "parliament" of dubious authority on 30 September 1399. Inserted in to the
Parliament Roll and immediately adopted as official, the "Record and Process"
quotes Henry as saying to those assembled:

> In the name off the ffadir, Sonne and Hooly Goost, I, Herry off
> Lancastre, clayme the Rewme off Englond, And the Crovne with
> alle the memberes and appurtenaunces. As I that am descendid by
> riht of lyne off the Bloode, komyng ffro the goode lorde Kyng Herry
> the thridde. And thurh that riht, that god off his grace hath sent to
> me, with helpe off my kynne and off my ffrendis to recover hit. The
> which Rewme was in point to be vndo ffor defaute of governaunce
> and goode lawe.[2]

In his assumption that Chaucer's envoy simply adopts Henry's "chalenge"
with slight embellishment, Strohm follows the lead of others who have written
about "To His Purse."[3] But in fact, on closer scrutiny, Chaucer's envoy begins
in a *wholly* unique fashion, by casting Henry as conqueror specifically "of Brutes
Albyon." The reference, as is always pointed out, is to the foundational myth
begun by Geoffrey of Monmouth that traces English civilization to the arrival
on the island of Brutus, great-grandson of the Trojan Aeneas. From his was the
name "Britain" derived.[4] Repeated and embroidered upon by many, including

---

[1] See his "Saving the Appearances: Chaucer's 'Purse' and the Fabrications of the Lancastrian Claim," chapter 4 in his *Huchon's Arrow: The Social Imagination of Fourteenth-Century
Texts* (Princeton, NJ: Princeton University Press, 1992), 75–94; quotation, 88.

[2] Text quoted from British Library MS Cotton Julius B.ii, as printed in *Chronicles of
London*, ed. C. L. Kingsford (Oxford: Oxford University Press, 1905; repr. London: Alan
Sutton, 1977), 43.

[3] E.g., M. Dominica Legge, " 'The Gracious Conqueror'," *Modern Language Notes* 68
(1953): 18–21; Florence R. Scott, "A New Look at 'The Complaint of Chaucer to His Empty
Purse'," *English Language Notes* 2 (1964): 81–87; Laila Z. Gross, in her notes to the poem in
The Riverside Chaucer.

[4] "Denique Brutus de nomine suo insulam Britoniam appellat sociosque suos Britones."
Historia regum Britannie of Geoffrey of Monmouth, I: Bern Burgerbibliothek, MS 568, ed.
Neil Wright (Cambridge: D. S. Brewer, 1984), I.16 (13).

Wace, Layamon and Higden (and translated by John Trevisa), and linked to the life of King Arthur, the Brutus story was familiar, it seems fair to say, to all but the most backward and isolated of late fourteenth-century Englishmen.[5] Clearly it was available to the Lancastrians.

What may be odd about it, however, is that *only* Chaucer uses the Brutus story to comment on Henry. This is true of the chroniclers, as well as the poets, although John Gower skims its surface in his *Cronica Tripertita* account of Henry's triumph, calling London "Troy" (I.58–60)[6]—but perhaps significantly not "New Troy," as Brutus did.[7] The Albion story seems like such an obvious "go-to" text for flattering an English ruler, especially in its Arthurian incarnation, as Spenser picked up on a century or two later. Yet neither Brutus nor Arthur figure in the comparisons heaped on Henry IV, or even Henry V, for whom, *pace* Hoccleve, the preferred conquering avatar is Alexander.[8] Probable reasons for this larger blankness are too numerous to consider here, but two points may have relevance for understanding "To His Purse." The first of these has to do with the Brutus–Albion story itself; the second with its originary connections to Arthur and consequent associative suggestions.

The key, perhaps, to what Chaucer is about in the first line of the envoy is the syntax. Usually the line is read, subliminally at least, so as to connect Brutus's conquering with Henry's. For Brutus was a conqueror, too: the island when he arrived with his wife and men was inhabited by giants, all of whom had to

---

[5] An example of how well-known was the story: other versions aside, Lister M. Matheson has stated flatly just of the Middle English prose *Brut*: "[it] survives in more manuscripts than any other Middle English work except two Wycliffite translations of the Bible." See his *The Prose Brut: The Development of a Middle English Chronicle* (Tempe, AZ: Medieval & Renaissance Texts and Studies, 1998), ix. He counts 180 English manuscripts, and an additional forty-nine in Anglo Norman and twenty in Latin (8).

[6] Not that the story wasn't well known, or important, to them: the chronicler Adam Usk, for example, breaks the account of his hair-raising escape from a Roman mob to identify the town of Alba through which he was passing (disguised as a common seaman) as "ubi Brutus, nepos Enee, rex Britonum primus, natus existiterat" ("where Brutus, the grandson of Aeneas, and the first king of the Britons, was born"); see *The Chronicle of Adam Usk 1377–1421*, ed. and trans. Chris Given-Wilson (Oxford: Clarendon Press, 1997), 204. For Gower see G. C. Macaulay, ed. *The Complete Works of John Gower*, 4 vols. (London: Oxford University Press, 1899-1902), IV, 316. (All quotations from the works of Gower, unless otherwise specified, are from Macaulay's edition.) Gower also prefaces the Prologue to the *Confessio Amantis* with Laitn verses locating his poem as a product of "Insula Bruti" (*Works* II, 1).

[7] Brutus's name for the city was Troia Nova—"New Troy," later transformed to "Trinovantum"; see *Historia regum Britannie*, I.17. That Gower knew this is certain: see *Vox Clamantis* I.880, prose heading: "nouam Troiam, id est ciuitatem Londoniarum." His reason for referring to London simply as "Troy" in the *Cronica* may have been metrical, but I am seldom persuaded by such arguments. A poet will always construct lines to include—or exclude—whatever is deemed important.

[8] E.g., *Regement of Princes*, 2038 ff.—although Hoccleve's motives are somewhat self-serving since, as he himself points out to Prince Henry, the *Regement* is partly a translation of the *Secretum Secretorum*. Hoccleve thus effectively casts himself as Aristotle to Hal's Alexander, with obvious immediate advantages for his project. Alexander is, however, something of a vexed figure when used in reference to Lancastrians: see my "Death Is a Lady: The *Regement of Princes* as Gendered Political Commentary," in *Studies in the Age of Chaucer* 26 (2004); for Gower's ambivalences, see below, and the discussion of Frank Grady, "The Lancastrian Gower and the Limits of Exemplarity," *Speculum* 70 (1995): 552–75.

be dispatched and the land cleansed before the civilizing process of proper city-building could commence.[9] The giants—or something like them—are essential in this process because at bottom the British/English historicization project embarked upon by Geoffrey of Monmouth and his cohort sets out, as do all foundational mythologies, the culture's claim to be recognized as a significant civilization.[10] As much as it does today for Western culture, for Geoffrey of Monmouth this meant conjoining his Britain to Greece and Rome of the epic tradition. Brought together in the figure of the noblest Greco-Trojan and city-founder Aeneas and transported to Britain in the person and ships of his great-grandson Brutus (who, along with his men, according to Geoffrey spoke "*curuum Grecum*"—"crooked Greek"),[11] it is that epic, classical world precisely that Geoffrey revivifies when he describes the first works of Brutus and his men:

> Agros incipiunt colere, domos aedificare, ita ut in breui tempore terram ab euo inhabitatam censeres.
> (They began to cultivate the fields, to build houses, such that in a short time you might think the country inhabited from earliest times.)[12]

Geoffrey's emphasis on a timeless appearance is significant, not merely be-cause no upstart outfit wants to look like one, but because it establishes visual credentials for a "real"—that is, Mediterranean—civilized life-way. Cereal agri-culture further connects Britain with civilization immemorial as, in classical progression, bucolic gives way to city-building:

> Diuiso tandem regno affectauit Brutus ciuitatem aedificare. Affec-tum itaque suum exequens circuiuit tocius patrie situm ut congruum locum inueniret.
> (Having viewed his kingdom, Brutus wished to build a city. Ac-cordingly he toured the circuit of the whole country looking for an appropriate site.)[13]

Nor should it be surprising that one more battle with the giants is necessary, culminating in a Herculean wrestling match (for "Gogmagog" read "Anteus"), before "New Troy" can be laid out.[14] The barbarity of the first inhabitants is requisite contrast to the refinement to follow.

---

[9] *Historia regum Britannie*, I.16.

[10] Geoffrey's project may in fact have been intentionally oppositional to contemporary de-pictions of the British peoples as savages: see J. Gillingham, "The Context and Purposes of Geoffrey of Monmouth's *History of the Kings of Britain*," *Anglo-Norman Studies* 13 (1990): 99–118.

[11] "Unde postmodum loquela gentis que prius Troiana siue curuum Grecum nuncupabatur dicta fuit Britann[c]a." *Historia regum Britannie*, p. 13, I.21.

[12] *Historia regum Britannie*, p. 13, I.21. Translation mine.

[13] *Historia regum Britannie*, p. 14, I.22. Translation mine. Note Geoffrey's use here—common in these passages related to Brutus—of "*patria*" forms. Gillingham, "Context and Purposes," makes the point (109) that "In Geoffrey's eyes town foundation is one of the proper activities of the good king. It often goes together with building roads, encouraging agriculture and issuing laws, —also, of course, an activity associated with the Romans."

[14] *Historia regum Britannie*, p. 13, I.21.

Indeed, the giants were apparently felt to be so necessary to an enlarging British/English historiography that in the late thirteenth century an Anglo-Norman poem, *Des Grantz Geanz*, was composed to explain how the giants got there to meet Brutus.[15] *Des Granz Geanz* tells the story of a group of sisters from Greece who, having plotted to murder their husbands, are set adrift and arrive on the British shore. Albina, the eldest and the leader, names the island "Albion" after herself. The women are visited by incubi, who father the giants upon them; incest subsequently produces more. Importantly, however, as the fruit of demonic and incestuous relations, the giants are so anti-social and violent that they have mostly slaughtered each other by the time Brutus and his Trojans arrive.[16] Soon added to the Anglo-Norman *Brut*, so that few extant copies are without it, and replicated in Latin and Middle English versions, the origin of the giants was a commonplace part of "Brutes Albyon" by the late fourteenth century.[17] Chaucer would have known the story—and so undoubtedly would Henry.[18]

The significance of the extended giants' narrative for mythic British/English history is two-fold: first, that, by so powerfully emphasizing the monstrous origin and brutality of those first inhabitants, it renders Brutus's civilizing achievement all the more marvelous, implying that in contrast his was a "golden age"; and second, the giants' tale serves as a dark reminder of how truly terrible things were in pre-Brutean Britain, and therefore of what horrors might await should history regress, and chaos come again. Figured into Galfredian history, it reinforces a downward curve there present which, from its Trojan premise to the demise of Arthur, is essentially tragic.[19]

---

[15] Ed. Georgine E. Brereton, *Medium Aevum Monographs* 2 (Oxford: Blackwell, 1937).

[16] The basic story has two elaborations. In one, the women are Greek, twenty-nine in number, and are prevented from murdering their husbands by the youngest sister, who reveals the plot. In the other, all thirty sisters carry out the murder successfully. In this version, the women are Syrian. See Brereton's introduction, *Des Grantz Geanz*, xxxv-vii, and Lesley Johnson, "Return to Albion," *Arthurian Literature* 13 (1995): 19–40.

[17] Matheson, *Prose Brut*, 2, notes that "the majority of the texts of the Anglo-Norman *Brut* are prefaced by [it]." For the Latin version, *De Origine Gigantum*, see James P. Carley and Julia Crick, "Constructing Albion's Past: An Annotated Edition of *De Origine Gigantum*," *Arthurian Literature* 13 (1995): 41–114. English versions infiltrate the chronicles into the fifteenth century: e.g., *Castleford's Chronicle*, ed. Caroline D. Eckhardt, EETS 305, 306 (Oxford, 1996).

[18] Lisa M. Ruch has suggested connecting the *Granz Geanz* story to Chaucer's incomplete "Legend of Hypermnestra" (*LGW* 2562–723) and to the "Man of Law's Tale"; see "Albina und ihre Schwestern: Ein Mythos in der mittelalterlichen Chronistik," in *Herrscher, Helden, Heilige*, ed. Ulrich Müller and Werner Wunderlich (St. Gallen: UVK, Fachverlag für Wissenschaft und Studium, 1996): 281–86. As for Henry, he was highly literate. According to K. B. MacFarlane, *Lancastrian Kings and Lollard Knights* (Oxford: Clarendon Press, 1972) "he valued books" and is reported to have passed a full morning reading in the library of Bardney Abbey; letters in his own hand survive in French and English, and notes in Latin pepper his private papers (23, 22).

[19] The point is made clearly and most recently by James Simpson: see *Reform and Cultural Revolution, Oxford English Literary History Volume 2. 1350–1547* (Oxford: Oxford University Press, 2002), Chapter 3: "The Tragic," 68–120; also suggestive are Nicholas Birns, "The Trojan Myth: Postmodern Reverberations," *Exemplaria* 5 (1993): 45–78; and Peter Stallybrass, "The World Turned Upside Down: Inversion, Gender and the State," in *The Matter of*

To be the "*conquerour* of Brutes Albyon" as Chaucer has it in "To His Purse," rather than Brutus himself, is thus something of a mixed compliment. Grammatically and syntactically the words insist, not on the continuation of civilization, but on its overthrow; nor is the thought that *Richard* might be Brutus if Henry is the *conqueror* of his Albion especially attractive, particularly given the political stakes in 1400—although the suggestion is clearly present. Moreover, to imagine further along such lines in context of the *Historia regum Britannie* is to equate Henry with the Saxons, who by murder, perfidy and theft of "gigantic" proportion were the only group to take Albion from the Britons.[20] In short, reading the envoy of "To His Purse" either backwards or forwards from Chaucer's opening line is no optimistic enterprise.

Nor do things brighten much for Henry if we take him for Arthur and see in his conquest the ultimate driving out of the Saxons and the dawn of chivalry at the Round Table. The problem is not simply that we all know how disastrously Camelot turns out—although perhaps that knowledge contributed to why no contemporary writer appears to have made the connection. Again, as with Brutus, it would seem an irresistible flattery to hail Henry as a newly-awakened Arthur come to reclaim his endangered kingdom.[21] Henry had, certainly, the chivalric presence and an international reputation as a jouster sufficient to recommend such praise.[22] But there may be better reason why not even—or rather, one might venture, *especially*—Henry's propagandists, searching as they were for historical-mythic analogies to burnish the usurper's image, dared to "play the Arthur–Henry card." Chaucer may, in fact, be digging up this particular body in the second line of the envoy, when he echoes Henry's claim to kingship by right of "lyne." Strohm is of course right about it, *prima facie*:

> Chaucer's references to "lyne" and to "verray" kingship seem a rough equivalent to Henry's own "right line of the blod" [in the "Record and Process"], though with the implied circumstances—that awkwardly concocted and inherently unpersuasive business about Edmund Crouchback—tacitly pushed even farther to the background than in Henry's own challenge.[23]

Difference: Materialist Feminist Criticism of Shakespeare, ed. Valerie Wayne (Hemel Hempsted: Harvester Wheatsheaf, 1991), 201–20. Both identify tendencies in violent societies to uphold violent originary myths by endorsing trajectories of division and discord.

[20]The story of the Saxons in Britain begins with the arrival of Hengist and Horsus, *Historia regum Britannie* VI.10. Geoffrey of course acknowledges the victory of Julius Caesar over the Britons (V.9–10), but almost incidentally, and does not treat the Romans as an occupying force. In Hoccleve's hands later, Julius Caesar joins Alexander as a paradigm for Prince Hal (*Regement of Princes*, 3246–48; 3271–304).

[21]Arthur *did* occur to the Chandos Herald, describing Henry's uncle Edward the Black Prince: see *The Life of the Black Prince by the Herald of Sir John Chandos*, ed. Mildred K. Pope and Eleanor C. Lodge (Oxford: Clarendon Press, 1910), ll. 52, 4099.

[22]On Henry's reputation, see MacFarlane, *Lancastrian Kings*, 37-38 and n. 1, citing contemporary French sources; and closer to home, see *Mum and the Sothsegger*, ll. 206–20, ed. Mabel Day and Robert Steele, EETS 199 (Oxford, 1936 [for 1934]).

[23]*Huchon's Arrow*, 88. An attempt was also made to discredit the legitimacy of Richard's birth, and his connection to the blood royal by questioning the legality of the Black Prince's marriage to, and the moral character of, Joan of Kent, Richard's mother; see K. P. Wenters-

The "business about Edmund Crouchback" was the rumor, purportedly urged first by Henry's father, John of Gaunt, that Edmund was actually the first-born son and heir of Henry III but was put aside secretly in favor of the younger Edward I, because of Edmund's deformity. "The advantage of this account," as Strohm remarks, "is that Edmund, as Duke of Lancaster, was great-grandfather of Duchess Blanche, Gaunt's wife and Henry's mother, and Edmund's reinstatement would thus enhance the matrilineal side of Henry's claim."[24] The story had made the rounds years before the accession, and was widely recognized as false.[25] The chronicler Usk, for one, offers a score of examples to disprove it, but religious houses around the country were ordered nonetheless to send their chronicles to Westminster to be searched by Henry's party for any evidentiary reference. Finding none, Usk reports, some of Henry's supporters in the drafting sessions of the "chalenge" still urged that it be used.[26]

And of course, used it was: cradle-swapping is the only thing Henry could have been hinting at when, in the "Record and Process" script, he claimed descent "by riht lyne off the Bloode, komyng ffro the goode lorde Kyng Herry the thridde"—no doubt to sharp intake of breath at his audacity in certain quarters of the hall. Apparently in the end, despite extensive recognition that the "Edmund Crouchback business" was a fudge, keeping mum about descent was deemed no option. Probably it was felt Henry had little choice but to address the issue somehow, since strictly speaking (to quote Nigel Saul) "Henry was not Richard's nearest male heir. That position was occupied by Edmund, earl of March, who was descended in the female line from Edward III's second son, whereas Duke Henry was descended from the third."[27] But the moment on 30 September must have been tense: unless the crowd in the great hall at Westminster could be brought to swallow a fudge so large, Henry's "chalenge" risked instant refutation on dynastic grounds alone.

That point once passed, however, and Henry's "eleccion" a *fait accompli*, the "Record and Process" version became official; and, in the manner of all such government "realities" actively foisted on the citizenry today as well as then, no doubt was left alone by the wise and the guilty, in hope of its fading quietly away. Interestingly, one way to impose that desired silence on the embarrassing "Crouchback" solution to the problem of descent was to *avoid* comparing Henry to Arthur. This is because most of Henry's direct line of *male* ancestors, which the Edward-I-for-Edmund-Crouchback swap was to consign to public

---

dorf, "The Clandestine Marriages of the Fair Maid of Kent," *Journal of Medieval History* 5 (1979): 203–31.

[24] *Huchon's Arrow*, 77.

[25] That is, in 1394; see the discussion of Sydney Armitage-Smith, *John of Gaunt: King of Castile and Leon, Duke of Aquitaine and Lancaster, Earl of Derby, Lincoln and Leicester, Seneschal of England* (New York: Barnes & Noble, 1964), 359–62.

[26] Usk, *Chronicle*, ed. and trans. Given-Wilson, 64–66. For the round-up of monastic chronicles for examination, see *The Chronicle of John Hardyng*, ed. Henry Ellis (London: Rivington, 1812), 353–54; and further James W. Sherborne, "Perjury and the Lancastrian Revolution of 1399," *Welsh History Review* 14 (1988): 217–41, especially 239.

[27] See Nigel Saul, *Richard II* (New Haven, CT: Yale University Press, 1997), 419.

forgetfulness, had associated themselves with Arthur, two of them—Edwards I and III—quite famously.[28]

To recall the Arthurian postures of two kings who, according to the "Crouch-back" solution, should not rightfully have ruled at all must have been, it is logical enough to assume, a risky business in 1400. Perhaps this is another reason why no contemporary comes even close to calling Henry an Arthur—and why Chaucer, if he is in fact suggesting a truth-telling context for "lyne" via extension of the odd syntax of "conquerour of Brutes Albyon," does so almost under erasure. Read together in such a manner, the first two acclamations in the envoy of "To His Purse" can be understood to cast doubt twice on Henry's right to rule.

And perhaps the third—the claim of "free eleccion"—does, too. More recent, less apologetic historians of the reign than Stubbs and Wylie have thoroughly debunked the Lancastrian narrative of Henry's "election" by "parliament."[29] Fifteenth-century accounts outside the sphere of Lancastrian influence have made it clear that the multitude assembled in the Great Hall at Westminster to hear Henry's "chalenge" on 30 September, and to shout him onto the throne thereafter, was no legal body.[30] It was allowed to become a mob,

---

[28] Edward I's verifiable associations with Arthur include holding "Round Tables" in Wales and Scotland, opening and himself examining the supposed graves of Arthur and Guinevere, possession among his books of an Arthurian romance, and applying Arthur's conquest of Scotland as a precedent in a letter to the pope in 1301. For some, including R. S. Loomis, "Edward I, Arthurian Enthusiast?" *Speculum* 28 (1953): 114–27, such details are telling. Others are less convinced, e.g., Michael Prestwich, *Edward I* (New Haven: Yale University Press, 1988), who concludes that "What is much less clear is the extent to which Edward saw himself in Arthurian terms: it was probably no more that a conceit he toyed with occasionally" (122). At the same time, however, Prestwich points out that "foreigners [i.e., Frenchmen] viewed him" in Arthurian terms, as did the contemporary Englishman Peter Langtoft (121). For present purposes, what the king thought of himself may be of less importance than how he was thought *of*, and remembered, by others. As for Edward III, Prestwich writes: "Edward III emulated his grandfather's [i.e., Edward I's] cult of the Arthurian legend. At Winchester a round table still survives, which was probably constructed early in his reign, and in 1344 at a great tournament held at Windsor it was decided to build a round house to hold a similar table. The king was clearly contemplating the foundation of a knightly order on the Arthurian model, but for some reason the scheme was not carried out, although some of the building work was done. Four years later the Order of the Garter was founded as a select brotherhood of twenty-six knights...." See *The Three Edwards: War and the State in England 1272–1377* (New York: St. Martin's Press, 1980), 204–5.

[29] William Stubbs, *The Constitutional History of England*, 3 vols. (Oxford: Clarendon Press, 1875–78), especially II, 532–33; J. H. Wylie, *The History of England under Henry IV*, 4 vols. (London: 1884–98). For more recent, critical views, see S. B. Chrimes, *English Constitutional Ideas in the Fifteenth Century* (Cambridge: Cambridge University Press, 1936), 106–16; H. G. Richardson, "Richard II's Last Parliament," *English Historical Review* 52 (1937): 39–47; Gaillard T. Lapsley, "Richard II's 'Last Parliament'," *English Historical Review* 53 (1938): 53–79; and Bertie Wilkinson, "The Deposition of Richard II and the Accession of Henry IV," *English Historical Review* 54 (1939): 215–39.

[30] Notably Jean Creton, *Chronique de la Traïson et Mort de Richard Deux Roy Dengleterre* (ed. Benjamin Williams [London: English Historical Society, 1846; repr. 1964]). See Lapsley, "Parliamentary Title," 448 and *passim*; M. V. Clarke and V. H. Galbraith, "The Deposition of Richard II," in *Fourteenth Century Studies by M. V. Clarke*, ed. L. S. Sutherland and May McKisack (Oxford: Clarendon Press, 1937), 53–98; MacFarlane, *Lancastrian Kings*, 54–55. It should be noted by way of balance that the accuracy of some non-Lancastrian French

thereby with no authority more than a gaggle of private citizens to witness re-port of Richard's deposition, let alone grant power to his successor.[31] Richard had no opportunity to respond to the "gravamina" laid against him—for rea-sons that must have been obvious even to the bishop of Carlisle Thomas Merks who, Jean Creton reports, fruitlessly registered his objection to the proceedings nonetheless.[32] The unofficial and unorthodox nature of the proceedings is also subtly but tellingly acknowledged by how the "Record and Process" is included into the Parliament Roll—as a description of events, rather than in the usual manner, as parliamentary transcription.[33]

For many Englishmen, particularly those whose legal or parliamentary ex-perience allowed them to see through the unprecedented tableau being orches-trated by Henry and Archbishop Arundel, the result was a clear awareness that the crown had been snatched by force and guile. Some of these responded by conspiring immediately to assassinate Henry—the variously called "Epiphany Rising" or "January Plot" of 1400 that ended with a parade of heads (a few be-longing to Chaucer's friends) through the London streets, and probably sealed Richard's fate.[34] The bloodiness of the plot's suppression doubtless intimidated many and taught others, notably the Percys, who rose against Henry in 1403, or a group of Franciscans who preached against Henry's accession in 1402, to wait for a better opportunity.[35] The usurper's response to the latter was an edict of May 1402 against divisive preaching which resulted in the arrest and trial of many friars.[36] How seriously king and chancellor took the Franciscans is measurable by the court's denial of benefit of clergy, and by Henry's own reported involvement in the interrogation of the Franciscan leader, one Richard (or Roger) Frisby. A contemporary account preserves their interchange, one

---

accounts has been held up to question: see J. J. N. Palmer, "The Authorship, Date and Historical Value of the French Chronicles on the Lancastrian Revolution: I and II," *Bulletin of the John Rylands Library* 61 (1978–79): 147–81. On the manner of acclamation by the crowd, see Saul's description, *Richard II*, 422–23.

[31] I borrow "mob" from MacFarlane, *Lancastrian Kings*, 54. See further Lapsley, "Parlia-mentary Title," 426 n. 2, and 433, quoting from Walsingham, *Annales Ricardi Secundi et Henrici Quarti*: "ad parliamentum Londoniis celebrandum . . . occurrerent."

[32] See Creton, *Traïson et Mort*, ed. Williams, 221–22. There is some division amongst historians as to the accuracy of this report—but it is the case that, as MacFarlane notes (*Lancastrian Kings*, 55), Merks lost his bishopric shortly after the coronation.

[33] The point is made by Lapsley, "Parliamentary Title," 424.

[34] Plans were made in December 1399; plotters included the deposed bishop Merks, William Colchester, abbot of Westminster, the earls of Kent, Rutland, Huntington and Salisbury, the Lord Despenser, Sir Thomas Blount and Sir Benedict Cely. See E. F. Jacob, *The Fifteenth Century 1399–1485* (Oxford: Clarendon Press, 1961), 24–25.

[35] Brady, "Lancastrian Gower," 574, has an excellent summary of events which brings the bloodshed home.

[36] On the whole question of developing opposition to Henry, especially making use of Richard's rumored survival, see Peter McNiven, "Rebellion, Sedition, and the Legend of Richard II's Survival in the Reigns of Henry IV and Henry V," *Bulletin of the John Ry-lands Library* 76 (1994): 93–117; Philip Morgan, "Henry IV and the Shadow of Richard II," in *Crown, Government and People in the Fifteenth Century*, ed. Rowena E. Archer (New York: St. Martin's Press, 1995), 1–31; and most recently Strohm, *England's Empty Throne: Usurpation and the Language of Legitimation, 1399–1422* (New Haven: Yale University Press, 1998), 101–27.

part of which is interesting in specific relation to Chaucer's envoy. Responding
to the friar's direct charge that "ye haue vsurpid the croune," Henry asserts:

> "I haue not vsurpid the croune, but I was chosen therto by elec-
> cioun." The maister ansuerde, "The eleccioun is noughte, livyng the
> trewe and lawful possessour; and yf he be ded, he is ded be you,
> and yf he be ded be you, ye haue lost all the righte and title that
> ye myght haue to the croune." Thanne saide the kyng to him, "Be
> myn hed thou shalt lese thyne hed."[37]

Striking here is the curt dismissal of Henry's assertion that "eleccioun" has
legitimized his authority. Friar Frisby cuts through the sham with a logic
irrefutable—save by beheading. And no doubt the friar spoke for the great
majority of Englishmen in 1400–1402. One has to wonder, faced with such
examples, *who* in England believed the Lancastrian farce of "eleccioun"? Not
Henry himself, certainly. Among all the charges laid at Henry's door, stupidity
was never one of them. Not as deep a schemer as Arundel, perhaps—but he
was a reader, with an apparent interest in philosophical argument.[38] In the
end, Henry IV was no dunce. He knew where his power came from, no less
than any modern candidate, packaged by his handlers. We could undoubtedly
imagine his bluff chafing at the tripartite "Record and Process" claim, with its
euphemism ("recovery") for conquest, its embarrassing "Crouchback" foolishness, if we didn't have Usk's eye-witness chronicle report as concrete evidence
that he did just that.

Henry's perceptivity has direct bearing on "To His Purse," of course, because
if my reading of the envoy is correct, and Chaucer did work a partisan second
level of meaning underneath the sycophantic surface—one which called into
question Henry's right to be hailed as "verray king" (l. 3)— would Henry have
noticed it, assuming of course that he ever read Chaucer's little poem? And if
Henry did perceive what Chaucer was up to, how would he have reacted? Just
as he did to Friar Frisby, perhaps?

Actually, to make matters worse, Henry might have had difficulty with "verray," too. "True" or "genuine" king was precisely what Richard, who had
stressed publicly the irrevocability of his God-bestowed authority, is reported
to have denied in the Tower to Henry's henchmen that a usurper could ever
attain. Everything points to the Lancastrians' early awareness of the problem,
and to their attempts to counter Richard's sacrality with suggestions of Henry's
own, from the texts preached on by Archbishop Arundel at the "election parliament" to Henry's carefully crafted opening words of the "Record and Process"

---

[37]See *An English Chronicle of the Reigns of Richard II, Henry IV, Henry V and Henry
VI, written before the year 1471*, ed. J. S. Davies, (London: Royal Historical Society, 1855),
25.

[38]On Henry's reading, see n. 16, above; Wylie, *Henry IV*, iv, 138, mentions his attending
lectures at the University of Paris, taking particular interest in debates of casuistry; Macfarlane, *Lancastrian Kings*, 23, calls him "that rare combination, the man of action who was
also an intellectual."

script ("In the name off the ffadir, Sonne and Hooly Goost, I, Herry of Lancastre, clayme....") to the altogether extraordinary coronation ceremony, in which Henry was anointed four times on his body while recumbent on cloth-of-gold and transported about the cathedral, as if to emphasize the unvolitional nature of his accession, to the use of the resurrected "oil of the Virgin" (so called) in the ceremony, and the rapid diffusion of its legend throughout the kingdom by Lancastrian agents.[39] Intriguingly, in the face of so many words and labors, that Henry's accession was the will of God is the one element from the Lancastrian "chalenge" that Chaucer does *not* mention in the envoy of "To His Purse."

It is easy to understand why, for Henry, it was essential that his reign (as Gower puts it) "stant ... of god and man confermed."[40] By far the thorniest question facing Henry's rule was whether replacing Richard as king was theologically tenable. Usurping the government clearly was—in effect it had been done before under the Appellants, of which Henry was one, in 1387–88. But Henry didn't want to rule in Richard's stead; he wanted to *be* Richard. That was the hitch, as Richard himself reportedly drove home to Henry's supporters in the Tower, in a confrontation over what the resignation they were demanding from him actually meant. Richard could swallow being deposed, and Henry taking over his powers—after all, he was used to that, and he had come back from it to rule again—but he argued that an anointed king could not, even if he wanted to, resign his sacral authority twice conferred, first implicitly, by God's favor in choosing him out of all men, and second directly, by the act of anointing itself.[41] English coronation theory, supported by the Common Law, took the anointing as the central moment of making the king, when the sevenfold gifts of the Holy Spirit are conferred and the royal "*persona laica*" is transformed into a "*persona mixta*."[42] "Nothing which goes before, and nothing which follows, can approach the anointing in significance ... the king is vested and adorned with the regalia because he is anointed ... he is not anointed in order that he may receive the regalia."[43] Richard was willing to acknowledge Henry as his successor, and to let him run the country while he lived; beyond that, however, he could not go. Nor might Lancastrian propaganda make the trouble vanish more than momentarily. The issue of sacrilege remained just under the surface

---

[39] Arundel's main text was I Samuel 9:17, which reported (in the words of the contemporary writer of MS Julius B.ii) "the wordes of the hyh Kyng spekyng to Samuel and teching hym whom he shulde ordeyne and putte Inne to governe the peple, whan the same peple asked a kyng to be yoven hem." See *Chronicles of London*, ed. Kingsford, 44; on the coronation, see 49. On the Lancastrian manipulation of the oil legend, see H. G. Wright, "The Protestation of Richard II in the Tower in September, 1399," *Bulletin of the John Rylands Library* 23 (1939): 151–65, pointing out (160–61) that the version fed to loyalist chroniclers like Walsingham was "adjusted" to make the prophecy seem more applicable to Henry.

[40] "To King Henry IV, In Praise of Peace," l. 14; in *Complete Works*, ed. Macaulay, III, 481.

[41] The story of the "*Protestatio regis Ricardi ante Resignationem*" has been assembled from several contemporary documents by Wright; see "The Protestation of Richard II," 151–65.

[42] See John Wickham Legg, *The Sacring of the English Kings* (London: Harrison & Sons, 1894), 3.

[43] Leopold G. W. Legg, *English Coronation Records* (London: Archibald Constable, 1901), xxxiv.

of Henry's rule until at last, after the protested execution of Archbishop Scrope in 1407, his illness brought the matter up again, to dog him to the grave.[44]

That Chaucer leaves God entirely out of his description of Henry's rise to power in the envoy of "To His Purse" might not be significant—one can't squeeze everything into a brief snippet of a poem. But the difference between a scoreless triple and a home run is just one base out of four: sometimes it's essential to make the rounds. For how Henry might have taken that omission, it may be important to imagine Chaucer's poem in light both of the sensitivities of the Lancastrian cabal to the issue of sacrilegious usurpation and of the competition. As to the latter, Henry was negotiating to lure Christine de Pisan from France, presumably to be glorified in a poem of hers, and Gower in 1400 was fulsomely celebrating Henry's accession, pointedly stressing its divine direction.[45]

So let us suppose a scenario: Chaucer, despite his several interactions with Henry over the years, is silent about the accession.[46] He's never been close to Henry—his wife Philippa was, after all, the sister of Henry's father's mistress and third spouse, not the usurper's mother, and he has had a long and loyal career in Richard's service. Until the certain news of Richard's death in February 1400, Chaucer, always the prudent court man, avoids commitment either way. But there is building pressure—from Gower, whose energies were liberated by the public success of Henry's "Record and Process" script, from the course of events (the bloody precedent of the "January Plotters" was lost on no one) and from the inner circle of Lancastrian strategists. Strohm has argued these included Henry himself. If so, it is then possible to see the usurper's oft-cited mandate of 9 November 1399, converting the £10 due Chaucer on his annuity from Richard into a gift from Henry, and likewise the 40 marks a year granted in February 1400 (but backdated to 13 October, the coronation), as carrots to break Chaucer's silence.

Was there a stick, too? Perhaps the fate of the "January Plotters" would have served a subtle man like Chaucer. All of them he undoubtedly knew; some of them were his friends. From his house on the abbey grounds at Westminster he could claim sanctuary, if need be, but this did not always work. (William Colchester, Westminster's abbot and technically Chaucer's landlord, was one of the plotters on trial.) What to do? Gower's effulgence is out of character for Chaucer; if he were asked, either on the advice of Gower himself or by others, to please the usurper by producing something similar, it seems unimaginable that he could muster it. Yet very likely it was necessary for Chaucer to send Henry

---

[44] On the national connection of Henry's mysterious sickness and sacrilege, see J. L. Kirby, *Henry IV of England* (London: Constable, 1970), 196–97. The killing of Scrope, over the objections of Arundel, marked a breaking-point in their alliance.

[45] On Henry's attempts to bring Christine to his court, see Wylie, *Henry IV*, iv, 136–37; and Strohm, *Huchon's Arrow*, 91–92. For Gower, see variously *Cronica Tripertita* III, ll. 316–23 and its gloss; "To King Henry IV, In Praise of Peace" l. 14.

[46] Kirby, *Henry IV*, 22, notes: "In 1395 William Loveney as clerk of the wardrobe bought 101 civet skins from Robert Markeley of London for the considerable sum of £8 8s. 4d in order to provide a scarlet gown for the poet at Henry's expense, and shortly afterwards Chaucer delivered £10 from Loveney into Henry's hands in London." See also *Chaucer Life-Records*, 275.

a poem, and after the death of Richard he may have seen no reason to hold out further.

In such circumstances, there is a perverse but rather noble irony in sending Henry an off-beat scrap of a begging poem. Here, if my reading of its lines is correct, a wicked idea took very subtle shape. Chaucer could see, from Gower's work if not simply from the "Record and Process" and talk about town, what elements were expected in a Lancastrian praise-poem. Some of this he could stomach, particularly if quietly undercut by the barbed direction of "Brutes Albyon." But the notion that God might sanction usurpation was impossible in conscience.

So Chaucer left it out. Or almost, anyway. God, I think, *is* present in the envoy, in the last two lines—although hardly in a way likely to satisfy Henry. Reading "To His Purse" in modern editions has accustomed most of us to see the text as follows (as in the *Riverside* edition):

> O conquerour of Brutes Albyon,
> Which that by lyne and free eleccion
> Been verray kyng, this song to yow I sende,
> And ye, that mowen all oure harmes amende,
> Have mynde upon my supplicacion.

But of course the various commas and period are all editorial, and *soto voce* support a particular interpretation. The manuscript Henry might have gotten probably looked more like this:

> O conquerour / of Brutes albyon
> Whiche that by lygne / and free eleccion
> Been verray kynge / this song to yow I sende
> And ye that mowen / alle oure harmes amende
> Haue mynde / vpon my supplicacion[47]

In such a text the breaks and pauses are the reader's to insert, with conse-quences, perhaps. It is clear that "yow" in line 3 refers to Henry—but does the "ye" in line 4 refer to him also? If a full stop is placed after "sende" in line 3, and a new sentence begun with "And" in line 4, one would have ended with the pair:

> And ye that mowen / alle oure harmes amende
> Haue mynde / vpon my supplicacion

Taken as a separate statement, and apart from the sentence of the first three lines, a reader's good first guess for the antecedent of "ye" would be God, a sovereign ruler whose legitimacy Chaucer never doubted. And if by "alle oure harmes amende" Chaucer meant rectification of rightful rule and an end

---

[47]Text from *A Variorum Edition of the Works of Geoffrey Chaucer*, 5: *The Minor Poems*, ed. George B. Pace and Alfred David (Norman, OK: University of Oklahoma Press, 1982), 131–32.

to usurpation, the little "Complaint to His Empty Purse" would be as subtle, subversive and dangerous a poem as Chaucer ever wrote.

Would "To His Purse" have succeeded with Henry, so encoded—or even read in the customary way? Beside Gower's "joyful noise" of the *Cronica Tripertita* and "In Praise of Peace," Chaucer's balade musters scarcely a squeak. Nor does it show Henry's "regne of god and man confirmed": it may, in fact, propose quite the opposite. Our lack of knowledge about whether Chaucer even sent the poem, or if so, whether Henry read it, is absolute. We do assume, however, that the envoy at least of "To His Purse" is Chaucer's last poetic utterance. One hopes the reason wasn't Henry's unexpected ability to read too keenly between the lines.[48]

* * *

Emerson Brown came from Puerto Rico to Stanford just in time for the demonstrations, the tear-gas and the teach-ins. Riding his thin-wheeled Italian racer about campus, Emerson was a tanned and near-equally lean figure who would show up when his presence (and his reasonable but impassioned voice raised in protest at acts of injustice) might be helpful. And it always was. He was the director of my senior Honors English thesis on Chaucer, and we talked in those days in equal parts politics and poetry. Among the many sensible and sensitive things he impressed upon me was the value of the small detail for the interpretation of literary (or political) texts. By re-reading the minutiae of Chaucer's little "To His Purse," to find the small gesture and play it out against the backdrop of times as parlous as those in which we met, it is my hope to have in some way built upon a career in scholarship, teaching and committed living so many knew for years as quintessentially "Emersonian."

---

[48] As indeed he may have: see Terry Jones, R. F. Yeager, Terry Dolan, Alan Fletcher and Juliette D'Or, *Who Murdered Chaucer? A Medieval Mystery* (London: Methuen, 2003).

Oral Performance

Chaucerian Sentences

Revisiting a "Crucial Passage" from the *Nun's Priest's Tale*

ALAN T. GAYLORD

Crucial passage: *NPT*

> "Now lat us speke of myrthe and stynte al this.
> Madame Pertelote, so have I blys,
> Of o thyng God hath sent me large grace
> For whan I se the beautee of youre face   4350
> Ye ben so scarlet reed aboute youre eyen
> It maketh al my drede for to dyen.
> For also siker as *In principio*,
> *Mulier est hominis confusio*—
> Madame, the sentence of this Latyn is   4355
> 'Womman is mannes joye and al his blys.'
> For whan I feel a-nyght youre softe syde,
> Al be it that I may nat on yow ryde
> For that oure perche is maad so narwe, allas,
> I am so ful of joye and of solas   4360
> That I deffie bothe swevene and dreem."[1]

4353–54: "The Italics used here for the Latin correspond to a change of script by the scribe" (Pearsall).

4355–56: "Owen . . . makes the neat point that both text and mistranslation are the same: woman is man's confusion *because* she is his joy and bliss"[2] (Pearsall).

4357–59: "These lines are omitted by Sisam as unseemly"[3] (Pearsall).

Robert Frost on "Confusio"

> The figure a poem makes. It begins in delight and ends in wisdom. . . .
> It begins in delight, it inclines to the impulse, it assumes direction
> with the first line laid down, it runs a course of lucky events, and

---

[1] The text of *NPT* quoted throughout is from the Hengwrt MS, as edited by Derek Pearsall in *A Variorum Edition of The Works of Geoffrey Chaucer*, Vol. 2, *The Canterbury Tales*, Part Nine, *The Nun's Priest's Tale* (Norman: University of Oklahoma Press, 1984).

[2] Charles A. Owen, Jr., *Pilgrimage and Storytelling in the* Canterbury Tales (Norman: University of Oklahoma Press), 137.

[3] *Chaucer: The Nun's Priest's Tale*, ed. Kenneth Sisam (Oxford: Clarendon Press, 1927).

ends in a clarification of life—not necessarily a great clarification, such as sects and cults are founded on, but in a momentary stay against confusion.... It finds its own name as it goes and discovers the best waiting for it in some final phrase at once wise and sad.[4]

Emerson Brown

If Chaucer is a great poet and not simply a wise and witty fellow who happened to write in verse, teachers and readers of Chaucer need to attend not only to what he says but to how he says it. We need to attend especially to passages where Chaucer does things that could not be done as well, or at all in prose.[5]

* * *

This essay attempts to define and illustrate "prosodic criticism" as an undeveloped and forgotten tool of close reading. It would seem to belong in the toolbox of New Criticism, but there are two problems with this: the New Critics when they entered the domain of medieval literature seemed to misplace that tool; furthermore, if their critical practice overlooked this category, so did the subsequent varieties of post-New-Criticism: even when later critics continued with their own modifications of close reading they did not propose to fill the prosodic gap. I shall argue that prosodic criticism now has an opportunity to rise from this neglect and do significant work with Chaucer's poetry, precisely because this kind of criticism has not been used up or disparaged, and, hence, once unwrapped, can be freshly applied.

My approach in this paper will be, first, diachronic, as I return to two critics, Charles Owen and Charles Muscatine, who were influential in bringing New Critical theory and practice to Chaucer studies and in beginning modern Chaucerian criticism "anew"; and, second, synchronic, as I revisit and re-analyze one of those "crucial passages" Owen had singled out from a tale that Muscatine also went on to write about with special wit and insight: the *Mulier est hominis confusio* passage from the *Nun's Priest's Tale*. A brief historical review will not discover the reasons for the omission of prosodic criticism, but it will allow us to see those places where close reading is throwing, we might say, a strong beam of light on the poetry that yet leaves some features in shadow. We can see just how the Chaucerian poesis is being defined for "modern" readers, and how an appropriate mode of close reading is demonstrated whose many virtues will yet leave unconsidered the metrical meanings that the shape and the sound of the Tale offer to our eyes and ears. I will be aiming to show how prosodic analysis can add some candlepower to the strong beam from that New Critical mode—how, at certain points, it can further illuminate, enrich, and even correct what has been said to have been seen.

---

[4]From "The Figure a Poem Makes" in Robert Frost's *Collected poems, prose & plays* (New York: Library of America, 1995), 777.

[5]"The Joy of Chaucer's Lydgate Lines", in *Essays on the Art of Chaucer's Verse*, ed. Alan T. Gaylord (New York & London: Routledge, 2001), 267.

I have cited above one of Robert Frost's best known descriptions of the writing (and then the reading) of a poem, because it links naturally to one aspect of the theme of *confusio*. It offers a semantic affinity to medieval uses of the term—not just flustered or disordered, but undone, confounded, brought to ruin. In its concept of a *momentary* stay it asserts the power of poetry to clarify—but not for much, not for long ("for once then, something"). And it does this within a metaphorical frame of prosodic description. I invoke this modern formulation at the beginning of a re-visit that will take us from the modern present to the medieval past, as we assess the charming confusions of this "crucial passage" resounding in the Nun's Priest's head and in our own.

I

Charles Owen became visible as a thinker and a resource in my early years of teaching, where, at the University of Michigan, I was given the usual variety of introductory courses, and where "close reading" was the procedure of choice. By this time, his essay had been reprinted, and in its clarity and in the enabling power of its generalizations, it was just the kind of thing the teacher of Chaucer could put into practice. By then, even though I had never taken a class where Brooks & Warren's *Understanding Poetry*[6] was the text, and did not teach a class where I assigned it, that set of methods and attitudes was pretty much what I was adopting. I was within the general discourse of New Criticism, and Charles Owen was speaking the same language.

His 1953 essay did not cite theoretical works or stick New Critical labels on everything. But his general vocabulary was familiar, as were his approaches to the poetic text. It began with a statement about complexities of narration and frame in the five passages he would discuss which "lead to a richness that defies final analysis but finds its most concentrated expression in passages that at once embody and expose the limited vision of created character and creating narrator."[7] He understands by "richness" a layering of theme and symbol that is defined by a series of related paradoxes, whose relationship to each other and to the reader are mediated by "irony." The reader discovers "multiple meanings" even as an aesthetic unity holds these in significant balance. And in certain cruxes, as Owen argues, that is, at points that are *crossings* or intersections of themes and symbols, one can find a metonymy of form and intention: in such passages the whole work can be apprehended in its tensions and textures.

It is the *Nun's Priest's Tale* that provides his fifth crucial passage—Chauntecler's concluding refutation of Pertelote's advice on dreams. Here, Owen argues, the central irony devolves from the cock's self-satisfied logic and the "deceitful flattery" he uses with his wife (with its warping of the *sentence* of the Latin

---

[6]Cleanth Brooks and Robert Penn Warren, *Understanding poetry; an anthology for college students* (New York: Holt, 1950).

[7]Charles A. Owen, Jr., "The Crucial Passages in Five of *The Canterbury Tales*: A Study in Irony and Symbol" *JEGP* 52 (1953): 294–311, cited from the reprint in *Chaucer: Modern Essays in Criticism*, ed. Edward Wagenknecht (New York: Oxford University Press,1959), 251–70, at p. 251.

he quotes), both of which reveal truths he does not recognize sufficiently to be
adequately warned when his unrecognized enemy, the fox, appears. "The cock
in effect wins the argument and forgets the dream that occasioned it" (265).
Furthermore, he has not taken to heart his maxim about *confusio*: "So far is
he from heeding the warning that the passage which contains it is full of the
uxorious passion usually attributed to Adam" (265).

"Mock-heroic" as narrative mode fits very nicely, of course, with this critical
discourse of paradox and ironies: "The exalted language and the deflating details
give the passage a quality that is typical of the whole poem" (266). Owen
indicates how the narrator, i.e., the Nun's Priest, "falls into overt criticism
of women.... at the expense of the complexity of his tale" (266). *Hominis
confusio*, Charles insists, "is man's own frailty" (267).

As I look back over this originary essay I see that the centrality of "irony"
depends upon a readerly calculation of logic and argument—upon what is dimly
descried but not understood, upon what is expected that is contradicted by experience. And I see that the reader is the one who discovers the mode of irony
in the role of metatextual "superior"-observer. But we are not yet working
with a foregrounded problematics of voice—how these issues are communicated,
heightened, embodied in a dialogics of speakers. That essay was one of the earliest Owen published; it is important for my discussion to mention two later
essays by him that were involved in some other crucial passages—rites of passage, let us say—of my own. In 1966 appeared his first piece of what I will call
prosodic criticism, "'Thy Drasty Rymyng ...'" published in *Studies in Philology* 63 (1966): 533–64. This was based on Chaucer's *Tale of Sir Thopas*; and I
took the concerns and methods there displayed as encouragement and passport
when I began my own work with the same tale.[8] The other essay, I am proud
yet sad to say, was published posthumously in the collection I have edited for
Routledge, *Essays on the Art of Chaucer's Verse*. Its title is "Chaucer's Witty
Prosody in the *General Prologue*":[9] and, after having worked through several
drafts with him, I can testify that it is a complete and fitting cap to one of the
major projects of his career.

It was always clear to Owen that prosodic considerations were broader than
"metrical analysis," and dealt with something wondrously alive, whose study
had to respond not only to patterns but to intricate reformatting of patterns
and subtle violations of norms. I quote here from his general remarks taken
from the beginning of this long essay:

> The wit in prosody ... is almost always dependent on context and
> meaning; it includes not just the humorous but the ingenious, the
> unexpectedly patterned. Rhythm in patterns of sound can even in-
> clude rhetorical and grammatical considerations. These observations

---

[8] Alan T. Gaylord, "Chaucer's Dainty 'Dogerel': The 'Elvyssh' Prosody of Sir Thopas,"
Studies in the Age of Chaucer 1 (1979): 83–104; "The Moment of *Sir Thopas*: Towards a
New Look at Chaucer's Language," *Chaucer Review* 16 (1982): 311–29; "The 'Miracle' of *Sir
Thopas*," *Studies in the Age of Chaucer* 6 (1984): 65–84.

[9] Charles A. Owen, Jr., "Chaucer's Witty Prosody in the General Prologue," in *Essays on
the Art of Chaucer's Verse* (see note 5 above), 339–78.

> have special relevance for poetry like Chaucer's, with its avoidance
> of system and its tendency to test meaning.   (339)

In his maturity as a critic, then, Owen would elect the prosodic avenue towards the text, using the notion of "wit" before "irony." In so doing, he stepped into the small but lively society of those who, like Emerson Brown, insisted on the central importance of the sound-shape of Chaucer's verse.

II

There is an interesting set of connections between Owen's readings of the *Nun's Priest's Tale* and those of Charles Muscatine, whose *Chaucer and the French Tradition* was judged, when it appeared in 1957, as one of the earliest, the most thorough, and perhaps the best, applications of New Criticism to the poetry of Chaucer.[10] The "Crucial Passages" essay was cited in Muscatine's notes; and again, when Owen revisited his thoughts on the *Nun's Priest's Tale* in his later book, *Pilgrimage and Storytelling in the* Canterbury Tales (1977), he noted there that "this reading of the Nun's Priest's Tale owes a special debt to Charles Muscatine" (231, n. 18).

In his Introduction, Muscatine stated that his study would

> provide data toward the theory that the perennial significance of
> great poems depends on the multiplicity of meanings they interre-
> late. One generation finds the *Troilus and Criseyde* a grave and
> serious tragedy. Another prizes it for its delicate comedy. Stylistic
> analysis will show that both of these attitudes are inherent in the
> poem, that they compose its irony.   (9)

He went on to observe: "Our own generation has necessarily its peculiar sensibility. To use such terms as 'irony,' 'ambiguity,' 'tension,' and 'paradox' in describing Chaucer's poetry is to bring to the subject our typical mid-century feeling for an unresolved dialectic" (9–10). Indeed, those are the terms generally seen as characterizing New Criticism, and "stylistic analysis" is the New Critical practice that applies them. It is part of my argument that for a variety of reasons, now mostly obscured, the New Critical legacy of "close reading" almost totally ignored prosodic criticism, and continues to do so. For the peculiar sensibility of "our generation," the one now marching into the twenty-first century, is less hostile to, than heedless of that poetic dimension I call Prosody. I shall be arguing that there remains plenty of room in contemporary "stylistic analysis" for prosodic analysis; and to sharpen and further define what I mean and what I aim at, I am going to move from Owen's early essay to Muscatine's, both because it can stand in for Owen's at most points, and because it more clearly represents a wide-ranging project of bringing modern stylistic analysis to the medieval verse of Chaucer. Furthermore, although what I shall be proposing does not appear in Owen's early essay, it does appear with major effect in his

---

[10]Charles Muscatine, *Chaucer and the French Tradition: A Study in Style and Meaning* (Berkeley and Los Angeles: University of California Press, 1957).

later work, so rather than developing a critique of his pioneer essay, I hope to go beyond it in a direction I believe he would approve.

In what follows, then, I am going to identify four aspects of Muscatine's criticism of Chaucer that I find illuminating and enjoyable, even as I propose certain ways I feel they need to be augmented and modified.

1. Generalizations about "style." I begin with the first of a series of economical generalizations which introduce Muscatine's discussion: "[The *Nun's Priest's Tale*] is above all brilliant, varied, a virtuoso performance.... [I]t fittingly serves to cap all of Chaucer's poetry. And so I put it last" (238). Yet how shall "performance" be defined, be illustrated? There are really only glints and flashes in the course of Muscatine's discussion.

   For example: "The shifting style and the succession of topics never rest long enough to serve a single view or a single doctrine or an unalterable judgment" (242). In this kind of discourse, the large category of "style" at once enables criticism and limits it. The cataloguing of techniques and effects, the identification of artistic choices in handling material, the description of diction and rhetoric—all these are comprehended in stylistic analysis. But they are elements of literary dissection or taxonomy. They identify theme, image, metaphor; *prosody* they do not identify. Whereas I want to gain a more immediate sense of "performance," not as an abstract theory of "the subject," but as an up-close description of events unrolling in time which are acted out in metrical space. That is a poetry that moves and breathes; that is Prosody.

2. Vivid metaphorical generalizations. Muscatine is always interesting, and usually authoritative, when he discusses French works and the French tradition behind Chaucer's poetry. When he comes to the connection between the *Nun's Priest's Tale* and the *Roman de Renart*, everything he says is worth heeding; it is what he does *not* say that is frustrating: "The humor of the *Nun's Priest's Tale* does not come at all as near to singeing its subjects; but this is the difference between the skirmishes preceding the war and the festive fireworks commemorating it in peace" (238). The sentence is an entertaining illustration of what this kind of discussion and its power of generalization can produce: the multifaceted figure, the metaphorical description. The "performance" is to be understood as fireworks celebrating the successful termination of hostilities, satire enfolded in carnival. Yet enjoy as we do the *critic's* performance, how much closer does that take us towards comprehending the performance in the poem?

3. Paradox, not Prosody. It could be replied that fireworks are best enjoyed from a distance. Up-close work seems to carry the risk of humorless dissection, or of being exploded along with the joke. As Muscatine writes, "The tale will betray with laughter any too-solemn scrutiny of its naked argument." Or as he will say a little later: "Unlike fable, the *Nun's Priest's Tale* does not so much make true and solemn assertions about life as it tests truths and tries out solemnities. If you are not careful, it will try

out your solemnity too; it is here, doubtless, trying out mine" (242). And he elaborates:

> The tale has recently been welcomed into the Marriage Group, but it says little about marriage that it does not unsay. With what marriage, indeed, can it be said to deal? The marriage of Chauntecleer in the varying lights of the poem is courtly and bourgeois, monogamous and polygamous, incestuous, and unsolemnized, a relationship of paramours.   (238)

More brilliant generalizing, with the familiar list of binaries, although the end of the series extends these into a list of paradoxes not all in pairs. We are a little farther from the actual performance, and the list serves to remind us of various moments in the performance, particular colors or emphases, which we can recall separately. But we are still removed from "a" performance. And I would add, that the sense I am proposing of prosodic performance is something vastly different from "naked argument." I am after the full-feathered poem.

4. "The Spirit of the Poem." I quote finally what might be called a "crucial passage" from Charles Muscatine, for it illustrates the wit of his writing, even as it brings together the terms and themes which, as he said, pleases the modern generation:

> the whole spirit of this poem is to erase or at least to overleap the boundaries: animal and human, fiction and truth severally join and separate, change partners and flirt here. The one constancy in the poem is this shifting of focus, the Chaucerian multiple perspective which itself virtually constitutes the theme. (239)

There is much to build on in this passage, and I would begin by proposing an annex to what Muscatine terms the "spirit of the poem." For as it is used here, the phrase addresses itself to an overall representation of the performance without addressing it up-close as something that lives and moves in a temporal dimension. These words amount to memories of the fireworks the day after the show. I do like the metaphors that provide a sense of the motility of the performance, with the double notions of dancing and looking through the viewfinder (what he will later call "complicated optics," 241), but they function for me as invitations to the dance rather than the dance itself. The "spirit of the poem," I would think, must include the way it *breathes.*

III

As an analytic category, "breathing" takes us into the essence of a poetic line and poetic measure, even as it normally contains more than a single sound or syllable; and it is the foundation of what our imagination perceives to be a voice. Thus I re-define "the spirit of the poem" as *the realization of a spoken performance by the imagination.*

If we stand at this "crucial passage" and pay attention to the many crossings we can see, we can entertain a metaphor of a stream of poetry, with ourselves at a ford. In which case, it is time to put our feet into the water.

Still within the metaphor of the fording of a stream, we must at once feel the current, which is the lively force of the breath and the progression of the verse that rides in and upon that breath.

The stream of breath in our crucial passage is strong and sustained, and the lines should be imagined as forceful but not violent, carrying easily several topics or objects, one visible, the other submerged. The strength comes from the will of the rooster and from his affections, in sentences that announce his resolve concerning his destiny. The visible parts are his "conclusiouns," and the submerged are his motives and his understandings.

I do not want to be trapped by the metaphor of the stream, so will leave it, even though there is a temptation to add, that in the middle of the stream would seem to stand the rock of *confusio.* But I do not think *confusio* is a rock, nor do I take it as dangerous or portentously thematic where it stands, even though it is foregrounded by means of its unusual riming and its prominent position in the only closed couplet in the passage. The final point I would make about the stream is that in our reading we should give ourselves up to the measured flow of the verse and try to have our analytic descriptions be answerable to the force and fluctuations of that carrier current. After breathing should come the categories of rhythm and measure, in which riming plays an important part. From here on, we must immerse ourselves in—do more than wade through—what we read. So we return to the master-metaphor of performance, the imagined sound of a voice and its sentences.

This "crucial passage" includes the usual forms of courteous address, but now announces and no longer argues: for it is Chauntecler's intent to close off what he had been saying and carry the two of them into calmer waters. It is a "carrying" that intends to ravish Pertelote away from any further debate, not without betraying within its performance of lordly omnipotence some signs of pettiness, of personal anxiety—as the prosody discloses.

The transition lines that precede this passage ride on a long breath that permits no pause:

> "Shortly I seye as for conclusioun
> That I shal han of this avysioun   4342
> Adversitee, and I seye forthermoor
> That I ne telle of laxatyves no stoor,
> For they ben venymes, I woot it wel;   4345
> I hem deffie, I love hem never a del."

Pearsall's lighter pointing at line 4343—the comma in place of Benson's semi-colon, is appropriate (and I would prefer a comma at the end of 4345 for the same reasons): the momentum of the progression from philosophy to medicine must not be broken, though the effect may make us wonder, in fact, if the second conclusion is of greater personal concern to Chauntecler than the first. He means, "I will now sum up briefly," but the drive of line 4341 is projected with wily force. Note the rhetoric of closure which links the strong "shortly" to the resonant "conclusióun," with its strong stress in the final syllable, riming with "avysióun" in the next line but then surging past line-end to put full force on what is concluded: "adversitée"—and the strong stress on its fourth syllable is enhanced by its placement within a regular series of alternating stresses—perfect "iambic pentameter," as one might say. The rhetorical cesura that follows can only be imagined as a quick gulp of breath, for what comes next is to feel like a rising point—"forthermoor"—not something lamely tacked on.

Perhaps subliminal in its effect is the insistent pecking of Chauntecler's ego: a redundancy of "I"s fills this passage with at least one first-person pronoun per line, most in normally unstressed (thesis) positions, but one ("that Í shal han") in the arsis position—making it clearer what (or who) the subject of this discourse really is.

If Chauntecler seems simply to be saying (just like a man?), "they're nasty things, those herbs, and I want nothing to do with them," his rhetoric assumes a posture of Embattled Rooster: for his most forceful verb comes from "defiance," the formal act of renouncing trust (OF *des-fier*) and a covenant relationship in and with one's lord. The placement of "I hem deffie" has the same force, the same placement before a rhetorical cesura, as line 4343's "adversitee." No one will lord it over *him*: a laxative will not be forced down *his* gullet.

Note, however, that what we may smile at as heroic hyperbole seems to be empirically based: for modern scholars are largely in agreement that if he took everything Pertelote proposed it would probably kill him (Pearsall 170-1, 198; Benson 938).

Chauntecler is almost but not quite telling her she is a poisoner, but the *not quite* is important. For one thing, we cannot be sure whether he knows the pharmacological details of each herb, or just doesn't like their tastes and their effects: a purgative is not necessarily a poison. And second, he is not starting a quarrel, he is correcting a misunderstanding—on her part, of course—and "concluding" his final response to her arguments.

So it is appropriate that, as a new beginning, he should now hasten to assure Pertelote of his love and regard:

> "Now let us speke of myrthe and stynte al this."   4347

In reproaching him for being unmanned by a bad dream, his wife had urged him to "Be myrie, housbonde!" (4158), and so he will be, but on his own terms. He will praise not her brains but her beauty, from which his mirth arises: "so have I blys." *Blys* is one of the cluster of words that carry the theme of *solas*, though its introduction here is in a relatively unmarked collocation that (lightly) means, "God help me"—that is, "so may I win heavenly bliss"—and is at once a prosodic spacer (for meter and rime) and a means of phatic emphasis. He is on his way to speaking of her beauty as God's gift to him and his *corage*; for he does not need her laxatives to be restored to true manhood, all he needs is to look at the irresistible scarlet about her eyes: "It maketh al my drede for to dyen." This is argument by flattery, as Owen and others have reminded us, but it hearkens back to the very beginning of their exchanges where she had reproached him for un-husbandlike cowardice ("Have ye no mannes herte and han a berd?" [4110]). The strong "now" is a sign of his sure hand, the foregrounded "myrthe" of his sexually energized courtesy, and the "stynte" of his firmness (i.e., no more need for debate): these strong beats comprise the assured pace of the master of this discourse.

It is important to notice the emotional impetus that carries over from Chauntecler's announced "conclusioun": for it becomes clear that he has not at all "stinted" the previous discussion. Feel the rhetorical energy of the following:

> "For also siker as *In principio*,"—

whose colloquial tone is accurately represented by Susan Cavanaugh, the editor of the Benson text of the *Nun's Priest's Tale*, as "It's as sure as Gospel truth (that) ...."; a similar formulation appears, with a bit more irony glistening on it, in the Priest's later words:

> This storie is also trewe, I undertake,
> As is the book of Launcelot de Lake   4402
> That wommen holde in ful gret reverence.

The "for" in "For also siker" is an important function-word, as most of Chaucer's logical connectives carry meaning even when they seem illogical. We may translate, "the reason I lose my fear when I gaze at your beauty is ...."; and so:

> "*Mulier est hominis confusio*—
> Madame, the sentence of this Latyn is   4355
> 'Womman is mannes joye and al his blys.'"

We stand at the crossings of the crux. In one stroke, Chauntecler has blithely illustrated his assurance—he is not confused about anything—even as he has created an echoing conundrum of multifarious confusions.

Prosodically, the ringing out of a whole line of Latin changes the texture of the discourse. Line 4354 is very unlike the glossing couplet that follows, for although the Latin has eleven syllables they fall in no pattern of alternating stress, and would sound like this: /xx x /xx x /xx, with the multisyllabic words establishing their separate weightiness by a kind of dactylic iteration (note Pearsall's comment on the handling of the Latin at this point in the manuscript). It is a macaronic moment, an assertion of authority that would sound strange and estranging to Chauntecler's lovely hen amidst her simples— until he unwraps it to discover a compliment as hyperbolic as his previous defiance was extravagant.

Of course this is a piece of self-satisfied irony and, at the literal level, a flagrant mistranslation; Pearsall's Variorum commentary takes us through all the responses of the critics (200–1), including this epitome of irony: "Owen makes the neat point that both text and mistranslation are the same: woman is man's confusion *because* she is his joy and bliss" (201).

But not quite so fast. There is more to consider that stems from the colloquial quality I have mentioned: for as Pearsall's notes make clear, the Latin *sentence* belongs to a monkish tradition of misogyny, with no real scriptural roots. It is like a line from a university drinking song making its way out of the *Carmina Burana* to reappear in the kinds of books Jankyn would want to collect and read to his Wife; and it belongs to the same level of diction as the use of "In Principio" as a popular charm and devotional cliché. Its prosodic wit arises not from any original diction, since "joy" and "bliss" are frequent doublets scattered in collocations throughout Chaucer's works; and even the rime is muted: *principio* and *confusio* are not perfect rimes (there is a better one in the Friar's portrait); nor is there thematic richness in riming *is* with *blys*—it is the startling appearance and cunning placement of *confusio*, the smiling impudence of the translation, that makes the whole sequence glow.

The lesson here is subtler, perhaps, in that its apparent aim is to produce a glow of joy and bliss, but its real motive is one of amorous polemic. Chauntecler is still recovering from Pertelote's forceful attack on his masculinity (4098–4110); her argument *ad hominem* is now being countered (in his mind) with a *force majeure*, an argument *ad mulierem* (or *ad gallinam*). She had challenged him to be a man, and he will be manly all right, reaching for a man's easy support in anti-feminism and falling back on his ready supply of testosterone. The point here is that although his program had begun with extremely bookish and clerical insistence on those authorities greater than the schoolboy's Cato—

> "By God, men may in olde bokes rede
> Of many a man moore of auctoritee   4165
> Than evere Caton was, so mote I thee,
> That al the revers seyn of his sentence...."

—it now sinks to self-serving academic folklore. And in its new shape it combines charm with malice; that is, the mis-translation, after all, purports to offer her his learning as an avowal of his love: this is what you women are, *all* our bliss. Yet what does the reversed Latin say, related to their particular situation? In spite of the Adamic and theological tendencies of that *confusio*, it has not been temptation or damnation that Pertelote has proffered; no, she has almost killed him with kindness. Thus he would seem to be saying to himself, if we did what you counseled we would be ruined [a general meaning for *confusio*]; but we are strong enough and smart enough to turn your unwitting venoms into sweetness. In such a buried sentence is found the greyn of his folly.

Into sweetness, into *solas*—for that is how Chauntecler reverses her *sentence*, as he goes on to say:

> "For whan I feel a-nyght youre softe syde,
> Al be it that I may nat on yow ryde
> For that oure perche is maad so narwe, allas,
> I am so ful of joye and of solas   4360
> That I deffie bothe swevene and dreem."

As it is placed syntactically, *solas* describes his most intense state and becomes his personal realization of *blys*. Yet what an extraordinary sequence this is! His masculine perspective on joy and bliss is of course sexual, which should come as no surprise, least of all to Pertelote; yet his venereal yearnings are here deferred and displaced. That is, even though he cannot "ryde" her as a cock, it is "whan I feel a-nyght youre softe syde" that he is filled with *solas*, filled so full "that I deffie bothe swevene and dreem."

Note that this long sentence has again begun with a "For." It is important to see the logic here, the last phase of what is now less an argument than a *captatio benevolentiae*, a kind of *sentence* from the whole fowl, the final words of one who has been misunderstood by a lover, has made it right, and now gathers the other into his embrace. So now, he once more stands defiant, but not *at* her but *with* her; she is being put in her place, which is close at his side.

Solas as I pointed out a long time ago, has always included the idea of some kind of comfort in its meanings, usually (but not always) the creature-kind.[11] And what Chauntecler is saying is that the comfort of Pertelote's presence, her soft pressure against him on their perch, gives him all the strength he needs to "defy," not laxatives now, but the fears of night and the portents of dreams. He does not recant his argument that the dreams are telling the truth, but he does not fear what will surely come. With this loving compliment, then, he has completely reversed, or "bouleversed," her earliest criticism of him as a faint-hearted coward.

At this point the careful reader of the whole fascicle may note an intertextual irony. For Chaucer's own tale in prose, the Melibee, had presented the moral allegory of a wife named Prudence who gave good counsel to Melibeus and saved him from confusion. I use the term advisedly: in order to be listened to, Prudence must first convince her husband that women can be good, can be discreet, can be wise, and can help their husbands. Near the end of an argument which completely convinces him, she says this:

> And mooreover, whan oure Lord hadde creat Adam, oure forme
> fader, he seyde in this wise:/ 'It is nat good to been a man al-
> loone; make we to hym an helpe semblable to hymself.'/ Heere may
> ye se that if that wommen were nat goode, and hir conseils goode
> and profitable,/ oure Lord God of hevene wolde nevere han wroght
> hem, ne called hem help of man, but rather confusioun of man./
> (1103–5, *Riverside* edition.)

In effect, through all his tumbling conclusions and his reversings, Chauntecler has re-discovered the theology of the helpmeet, inadvertently refuting a second time his Latin *sentence*.

It is a sweet moment, its argument at a calm point at the edge of dawn, with Chauntecler's performance of masculinity nearly at rest. What meanings are to be found here are muffled, since one creature's understanding has been played

---

[11] *"Sentence* and *Solaas* in Fragment VII of the *Canterbury Tales*: Harry Bailly as Horseback Editor," *PMLA* 82 (1967): 226–35, p. 230

with, and the other's has been dimmed with self-regard. Yet there is wisdom, and there is sadness—the end of the passage is wise for its balance, but sad for its but momentary stay against confusion.

Daybreak will come, Chauntecler will resume his offices with regal vigor, and Pertelote will not be heard from again until she shrieks with mock-epic alarm at the catastrophe of her husband's reckless vanity. Confusion will break upon the barnyard like Muscatine's fireworks. Yet (for this is a comedy, not a tragedy) all will not quite be lost. And there will be indeterminate acres of *moralitee* to be harvested.

IV

My application of prosodic criticism to fifteen lines from the middle of the *Nun's Priest's Tale* can only serve, at best, as a preliminary report towards the great gathering and sifting of *fruyt* and *chaf* at the end. If it is a crucial passage, what it reveals is a style of performance rather than a set of syllogisms, wise or foolish, that try to stack up as the "best" sentences worthy of a dinner at the Tabard. Yet even this short exercise offers some additions and some corrections to that body of criticism displayed in the commentary of Pearsall's Variorum edition.

1. Starting close to home: it is not correct to say, "The cock in effect wins the argument and forgets the dream that occasioned it" (Owen, "The Crucial Passages," 265). When we get inside that argument, it turns into performance, one that does not so much "win" an argument as overwhelm it; furthermore, Chauntecler has not forgotten the dream, but rather has lost his fear of it. He has not taken Pertelote's advice; he has taken her presence, not her herbs, as his comfort.

2. What Muscatine described as "our typical mid-century feeling for an unresolved dialectic" seems to have developed, as post-modern developed from modern, into a passionate predilection fifty years later for authorless works of shimmering indeterminacy. *Mirabile dictu*, some of that shows up in our crucial passage, if in its own sweet way. There are at least three authors at work in its performance, and we must count the gravitational attraction of Pertelote as another force, if not an actively continuing voice. And to the question, how much confusion is realized and then held off by means of the prosody in this passage? the answer must come: a delicious amount, a comic and melancholy amount, poised at a momentary pause—rough, tender, ambivalent, fugitive, ironic. One long breath, trembling towards insight.

3. With regard to *sentence* and *solas*, the thematic armature of the fascicle that is Fragment VII, the (cautionary) lesson has to do with a surfeit of binaries and the fatuous sounding of "sentences." There is only one truly resounding *sentence* in this passage, foregrounded by the prosody, and all the game is to become aware of how, as it reverses other sentences, it reverses itself. Yet it is comfortable to see how this proceeds, for the

argument that flows through the lines is not one that devours meaning. The sport is not the elusions of Truth, but the illusions of the Declarers of Truth. "If you are not careful, it will try out your solemnity ...; it is here, doubtless, trying out mine."

We are of the tribe of Chauntecler, trying to sing amidst bad dreams, and grateful for a little friendly pressure on the side. It is our fate to be the more foolish, the more we asseverate. It is likely to be our mother-wit more than our profundity of learning that will save us, not to mention the grace of God. But as Emerson Brown would surely say, Taketh the fruyt, and lat the chaf be stille.[12]

---

[12] An earlier version of this paper was delivered at a session of the Medieval Institute at Kalamazoo, May, 2000. I wish to thank my colleague, Peter Travis (*NPT*-Meister), for his helpful reading of an earlier draft.

Reading Chaucer's Latin Aloud

Michael W. Twomey

Introduction

Anyone who has read Chaucer aloud as a prelector (reader before an audience), or taught Chaucer's pronunciation to others, has had to confront the problem of how to pronounce the many Latin words, phrases, and sentences in Chaucer's works.[1] It is obviously incorrect to assume that Chaucer's Latin pronunciation was either the restored classical or the ecclesiastical style, by which for example *vincit* in the General Prologue's "*amor vincit omnia*" (I 162) is either restored classical ['wɪnkɪt] or ecclesiastical ['vɪntʃɪt]. How, then, do we derive rules for pronouncing Chaucer's Latin?

By all accounts, the pronunciation of medieval Latin in England was influenced by the pronunciation of the vernacular—i.e., Anglo-Saxon before the Norman Conquest, Middle English and Anglo-Norman French after the Conquest, and Middle English from the fourteenth century, when English superseded French as the dominant vernacular.[2] The situation is not entirely as simple as that, however. Complicating it is the presence late into the Middle Ages of Latin verse attempting to follow the classical rules of scansion (e.g., John Gower's Latin verses in the *Confessio Amantis*), which indicates a knowledge of quantitative distinctions and possibly of other features of classical

---

[1] I adopt the term "prelector" from Joyce Coleman, *Public Reading and the Reading Public in Late Medieval England and France*, Cambridge Studies in Medieval Literature 29 (Cambridge: Cambridge University Press, 1996), especially chapters 1, 2, 4 and 7, which discuss theory, terminology, medieval evidence, and non-Chaucerian medieval English literature, respectively. Coleman adopts the term "prelection" (p. 35) from John of Salisbury's *Metalogicon*, and she uses "prelector" to refer to someone reading aloud before an audience.

[2] The scheme of Latin pronunciation in England that is used in the present essay is based on the following: A. G. Rigg, "Orthography and Pronunciation," in F. A. C. Mantello and A. G. Rigg, eds., *Medieval Latin: An Introduction and Bibliographical Guide* (Washington, D. C.: Catholic University of America Press, 1996), 79–82; A. G. Rigg, "Anglo-Latin," in Timothy J. McGee, with A. G. Rigg and David N. Klausner, eds., *Singing Early Music: The Pronunciation of European Languages in the Late Middle Ages and the Renaissance* (Bloomington, Ind.: Indiana UP, 1996), 46–61; A. G. Rigg, *A History of Anglo-Latin Literature, 1066–1422* (Cambridge: Cambridge University Press, 1992), "Appendix: Metre," 313–29; W. Sidney Allen, *Vox Latina: The Pronunciation of Classical Latin*, 2nd ed. (Cambridge: Cambridge University Press, 1978; repr. 1999), Appendix B, "The Pronunciation of Latin in England," 102–10; G. Herbert Fowler, "Notes on the Pronunciation of Medieval Latin in England," *History* NS 22 (1937): 97–109. Rigg, "Anglo-Latin," 47–56, discusses several forms of evidence that we can use to reconstruct the pronunciation of Latin in England: rhyme, alliteration, spelling, loanwords, comparative analysis, post-Reformation authorities, and modern legal Latin (which reflects post-Reformation, post-Great-Vowel-Shift pronunciation).

pronunciation.[3] Rigg posits two styles of Latin pronunciation—one, more formal, that aspired to classical norms, and the other, less formal, that was pulled into the orbit of vernacular norms—but the distinction between the two styles is chiefly vowel quantity ("Orthography and Pronunciation," 80–81).

The problem lies in determining just what the influence of the vernacular would have been. Because of the Norman Conquest, England lay along the fault line that divided northern and southern pronunciation of Latin—that is, Germanic-speaking countries vs. Romance-speaking countries. Before the Norman Conquest, England was in the Germanic camp. Under the apparent influence of the Germanic Stress Rule, the Anglo-Saxons would lengthen vowels in the initial syllable of disyllabic words such as *pater* whose classical pronunciation calls for a short vowel. Under the influence of their own vernacular practices, the Anglo-Saxons would pronounce *g* before a front vowel as a semivowel [y] and they would voice intervocalic *s* to [z].[4] After the Conquest, when Latin was taught by French schoolmasters, French pronunciations began to be introduced. For example, *g* before a front vowel now became the affricate [dʒ] as in Modern English *gem* and *gin*.[5] Despite this French influence on Anglo-Latin, for the twelfth and thirteenth centuries, it is not always clear whether to use Middle English or Anglo-Norman pronunciation for Anglo-Latin. For example, the Latin relative pronoun *qui* might be French [kiː] or English/classical Latin [kwiː].

From the fifteenth century through the Reformation the situation is also complex. During the period of the Great Vowel Shift, which was under way by the mid fifteenth century, Latin long vowels must have kept pace with English long vowels, since at the end of the shift the Latin long vowels are pronounced as English long vowels, i.e., as in "old Latin" and legal Latin. For example, after the shift, *"Deus hic"* in the *Summoner's Tale* (III 1770) would be pronounced [ˈdiːʊs haik]. But the Great Vowel Shift is only one of several influences on English pronunciation of Latin in this period. In the sixteenth century, the Reformation dispersed English Catholics to various Continental lands where they would have acquired Continental Latin pronunciation, including the reformed classical pronunciation promoted by Erasmus.[6] When these Catholics brought

---

[3]Latin scansion is summarized in Rigg, *A History*, "Appendix: Metre," 313–29. An excellent study of Gower's verses in particular is Siân Echard and Claire Fanger, *The Latin Verses in the Confessio Amantis: An Annotated Translation*, with a preface by A. G. Rigg (East Lansing: Colleagues Press, 1991).

[4]The Germanic Stress Rule describes the tendency in Germanic languages to stress the initial syllable in polysyllabic words. See Roger Lass, "Phonology and Morphology," in *The Cambridge History of the English Language*, ed. Richard M. Hogg and Norman Blake, 2 vols. (Cambridge: Cambridge University Press, 1992) 2: 23–155, here citing 85–90. On Anglo-Saxon pronunciation of Latin, see Allen, *Vox Latina*, "Appendix B," 102, and Fowler, "Notes on the Pronunciation," 104.

[5]Allen, *Vox Latina*, "Appendix B," 102, and Fowler, "Notes on the Pronunciation," 100, 104.

[6]Erasmus, *De recta Latini Graecique sermonis pronuntiatione* (1528). Erasmus was responding not to the Counter-Reformation but to the linguistic confusion resulting from the plethora of Latin pronunciations in use on the Continent by the early sixteenth century. On the rise and fall of Erasmus's reformed pronunciation at Cambridge University in the sixteenth

their Continental Latin back to England with them under Queen Mary, there would have been a number of competing systems in play.

We can ascertain the Latin pronunciation of fourteenth-century England with a little more certainty than we can ascertain the Latin pronunciation of the periods before or afterwards, and the end of the fourteenth century, the period of Chaucer's literary career, is the period of greatest certainty because by this time English as the dominant vernacular is the chief vernacular influence. At around 1400, the Great Vowel Shift had not yet begun—or at least we are fairly sure that Chaucer's conservative pronunciation does not give evidence of it.[7]

Since the *Canterbury Tales* are the usual vehicle for teaching Chaucer in schools, the *Canterbury Tales* are particularly useful for glossing the pronunciation of Chaucer's Latin for teachers and other prelectors. This guide to pronunciation in the *Tales* follows Rigg's summary of Latin pronunciation in medieval England, "Anglo-Latin," 49–56, to which the reader is directed for a fuller explanation of rules and caveats. Illustrations are taken from the *Riverside Chaucer*. Since it is based on an edited text, the following pronunciation guide does not consider manuscript variants. Transcriptions use the International Phonetic Alphabet and are approximate. Parameters:

- Only words that occur in the Latin of the *CT* are glossed, which means that certain sounds occurring elsewhere in Anglo-Latin, even in Chaucer's other works, are excluded. Sounds unattested in the *CT* are noted where relevant in the General Rules and in the footnotes.

- Throughout it is presumed that Chaucer's lines are metrically regular. How scansion may suggest Latin pronunciation and stress is discussed in section 3. Other special cases are discussed in section 4.

- Long and short vowels from Classical Latin do not simply carry over into Chaucer's pronunciation. For general rules describing vowel quantity, see below, section 2.

- Although they may in fact be scribal rather than authorial, textual divisions from the manuscripts and used in editions have been included nevertheless, since in reading Chaucer aloud, a prelector might use them as transitions. Such passages are not numbered in the *Riverside* edition; here they are identified by the line before which they occur.

- The italicized Latin words and phrases highlighted by the editors of the *Riverside* edition are not presumed to constitute the complete set of Chaucerian Latin in the *CT*. Other Latin words, chiefly names, occurring in their Latin forms may very well be considered Latin rather than English. Since in these cases it is not possible to distinguish Latin from

---

century via John Cheke, the first Regius Professor of Greek, and Thomas Smith, the first Regius Professor of Civil Law, see Allen, *Vox Latina*, "Appendix B," 103–05.

[7]See Jeremy Smith, *An Historical Study of English: Function, Form, and Change* (London and New York: Routledge, 1996), 86–111.

English forms, and in any case there would often be no difference in pronunciation, additional words from this category are occasionally included here without comment.

Abbreviations

C	consonant
c-	initial consonant
-c-	medial consonant
-c	final consonant
CL	Classical Latin
CT	*Canterbury Tales*
ME	Middle English
PDE	Present-Day English
V	vowel

Symbols

' is placed before a syllable receiving primary stress
· is equivalent to a diaeresis, indicating syllable boundary between vowels
ː is placed after a long vowel to indicate length

1. Consonants

General rules

- The consonants *b, d, f, l, m, n, p, r, t, x, z* have their CL (= ME) values.

- Other consonants and consonant combinations are illustrated below, in Table 1.

- Influence of front vowels and liquids: *c, g, sc* are "hard" [k, g, sk] before back vowels *a, o, u,* and liquids *l, r*; but "soft" [s, ʤ, s] before front vowels *e, i.* Hence *Significavit* (GP I 662), *corpus* (ShipT VII 435), *Cupiditas* (PardPro VI 334), *Claudius* (MkT VII 2335), *Cresus* (MkT VII 2727); *interrogate* (ParsT X 75), *Nabugodonosor* (MkT VII 2145), *Augustinus* (ParsT X 754); but *celo* (ParsT X 597), *vincit* (GP I 162); *Angelus ad virginem* (MilT I 3216); *Scithice* (KnT before I 859). Other combinations are unattested in the *CT*.

Illustrations of consonants: See Table 1, pp. 186–87.

2. Vowels

General rules

- Long vowels occurring prior to and in antepenults are shortened, e.g., [trɪsˈtɪsɪ·a] for CL *trīstitia*.

- Vowels directly preceding consonant pairs and clusters are shortened, e.g., [ˈsapɪ·ɛns] for CL *sapiēns*.

- Short vowels occurring in the open-syllables of disyllabic words are length-ened, e.g., ['pɑːtɛr] for CL *pater*.[8]

Illustrations of stressed and unstressed vowels, diphthongs and diaereses: See Table 2, pp. 188–89.

3. Pronunciations inferred from scansion

KnT I 1785, etc. *Benedicite(e)*: In order to preserve the scansion of Chaucer's iambic, ten-syllable line, the ejaculation *benedicite!* must usually have three syllables rather than the full five syllables it has in I 1785. The final *e* must be pronounced [eː] rather than [iː] in order to rhyme with [eː] in the English words with which it is paired in couplets. The double *ee* spelling, adopted in editions from scribal practice in Chaucer manuscripts, as well as the "mascu-line" syllable that ends the line, also prompt the prelector to lengthen the vowel; hence, ['bɛndɪsteː], as suggested by the spelling *bendiste* in Tr 1.780. In FrT III 1456, therefore, *sumonour* is probably disyllabic: "'A!' quod this somonour, 'benedicite! What sey ye?'"

MLT II 93 Methamorphosios woot what I mene: In order for the line to scan, *Methamorphosios* must be stressed on the second, fourth, and sixth sylla-bles; thus: "*Methámorphósiós* woot whát I méne." By the rule of the antepenult primary stress would fall on the fourth syllable, while secondary stress would be on the first syllable. One can also pronounce *Methamorphosios* as two dactyls.

WBPro III 608 I hadde the beste quoniam myghte be: Strict metrical practice would require *quoniam* to be disyllabic, i.e., ['kɔnjam]; thus: "I hádde the béste quóniam mýghte bé." For two reasons, it seems more likely that trisyl-labic ['kɔnɪ·am] is correct. One is the importance of preserving the association with the French slang term *cony*, which ends in [ɪ]. The other is that Chaucer does not always follow strict metrical practice. In this same line, disyllabic *hadde* must fit the space of a monosyllable, and even so, the line ends on a strong stress rather than a weak one: I hádde the béste quóniam mýghte bé.

SumT III 2075 Syngeth *Placebo* and 'I shal, if I kan': Scansion requires treating *syngeth* as one syllable and stressing *Placebo* on the first syllable; thus: "Syng'th Plácebó and 'Í shal, if I kán." Classical pronunciation would stress the penult, which is long, i.e., *placēbō*. So also MerT IV 1476, "Of whíche that óon was cléped Plácebo," and so presumably ParsT X 617, "Flatereres been the develes chapelleyns, that syngen evere Plácebo."[9]

4. Special cases

See p. 190 below.

---

[8]This rule follows Middle English Open-Syllable Lengthening (MEOSL), which began in the thirteenth century and was still under way in Chaucer's time. See Smith, *Historical Study of English*, 96–98.

[9]Shifting the stress to the first syllable of a classical name is quite normal for Chaucer; e.g., *Alcyone* in BD 76, 220, etc.; *Achilles* in CT II 198 and VII 3148; *Medea* in CT I 1944; but not *Antiochus* in MkT VII 257. I am grateful to Winthrop Wetherbee for this observation.

Table 1: Consonants *(continued on facing page)*

c + a,o,u	[k]	*corpus*	ˈkɔrpʊs
c + e,i	[s]	*vincit*	ˈvɪnsɪt
cc + e,i	[ks]	*accidia*	akˈsɪdɪ·a
ch	[k]⁹	*Anthiochus*	anˈtɪ·ɔkʊs
ci + V	[sɪ]¹⁰	*tristicia*	trɪsˈtɪsɪ·a
-c	[k]	*hic*	ɪk
-d	[t]¹¹	*ad*	at
g + a,o,u	[g]¹²	*interrogate*	ɪntɛrɔˈgaːte
g + e,i	[ʤ]	*virginem*	ˈvɪrʤɪnɛm
gn	[ŋgn]	*Significavit*	sɪŋgnɪfɪˈkaːvɪt
h	[-]¹³	*hic*	ɪk
i-/j- + V	[ʤ]¹⁴	*Judicum*	ˈʤʏdɪkʊm
Ih/Jh	[ʤ]	in *Jhesus*	ˈʤɛːzʊs
ph	[f]¹⁵	*Phebus*	ˈfɛbʊs
qu + a,e,i	[kw]	*quam*	kwɔm
qu + o,u	[k]	*quoniam*	ˈkɔnɪam
V + s + V	[z]	*Jhesus*	ˈʤɛːzʊs
sc + e,i	[s]	*Scithero*	ˈsɪtɛro
-ti + V	[sɪ]¹⁶	*Penitentie*	pɛnɪˈtɛnsie
th	[t]	*Scithice*	ˈsɪtɪse
v	[v]	*vias*	ˈvɪas
x	[ks]¹⁷	*explicit*	ɛksˈplɪsɪt
z	[z]¹⁸	*Nazarenus*	nazaˈrɛːnʊs

[9] Rigg, "Anglo-Latin," 51: "In *michi, nichil* (normal Medieval spellings for Classical *mihi, nihil*), it is probably the palatal spirant [ç]: [mɪːçɪ], [nɪːçɪl]" (unattested in the *CT*).

[10] *-ci-* and *-ti-* are homonymns when *-ci-* replaces CL *-ti-*, e.g., *tercia* (KnT before I 1881).

[11] This sound is not so much a marked [t] as an unvoiced, unstressed [d].

[12] Also, g + r, l [g] (unattested in the *CT*).

[13] Rigg, "Anglo-Latin," 51: "This is not a consonant in Medieval or Renaissance Latin, and there is strong evidence that it was often not pronounced at all," e.g., it is added in some words and omitted in others. Hence *exametron* for *hexametron* (MkT VII 1979) and *Oloferno* for *Holoferno* (MkT before VII 2551). In personal and place names such as *Hierusalem, Hiericho,* and *Hieronymus, hier-* is [ʤɛr-].

[14] Rigg, "Anglo-Latin," 51: "Similarly, intervocalic *i* is [ʤ] in *cuius* [kʏʤʊs], *eius* [eʤʊs]" (but unattested in the *CT*).

[15] Rigg, "Anglo-Latin," 52: "[f] except in the word *sphera* (Classical *sphaera*), whose common spelling *spera* indicates [p]" (but unattested in the *CT*).

[16] Rigg, "Anglo-Latin," 53: After *s* and *x*, *ti* remains [tɪ] (e.g., *Questio* in GP I 646, but *-xti-* is unattested in the *CT*.

[17] Rigg, "Anglo-Latin," 53: "The group *exst- ext-*, is sometimes simplified to [ɛst]."

[18] Rigg, "Anglo-Latin," 53: "This occurs only in words of Hebrew or Greek origin," but cf. *Pize* in MkT before VII 2407, *De Hugelino Comite de Pize.*

Table 1 *(continued)*

'Wel seyd, by *corpus dominus*'	ShipT VII 435
And after *Amor vincit omnia*	GP I 162
Sequitur de Accidia	ParsT before X 677
What nedeth it of kyng Anthiochus	MkT VII 257
swich as is cleped *tristicia*	ParsT X 725
'*Deus hic!*' quod he	SumT III 1770
And *Angelus ad virginem* he song	MilT I 3216
et interrogate de viis antiquis	ParsT X 75
And *Angelus ad virginem* he song	MilT I 3216
And also war hym of a *Significavit*	GP I 662
'*Deus hic!*' quod he	SumT III 1770
as *Judicum* can telle	MkT VII 2046
Jhesus Nazarenus rex Judeorum	ParsT X 284
Whan *Phebus* dwelled heere	MancT IX 105
quam ponit frater Jacobus	SNPro before VIII 85
I hadde the beste *quoniam* myghte be	WBPro III 608
And *Jhesus, filius Syrak*	MerT IV 2250
Marcus Tullius Scithero	FranPro V 722
Explicit prima pars Penitentie	ParsT before X 316
Scithice post aspera gentis	KnT before I 859
State super vias	ParsT before X 75
Explicit prima pars	KnT before I 1355
Jhesus Nazarenus rex Judeorum	ParsT X 284

Table 2: Vowels *(continued on facing page)*

Stressed vowels	Long	(open syllables)	
a	[ɑː]	*radix*	'rɑːdɪks
e	[ɛː]	*Jhesus*	'ʤɛːzʊs
i	[iː]	*Titus*	'tiːtʊs
o	[ɔː]	*nomen*	'nɔːmɛn
u	[ʏː]	*Luna*	'lʏːna

Stressed vowels	Short	(closed syllables)	
a	[a]	*Marcus*	'markʊs
e	[ɛ]	*vestris*	'vɛstrɪs
i	[ɪ]	*libro*	'lɪbrɔː
o	[ɔ]	*noster*	'nɔstɛr
u	[ʊ]	*secunda*	sɛ'kʊnda

Unstressed vowels	Non-final		
a	[a]	*Sathanas*	'satanas
e	[e][19]	*eructavit*	erʊk'taːvɪt
i	[ɪ]	*principio*	prɪn'sɪpio
o	[ɔ]	*interrogate*	ɪntɛrɔ'gɑːte
u	[ʊ]	*ambulate*	ambʊ'lɑːte

Unstressed vowels	Final	(open)	
a	[a]	*omnia*	'ɔmnɪa
e	[e]	*patre*	'pɑtre
i	[iː][20]	*Exodi*	'ɛksɔdiː
o	[ɔː][21]	*nono*	'nɔːnɔː
u	[y][22]	—	—

Diphthongs and diaereses			
au	[aʊ]	*laurigero*	laʊ'rɪʤɛroː
eu	[e·ʊ]	*Deus*	'de·ʊs

---

[19] Rigg, "Anglo-Latin," 54: "[ɛː]; probably [e] in open syllables, as this would be the sound most likely to raise to [ɪ] in the seventeenth century," i.e., because of the Great Vowel Shift.

[20] Rigg, "Anglo-Latin," 55: "Perhaps [iː]," without explanation.

[21] Rigg, "Anglo-Latin," 55: "[ɔː] until about 1400, [oː] thereafter." I have opted for the more conservative pronunciation since Chaucer's phonetic formation would have taken place earlier in the fourteenth century.

[22] Rigg, "Anglo-Latin," 55: "Perhaps [y], e.g., [mɑːny] for *manu*, but this is a guess."

Table 2 *(continued)*

Radix malorum est Cupiditas	PardPro VI 334
And *Jhesus, filius Syrak*	MerT IV 2250
Ther was, as telleth *Titus Livius*	PhyT VI 1
Non est aliud nomen sub celo	ParsT X 597
That out of *Sol* and *Luna* were ydrawe	CYT VIII 1440
Marcus Tullius Scithero	FranPro V 722
et invenietis refrigerium animabus vestris	ParsT X 75
Augustinus, De Civitate, libro nono	ParsT X 754
'Now, *Pater noster*, clom!' seyde Nicholay	MilT I 3638,
Sequitur pars secunda	KnT before I 1355
My soule bitake I unto *Sathanas*	MilT I 3750
Lo, 'buf,' they seye, '*cor meum eructavit!*'	SumT III 1934
For al so siker as *In principio*	NPT VII 3163
et interrogate de viis antiquis	ParsT X 75
et ambulate in ea	ParsT X 75
And after *Amor vincit omnia*	GP I 162
With *qui cum patre* forth his wey he wente	SumT III 1734
in *Exodi capitulo vicesimo*	ParsT X 750
Genesis nono	ParsT X 755
(not attested in *CT*)	
Prelia, laurigero, &c.	KnT before I 859
'*Deus hic!*' quod he	SumT III 1770

Special cases

GP I 662 And also war hym of a *Significavit*: The rhyme of *Significavit* with "savith" in the previous line ("For curs wol slee right as assoillyng savith") implies that "savith" ended in [t].

KnT before I 859 Iamque domos patrias, Scithice post aspera gentis / Prelia, laurigero, &c. (Statius, *Thebaid*, 12.519–20): The hexameter may have called for heightened attention to vowel quantity.

MilT I 3638 'Now, *Pater-noster*, clom!' seyde Nicholay: The initial vowel *a* in *pater* is lengthened, hence ['pɑːtɛr] (Vowels, General Rules).

MLEpi II 1189 Ne phislyas, ne termes queinte of lawe: *Phislyas*, perhaps pronounced ['fɪslɪ·as] is a *locus desperatus*; there are numerous variants in the manuscripts, and there is no agreement as to its meaning, although the Shipman, who speaks this line, seems to consider it Latin ("Ther is but litel Latyn in my mawe," II 1190). It is therefore tempting to consider it a deliberately unlearned form.

WBPro III 619 Yet have I Martes mark upon my face: *Martes* is a macaronic construction composed of the Latin stem (*Mart-* from *Mars, Martis*, 3rd declension) and the English gentive singular (*-es*).

SumT III 2222 In ars-metrike shal ther no man fynde: *Ars metrike* [ars 'mɛtrɪkə] is a macaronic form deriving by folk etymology from a presumed Latin *ars metrica* (see *OED, arithmetic, n.*[1]). Strict scansion would require stress on the second syllable of *metrike*—i.e., " 'In árs-metríke shál ther nó man fýnd"—although since Latin *metrica* is properly stressed on the first syllable, the scansion is more likely *árs-métrike*.

NPT VII 3163–64 For al so siker as *In principio* / *Mulier est hominis confusio*: The Latin in these lines cannot be forced neatly into the iambic pentameter mold, as each line has eleven syllables rather than ten and the stresses fall in such a way as to make it impossible to follow the norms of Chaucer's English line. One solution is to use a trochaic meter, thus: *Ín principió / Múliér est hóminís confúsió*. Another solution would be to observe ordinary Latin stress, thus: *In princípio / Múlier est hóminis confúsio*. Which one the prelector chooses will doubtless depend on his idea of Chanticleer's (and the Nun's Priest's) tone in this passage.[23]

---

[23]This article was inspired by a number of spirited conversations about reading Chaucer aloud that I enjoyed with Emerson Brown at his *cabaña* on Cayuga Lake, where he and his wife Cindy would summer. I offer it in tribute to Emerson's passions for Chaucer and for the Latin language.

Editing and Annotating

Where's the Point?
Punctuating Chaucer's *Canterbury Tales*

PETER G. BEIDLER

An essay on punctuating Chaucer is appropriate in a volume honoring Emerson Brown, Jr., whose essay on a possible error in punctuation in the *Knight's Tale*[1] got many Chaucerians thinking about challenging the pointing done by powerful editors. It always comes as a surprise to my Chaucer students to learn that 600 years ago Chaucer did not know, and did not use, punctuation marks as we know them now. The many manuscripts of Chaucer's verse give us columns of verse with no periods, commas, question marks, exclamation marks, semicolons, colons, dashes, apostrophes, or consistent paragraph markers. To be sure, there is an occasional raised point that we have come to call a "punctus," and that punctus may be related in some way to the modern period, but there are few puncti in the manuscripts, and those we do find rarely appear where we would put periods. There are lots of virgules, or slash marks [/], in the manuscripts. In most lines we find at least one virgule, in some two. These may be the ancestors of the modern comma, since the virgules sometimes seem to mark a caesura or pause in the line. They almost never come at the end of the line, however, even when we would require a comma there. There are also in the manuscripts some paragraph markers [¶]. These serve as a kind of punctuation mark, and some of those are at places where we might indent for paragraphs. The punctus, the virgule, and the paragraph marker, however, are inconsistently used. That they vary in use from manuscript to manuscript suggests that at least some of them are scribal rather than Chaucerian marks. We do not have a single document that we *know* was from Chaucer's own hand. To the extent that we have any punctuation at all in the surviving manuscripts, then, the punctus, the virgule, and the paragraph marker are the only marks we find, and those were quite possibly put there by a scribe rather than by Chaucer.

Where, then, does the punctuation in modern editions, using marks that Chaucer had never heard of, come from? The answer is simple enough: the

---

[1] "The *Knight's Tale*, 2639: Guilt by Punctuation," *Chaucer Review* 21 (1986): 133–41. Following Brown's lead, others have suggested repunctuating or even unpunctuating Chaucer. See, for example, Howell Chickering's "Unpunctuating Chaucer," *Chaucer Review* 25 (1990): 96–109, and D. Thomas Hanks, Jr., Arminda Kamphausen, and James Wheeler, "Circling Back in Chaucer's *Canterbury Tales*: On Punctuation, Misreading, and Reader Response," *Chaucer Yearbook* 3 (1996): 35–53. Few earlier studies challenged the standard punctuation of modern editions. A notable exception is Albert E. Hartung's "Inappropriate Pointing in the *Canon's Yeoman's Tale*, G 1236–1239," *PMLA* 77 (1962): 508–9.

punctuation comes from modern editors of Chaucer, most of whom take their lead from earlier editors of Chaucer, dating back as far as Thynne's sixteenth-century and Speght's seventeenth-century editions. Indeed, one of the most important services that a modern editor performs is to insert the kind of punctuation and paragraphing that will help modern readers, most of them college students, read Chaucer with comparative ease. These modern editors perform an important function, of course, because we teachers want to do all we can to help students understand and take delight in Chaucerian plots, characterization, humor, meaning, and subtlety. Still, modern editors sometimes get the punctuation wrong, and in doing so they mislead or confuse modern readers.

In this essay I present four examples that show the possible errors of modern editors' ways and the importance of a critical reading of all modern punctuation. Of these four, two are from the *Knight's Tale*, one from the *Franklin's Tale*, and one from the *Shipman's Tale*. I close with a challenge to Chaucerians and their students to rethink the standard punctuation of three sets of lines in the *Miller's Tale*. All arguments for one punctuation rather than another should be based not on what punctuation Chaucer used, but on how modern punctuation serves best to bring out the meaning that Chaucer most likely intended and would have presumably made clear through intonation, emphasis, and pause in an oral reading of his works.[2] Even to guess what Chaucer had in mind, we need to understand the context of any passages we discuss.

Emily speaks to Diana

Just before the tournament in the *Knight's Tale*, Emily prays to Diana, the chaste goddess of virginity, asking that she not have to marry either of the young knights who want to take her virginity in marriage. In the *Riverside* her lines to Diana read thus:

> "Syn thou art mayde and kepere of us alle,
> My maydenhede thou kepe and wel conserve,
> And whil I lyve, a mayde I wol thee serve."   (I 2328–30)

I propose an alternative punctuation by moving the comma in the third of those lines two words to the right.

> *Proposed*:
> "Syn thou art mayde and kepere of us alle,
> My maydenhede thou kepe and wel conserve,
> And whil I lyve a mayde, I wol thee serve."   (I 2328–30)

In the *Riverside* punctuation, Emily promises, in exchange for Diana's protecting her maidenhead, to serve Diana as a maiden as long as she lives: "And as

---

[2] I am skeptical of the view that students should be asked to read Chaucer in texts with no modern punctuation. It may be that any decision about punctuation can obscure a possible ambiguity, but surely in reading his texts aloud Chaucer would have indicated what his primary meanings were. The job of modern editors is to provide punctuation that will help students understand texts as Chaucer most likely wanted them to be understood. Scholars, of course, can profitably use unpunctuated texts.

long as I live, I will serve you as a maiden." In my reading, Emily promises, in exchange for Diana's protecting her maidenhead, to serve Diana as long as she is a virgin: "And so long as I live as a maiden, I will serve you."

The changed punctuation changes the meaning of the word "while." According to the *Riverside* punctuation, "while" means "as long as." According to the punctuation I propose, "while" means "*so* long as." If he were reading the text out loud, Chaucer would have made his meaning clear by pausing either after "live" or "maid." The manuscripts themselves can offer no help since there were no commas in the line. It is purely a matter of deciding which reading makes the most sense. For me the alternative reading makes more sense. Why would Emily promise that as long as she gets to keep her maidenhead she will serve Diana as a maiden? Those who serve Diana are, by definition, maidens, so little is gained by Emily's stipulating that she will serve Diana as a maiden. It makes more sense for Emily to promise to serve Diana *if* she remains a maiden: "And so long as I live as a maiden, I will serve you." Not only is that a more realistic promise, since she promises to serve Diana only so long as she remains a maiden, but it also carries with it an implied request for Diana's protection not just this once, but on into the future, as well: "I will serve you only if you help me to continue to live as a maiden." I prefer this reading, also, because it gives Emily a bit more personality. There may, after all, be implied in her promise not merely a plea for continued protection from Diana, but also a veiled threat, as well: "If you do not offer me protection from the unchaste desires of these men, Diana, I will no longer serve you."

Saturn speaks to Venus

There is great rejoicing when Arcite wins the tournament near the end of the *Knight's Tale*. The people celebrate noisily to honor Arcite's winning in combat the hand of the fair Emily. Palamon, of course, is disappointed and confused. Venus herself is also upset at the outcome, since she had promised Palamon that he would get Emily. Venus, weeping and distraught, takes her case directly to her father Saturn. The mighty Saturn hears her, but tells her to hold her peace because she will have her way yet. Here is the *Riverside* passage:

> Saturnus seyde, "Doghter, hoold thy pees!
> Mars hath his wille, his knyght hath all his boone,
> And, by myn heed, thow shalt been esed soone."
> The trompours, with the loude mynstralcie,
> The heraudes, that ful loude yelle and crie,
> Been in hire wele for joye of daun Arcite.
> But herkneth me, and stynteth noyse a lite,
> Which a myracle ther bifel anon.   (I 2668–75)

The main problem with the *Riverside* punctuation is that in the next to last line above, "me" must refer to the narrator, the Knight himself. "Listen to me," says the Knight, "and stop your noise." To whom is the Knight speaking here? The only possible answer, in the *Riverside*, is the other twenty-odd pilgrims, who have presumably been making a lot of noise. Chaucer never tells us, however,

that the other pilgrims have been noisy, and indeed they have nothing to be
noisy about. Why would the pilgrims noisily cheer Arcite's success in battle? If
they don't react to anything else in the tale, why would they react here, even
if they were on Arcite's side, which they probably would not have been?[3] And
even if they did react noisily, it seems distinctly out of character for the gentle
pilgrim Knight to tell them to shush up and "herkneth me." He is, after all, a
polite and gentle sort of chap unlikely to speak villainously to others:

> And though that he were worthy, he was wys,
> And of his port as meeke as is a mayde.
> He nevere yet no vileynye ne sayde
> In al his lyf unto no maner wight.
> He was a verray, parfit gentil knyght.[4]   (I 68–72)

But if we take the close-quotation mark from the end of line I 2870 and move
it to the end of I 2874, then Saturn becomes the speaker of the lines, which he
addresses still to his distraught daughter Venus.

> *Proposed*:
> Saturnus seyde, "Doghter, hoold thy pees.
> Mars hath his wille. His knyght hath all his boone.
> And, by myn heed, thow shalt been esed soone.
> The trompours, with the loude mynstralcie,
> The heraudes, that ful loude yelle and crie,
> Been in hire wele for joye of daun Arcite.
> But herkneth me, and stynteth noyse a lite."
> Which a myracle ther bifel anon.   (I 2668–75)

In my punctuation, Saturn speaks seven lines to Venus, not three, and in doing
so makes it quite clear who the "me" of the seventh line is. It is not a belligerent
Knight telling his fellow pilgrims to be quiet and listen to him, but a kindly Saturn telling his distraught and weeping daughter to do so, because he knows that
the joyous trumpeters and musicians down there proclaiming Arcite's victory
will soon stop their celebrating when a big surprise comes. It would be perfectly
in character for Saturn, the wisest and most powerful of the planetary gods, to
show a bit of gentle impatience with his weeping daughter as he reassures her
that she will get her way in the end.

---

[3] Chaucer, after all, changed the events of Boccaccio's *Teseide* to make Palamon the one
who deserves Emily by seeing her first, praying more wisely, and being a hero defeated not by
a horse bite but by a gang of twenty.

[4] Once we begin to question the standard punctuation, it is difficult not to meddle with it.
These lines, for example, might be repunctuated thus, though in this case the difference in
actual meaning is minimal:

> And though that he were worthy, he was wys.
> And, of his port as meeke as is a mayde,
> He nevere yet no vileynye ne sayde
> In al his lyf, unto no maner wight.
> He was a verray, parfit, gentil knyght.   (I 68–72)

My punctuation not only gets rid of the confusing equation of "me" with the Knight and of the Knight's curious admonition to his fellow pilgrims to be quiet, but has the additional advantage of lending a nice balance to Saturn's speech to his daughter. It starts with his telling her to hold her peace, and ends with his telling her to be quiet.[5] In my punctuation, the final line in the passage makes sense as the first line of the Knight's transition to the next section after Saturn's speech ends: "What a miracle comes next," he says. The "miracle" he refers to is that Saturn sends a fury from hell to frighten the victorious Arcite's horse, which then rears back and kills Arcite. The miracle of the fury brings an end to Venus's grief and lets her make good on her promise to Palamon.

Aurelius speaks to Dorigen

Near the end of the *Franklin's Tale*, the young lover Aurelius, upon learning from Dorigen that her husband Arveragus has sent his wife to keep her promise, feels pity for Dorigen, respect for Arveragus, and shame for his own selfish actions. He decides to follow Arveragus's lead and do the right thing. His speech to Dorigen ends thus in the *Riverside*:

> "I yow relesse, madame, into youre hond
> Quyt every serement and every bond
> That ye han maad to me as heerbiforn,
> Sith thilke tyme which that ye were born.
> My trouthe I plighte, I shal yow never repreve
> Of no biheste, and heere I take my leve,
> As of the treweste and the beste wyf
> That evere yet I knew in al my lyf.
> But every wyf be war of hire biheeste!
> On Dorigen remembreth, atte leeste.
> Thus kan a squier doon a gentil dede
> As wel as kan a knyght, withouten drede."   (V 1533–44)

It is a moving speech that Aurelius makes, but the last four lines of it are not his to deliver. A modern editor has through punctuation misascribed them to him. Those last four lines make no sense in his mouth. Why would the lovesick Aurelius, having made a decision to give up the object of his love just when she is within his reach, warn other wives to beware of making promises like hers? It makes no sense for him to be thinking of other wives at all. Why would he in one breath praise her for being the "treweste and the beste wyf" he has ever known (V 1549), and in the next breath exhort other wives not to make promises like the one she made to him? If he did want to make such a statement, why would

---

[5]I have made some other changes, also, by removing the exclamation mark at the end of line 2668, thus making Saturn less harsh and more loving, by removing what we now call a comma splice in line 2669, by moving the paragraph indent at line 2671, making the seven lines one unbroken speech, and putting it before line 2675. Teachers might want to debate with students these smaller changes—and others they might want to suggest. Incidentally, I am aware that it may be unusual for Saturn to use the plural "herkneth" and "stynteth" in this line to speak in the imperative to his daughter, but I am not sure Chaucer would have been such a stickler for the finer points of grammar.

he make it in a speech to her as the sole listener rather than to other wives? And even if he wanted to make such a speech to her, why would he tell other wives to "be war of *hire* biheeste" rather than to "be war of *youre* biheeste"?

There are other problems with having Aurelius deliver those four lines. The most obvious problem is that the *Riverside* has him praise himself by saying, "Thus kan a squier doon a gentil dede" (V 1543). Such self-praise is out of character for a young man who has just learned the most important lesson and made the defining decision of his young life. Surely we are to admire his humility and wisdom and good judgment here, not watch him pat himself on the back for being every bit as noble as a knight.

Those four lines, however, are entirely appropriate in the mouth of the Franklin, the teller of the story. He has, after all, been critical of Dorigen before—critical of her impatience with the rocks and of her complaining nature— so it would be entirely appropriate for him to use her here as an example to other wives of the disastrous consequences that come from making rash promises to would-be lovers. Similarly, this Franklin, who is impatient with his own son and wishes that he would "comune with any gentil wight / Where he myghte lerne gentillesse aright" (V 693–94), would be eager to point out that in his tale young men can learn proper behavior by paying attention to the good examples of knights: "Thus kan a squier doon a gentil dede / As wel as kan a knyght" (V 1543–44). I would, then, render the passage differently. A careful reader will notice that in the following repunctuation of the passage, I have made a few more changes in pointing, though none as significant as moving the closing quotation mark four lines forward.

> *Proposed*:
> "I yow relesse, madame, into youre hond,
> Quyt every serement and every bond
> That ye han maad to me as heerbiforn
> Sith thilke tyme which that ye were born.
> My trouthe I plighte, I shal yow never repreve
> Of no biheste. And heere I take my leve
> As of the treweste and the beste wyf
> That evere yet I knew in al my lyf."
>   But every wyf be war of hire biheeste—
> On Dorigen remembreth, atte leeste.
> Thus kan a squier doon a gentil dede
> As wel as kan a knyght, withouten drede.   (V 1533–44)

In my reading, the Franklin takes gentle issue with one of his own characters. Aurelius takes his leave of the truest and best wife he has ever knows, but the Franklin offers a closing caution to all wives to beware of making foolish promises like Dorigen's and to all young men to learn from the example of gentle knights.

Daun John speaks to the Wife of Saint Denis

At the beginning of the garden scene in the *Shipman's Tale*, the wife of the merchant of Saint Denis comes up to daun John and speaks to him. The lines run thus in the *Riverside*:

> "O deere cosyn myn, daun John," she sayde,
> "What eyleth yow so rathe for to ryse?"
>   "Nece," quod he, "it oghte ynough suffis
> Fyve houres for to slepe upon a nyght,
> ....
> But deere nece, why be ye so pale?
> I trowe, certes, that oure goode man
> Hath yow laboured sith the nyght bigan
> That yow were nede to resten hastily."   (VII 98–101, 106–9)[6]

Every modern edition agrees in punctuating the lines thus, or very nearly thus.[7] The sense of the passage, then, is, " 'Oh my dear cousin, sir John,' she said. 'What ails you that you rise so early?' 'Niece,' he replied, 'five hours of sleep at night is sufficient.... But, dear niece, why are you so pale? I'll bet your husband has been keeping you busy in bed since the night began!' " Three problems, however, immediately surface with this reading. First, why would the wife be surprised at finding the monk out saying his devotions early in the morning? Monks, after all, are required to get up early to say their devotions, so there is nothing for her to be puzzled about. Second, why does she ask him what ails him? The monk is not ailing at all, and the rest of the garden scene shows him to be healthy and relaxed. Third, how are we to make sense of the monk's answering her question about what ails him by saying that five hours is enough sleep? We are presumably to read the monk's reply as self-righteous bragging about how few hours of sleep pious monks need, because sleep takes away from their good works and their prayerful service to Jesus, but in fact he never does answer what ails him, and her question remains as puzzling as his non-answer.

---

[6] For the sake of simplicity, I have removed from consideration the monk's four-line statement to the wife about how tired old wedded men, who lie cowering like hound-harassed rabbits in a furrow, need more sleep than the five hours. That passage does not affect my argument.

[7] Both the Hengwrt and the Ellesmere scribes have seemed to suggest through paragraph markers that line 100 should start a new speech with the word "Nece." Modern editors, perhaps having seen that marker, may well have assumed that the mark was Chaucer's own and punctuated the passage accordingly. I suggest, however, that the positioning of the paragraph markers may well have been a scribal error that later editors picked up on. The Hengwrt MS has 37 such markers in the *Shipman's Tale*, while the Ellesmere has 36. But only 30 of those appear in the same places in the two versions. The Hengwrt has seven paragraph markers that the Ellesmere does not have, and the Ellesmere has six that the Hengwrt does not have. If, as most scholars now assume, the same scribe copied both the Hengwrt and the Ellesmere, it is interesting that he felt free to place the paragraph markers in somewhat different places in the two manuscripts. For example, while the Hengwrt has a marker at the start of line 98, with the wife's speech, the Ellesmere does not. We need not, then, be controlled in our reading by scribal paragraphing in the manuscripts.

I propose an alternative punctuation, and thus an alternative reading of the lines. My reading is accomplished by altering the punctuation slightly, ending the wife's speech in the first line (98) and giving the second line to the monk.

> *Proposed*:
> "O deere cosyn myn, daun John," she sayde.
> "What eyleth yow so rathe for to ryse,
> Nece?" quod he. "It oghte ynough suffise
> Fyve houres for to slepe upon a nyght,
> ....
> But deere nece, why be ye so pale?
> I trowe, certes, that oure goode man
> Hath yow laboured sith the nyght bigan
> That yow were nede to resten hastily."   (VII 98–101, 106–9)

By changing only the punctuation, I have removed the three problems with the standard reading. In my alternative reading, the wife says only six words, presumably with a sad sigh: "Oh my dear cousin, sir John." The distress in that short speech signals to the monk that something is troubling her, and *he* then speaks the next line, asking what ails *her* that she is up so early.[8] Changing the punctuation gets rid of the first problem—why the wife asks him why he is up early—because in my alternative reading *he* asks *her* the question. While it is perfectly usual for a monk to be up early saying his morning devotions, it might well be unusual for *her* to be up so early unless something is wrong. Changing the punctuation also gets rid of the second problem—why the *wife* asks the *monk* what ails him when nothing does ail him. Rather, in my alternative reading, the *monk* asks the *wife* why she is ailing—a reasonable question since she *is* "ailing." Not only is she pale, but we soon discover that she is unhappy with her marital condition. Later lines reveal that she is distraught about her debts and the alleged failings of her husband: his stinginess, his incapacity in bed, and so on—the "thynges sixe" of lines VII 174–77. These are ailments enough for the wife of the merchant of St. Denis. As for the third problem—why in reply to her question about what ails him daun John says that five hours is enough sleep—that problem disappears also with my alternative punctuation. The monk's response makes sense as a response to *his* question about what ails *her*. He says, in effect, "What ails you that you are up so early? Five hours ought to be enough sleep, but you look awfully pale. I'll bet I know: your husband kept you working all night in bed! That's why you did not get five hours of sleep and look so pale."

---

[8]The closest analogue to the *Shipman's Tale*, Boccaccio's *Decameron* VIII, 1, cannot guide us here, since in it there is no garden meeting and no conversation between Ambruogia and Gulfardo, the German soldier who wants to become her lover. In the thirteenth-century Old French tale *Aloul*, however, a lustful clergyman and a distraught wife meet early in the morning in an orchard. In a situation curiously parallel to the garden scene in the *Shipman's Tale*, the clergyman opens the conversation by asking the pretty wife why she is up so early (see line 69). *Aloul* is conveniently translated by John DuVal in *Fabliaux, Fair and Foul* (Binghamton: MRTS, 1992), 107–29.

I emphasize here that I have not changed the words or the word order at all, but only the editorially-inserted punctuation. That is, I propose not an emendation to what Chaucer wrote, but only an alteration in the punctuation that modern editors have supplied.

Does it make any difference, since readers have been making what they thought was perfectly good sense of the passage for some six centuries? I think so. By altering the punctuation we have not only made the passage more logical, but we have also corrected the characterization of the monk. Instead of listening to her question about what ails him, daun John takes the lead by asking her a question, and in so doing shows at least the appearance of concern for her: "What is ailing you, dear niece? Has your husband been working you too hard in bed all night?" His question, then, is less an expression of concern than an invitation to her to talk about her sex life—and she immediately does: "Nay, cosyn myn, it stant nat so with me" (VII 114). His question and his own hinted answer are therefore his own sleazy moves towards seduction. By altering the punctuation, we have also altered the characterization of the wife. No longer asking the monk a meaningless question about what ails him when nothing does, she stops short with a self-pitying address and lets *him* inquire what ails *her*. Her opening words, then, are the lament of a woman in distress, a plea for help. Instead of asking a question that shows her concern for his welfare, she draws attention to her own sad condition.

My interest in repunctuating Chaucer is in part a pedagogical one. It is less that I want the rest of the world to punctuate Chaucer my way than that I want to encourage teachers to discuss with their students the importance of proper punctuation in general and the proper punctuation of Chaucerian texts in particular. We all know that punctuation alters meaning, but not all students quite understand that. I close by suggesting three alternatives to the standard punctuation of one of the Chaucerian tales that our students enjoy the most, the *Miller's Tale*. I have reasons for proposing the three repunctuations, but I do not state them here, thinking that perhaps teachers might like to invite students to argue the punctuation out and reach their own conclusions. In fact, if I were re-editing the *Miller's Tale*, I would adopt only two of the three alternative punctuations that I propose here. My purpose here is not to insist that the standard punctuation be changed, but to encourage teachers and students to argue for or against that standard punctuation, and in doing so learn that punctuation does matter.

Alison speaks to Nicholas

When Nicholas grabs Alison and commands that she give him her love, the startled Alison springs like a colt and twists out of his grip. Here is the *Riverside* passsage:

> And seyde, "I wol nat kisse thee, by my fey!
> Why, lat be!" quod she. "Lat be, Nicholas,
> Or I wol crie 'out, harrow' and 'allas'!
> Do wey youre handes, for youre curteisye!"   (I 3284–87)

I propose an alternative punctuation that includes the last line as part of what she threatens to cry out.

> *Proposed*:
> And seyde, "I wol nat kisse thee, by my fey.
> Why, lat be," quod she, "lat be, Nicholas,
> Or I wol crie 'out, harrow, and allas,
> Do wey youre handes, for youre curteisye!'"   (I 3284–87)

Alison speaks to John

Part of Absolon's attempt to seduce the fair Alison in the *Miller's Tale* is his two-line song to her outside her bedroom window. Here is the *Riverside* reading:

> He syngeth in his voys gentil and smal,
> "Now, deere lady, if thy wille be,
> I praye yow that ye wole rewe on me."   (I 3360–62)

Sleeping next to Alison, John hears the song and speaks to his wife about it:

> "What! Alison! Herestow nat Absolon,
> That chaunteth thus under oure boures wal?"   (I 3366–67)

In the *Riverside* punctuation, Alison replies with one line:

> "Yis, God woot, John, I heere it every deel."   (I 3369)

I propose that we give her a second line by moving the closing quotation mark to the end of the next line, so that the whole passage reads differently.

> *Proposed*:
> He syngeth in his voys gentil and smal,
> "Now, deere lady, if thy wille be,
> I praye yow that ye wole rewe on me,"
> Ful wel acordaunt to his gyternynge.
> This carpenter awook and herde him synge
> And spak unto his wyf and seyde anon,
> "What, Alison, herestow nat Absolon
> That chaunteth thus under oure boures wal?"
> And she answerde her housbonde therwithal,
> "Yis, God woot, John, I heere it every deel.
> This passeth forth. What wol ye bet than weel?"   (I 3360–70)

Nicholas speaks to John

When he gives his prediction to John about what will happen the night of the flood, Nicholas talks about what to do with the axe once the waters rise. Again, I give the *Riverside* version:

> "And breke an hole an heigh, upon the gable,
> Unto the gardyn-ward, over the stable,

> That we may frely passen forth oure way,
> Whan that the grete shour is goon away.
> Thanne shaltou swymme as myrie, I undertake,
> As dooth the white doke after hire drake." (I 3571–76)

I propose that we change the comma to a period at the end of I 3573 and remove the period at the end of I 3574.

> *Proposed*:
> "And breke an hole an heigh, upon the gable,
> Unto the gardyn-ward, over the stable,
> That we may frely passen forth oure way.
> Whan that the grete shour is goon away
> Thanne shaltou swymme as myrie, I undertake,
> As dooth the white doke after hire drake." (I 3571–76)

Conclusion

My larger point is not that I am right in punctuating these passages in particular ways, but that we should as teachers of Chaucer be aware that modern editors can misguide both us and our students. There is pedagogical usefulness in letting our students know that the punctuation in modern editions is not Chaucerian and in giving modern students some unpunctuated Chaucerian lines and letting them come up with, and argue for, their own punctuation of those lines. I can think of no better way to end than by quoting Emerson Brown: "I am not prepared to advocate removing punctuation from classroom texts, but we might at least think about the problem and experiment some. Let's see how well our students can cope with passages transcribed from the manuscripts. They may surprise us" (p. 139). And they may also come to see, perhaps for the first time, that in their own sentences as well as Chaucer's, punctuation absolutely affects meaning. One misplaced comma or quotation mark can make all the difference. I think Emerson would have agreed that that is an important point.

Annotating Chaucer
Some Corrections and Additions

DANIEL J. RANSOM

Emerson Brown took special pleasure in unearthing medieval lore concerning classical and biblical references made by Chaucer, an effort that is vital in recreating a proper interpretive context for Chaucer's allusions. Emerson taught us to see more clearly what Chaucer may have meant, or what his contemporary audience may have understood, when he made Pavia the setting of the *Merchant's Tale*, introduced the figure of Priapus, or alluded to biblical heroines such as Judith and Esther.[1] Perhaps by a kind of osmosis (Emerson was my teacher in 1971–73), I find that I too enjoy this sort of work. In vetting, redacting, and contributing to the Chaucer Encyclopedia (a project still ongoing), I have uncovered noteworthy information about some of Chaucer's references, much of it corrective. A volume dedicated to Emerson's memory seems a perfect place to share some of this information. I will begin with a small but characteristic amendment.

In the *House of Fame* (1469) Chaucer refers to "Guydo ... de Columpnis" (Guido delle **Colonne**). The surname is problematic. F. P. Magoun states that it derives "almost certainly" from Colonna, the name of a great Roman family whose founder was lord of the city Colonna (fifteen miles southeast of Rome). The plural form in Guido's name means then "(one) of the Colonna family."[2] Magoun quotes N. E. Griffin on this point, but Griffin actually casts doubt on such an interpretation ("a belief on the part of later scribes" copying legal documents with Guido's name on them).[3] Indeed, Griffin cites G. A. Cesareo, who champions the idea that Guido's surname derives from place names on the strait of Messina, not from the Roman family name. Cesareo quotes Petrarch, who in a comment on *Aeneid* 3.411 observes that his contemporaries refer to Messina as Columna (though he finds no ancient authority for this identification), and that directly across the Strait of Messina (on the toe of Italy) is a

---

[1] See Emerson Brown, Jr., "*The Merchant's Tale*: Why Was Januarie Born 'Of Pavye'?" *Neuphilologische Mitteilungen* 71 (1970): 654–58; "*Hortus Inconclusus*: The Significance of Priapus and Pyramus and Thisbe in the *Merchant's Tale*," *Chaucer Review* 4 (1970): 31–40; "Biblical Women in the *Merchant's Tale*: Feminism, Antifeminism, and Beyond," *Viator* 5 (1974): 387–412.

[2] Francis P. Magoun, Jr., *A Chaucer Gazeteer* (Chicago: University of Chicago Press, 1961), 57–58.

[3] Nathaniel Edward Griffin, ed., *Guido de Columnis, Historia Destructionis Troiae* (Cambridge, Mass.: The Mediaeval Academy of America, 1936), xvi.

place called Columna Regia (an ancient name), the crossing point for those who wish to travel from Italy to Sicily.[4] As Magoun himself notes, Guido lived at Messina. It should be pointed out too that in his *Historia Destructionis Troiae*, ch. 13 (Griffin ed., pp. 113–14), Guido refers to a place on the southern coast of Sicily as "locus ... Columnarum." Guido reports but dismisses the local legend that this place name arose from pillars set there by Hercules.

The legend to which Guido refers arises no doubt because in classical sources Hercules is said to have set up monuments **(Pillars of Hercules)** to mark the extent of his travels or to commemorate some of his great deeds. In the *Monk's Tale* (VII 2117–18) Chaucer alludes to the most famous of these structures: "At bothe the worldes endes ... / In stide of boundes he a pileer sette." The reference is somewhat opaque for several reasons. If one takes "bothe the worldes endes" to mean east and west, then Chaucer's language implies that there is one pillar at each position. But typically each boundary is said to be marked by two columns: the twin pillars at the Strait of Gibraltar, which were thought to mark the westernmost limit of human habitation, and a corresponding, but less familiar, pair of columns supposed to stand at the far eastern limit in India. An added difficulty is that, whereas the markers in the east are literally pillars, one made of gold and one of silver,[5] those in the west are either *columnae* in fact or promontories, Gibraltar and Septe (also called Calpe and Abyla), merely designated as pillars. The latter notion, well known now but somewhat arcane in the Middle Ages, is reported by Pliny (*Natural History* 3.1.3–4) and also by Martianus Capella (*De nuptiis* 6.624–25), who notes the tradition that the promontories, once joined, were separated by Hercules to allow Ocean to flow into the Mediterranean Sea.[6] Boccaccio (*Genealogia Deorum* 10, *proemium*; and 13.1) quotes Seneca and the geographer Pomponius Mela to this effect.[7] Brunetto Latini (*Tresor* 1.123.23) seems to meld the two traditions by indicating that Hercules placed columns on the promontories.[8] The more common

---

[4]G. A. Cesareo, *Le origini della poesia lirica e la poesia Siciliana sotto gli Svevi*, 2nd ed. (Milan: Remo Sandron, 1924), 149–56. The same suggestion was made earlier by Egidio Gorra, *Testi inediti de storia Trojana* (Turin: Ermanno Loescher, 1887), 137, n. 2. Pliny mentions Columna Regia three times in his *Natural History* 3.71, 73, 86 (Loeb 352, pp. 54–55, 64–65). It is noted twice in a 6th-century *Cosmographia* (4.32, 5.2) written in Ravenna (and in a 12th-century redaction of this work, *Geographica* 31, 73): see *Ravennatis Anonymi Cosmographia et Guidonis Geographica*, ed. M. Pinder and G. Parthey (1860; reprint, Aalen: O. Zeller, 1962).

[5]See G. L. Kittredge, "The Pillars of Hercules and Chaucer's 'Trophee,'" in *Putnam Anniversary Volume: Anthropological Essays Presented to Frederic Ward Putnam* (New York: G. E. Stechert, 1909), 545–57.

[6]See William Harris Stahl and Richard Johnson, trans., *The Marriage of Philology and Mercury*, vol. 2 of *Martianus Capella and the Seven Liberal Arts* (New York: Columbia University Press, 1977), 231–32.

[7]Vincenzo Romano, ed., *Giovanni Boccaccio, Genealogie Deorum Gentilium Libri*, 2 vols. (Bari: Gius. Laterza & Sons, 1951), 2.485, 635. Seneca, who was born in Spain, records the tradition in *Hercules Furens*, lines 235–38. Pomponius Mela, who was from the area of Gibraltar, refers to the mountains surrounding the strait as Columnae Herculis and relates the fable in *De Chorographia* 1.5.27; cf. 2.6.95. See A. Silberman, ed. and trans., *Pomponius Mela: Chorographie* (Paris: Société d'Édition "Les Belles Lettres," 1988), 9, 59.

[8]Not having access to the standard edition by Francis J. Carmody (Berkeley: University

medieval notion was that Hercules set up actual pillars on *Gades*, modern Cadiz, supposedly an island situated in (but Cadiz is actually well northwest of) the Strait of Gibraltar, *fretus Gaditanus*.[9] In fact medieval maps such as the 13th-century Hereford map and the 14th-century Higden map depict columns set up on an island Cadiz.[10] Furthermore, in some manuscripts of Walter Map's *Epistola Valerii ad Rufinum* a gloss of the phrase "a Gadibus Herculis" identifies Gades as a city ("urbs") in which Hercules placed "columpnas," beyond the western edge of Africa; it also explains that "gades herculis" are images ("ymagines") that Hercules erected in the west ("parte occidentali") and in the east ("parte orientali").[11]

Another lapse or confusion in the Hercules tradition involves his **Twelve Labors**. Hyginus (*Fabulae*, no. 30) sets forth the ancient topos and canon (cf. Seneca, *Hercules Furens* 222–48), though not in the now standard order.[12] Virgil, *Aeneid* 8.291–93, indicates that Eurystheus (king of Mycenae and taskmaster of the hero) commands Hercules to perform the labors. Eurystheus's power to make such demands is explained by Servius (comment on *Georgics* 3.4),[13] who in turn is quoted by Lactantius Placidus (comment on Statius's *Thebaid* 6.289 [311]);[14] cf. Ovid, *Heroides* 9.5–7. But medieval writers show little awareness of these matters, and their allusions to twelve labors (e.g., Walter Map, *Epistola Valerii*, "duodecim inhumanos labores," whence *Roman de la Rose* 9161–64, "il vainqui .XII. horrible montres")[15] are unlikely to echo the classical canon, which was not universally recognized even in antiquity— e.g., Virgil's reference to Eurystheus speaks of a thousand labors imposed on Hercules. Such allusions are likely to reflect the "duri ... labores" recorded

---

of California Press, 1948), I cite P. Chabaille, ed., *Li livres dou tresor par Brunetto Latini* (Paris: Imprimerie Impériale, 1863), 168 (Chabaille 1.4.124 = Carmody 1.123.23).

[9]On Gades and its pillars, cf. Martianus, 6.611 (Stahl and Johnson, 228); Isidore, *Etymologiae*, 13.15.2, 14.6.7, in W. M. Lindsay, ed., *Isidori Hispalensis Episcopi, Etymologiarvm sive Originvm Libri XX*, 2 vols. (Oxford: Clarendon Press, 1911); Bartholomeus Anglicus, *De propretatibus rerum* 15.67, in *On the Properties of Things: John Trevisa's translation of Bartholmæus Anglicus De Proprietatibus Rerum, A Critical Text*, 2 vols. (Oxford: Clarendon Press, 1975), 2.764; Guido, *HDT*, ch. 1 (ed. Griffin, 9–10). See also the note by Mary Elizabeth Meek, trans., *Historia Destructionis Troiae* (Bloomington: Indiana University Press, 1974), 272.

[10]See P. D. A. Harvey, *Mappa Mundi: The Hereford World Map* (London: The British Library, 1996), page preceding p. 1 (Hereford map) and p. 20 (Higden map); cf. too p. 28 (Psalter map).

[11]See Robert A. Pratt, "Chaucer and the Pillars of Hercules," in Lillian B. Lawler et al. eds., *Studies in Honor of Ullman* (St. Louis, Mo.: The Classical Bulletin, St. Louis University, 1960), 118–25.

[12]Mary Grant, trans., *The Myths of Hyginus* (Lawrence: University of Kansas Publications, 1960), 47–48. The content of Seneca's list differs only in the replacement of Cerberus with reference to the creation of the Strait of Gibraltar (see above, note 7).

[13]Georg Thilo and Hermann Hagen, eds., *Servii Grammatici qui feruntur in Vergilii carmina commentarii*, 3 vols. (Leipzig: B. G. Teubner, 1881–1902; reprint, 1923–27), 3.272.

[14]Ricardus Jahnke, ed., *Lactantii Placidi Commentarios in Statii Thebaida et Commentarium in Achilleida* (Leipzig: B. G. Teubner, 1898).

[15]For text and translation of the *Epistola Valerii*, see Ralph Hanna III and Traugott Lawler, eds., *Jankyn's Book of Wikked Wyves* (Athens, Ga., and London: University of Georgia Press, 1997), 140–41. For *RR* see Félix Lecoy, ed., *Guillaume de Lorris et Jean de Meun, Le Roman de la Rose*, 3 vols. (Paris: Librairie Honoré Champion, 1970–73), and Lecoy's note at 2.276.

by Boethius in *De consolatione philosophiae* 4m7. The Boethian list includes seven labors from the classical canon (not presented in the following canonical order): Hercules kills the Nemean lion (cf. *Troilus and Criseyde* 2.32), drives off the Stymphalian birds, acquires the golden apples of the Hesperides, captures Cerberus, slays Diomedes of Thrace, quells the Hydra, and captures the Erymanthean boar. Instead of canonical labors involving the Ceryneian stag, the Augean stables, the bull of Pasiphae, the belt of Hippolyte, and the monster Geryon, Boethius records five other achievements: Hercules "tames" the centaurs, defeats Achelous, slays Antaeus and Cacus, and holds the sky on his neck (to give relief to Atlas). Nicholas Trevet, commenting on the Boethian passage, observes that different lists are offered by Claudian, *De raptu Prosperpinae* (see 2.9–12, 29–48), and by Ovid, *Metamorphoses* 9 (182–98).[16] Boccaccio (*Gen. Deor.* 13.1), reporting that nearly everyone speaks of twelve labors, enumerates thirty-one; six of these he draws from Ovid, and twelve from Seneca (*Hercules Furens*). See also commentary appended to Servius's annotation of *Aeneid* 8.299 (Thilo and Hagen, 2.241–43); and Ranulph Higden, *Polychronicon* 2.17.[17]

Two of the feats recorded by Boethius require comment here. First, to explain Hercules's **taming of the centaurs,** W. W. Skeat offers two incompatible notes. Commenting on *Monk's Tale* VII 2099, "of Centauros leyde the boost adoun," he states: "Hercules slew Pholus the centaur; and (by accident) Chiron. His slaughter of the centaur Nessus ultimately brought about his own death; cf. l. 3318." But in a note to *Boece* 4m7 ("dawntide the proude Centauris"), he reports: "Hercules was present at the fight between the Centauri and Lapithae; Ovid, Met. xii. 541; ix. 191."[18] In commenting on the *Monk's Tale* passage, F. N. Robinson points to Pholus and Nessus; Susan H. Cavenaugh, to Pholus and Chiron.[19] Trevet's comment on 4m7 also adduces Chiron and Nessus, but these instances are not really germane for two reasons. One, the death of Chiron was an accident (as Trevet acknowledges), not the result of an intention to subdue his pride.[20] Two, the taming of the centaurs would be the only example

---

[16]Trevet's gloss is reproduced in Edmund Taite Silk, "Cambridge Ms. Ii.3.21 and the Relation of Chaucer's *Boethius* to Trivet and Jean De Meung" (dissertation, Yale University, 1930), 612–20. His references to Claudian and Ovid are on p. 612.

[17]Churchill Babington and J. R. Lumby, eds., *Polychronicon Ranulphi Higden, together with the English Translations of John Trevisa and of an Unknown Writer of the Fifteenth Century,* 9 vols. (London, 1865–86), 2.356–63.

[18]Walter W. Skeat, ed., *The Complete Works of Geoffrey Chaucer,* 6 vols. (Oxford: Clarendon Press, 1894), 5.232 and 2.453. The annotation for *Bo* was actually written later than that for *MkT*, which appears (without mention of Nessus) in Skeat's edition of selected Canterbury tales (Oxford: Clarendon Press, 1874; 9th ed. 1906), 179. It seems odd that in the *Complete Works* Skeat would amend his *MkT* note by adding reference to Nessus instead of directing readers to his more suitable comment on the *Bo* passage. The *MkT* passage, of course, also depends on Boethius.

[19]Robinson, ed., *The Complete Works of Geoffrey Chaucer* (Boston: Houghton Mifflin, 1933; 2nd ed. 1957); Cavenaugh in the Riverside edition, and reprinted in Larry D. Benson, ed., *Geoffrey Chaucer*: The Canterbury Tales *Complete* (Boston: Houghton Mifflin, 2000).

[20]Chiron was immortal but, when accidentally pricked by Hercules's arrow tipped with the Hydra's poison, he suffered such pain that the gods granted his request to die. See Ovid, *Met.* 2.649–55 and *Fasti* 5.397–414, referred to in Trevet's gloss (Silk, p. 613); also Boccaccio, *Gen. Deor.* 8.8.

in Boethius's list of Hercules's accomplishments that did not refer to a single episode in the hero's career. Even if one eliminates Chiron and Nessus, there is still a question as to what episode Boethius meant to refer to, and whether Chaucer would have recognized the allusion. Was it the story of Pholus or of the Lapithae? Albert C. Baugh and John H. Fisher hint at the former in their notes to the *Monk's Tale*,[21] but the battle over a cask of wine to which they refer is narrated only in Greek texts, and the tradition seems to have had in Latin literature neither an explicit transmission nor an explicit relation to Pholus.[22] Virgil, for example, attributes the death of Pholus once to Hercules and once to Bacchus, without any explanation in either instance. Servius's comment on *Aeneid* 8.294 and supplements to it and to his commentary on the *Georgics* (see 2.456) highlight the problematic nature of Virgil's references. Lactantius Placidus encounters the same difficulty in commenting on Statius's *Achilleida* 238. These commentaries point out that Pholus was the host, not the enemy, of Hercules (cf. Lucan, *Pharsalia* 6.291), and that after Hercules had fought and killed other centaurs, Pholus died by accident when handling one of the hero's poisoned arrows (a recapitulation of the Chiron legend). Elimination of Pholus and the wine cask still leaves three possible identifications of the reference. One is the episode in which Hercules kills Eurytus (Eurytion) and other centaurs to secure Deianira as his bride; a second possibility, intimated by Ovid, is that Hercules aided the Lapiths in their battle against centaurs who disrupted the wedding of Pirithous and Hippodamia.[23] Trevet (Silk, 613), apparently not knowing the Pholus legend, invents a third interpretation: citing Claudian's *De raptu*, Book 2 (preface, line 44) and *Met.* 15 (line 283), he states that at palaestral games on Mount Pholoë violence broke out and Hercules wounded many centaurs with his arrows. In short, there is no easy gloss to Chaucer's uses of Boethius's allusion.

The other feat in Boethius's list that deserves remark is the episode in which **Hercules holds up the sky** (cf. Ovid, *Met.* 9.198; Seneca, *Hercules Furens* 69–72). Baugh and Fisher comment (on *MkT* VII 2110) that Hercules performs

---

[21] Albert C. Baugh, ed., *Chaucer's Major Poetry* (New York: Appleton-Century-Crofts, 1963); John H. Fisher, ed., *The Complete Poetry and Prose of Geoffrey Chaucer* (New York: Holt, Rinehart and Winston, 1977; 2nd ed. 1989).

[22] See for example the entries "Kentauren" and "Pholos" in W. H. Roscher, ed., *Ausführliches Lexikon der Griechischen und Römischen Mythologie*, 6 vols. (Leipzig: B. G. Teubner, 1884–1921), 2.1040–48, 3.2416–23.

[23] For Eurytus and Deianira see Hyginus, *Fab.* 33; Lactantius, on *Theb.* 5.263; Boccaccio, *Gen. Deor.* 9.29. These authorities (Hyginus and Lactantius by later redaction) compare this legend with the battle fought between centaurs and Lapiths, but only Boccaccio states (at *Gen. Deor.* 31.1; ed. Romano, p. 635, lines 23–26) that Hercules participated in the Lapith melee. He derives this idea from Ovid, *Met.* 9.191, as Skeat does. But Skeat seems to recognize that this citation is not probative without relation to an inference drawn from *Met.* 12.536–41. Robinson (ed., notes to *Bo*) cites only the latter passage; the Riverside edition ignores the Lapith hypothesis entirely. That Ovid intended the inference is suggested in *Heroides* 9.99–100, which sets Hercules's conflict with centaurs in Thessaly (where Pirithous's wedding took place). But this hint is complicated by his reference (*Met.* 15.281–84) to the river Anigrus (in Elis), where the centaurs bathed the wounds that Hercules inflicted upon them. The Pholus and Eurytus incidents occurred in Arcadia (on Mount Pholoë) and Calydon, respectively, both (especially Arcadia) much closer than Thessaly to the Anigrus.

this act as part of his effort to acquire the apples of the Hesperides. While this idea is available in the Greek tradition, Latin references seem never to express such a relation.[24] Indeed, Boethius clearly separates the two deeds, as does Ovid, *Met.* 9.189–98, who at 4.627–62 makes plain that Atlas would not have wanted to help Hercules to this end. Boccaccio, *Gen. Deor.* 13.1 (ed. Romano, p. 636, lines 13–21) offers two causes for the task, neither involving the golden apples; for one he cites "Anselmus" (i.e., Honorius), *De imagine mundi* 1.111 (PL 172.144):[25] Hercules helps Atlas hold up the sky as part of a strategy employed in the war of the giants and the gods. The other "vulgatior" fable is that Hercules assumed the burden so that a tired Atlas could shift it from one shoulder to the other. Trevet (ed. Silk, p. 618) seems to fuse these two scenarios. Clearly, when annotating Chaucer's allusions one must take care not to rely on modern handbooks of classical lore, which tend to offer synopses that do not differentiate between Greek and Latin sources.[26]

The difficulty of assessing classical lore is more forcibly apparent in modern annotation of Chaucer's reference to **Lucia** in the *Wife of Bath's Prologue*. Following the suggestion of Thomas Lounsbury, Skeat and subsequent editors have identified her as the wife of Lucretius, the Epicurean philosopher and poet of ancient Rome.[27] Lucia, writes Chaucer (*WBP* 747–56), was a "likerous" wife who gave her husband what she thought was a love potion (to make him remain faithful), but in fact it was a deadly poison. Chaucer pairs her with Livia, which makes clear that he derives his brief anecdotes about them from Walter Map (*Epistola Valerii ad Rufinum*, in *De nugis curialium* 4.3), who names the two women Livia and Lucilia. All of Map's surrounding exempla are drawn from classical lore; only Lucilia lacks a historical or literary pedigree, which was created only by a later accident of literary history. As it happens, some medieval manuscripts of Map's *Epistola* attributed that work to St. Jerome, and it was subsequently printed among Jerome's writings (see Hanna and Lawler, 61–62). Renaissance scholars (Pietro Crinito and after him Joseph Justus Scaliger) matched the passage in the *Epistola* with a report made by Jerome (in his

---

[24]See, for example, Franz Bömer, *P. Ovidius Naso, Metamorphosen: Kommentar*, 7 vols. (Heidelberg: Carl Winter, 1969–86), 4.337; Bömer remarks that "die Erwähnung des Atlas-Abenteuers in der klassischen lateinischen Dichtung ist relativ selten und topisch."

[25]For other editions and versions of the *Imago mundi*, see Michael W. Twomey, in R. E Kaske, *Medieval Christian Literary Imagery: A Guide to Interpretation* (Toronto: University of Toronto Press, 1988), 189–90. On Honorius, see below, note 31.

[26]Another example of this problem may be seen in Jacqueline de Weever's identification of Hero (named in *LGW* F 263, G 217) as "a priestess of Venus's temple at Sestos"; see *Chaucer Name Dictionary* (New York: Garland, 1988), 138. I have not found Latin sources for that information.

[27]See Thomas R. Lounsbury, *Studies in Chaucer, His Life and Writings*, 3 vols. (1892; reprint, New York: Russell & Russell, 1962), 2.369–70. The error persists even in Benson, ed. (New York, 2000), though Hanna and Lawler, who edit and translate Map's "Dissuasio Valerii ad Rufinum" (see especially 138–41), observe (214) that Lucilia "is apparently Map's invention." The problem with the identification was hinted at much earlier in Frederick Tupper and Marbury Bladen Ogle, trans., *Master Walter Map's Book* De Nugis Curialium *(Courtiers' Trifles)* (London: Chatto & Windus, 1924); while their index of names (353) lists "Lucilia, the wife of Lucretius," their annotation of the passage states (337): "Lucilia was the imaginary wife of Lucretius.... Map seems the sponsor of Lucilia."

additions to the *Chronicon* of Eusebius) which states that Lucretius was driven mad by a love philter and eventually committed suicide. Apparently this conflation took on a life of its own, even though Erasmus had by 1516 relegated the *Epistola* to the slag heap of works spuriously ascribed to Jerome,[28] and thus, presumably, it accounts for the first line of Tennyson's *Lucretius* (1868)— "Lucilia, wedded to Lucretius, found."[29] Lounsbury cites Tennyson, and owing to him modern editions of Chaucer regularly and wrongly identify Lucia as the wife of Lucretius.

Lucia may be a phantom name, but at least it is in Chaucer's text. More spectral is Chaucer's possible allusion to a by-name of the god of war: in *The Complaint of Mars* Chaucer writes of Mars (99–103):

> He throweth on his helm of huge wyghte,
> And girt him with his swerd, and in his hond
> His myghty spere, as he was wont to fyghte,
> He shaketh so that almost hit towond,
> Ful hevy was he to walken over lond.

In Latin texts **Mars** is also called **Gradivus**, a name variously etymologized and each etymology hinted at in Chaucer's depiction. Scholia attached to Servius's comment on *Aeneid* 3.35 derive the name from *gravis deus*, the heavy god (Chaucer refers again to Mars's "hevy armure" at line 130). Ovid, *Fasti* 3.169–74 ("Gradive ... gressus"), implies that *gradivus* comes from *gradiri*, to walk or march (cf. Isidore, *Etymologiae* 8.11.52). John the Scot and Remigius of Auxerre, each glossing Martianus Capella's *De nuptiis* (1.4), add to the marching-god idea an alternative derivation from Greek κράτοσ (powerful). Remigius offers yet a third possibility: *gradein* (Greek κραδαίνω), to shake or brandish, "id est a vibratione hastae" ("that is, from the vibration of a spear").[30]

---

[28]On the Renaissance linking of information in Jerome's *Chronicon* and Map's *Epistola*, see Cyril Bailey, ed., *Titi Lvcreti Cari, De Revm Natvra, Libri sex* (Oxford: Clarendon Press, 1947; corrected reprint, 1972), 10–11; and Karl Lachmann, *In T. Lucretii Cari* De Rerum Natura Libros *Commentarius*, 3rd ed. (Berlin: George Reimer, 1866), 62–63. Hanna and Lawler, 62 (n. 125), provide the information about Erasmus and indicate that even in the 19th century Map's *Epistola* was still being printed among the Jerome apocrypha (PL 30.254–61).

[29]It would be interesting to discover more about the genesis of Tennyson's poem. A reviser of Thomas Creech's English translation of Lucretius (6th ed., London: T. Warner and J. Walthoe, 1722) states plainly that there is no authority for naming the poet's "Mistress, or his Wife, Lucilia" (vol. 1, "Life of Lucretius, pages a3v–a4r). On the other hand, Michael Maittaire's edition of Lucretius (London: Jacob Tonson & John Watts, 1713) includes a biography of the poet that attributes to Lilio Gregorio Giraldi (and not to Pietro Crinito, who is also quoted) the following information (p. A8v): "Sunt, qui ex Hieronymi verbis ad Ruffinum putent Luciliam amicam poculum dedisse Lucretio. Lucilia, inquit, decepta furorem propinavit, pro amoris poculo" ("There are those who may suppose from Jerome's words to Rufinus that the lover who gave the drink to Lucretius was [called] Lucilia. Lucilia, he says, being deceived, hastened [the poet's] madness by way of a love potion").

[30]Isidore's statement about walking vigorously is repeated in the scholia attached to Servius and by Rhabanus Maurus, *De universo* 15.6 (PL 111.430B), which in turn is cited by Boccaccio, *Gen. Deor.* 9.3 (ed. Romano, p. 450, lines 15–16). Boccaccio does not adduce the other etymologies. How might Chaucer have come by them, if he did? He might well have seen glossed copies of Martianus Capella's *De nuptiis*. For the glosses by John the Scot and

That Chaucer could make such subtle allusions is supported by an easier example, this one a reference to **Ninus**, reputedly the first king of the Assyrians (d. 810 B.C.) and husband of Semiramis. In the *Legend of Good Women* (784–85) Chaucer follows Ovid (*Met.* 4.88) in stating that Ninus's grave is in a field outside Babylon; Chaucer adds to Ovid's information that idol-worshipping pagans used to be buried in fields. The inference about burial places remains mysterious, but the association of Ninus with idol worship is readily explained. Jerome, in his commentary on Hosea (Osee 2:16–17; PL 25.838), states that Ninus deified his father Belus (whence Baal) and thus created idol worship. This information is repeated by Isidore, *Etymologiae* 8.11.23; Honorius, *Elucidarium* 2.21 (PL 172.1151);[31] Higden, *Polychronicon* 2.9 (ed. Babington, vol. 2, pp. 78–79); Vincent of Beauvais, *Speculum historiale* 1.102;[32] and Guido delle Colonne, *Historia Destructionis Troiae*, ch. 10 (ed. Griffin, pp. 94–95; trans. Meek, lines 141–55).

By tracking in medieval authorities the topics to which Chaucer alludes, it may be possible to find hints of **verbal influence**. For example, the life of **Hannibal**, the great Carthaginian general, was available to Chaucer in Livy, *Ab urbe condita*, Bks. 21–30; Orosius, *Historiarum libri septem* 4.14–20; Vincent of Beauvais, *Speculum historiale* 5.40–59; Higden, *Polychronicon* 3.33–34; Boccaccio, *De Casibus Virorum*, ch. 5. In the *Man of Law's Tale* (II 290–91) Chaucer says that "Hanybal" vanquished the Romans three times. Among the writers named above only Vincent of Beauvais offers the same succinct enumeration; chapter 42, "De Trina victoria Annibalis," begins: "Eo tempore Romani ab Annibale ter victi leguntur" ("in that time the Romans are reported to have been conquered by Hannibal three times"). A second example may occur in the *Nun's Priest's Tale* (VII 3367), where Chaucer says that **Hasdrubal's wife**, "ful of torment and of rage," threw herself into the fire of burning Carthage. His language seems to echo a phrase, "dolore sed ... furore," used in narratives supplied by Orosius (*Hist.* 4.23; PL 31.916), Vincent (*Spec. hist.* 5.78), and Higden (*Poly.* 3.36; ed. vol. 4, 128). Perhaps less telling is Chaucer's language in describing **Xantippe** (*WBP* 728–29), who cast "pisse" on Socrates's head. The anecdote is borrowed from Jerome (*Adversus Jovinianum* 1.48), whose corresponding phrase is "aqua immunda" (ed. Hanna and Lawler, 177,

---

Remigius of Auxerre, see Jane Chance, *Medieval Mythography, from Roman North Africa to the School of Chartres, A.D. 433–1177* (Gainesville: University of Florida Press, 1994), 570, n. 44; her reference number 5.19 identifies page and line in the edition of Martianus by Adolfus Dick (1925; reprint, Stuttgart: B. G. Teubner, 1969). Thomas Walsingham, *Archana Deorum* 1.16 (ed. Robert A. van Kluyve, Durham, N.C.: Duke University Press, 1968, 25), drawing from the Third Vatican Mythographer (van Kluyve's note), adds to the "walking" etymology a dim echo of the κράτοσ (powerful) one: "eo quod gradatim pergitur in prelium, vel quasi gratus divus, id est potens deus" ("because he proceeds step by step into battle or as if a welcome deity, that is, a *powerful* god" [my emphasis]).

[31] For recent bibliography on Honorius (formerly associated with the town of Autun) and his immensely popular work, see C. W. Marx, "An Abbreviated Middle English Prose translation of the *Elucidarius*," *Leeds Studies in English* n.s. 31 (2000): 1–53.

[32] Vincentius Burgundus (Bellovacensis), *Speculum historiale*, vol. 4 of *Speculum quadruplex* or *Speculum maius* (Douai: Balthazar Beller, 1624; reprint, Graz: Akademische Druck- u. Verlagsanstalt, 1964–65).

line 259). Either Chaucer understood that "unclean water" was a euphemism or he knew versions of the anecdote that made the interpretation clear. For example, John of Salisbury substitutes the somewhat arcane "lotium" (*Policraticus* 8.11); Higden employs the more obvious "urina" (*Poly.* 3.18).[33]

Re-examination of proposed identifications can also lead to a reassessment of their appropriateness. For instance, annotators of Chaucer routinely identify two separate personages named Minos, and one personage named Nebuchadnezzar, whereas in fact it is more proper to refer to one Minos and two Nebuchadnezzars. While one ancient (and obscure) tradition separated **Minos** brother of Rhadamanthus and judge of the underworld from the husband of Pasiphae, and presented the latter as grandson of the former, the prevalent tradition, ancient and medieval, treated the brother of Rhadamanthus and the husband of Pasiphae as one and the same.[34] The opposite fate befalls annotation of **Nebuchadnezzar**. In the *Monk's Tale* Chaucer tells the story of the famous Babylonian king (VII 2143–82) and refers again to "Nabugodonosor" in the story of Holofernes (VII 2562–63). He says nothing in the second instance to distinguish this Nebuchadnezzar from the one treated earlier, and no annotator of Chaucer gives the matter a second thought. However, the Book of Judith, source for Chaucer's treatment of Holofernes, describes its Nebuchadnezzar, not as a king of Babylon, but as king of the Assyrians and ruler of Nineveh. Medieval commentators make clear that the latter is to be identified with Cambyses, who lived two generations after the Babylonian king.[35]

One other proper name worth pausing over is that of **Chrysippus**, whom Chaucer encountered in reading Jerome's *Adversus Jovinianum*, and hence it appears in the *Wife of Bath's Prologue* (677). Chrysippus, a Greek Stoic philosopher, was not well known in the Middle Ages, but thanks to dozens of references to him in works by Latin writers of late antiquity (Jerome, for example, mentions him at least six other times),[36] his name does appear in medieval works

---

[33]Clemens C. I. Webb, ed., *Ioannis Saresberiensis Episcopi Carnotensis Policratici sive De Nugis Curialium et Vestigiis Philosophrum Libri VIII*, 2 vols. (Oxford: Clarendon Press, 1909; reprint, New York: Arno, 1979), 2.301, line 14. Trevisa's translation of Higden has "pisse"; see ed., 3: 284–85.

[34]Skeat (3.333), commenting on the *Legend of Good Women* lines 1886ff., states without explanation that Chaucer "has confused the two kings of this name [Minos]." Notes to this passage in the editions of Robinson (1933, 1957), expanded in the Riverside edition (1987), suggest that this treatment was a medieval aberration, but in fact it merely recapitulates the standard view of antiquity. See, for example, the Pauly-Wissowa *Real-Encyclopädie der classischen Altertumswissenschaft*, vol. 15, part 2 (new ed., Stuttgart: J. B. Metzlersche Verlagsbuchhandlung, 1932), column 1894, which reports that one finds in ancient texts a "merkwürdige Seltenheit der Spaltung des M[inos] in zwei Homonyme." The split is explained as an attempt to deal with incompatible traditions that attached to the one figure.

[35]According to Jerome, the Assyrian Nebuchadnezzar in the Book of Judith (1:5) is not the famed Babylonian king but a later potentate to be identified with Cambyses: see Jerome's translation of Eusebius's *Chronicon* (PL 27.378). Compare too Peter Comestor, *Historia scholastica*, preface to the Book of Judith (PL 198.1475); Vincent of Beauvais, *Spec. hist.* 3.19–20, 22; and Higden, *Poly.* 2.8 and 3.8 (ed., 2: 260–63; 3: 170–71). Whether Chaucer appreciated this distinction one can only guess; he tells an anecdote about Cambyses in *SumT* III 2043–74.

[36]For incomplete listings of ancient references to Chrysippus, see *Stoicorum Veterum*

of philosophical bent: e.g., Alan of Lille's *Anticlaudianus* (twice); John of Salisbury's *Policraticus* (five times); Dante's *De monarchia* (once); Boccaccio's *Genealogia Deorum* (six times). These medieval references offer scraps of information, some unverifiable. A fuller treatment is provided by Vincent of Beauvais (*Spec. hist.* 5.26–28), who quotes from several identified classical sources. It seems likely, moreover, that Chaucer also encountered Chrysippus's name in one of Horace's *Epistles* (1.2.4), probably as quoted in John of Salisbury's *Policraticus* 7.9, where the name appears three lines after a reference to Lollius.

I will conclude this series of annotative adjustments by returning to the topic of place names, specifically places in England. First let us consider Chaucer's measure of the Pardoner's excellence: "But of his craft, fro Berwyk into Ware / Ne was ther swich another pardoner" (I 692–93). Skeat confidently identifies these places with **Berwick**-on-Tweed, the northern-most city of medieval England, and Ware, Hertfordshire (some twenty-three miles north of London). Manly[37] and Magoun, and later editors, feel less certain because England had in it two other Wares and several other Berwicks: "any real certainty seems all but hopeless," says Magoun (*Gazeteer* 31). But I think such a view is unnecessarily despondent. The Hertfordshire **Ware**, one may note, had a particularly important connection to London. It was a major depot for grain that was shipped down the river Lea to Stratford-at-Bow (home of Chaucer's Prioress), where the grain was processed in mills and ovens that provided London (three miles east) with flour and bread.[38] Similarly, Berwick-on-Tweed was not only the most prominent of England's Berwicks, it also had a conspicuous history. Recaptured from the Scots in 1333, Berwick remained a focal point in English–Scottish relations; it was for instance a staging point for Richard II's abortive campaign against Scotland in 1385.[39] Noteworthy too is a plate made for the Painswick astrolabe, at Merton College (Oxford) in the 14th century: it is marked on one side expressly for the latitude of London and on the other for that of Berwick,[40] clearly indicating that Berwick-on-Tweed was looked upon as a proper limit.

Trouble seems to follow the Pardoner and the place names associated with him. But whereas scholars multiply the possibilities for Berwick and Ware, they steadfastly choose the path less traveled in annotating the Pardoner's reference to wine sold "in Fysshstrete or in Chepe" (*Pardoner's Tale* VI 564). The former is regularly identified as Fish Hill Street (also called Bridge Street), which led north from London Bridge and intersected **Eastcheap**. It is possible, however, that Chaucer meant a reference to "Old" or "West" **Fish Street**, a central

---

Fragmenta, compiled by Johann von Arnim in 3 vols. (Leipzig: B. G. Teubner, 1903–05), with indices provided by Maximilian Adler in a 4th vol. (1924).

[37] John Matthews Manly, ed., *Canterbury Tales by Geoffrey Chaucer* (New York: Henry Holt, 1928), 537.

[38] On the commercial link between Ware and London, see K. G. T. McDonnell, *Medieval London Suburbs* (London: Phillimore, 1978), 73–79.

[39] See May McKisack, *The Fourteenth Century, 1307–1399.* Oxford: Clarendon Press, 1959), 439–40.

[40] See Sigmund Eisner, ed., *A Treatise on the Astrolabe. A Variorum Edition of the Works of Geoffrey Chaucer,* vol. 6, part 1 (Norman: University of Oklahoma Press, 2002), 11. Berwick-on-Tweed is the only Berwick at the indicated latitude of 57°.

section of Knightrider Street, an east-west throughway at the north edge of the Vintry and just south of **Cheapside** (which Chaucer calls "Chepe" at *Cook's Tale* I 4377). The retail sale of fish was authorized along both streets, hence their names, and each area was known (in the Renaissance, at least) for its taverns.[41]

How important is it to know such things? Should we ask whether by the 14th century there was a wooden bridge at **Deptford** (*GP* 822; "deep ford"), where the pilgrims had to cross the Ravensbourne,[42] or whether the Canterbury road was paved in **Sittingbourne** (*WBP* 847).[43] I don't know that such details will precipitate any fundamental shifts in the way that we regard Chaucer or read his works. But as Linne Mooney has recently shown in discovering the identity of Chaucer's scribe Adam,[44] the big picture can be changed by looking through a microscope. I hope that the bits and pieces offered here will encourage further nano-research, and that one day it will permit a fuller, more exact appreciation of a poet who amply repays re-examination and deserves a closer look.

---

[41] On the two Fish Streets, see Eilert Ekwall, *Street-Names of the City of London* (Oxford: Clarendon Press, 1954), 30–31, 72–75. See also Henry B. Wheatley, *London Past and Present* (London: John Murray, 1891; reprint, Detroit: Singing Tree Press, 1968), 3.45–47; and cf. quotations in *MED*, s.v. *fish* n. 5. (cc). For good maps that show the location of each street, see Hugh Clout, ed., *The Times London History Atlas* (New York: HarperCollins, 1991), 49–53.

[42] Howard Loxton, *Pilgrimage to Canterbury* (Newton Abbot & London: David & Charles; Totowa, N. J.: Rowman & Littlefield, 1978), 151, indicates that there was such a bridge, perhaps making a reasonable assumption based on a source such as William Lambard (d. 1601), who says in his *Perambulation of Kent* (London: Matthew Walbancke, and Dan. Pakeman, 1656), 469, that the wooden bridge there "was lately reedified."

[43] For lack of paving in Sittingbourne, see Edward Hasted, *The History and Topograpical Survey of the County of Kent*, 2nd ed., 12 vols. (Canterbury: W. Bristow, 1797–1801), 6.152; also *The Victoria History of the County of Kent* (The Victoria History of the Counties of England), 3 vols. (London: Archibald Constable, and St. Catherine Press, 1908–1932), 3.96.

[44] In a presentation given at the New Chaucer Society congress in Glasgow, 17 July 2004.

Philosophical and Scriptural Topics

Chaucer, Auctoritas, and the Problem of Pain

D. Thomas Hanks, Jr.

When one hears "the problem of pain," one thinks of philosophy, perhaps of The Book of Job, and almost certainly of theology. The problem of pain has doubtless haunted humans since we developed thinking powers; it certainly haunts modern scholars. In fact, the problem of pain (or the problem of evil) engrosses so many that an MLA computer-search for books, articles, and dissertations on this topic turns up 890 separate entries between 1990 and January 2004 (though, to be sure, many of these simply address either evil or pain). In 2003 alone, one entire issue of *Hypatia: A Journal of Feminist Philosophy* and part of another were devoted to "Feminist Philosophy and the Problem of Evil" (*Hypatia* 18.1 [Winter 2003] and 18.2 [Spring 2003]). The journal *Rhetoric and Public Affairs*, not to be behindhand, carried in the same year seven such titles as Ned Vankevich's "Confronting the Uncomfortable: Postmodernity and the Quandary of Evil" (*Rhetoric and Public Affairs* 6.3 [Fall 2003]: 554–66). The MLA search produces forty-three titles on this topic just for 2003, some exclusively literary—e.g., Clementina R. Adams, "The Existential Dilemma of Good and Evil: The Inner Soul of the Individual and Society in the Struggle for Survival in *La ventana abierta* by Ramón Fonseca Mora" in *Diáspora: Journal of the Annual Afro-Hispanic Literature and Culture Conference* 13 (2003): 54–61.

Chaucerians, however, seem less interested in the problem of pain or evil. Again searching the MLA database under this topic (1990–2004) with "Chaucer" added, one finds only one essay: the improbably–named "Chaucer and the Goats of Creation" by Gloria Cigman.[1] Throughout this essay I shall suggest that Chaucer gives far more attention to the problem of pain in his *Canterbury Tales* than succeeding generations of scholars have noted; I shall first, however, suggest that he appropriates a near-biblical authority for his Tales.

Twice in Chaucer's *Canterbury Tales* a narrator claims the highest possible status for his writings. The first claim appears in the *Nun's Priest's Tale*. There, the priest–narrator concludes,

> But ye that holden this tale a folye,
> As of a fox, or of a cok and hen,

---

[1] *Literature & Theology: An International Journal of Theory, Criticism and Culture* 5.2 (June 1991): 162–80.

Taketh the moralite, goode men.
For Seint Paul seith that *al that writen is,*
To oure doctrine it is ywrite, ywis;
Taketh the fruyt, and lat the chaf be stille.

(VII 3438—43; emphasis mine)

The second narrator is Chaucer himself, in his authorial persona. His claim, almost identical with the Nun's Priest's, appears in his *Retraction*:

For oure book seith, 'Al that is writen is writen
For oure doctrine,' and that is myn entente.   (X 1083)

This claim combines two biblical passages: Second Timothy 3:16 and Romans 15:4.[2] I quote the two from the Vulgate:

2 Timothy 3:16
[16] omnis scriptura divinitus inspirata et utilis ad docendum ad arguendum ad corrigendum ad erudiendum in iustitia
[17] ut perfectus sit homo Dei ad omne opus bonum instructus
(All that is written is inspired by God and useful for teaching, for debating, for correcting, and for training in righteousness, so that the man of God may be perfect and instructed for every good work.)

Romans 15:4
quaecumque enim scripta sunt ad nostram doctrinam scripta sunt ut per patientiam et consolationem scripturarum spem habeamus
(for whatever things have been written have been written for our doctrine so that through patience and the consolation of the writings we might have hope.)[3]

Chaucer seems to have taken "omnis scriptura" from Second Timothy, and "ad nostram doctrinam" from Romans. The central phrases in both passages are ambiguous: "omnis scriptura" or "quaecumque ... scripta sunt" contain forms of the verb "scribere" (to write), and mean in isolation "all written (things)" or "whatever has been written." By translators, the term has either been anglicized to "scripture," synonymous with "holy Word," or rendered as "whatsoever things were written."[4] For the Chaucer of the Retraction, if we are to believe

---

[2]Lawrence Besserman suggests the Romans passage alone as Chaucer's source: *Chaucer's Biblical Poetics* (Norman, Oklahoma: University of Oklahoma Press, 1998), p. 58. Nicholas Watson agrees with Besserman: "Christian Ideologies," in *A Companion to Chaucer*, ed. Peter Brown (Oxford: Blackwell, 2000), 75–89; see p. 75 for the reference to Romans.

[3]Vulgate passages reached through "Latina" on: http://www.biblegateway.com/versions/ (checked 3 January 2005). The Vulgate present on the Bible Gateway website is the fourth edition of the *Biblia Sacra iuxta vulgatam versionem*. Originally published in 1969, the fourth edition was released in 1994.

[4]The King James Version (KJV) translates the passages as follows:

2 Timothy 3:16–17: All *scripture* is given by inspiration of God, and is profitable for doctrine, for reproof, for correction, for instruction in righteousness: (17) That the man of God may be perfect, throughly furnished unto all good works. (emphasis added)

this statement, the latter reading is preferable: "*All* that is written, is written for our doctrine"—including, of course, the *Canterbury Tales*.

For Nicholas Watson (see note 2) these words of Chaucer's have been "among the most annoying Chaucer wrote," because they impose "a seemingly monolithic didacticism" either on all of the *Canterbury Tales* or at least on the *Parson's Tale*, in either case substituting a Robertsonian singleness of reading for "the multiplicity for which he is famous" (75). *Pace* Watson, one can read these claims in at least two other ways: one can see in this twice-made claim either Chaucer's assertion that all writing—not only his *Tales* or his *Parson's Tale* alone, but all writing—is somehow equal to the Bible in authority; or (more plausibly) one can see a bold assertion that his own writing in the *Tales* partakes of the *auctoritas* accorded the Bible—not only in the *Parson's Tale*, but also in the *Nun's Priest's Tale* and therefore presumably throughout the *Tales*.[5]

Given Chaucer's bold claim to biblical *auctoritas*, it is not surprising to see him examining biblical themes. The tales usually termed "the religious tales" certainly raise such themes: Walter's testing of Griselda in the *Clerk's Tale* struck the Clerk–Narrator himself as a metaphor for God's testing of humans (IV 1142–62); the Man of Law compares his Custance to biblical figures like Daniel or Jonah (II 473–87); the Prioress and Second Nun alike begin their tales with liturgical echoes and/or passages from the Psalms; the *Monk's Tale*, though drearily uninformed by grace, nonetheless discourses within the Christian framework; the *Physician's Tale* follows the form of the martyr-tale, though set in a non-Christian land and time; and, of course, *Melibee* and the *Parson's Tale* are riddled with biblical references, as well as with themes such as forgiveness of enemies and avoidance of sin.[6]

> Romans 15:4: For *whatsoever things were written aforetime* were written for our learning, that we through patience and comfort of *the scriptures* might have hope. (emphasis added)

The New Revised Standard Version presents the two passages almost identically:

> 2 Timothy 3:16–17: All *scripture* is inspired by God and is useful for teaching, for reproof, for correction, and for training in righteousness, (17) so that everyone who belongs to God may be proficient, equipped for every good work. (emphasis added)
>
> Romans 15:4: For *whatever was written in former days* was written for our instruction, so that by steadfastness and by the encouragement of *the scriptures* we might have hope. (emphasis added)

[5] Derek Pearsall discusses this passage in "Chaucer's Religious Tales: A Question of Genre," in *Chaucer's Religious Tales*, ed. C. David Benson and Elizabeth Robertson (Cambridge: D. S. Brewer, 1990), 14. He suggests that since Chaucer first cites this doctrine, then revokes those of the *Canterbury Tales* that "sownen into synne"—whatever tales those might be—the revoked tales must be thought of as "unedifying" as doctrine.

[6] Pearsall lists eight religious tales the *Prioress's Tale*, the *Second Nun's Tale*, the *Man of Law's Tale*, the *Clerk's Tale*, the *Physician's Tale*, the *Monk's Tale*, *Chaucer's Tale of Melibee*, and the *Parson's Tale*): Derek Pearsall, *The Canterbury Tales* (London: Allen & Unwin, 1985), 244–46. More recently, he has repeated his list and defined as generically religious all those tales "predicated upon the assumption that the significance of human life is in the transcending of its secular limitation through Christian faith," with the "purest" example being the *Second Nun's Tale*, followed by the *Man of Law's Tale*, the *Prioress's Tale*, the *Clerk's Tale*, the *Parson's Tale*, the *Monk's Tale*, *Chaucer's Tale of Melibee*, and even the

Indeed, the thematic density of the eight "religious" tales seems to have persuaded many (most?) modern readers of Chaucer that the Christian context of his time has been almost entirely confined to these eight tales, and that the other tales make only passing references to Christian elements (as in the closing prayers of several of the tales, or as in the Pardoner's hypocritical citation of biblical precedent for his authority). Conversely, several scholars have suggested that, in one way or another, the *Tales'* embodiment of their Christian context goes well beyond the eight "religious" tales; they suggest, indeed, that Chaucer establishes a web of Christian and biblical references throughout his Tales. I pause to review their work below.

I again mention Derek Pearsall (see notes 5 and 6), who finds Christian references in most of the tales. I next note what is still called "Robertsonianism," which was the twentieth century's most obviously Christian approach to the *Canterbury Tales*. The eponymous founder of the movement, D. W. Robertson, Jr., in his *Preface to Chaucer* (Princeton: Princeton University Press, 1962), suggests that the *Tales* are to be read as Christian allegories. The Wife of Bath, for example, is to Robertson the allegorical example of various forms of concupiscence ("hopelessly carnal," 317); she appears as an awful example of spiritual misguidedness, misquoting the Bible and leading an existence exactly opposite to the proper Christian role for wives (317–31). Bernard F. Huppé and Robertson produced an ingenious and well-reasoned book on the topic: *Fruyt and Chaf: Studies in Chaucer's Allegories* (Port Washington, NY: Kennikat Press, 1963). Robertsonianism is widely deplored by many Chaucerians, but still exerts considerable influence. As the deplorers have pointed out, the allegorical approach can come to flatten the *Tales* into a series of sermons; most readers feel that they are more, or at least other, than sermons. The backlash against this view has perhaps curtailed investigation into the interactions of the Christian and the secular in the *Tales*; a pre-*Preface* work that exemplifies the fruitfulness of such investigation is Arthur W. Hoffman, "Chaucer's Prologue to Pilgrimage: The Two Voices," easily available in *Chaucer: Modern Essays in Criticism*, ed. Edward Wagenknecht (London: Oxford University Press, 1959), 30–45.

Several books, and many articles, have addressed issues of Christianity in the *Tales*. Ruth Ames's book approaches Chaucer's works from a straightforward Christian viewpoint: *God's Plenty: Chaucer's Christian Humanism* (Chicago: Loyola University Press, 1984). More recently, John M. Hill has explored "The Poetics of Reverence and Delight" (subtitle) in his *Chaucerian Belief* (New Haven: Yale University Press, 1991), where he suggests that in the *Tales* overall Chaucer poses "relations between feeling, belief, and perception in teller after teller" (23). It is not clear, however, what the tellers believe in; though Hill continues to repeat such statements as "the tales ... are arenas for the episte-mological play of wonder, feeling, and belief" (94), such terms as "Christian"

Physician's Tale (though this last may simply be "a failure"); the list appears in "Chaucer's Religious Tales: A Question of Genre" in *Chaucer's Religious Tales*, 16. Interestingly, in this essay he suggests that *All* of the *Canterbury Tales* can be seen as religious "by virtue of their historical context" (13). He rather scouts this approach, but eventually agrees that Christianity is relevant to all the tales except *Thopas* (15).

or "God" (except for the God of Love) do not appear in his index. Still more recently, Robert Boenig has written of Chaucer's aligning himself with a "mystical environment" in *Chaucer and the Mystics*: The Canterbury Tales *and the Genre of Devotional Prose* (Lewisburg: Bucknell University Press; London: Associated University Presses, 1995), 169. He finds many parallels between the *Canterbury Tales* and the genre of devotional prose, as his subtitle announces. More recently still, an important book on Chaucer's *Parson's Tale* necessarily raises issues of Christianity: *Closure in the* Canterbury Tales : *The Role of* The Parson's Tale, ed. David Raybin and Linda Tarte Holley (Kalamazoo, Mich.: Medieval Institute Publications, 2000).

Many articles likewise illustrate a continuing interest in Chaucer and Christianity. One of the more luminous is Linda Georgianna's "Love So Dearly Bought: The Terms of Redemption in *The Canterbury Tales*," *Studies in the Age of Chaucer* 12 (1990): 85–116, in which she examines Chaucer's treatment of pilgrimage in the *Tales* and concludes that though he consistently writes of pilgrimage and of redemption in terms of commercial exchange (e.g., Christ has "boghte" sinners with his blood), he nonetheless "treats the practice of pilgrimage . . . as an appropriate extension of the theology of redemption and forgiveness" (97–98). Georgianna surveys the *Tales* in general, noting a widespread use of the language of commercial exchange for redemption, but argues for a final statement in the *Parson's Tale* in favor of traditional redemption based on the Word, not on the pocketbook.

Appearing at the same time, Przemyslaw Mroczkowski's "Faith and the Critical Spirit in Chaucer and His Time" in *Religion in the Poetry and Drama of the Late Middle Ages in England,* ed. Piero Boitani and Anna Torti (Cambridge: D. S. Brewer, 1990), 83–100, surveys not only the European and English religious context of Chaucer's times, but all of Chaucer's works as well in a treatment necessarily broad. He concludes that Chaucer was "a thinking, indeed shrewd educated layman, basically content to accept the requirements of his faith together with his 'non-specialist' status, who also understands the accompanying intellectual difficulties experienced by many in his time but will not voice them aggressively or peremptorily"—a philosophical stance perhaps tempered by Chaucer's caution in the face of possible Churchly opposition to clearly-stated scepticism, he adds (99). I share Mroczkowski's view of Chaucer as questioning fideist, though I shall argue that he voices "intellectual difficulties" more clearly than Mroczkowski suggests.

An older article too little noted is W. Meredith Thompson, "Chaucer's Translation of the Bible," in *English and Medieval Studies Presented to J. R. R. Tolkien on the Occasion of His Seventieth Birthday,* ed. Norman Davis and C. L. Wrenn (London: George Allen & Unwin, 1962), 183–99. Thompson notes how very much of the Vulgate Chaucer translates, and the many contexts in which Chaucer uses the Bible as a source.

And, finally, I note that many articles, like Lee Patterson's " 'The Living Witnesses of Our Redemption': Martyrdom and Imitation in Chaucer's Prioress's Tale," *Journal of Medieval and Early Modern Studies* 31.3 (2001): 507–60, discuss Christianity in the context of a single tale or of a few tales.

In sum, the above-noted scholars suggest that a myriad of Christian themes and references appear throughout the *Canterbury Tales*. One of those themes which has been too little discussed is Chaucer's examination of the problem of pain.

I

The *locus classicus* for the problem of pain in the Western Christian tradition is the Book of Job. The book opens with God's asking Satan to consider God's servant Job, who is perfectly godly; Satan tartly replies that Job is not perfect for nothing, since God has given him so much. Should God remove Job's riches and family, Satan avers, he would waver and fall. God, interested in the challenge, allows Satan to test Job—who promptly loses riches, children, and finally health at Satan's hands (he develops "sore boils" over his entire body: Job 2:7; biblical quotations come from KJV unless otherwise stated). Job remains faithful, saying only "the LORD gave, and the LORD hath taken away; blessed be the name of the LORD" (1:21).

Several friends come to "comfort" Job; they do so by assuring him that since he has lost so much of worldly goods, he must have sinned: God punishes only the unrighteous. Job, indignant, says again and again that he has *not* sinned— that God is persecuting him unjustly. The entire debate appears encapsulated in a statement by Bildad followed by a later response from Job: in Job 8:3 Bildad asks, "Doth God pervert judgment? or doth the Almighty pervert justice?" Job eventually responds, "[God] destroyeth the perfect and the wicked" (9:22).

Eventually, God returns Job's wealth, and new and better children to replace those whom God allowed to be killed. Job's question about undeserved pain stands, however—and, astonishingly, God takes Job's side in the debate. Addressing Job's non-comforters, "the LORD said to Eliphaz ... 'My wrath is kindled against thee and against thy two friends; for ye have not spoken of me the thing that is right, as my servant Job hath'" (42:7).

I summarize the Job story at such length for two reasons. First, the story was part of the daily experience of many medieval Christians. As Lawrence Besserman points out, most regular clergy and many lay persons experienced the Book of Job daily, in truncated form; portions of six chapters of the book appeared in the liturgy in the Matins of the Dead, recited daily at 9 p.m., midnight, and 3 a.m.[7] My second reason for summarizing the story is that so many of the elements of the summary appear in Chaucer's *Tales*, as appears below. Job's story was not generally read as an indictment of a seemingly-capricious God in the Middle Ages, and it is not often read that way today. Nonetheless, an indictment it is. It states the problem of pain in a Godly context: if God is, and if God values virtue, and if God rules, why does God allow pain to befall those who lead "blameless and upright" lives (Job 1:1) and

---

[7]Lawrence Besserman, *The Legend of Job in the Middle Ages* (Cambridge, Mass.: Harvard University Press, 1979), 58. Besserman further reports a flowering of European vernacular writing about Job in the fourteenth and fifteenth centuries (75). The chief English works, the *Pety Iob* and an early-fifteenth-century *Paraphrase* of much of the Old Testament, both use Job as an exemplar of meekness and obedience to God.

who worship God? For the *Tales*, only Mary Edith Thomas and Ruth Ames have raised this God–pain issue in a context broader than a single tale; I summarize their comments below.

Thomas raises the issue as the "problem ... of God's justice" in her *Medieval Skepticism and Chaucer* (1950; reprint, New York: Cooper Square, 1971), 124. Beginning with the *Knight's Tale*, Thomas discusses the problem of reconciling "the existence of evil with a divine plan" (124). She touches upon the *Knight's Tale*, the "grisly feendly rokkes blake" of the *Franklin's Tale*, and Custance's plight in the *Man of Law's Tale* (124–31). I have perhaps cast my net more widely in this essay, but to Thomas must go the credit for first raising this issue for the *Canterbury Tales* in a manner more comprehensive than had occurred before.

Ames discusses the issue, in a chapter which she terms "The Problem of Evil," in *God's Plenty: Chaucer's Christian Humanism* (Chicago: Loyola University Press, 1984), 227–52. She notes that Chaucer raises the problem often in his works, and that his characters cannot solve it. She is certain, however, that Chaucer is not "a skeptic or a determinist" (227). As do I, she sees the problem of pain in the *Knight's Tale* (the only tale she considers for the problem of pain), but considers the problem solved within the tale. To be sure, Palamon and Arcite do not solve it—they are no greater philosophers than the Knight–Narrator himself, who is to Ames "not much of a philosopher" (234). The Knight's Theseus, however, thinks that he solves the problem as he sums up Boethius' *Consolation* in the tones of Ben Franklin: Lady Philosophy adapted to the meanest understanding (235–36). This, for Ames, settles the matter. She turns to *Troilus and Criseyde*, touches upon the *Nun's Priest's Tale* as parody, quickly notes the appearance of the problem of pain in the *Man of Law's Tale*, the *Franklin's Tale*, and a few others (but not the *Clerk's Tale*), discusses the role of "the devil" in causing the various evils from which the characters suffer, and concludes that "the force of circumstance is strong, but ... the characters are responsible for their handling of the evil that descends upon them" (251). In short, they have free moral choice; they can always choose to do good in the face of evil (252). I have to think this a facile solution to the problem of pain; it shifts the grounds of the argument. To be obvious: if God is good, why does evil descend on, for example, Custance?

I am pleased that Thomas and Ames have perceived this issue in the *Tales*; their treatment is sufficiently general, however, that it seems useful to develop the topic more fully. I develop that topic by suggesting that Chaucer raises the issue of the problem of pain regularly in his *Canterbury Tales*, and that he raises the issue in a Christian context—often in the context of the Book of Job as read by Christians.

II

Chaucer first puts the problem of pain into a Christian context in his putatively-pagan *Knight's Tale*. The problem appears succinctly implied in two questions which govern my approach to the tale: Palamon first asks,

> What governance is in this *prescience*,
> That giltelees tormenteth innocence?
>
> (I 1313–14; my emphasis)

Arcite, innocent but dying young, asks the second question:

> "What is this world? What asketh men to have?
> Now with his love, now in his colde grave
> Allone, withouten any compaignye."   (2777—79)

One answer to the young knights' two questions begins with the narrator's comment about destiny and God's providence:

> The destinee, ministre general,
> That executeth in the world over al
> The purveiaunce that God hath seyn biforn,
> So strong it is that, though the world had sworn
> The contrarie of a thyng by ye or nay,
> Yet somtyme it shal fallen on a day
> That falleth nat eft withinne a thousand yeer.
> For certeinly, oure appetites heer,
> Be it of werre, or pees, or hate, or love,
> Al is this reuled by the sighte above.   (1663–72)

The passage derives from Boethius' *Consolation of Philosophy* (Bk IV, Prose 6). There and elsewhere, Boethius' Lady Philosophy points out that God rules all, and that nothing occurs outside of God's providence; here, Chaucer's Knight says likewise, closing with the definite statement,

> Be it of werre, or pees, or hate, or love,
> *Al* is this reuled by the sighte above.
>
> (1671–72; my emphasis)

To the Knight–Narrator, then, God rules all. To be sure, his Theseus will later attribute this rule to Jupiter—but the pagan disguise is thin. It is "The purveiaunce that *God* hath seyn biforn" that the Knight suggests as the answer to the queries of the tormented Palamon, of the dying Arcite: God has ordained what is happening to you. In the context of his tale, this becomes a Job-like indictment of God—at least, from the perspective of these two young men.

That perspective begins to appear in the two long complaints by Arcite and Palamon after Arcite is taken out of prison and exiled from Athens. Arcite begins his complaint with another reflection derived from the *Consolation of Philosophy*. First bewailing the loss of the sight of Emelye from his prison tower, he then turns to a wider reflection concerning the Providence of God, or of Fortune:

> "Allas, why pleynen folk so in commune
> *On purveiaunce of God, or of Fortune,*

> That yeveth hem ful ofte in many a gyse
> Wel bettre than they kan hemself devyse?"
>
> (1251–54; emphasis mine)

Arcite here introduces a theist, if not Christian, theme straight out of Boethius. It begins to look like a Christian theme just a few lines later, when Arcite adds to his complaint, "We witen nat what thing we preyen heere … " (1260), reflecting Romans 8:26, which in the Vulgate appears as "quid oremus sicut oportet nescimus" (what we ought to pray we do not know).

Palamon mirrors Arcite's complaint. He, too, begins with Boethius, complaining that the force that governs the world (here identified with "crueel goddes," 1303)—that this governing force, prescient as it is (1313), nonetheless not only *allows* the innocent to suffer, as Boethius suggests (Book I, Meter 5), but actively "tormenteth innocence" (1314—a phrase reminiscent of Job).[8] Note, too, that though it begins with Boethius, the passage soon turns like Arcite's to a Christian reflection—in fact, it turns to two Christian reflections. The first echoes Ecclesiastes: "For slayn is man right as another beest" (1309) alludes to Ecclesiastes 3:18–19, which contains "I said in my heart with regard to human beings that God is testing them to show that they are but animals. For the fate of humans and the fate of animals is the same; as one dies, so dies the other" (NRSV). Palamon's comment particularly appears as a biblical reference in the context of 1313–20, lines which clearly refer to Purgatory—a surprising reference to come from pagan Palamon. In these lines Palamon complains that humans, "for Goddes sake," must govern their own will, whereas animals are free to do as they please—and nonetheless, a human "after his deeth moot wepe and pleyne" (1320).[9] Each young lover, then, begins his complaint with a Boethian reflection, but each soon turns to a Christian, and to a biblical, allusion. Note that Palamon closes his *planctus* with an outright statement of the problem of pain:

> "The answere of this lete I to dyvynys,
> But wel I woot that in this world greet pyne ys." (1323–24)

Chaucer, first having used his Knight–Narrator to establish the view that God's Providence rules every human activity (recall "Al is this reuled by the sighte above," I 1672), questions the beneficence of that Providence in the complaints of the two lovers, and closes their complaints with Palamon's stating the problem of pain. Theseus' answer to the problem at the tale's close—that this is just the way Jupiter does things, and we have to make the best of it—may seem, as Helen Cooper has suggested, "an exercise in patching grief with

---

[8] As Helen Cooper has suggested, this passage "strengthens the sense of malevolent forces at work in the world." Helen Cooper, *Oxford Guides to Chaucer: The Canterbury Tales*, 2nd edn. (Oxford: Oxford University Press, 1996), 70.

[9] John C. Zhang, in "Writing in Lines 1303–27 of The Knight's Tale," *English Language Notes* 26 (June 1989): 1–5, suggests that this passage shows Chaucer's voice, not the voice of the Knight–Narrator or of Palamon. Zhang finds the reference to suffering after death inappropriate to the "pagan" Palamon, and likewise inappropriate to the Knight, who as a noble Knight could expect to enter heaven after death. Zhang has overlooked the concept of Purgatory, which was of course a constant in the minds of medieval Christians.

proverbs" (*The Canterbury Tales*, 79);[10] Egeus' solution is more in line with Chaucer's contemporary Christian world, as he suggests that "This world nys but a thurghfare ful of wo, / And we been pilgrymes, passynge to and fro. / Deeth is an ende of every worldly soore" (2847–49). The Knight–Narrator, however, takes back whatever comfort one may find in Egeus' comment: rather than suggesting that Christian comforts will follow Arcite's death, he merely states that Arcite's spirit "chaunged hous" to go "I kan nat tellen wher" (2809–10). In a highly Chaucerian move, he does not deny the Christian happy ending; he simply refuses to comment. "I nam no divinistre," he reports (2811), and leaves Arcite "coold" (2815).[11]

As all know, Egeus' conclusion, and the *Knight's Tale* in general, take place in a pagan world.[12] Chaucer, however, has inset Christian references into this pagan world; he is not just examining the lost-ness of humans in a pagan world, as many have suggested,[13] but rather he delicately suggests that in his audience's Christian world, where all are pilgrims on the road to the Heavenly Jerusalem, the problem of pain nonetheless, and insolubly, appears.[14]

The problem reappears in the Man of Law's relentlessly Christian tale of Custance. Poor Custance travels continually in a rudderless ship, both metaphorically and literally; hers is a determinate world, one wherein "Goddes sonde"— what God sends—is the determining factor. Thus when the Man-of-Law–Narrator asks why Custance was not slain at a feast along with the Sultan her husband and most of his guests, he responds that she was preserved because "God liste to shewe his wonderful myracle / In hire, for we sholde seen his myghty werkis" (II 477–78).[15] Indeed, God very quickly becomes the motive

---

[10]Nicholas Watson likewise finds Theseus' attempt to "justify the order of the cosmos in the limited Boethian terms available to him" a signal failure ("Christian Ideologies," 79).

[11]Mary Edith Thomas suggests that Chaucer raises the problem of the "righteous heathen" in this passage, and that his audience would have recognized that problem in his terms (*Medieval Skepticism and Chaucer*, 104–6). Thomas also sees the problem of pain reflected in Palamon's speeches in his prison soliloquy: she concludes that "Palamon could give the riddle of life over to the theologians, but he could not believe in a just providence" (128). She does not carry her discussion of the problem of pain further with respect to the *Knight's Tale*.

[12]Pearsall echoes a common assertion that the *Knight's Tale* and *Franklin's Tale* are "deliberately set in pre-Christian or pagan times" ("Chaucer's Religious Tales," 15). The *Knight's Tale*, he further suggests, shows humans without God, and inhabiting a world much like that of *Lear*. He adds, "our consciousness of what is absent, of the immanence of a Christian view of man and the world as we read of men and worlds supposedly benighted, is a very present part of our experience of these poems" (15). Much earlier, Roger Ellis suggested that the *Knight's Tale* "treats religious questions seriously, but ... does not actively engage with specifically Christian language or reference": *Patterns of Religious Narrative in the* Canterbury Tales (Totowa, NJ: Barnes & Noble, 1986), 15.

[13]Two examples from many are Pearsall as above and in his *The Canterbury Tales*, 120; see also Cooper, *The Canterbury Tales*, 81–82.

[14]Charles A. Owen, Jr., has noted "The Problem of Free Will in Chaucer's Narratives," *Philological Quarterly* 46 (1967): 433–56. For the *Knight's Tale*, he notes the Boethian determinism of Godly rule, but does not touch upon what I see as the explicitly Christian nature of the discussion in the tale (435–39).

[15]Dorothy Bethurum Loomis suggests that these words mark the point at which the earlier astrological determinism of the tale comes to an end, and God steps in to reverse the disastrous trend brought about by the stars ("Constance and the Stars" in *Chaucerian Problems*

power behind all the actions of the *Man of Law's Tale* (though sometimes Jesus or Mary gets credit as well); again and again, the Man of Law asks who preserved Daniel (II 473–75), or Jonah (II 486–87), or Mary of Egypt (II 500–501), or David confronting Goliath (II 934–36), or Judith (II 939–42). For that matter, he asks, who preserved Custance from rape by the apostate steward (II 920–45)? In each case, the answer is God—or, in the instance of the attempted rape, Mary and Jesus (II 920, 924) as well as God (II 945).

Chaucer's Custance differs greatly from the Constance of his source, Nicholas Trivet's Anglo-Norman *Chronicle*. Custance is much more God's puppet than was Trivet's Constance, as a comparison of the tale with Trivet's version quickly shows.[16] Custance's puppet status does not preserve her, however. Woe ever follows joy in Custance's world, pre-determined at first by the stars and then by God: "God liste to shewe his wonderful myracle / In hire, for we sholde seen his myghty werkis" (II 477–78). Owing to the machinations of her wicked mother-in-law, Custance is once again set adrift on the high seas. The constable ordered to set her adrift alludes to the problem of pain as he follows his orders:

> "O myghty God, if that it be thy wille,
> Sith thou art rightful juge, how may it be
> That thou wolt suffren innocentz to spille,
> And wikked folk regne in prosperitee?"   (II 813–16)[17]

In the same scene, before being again set adrift, Custance makes it clear that she is aware of the injustice being visited upon her child and herself, though she directs her comments to her child alone:

> "O litel child, allas! What is thy gilt,
> That nevere wroghtest synne as yet, pardee?
> Why wil thyn harde fader han thee spilt?"   (II 855–57)

In the first of the two passages, the constable asks how a "rightful" God can suffer the innocent to suffer; forty lines later, Custance asks her baby why its father persecutes his guiltless child. The questions are obviously related, and

---

and Perspectives, ed. Edward Vasta and Zacharias Thundy [Notre Dame, Ind., and London: University of Notre Dame Press, 1979], 217).

[16] For just one instance, compare the openings to each account. Trivet's Constance meets the Syrian merchants who have heard of her beauty and goodness; she preaches to them and converts them. Chaucer makes his Custance passive as the tale opens; the Syrian merchants merely hear of Custance's virtue and beauty and report them to the Sultan. See Nicholas Trivet, *Chronicle*, in Margaret Schlauch, "The Man of Law's Tale," in *Sources and Analogues of Chaucer's* Canterbury Tales, ed. W. F. Bryan and Germaine Dempster (1941; reprint, Atlantic Highlands, NJ: Humanities Press, 1958), 155–206. Constance's conversion of the Syrian merchants occurs on p. 165: "e quant ele entendi qil estoient paens, lour prescha la fey Cristienn. E puis qil auoient assentu a la fey, les fist baptizer" [and when she understood that they were pagans, she preached to them the Christian faith. Then as soon as they had assented to the faith, she had them baptized].

[17] Patricia J. Eberle's explanatory note to lines 813–16 in the *Riverside Chaucer* (p. 861) identifies the passage as a "Boethian echo" of the *Consolation*, Book 1, Meter 5, lines 34–46, and Book 4, Prose 1, lines 19–31, which it is. The passage also echoes a constant refrain in the Book of Job, which Eberle does not point out.

equally unanswerable. The Man of Law does not give an answer; that is, he gives no answer beyond "God liste" (II 477). Chaucer raises the question, but leaves it unresolved. One could argue, of course, that "things work out all right at the end" in the *Man of Law's Tale*—but to argue so, one must ignore more than eight years of Custance's rudderless voyaging (II 499, 901), ignore her arraignment for murder (II 596–689), ignore the attempted rape she suffers (II 904–45), and—surely worst of all—ignore what she thinks is her husband's order that she be sent to her death drifting once more on the sea (II 792ff). It is not an easy life, being Custance. God is always sending her more disaster.

That word "send," or its derivative "sonde"—that which is sent—appears eleven times in the *Man of Law's Tale* referring to what God (or Jesus) has ordained (in II 504, 523, 760, 766, 826, 902, 943, 945, 1041, 1042, and 1160). Many other episodes close or open with the comment that God, or Jesus, or even Mary, is aiding Custance, or guiding her, or sending a huge hand down from heaven to smite one of her detractors (II 666–76). Negating the opening lines' comments on astral determinism, the latter two-thirds of the tale show that God rules every particular of Custance's world; Custance has as much reason to question what God sends her as did Job. She never does. Her first readers may have done so, or they may have joined the Man of Law in his mindless assertion that so long as "it lyked God" to do these things, then that's just fine. It seems clear, however, that the Chaucer who raised the problem of pain in his first tale is still pursuing it here.[18]

---

[18] Paul Ruggiers suggested long ago in his *The Art of the* Canterbury Tales (Madison: University of Wisconsin Press, 1965) that "the outrageous and fantastic episodes" of the tale require the intervention of God to resolve them; it is this "Higher Power whose influence molds the life of this Christian woman, and provides, from the point of view of the plot, its informing spirit" (171). He does not suggest that Chaucer questions this view in any way. Ruggiers, like many a reader since, sees this tale as simply "the vehicle for the more credulous kind of religious element"; "the overwhelming effect," he adds, "is that of religious enthusiasm and insistence" (171). Jill Mann, in "Suffering Woman, Suffering God" (chapter four of her *Geoffrey Chaucer*, Atlantic Highlands, NJ: Humanist Press, 1991, 128–64), notes the Godly determinism which shapes the tale (131–34). Like me, she sees that explicit determinism as the major shaping force in the tale, and notes that it raises the question of suffering "on a metaphysical level." She adds that this question admits of no final answer—but, she continues, *MLT* answers it "on the emotional, experiential level of Christianity itself, by locating God *in* the suffering" (Mann's emphasis; 134–35). Mann finds her evidence for this assertion chiefly in Custance's reference to the Cross in lines 841–47 (quoted on p. 135). She suggests later in her article that both Custance and Griselda typify the statement made in the Cross: "the suffering that God 'allows' is visited on himself [sic]" (163). Custance, then, typifies the patience of the ideal Christian—as does Griselda, Mann later concludes (see below). See also Mann's Presidential Address to the New Chaucer Society (1994) in *Studies in the Age of Chaucer* 17 (1995): 5–19. Titled "Chaucer and Atheism," the essay notes in passing her conclusions in the earlier book: see pp. 16–17. More recently, Helen Cooper has not seen the juxtaposition of God's will with disaster as an expression of scepticism; rather, she suggests another view of this discordant juxtaposition: that Chaucer's contrasting the world of hagiography with the world of tragedy results in setting up "generically incompatible views of the world[, thus allowing] a pattern of relativity, and therefore of fullness of vision, [to] emerge from the juxtaposition" (*The Canterbury Tales*, 132). I do not quite agree; to use Cooper's terms, I think the world of tragedy here questions the world of hagiography.

Custance's problem of pain reappears in the *Clerk's Tale*, which recalls Job to us not once but three times.[19] Chaucer's source for the tale, Petrarch's *Epistolae Seniles* (XVII.3), alludes to The Book of Job at one point: his Griselda states "Nuda e domo patris egressa, nuda itidem revertar" (naked I left my father's home, nude I return there—an allusion to Job 1:21.)[20] Chaucer's Griselda repeats the allusion with " 'Naked out of my fadres hous ... I cam, and naked moot I turne agayn' " (IV 871–72).

Following this near-quotation from Job, Chaucer then adds an allusion to Job not in his source, and finally adds a straightforward reference to the ancient story.

The added allusion appears in Janicula's response to the Marquis Walter's divorce of Janicula's daughter, Griselda:

> Hir fader, that this tidynge herde anoon,
> Curseth the day and tyme that Nature
> Shoop hym to been a lyves creature. (IV 901–3)

One hears a clear echo of Job 3:3: "pereat dies in qua natus sum et nox in qua dictum est conceptus est homo" (may the day perish in which I was born and the night in which it was said a man has been conceived).

Finally, as if fully to clarify his interest in Job (and in the problem of pain), Chaucer adds a straightforward reference:

> Men speke of Job, and moost for his humblesse,
> As clerkes, whan hem list, konne wel endite,
> Namely of men, but as in soothfastnesse,
> Though clerkes preise wommen but a lite,
> Ther kan no man in humblesse hym acquite
> As womman kan, ne kan been half so trewe
> As wommen been, but it be falle of newe. (IV 932–38)

As George Lyman Kittredge suggested long ago, this speech controverts the Wife of Bath's claim that clerks never speak well of women.[21] The speech also makes

---

[19]Besserman notes, in *The Legend of Job in the Middle Ages*, that Chaucer refers to the Book of Job in the *Clerk's Tale*; Besserman cites the references which I also note below. He suggests that Chaucer splits the traditional Job into two: the impatient Job becomes Janicula (who curses the day he was born, as Job does); the meek Job becomes Griselda (Besserman, 111–12). Besserman adds that the use of Job to promote the idea of a patient wife is new to medieval literature, and unique to Chaucer (113).

[20]From Petrarch's *Epistolae Seniles* (XVII.3) in J. Burke Severs, *The Literary Relationships of Chaucer's Clerkes Tale* (New Haven: Yale University Press, 1942), 280, line 29. The nearly identical passage in the Vulgate reads, " ... nudus egressus sum de utero matris meae et nudus revertar illuc" (naked I issued from the womb of my mother, and naked I shall return there—Job 1:21).

[21]
> For trusteth wel, it is an impossible
> That any clerk wol speke good of wyves,
> But if it be of hooly seintes lyves,
> Ne of noon oother womman never the mo. (III 688–91)

Kittredge's comments on the Wyf appear in *Chaucer and His Poetry* (1915; reprint, Cambridge, Mass.: Harvard University Press, 1970), 185–211; Kittredge discusses the Clerk's responding to the Wyf on pp. 194–95.

evident Chaucer's interest in the applicability of the Book of Job to his story of Griselda. God allowed the ultra-virtuous Job to be persecuted, seemingly out of caprice; Walter does likewise to Griselda.

These passages show that Chaucer saw the Book of Job reflected in Petrarch's tale, though Petrarch did not explicitly mention it. Not only did Chaucer quote the two lines from Petrarch which paraphrase a passage in Job, he added the two passages of his own which either use or cite Job as a source. Moreover, Chaucer's Clerk adds to his tale a moral embodying the medieval view of Job:

> For sith a womman was so pacient
> Unto a mortal man, wel moore us oghte
> Receyven al in gree that God us sent.   (1149–51)

Here—though not earlier, where he inveighed against Walter's cruelty—here, Chaucer's Clerk seems perfectly comfortable with the problem of pain; if, indeed, it pleases God to send us grief like that which he sent Griselda, we must simply receive that grief in patience—like Job, if you think in terms like "the patience of Job." (One recalls that the root of the word "patience" is *patior*, meaning "to suffer.")[22] I must add that almost no student of mine to date has ever failed to react to the tale as portraying Griselda as a dishrag and Walter as a jerk. It is only after they realize that the Clerk parallels Walter with God that they draw back from their position, with great uneasiness. They do not want to see God portrayed as pointlessly cruel. This point—Walter's identification with God—has been much debated by Chaucerians. In three particularly important articles, Robert O. Stepsis, David C. Steinmetz, and Rodney Delasanta have debated the degree to which Chaucer embodied in the *Clerk's Tale* the Ockhamist-Nominalist concept of God's absolute power, or *potentia absoluta*. Their conclusions differ, but all three unite in agreeing that Chaucer engages the problem of pain in the *Clerk's Tale*, and that the problem is difficult to solve.[23] All three also agree that Walter represents God in the tale. Here, Chaucer is bolder in his *Clerk's Tale* than my students (who are mostly professing Christians) want him to be. I have to wonder how thoughtful Christians of

---

[22] Paul Ruggiers, again in his *The Art of* The Canterbury Tales, has been so impressed by the Clerk's closing moral that he concludes that the tale is "anagogical," an allegorical tale having to do with the soul's response to God in its progress to the afterlife (219). As he puts it,

> Allowing Griselda to suggest symbolically suffering humanity in much the same way that Job does, and allowing Walter to suggest the seemingly capricious hand of God visiting oppression upon one of the faithful, help to supply the justifications for which so many readers strain (220).

The tale is, he suggests, "vastly more austere" than the *Man of Law's Tale* (224). Cooper, too, sees the Christian reading, and suggests that though it is less of a theme than that of natural "gentilesse," the theme of necessary obedience to God nonetheless appears in it (*The Canterbury Tales*, 196–97).

[23] Robert Stepsis, "*Potentia Absoluta* and the *Clerk's Tale*," *Chaucer Review* 10 (1975–76): 129–46; David C. Steinmetz, "Late Medieval Nominalism and the *Clerk's Tale*," *Chaucer Review* 12 (1977): 38–54; Rodney Delasanta, "Nominalism and the *Clerk's Tale* Revisited," *Chaucer Review* 31 (1997): 209–31.

his own time received Chaucer's *Clerk's Tale*. (Jill Mann has noted the modern reluctance to perceive Walter as echoing "the God who inflicts suffering and death on his children," but herself suggests that the Christ-like suffering of Griselda—as of Custance—mirrors the suffering God embodied in the crucified Christ, while at the same time the woeful situations of the two are directly caused by the God who does, indeed, inflict suffering upon God's children. Both Custance and Griselda are ideal Christians in their steadfast faith, she concludes—and they are at the same time types of the embodied God–Christ in their suffering.)[24]

Chaucer once again touches upon Job's problem of pain in the *Franklin's Tale*. Recall Dorigen's agonized musings upon the black rocks off the coast of Armorica (I quote the entire 36 lines):

> But whan she saugh the grisly rokkes blake,
> For verray feere so wolde hir herte quake   860
> That on hire feet she myghte hire noght sustene.
> Thanne wolde she sitte adoun upon the grene,
> And pitously into the see biholde,
> And seyn right thus, with sorweful sikes colde—
> "Eterne God, that thurgh thy purveiaunce   865
> Ledest the world by certein governaunce,
> In ydel, as men seyn, ye no thyng make.
> But, Lord, thise grisly feendly rokkes blake,
> That semen rather a foul confusion
> Of werk than any fair creacion   870
> Of swich a parfit wys God and a stable,
> Why han ye wroght this werk unresonable?
> For by this werk, south, north, ne west, ne eest,
> Ther nys yfostred man, ne bryd, ne beest;
> It dooth no good, to my wit, but anoyeth.   875
> Se ye nat, Lord, how mankynde it destroyeth?
> An hundred thousand bodyes of mankynde
> Han rokkes slayn, al be they nat in mynde,
> Which mankynde is so fair part of thy werk
> That thou it madest lyk to thyn owene merk.   880
> Thanne semed it ye hadde a greet chiertee
> Toward mankynde; but how thanne may it bee
> That ye swiche meenes make it to destroyen,
> Whiche meenes do no good, but evere anoyen?
> I woot wel clerkes wol seyn as hem leste,   885
> By argumentz, that al is for the beste,
> Though I ne kan the causes nat yknowe.
> But thilke God that made wynd to blowe
> As kepe my lord! This my conclusion.

---

[24] For the *Clerk's Tale* as for the *Man of Law's Tale* see the references to Jill Mann's work in n. 18 above.

To clerkes lete I al disputison.   890
But wolde God that alle thise rokkes blake
Were sonken into helle for his sake!
Thise rokkes sleen myn herte for the feere."
Thus wolde she seyn, with many a pitous teere.   (859–94)

A quick glance back at the *Knight's Tale* shows that central elements of the material there appear likewise in Dorigen's complaint. Both Chaucer's Knight and Arcite note God's "prescience" or "purveiaunce," as Dorigen does here (V 865); moreover, where Palamon leaves the answer "to dyvynys," Dorigen leaves it "to clerkes" (V 890). The problem is the same in each tale.[25]

III

To summarize: Chaucer has claimed for himself the authority of holy writ—"Al that is writen is writen for oure doctrine." A thematic element of his *Canterbury Tales* seldom commented upon is the problem of pain. He does not solve that problem, or unravel the doctrine; he doesn't answer the question he raises. Whether in the *Knight's Tale*, the *Man of Law's Tale*, the *Clerk's Tale*, or the *Franklin's Tale*, his narrators and characters simply raise the issue, then leave it. He even raises (and abandons) the problem of pain in his constantly-chuckling *Nun's Priest's Tale*, introducing the tragicomedy of Chaunticleer's encounter with Daun Russell the fox by first solemnly intoning an echo from the *Knight's* and *Franklin's Tales*: "what that God forwoot moot nedes bee" (VII 3234). He hastily drops the issue, however, disavowing any serious intent in a great rhetorical flurry which first cites Augustine, Boethius, and Bradwardine but closes by averring "I wol not han to do of swich mateere; / My tale is of a cok ... / That tok his conseil of his wyf, with sorwe" (3251–53).

That Chaucer raises an issue but refuses to resolve it should not surprise us; Chaucer's practice in the *Tales* is to leave his pilgrims travelling on a road which he has marked out, but whose goal remains unreached. His fictional pilgrims may find this frustrating; readers have found it stimulating. To my mind, Chaucer's use of Christian allusion to raise the issue of the problem of pain is likewise both frustrating and stimulating.[26] I am frustrated in that Chaucer does not resolve his treatment of the problem. Claiming the *auctoritas* of scripture, he refuses to give an authoritative pronouncement on this issue. His Arcite remains irremediably dead and alone in the cold grave he complains

---

[25] Ruggiers notes in *The Art of* The Canterbury Tales that the "complaint" passage is "Boethian in tone" (230) in stating that the world is governed by God's providence, and that all things have a "use or function" (231). Dorigen's complaint is her own, he suggests, but it portrays "the problem of evil, of personal freedom and responsibility" (231). The only way this problem of evil can be solved in this tale is for each of the male characters to act according to "the principles of honor and generosity" (234). They do so, beginning with Arveragus: his act spurs a similar act by Aurelius, which in turn causes the magician to relent and act with equally honorable generosity. The problem of pain is for Ruggiers solved through human acts.

[26] Nicholas Watson uses the term "quizzical" as one of a group of adjectives qualifying Chaucer's approach to Christianity in the *Tales*; the others are "believing, fascinated,... and uncertain" ("Christian Ideologies," 86).

of, and Theseus' statement that "That's just the way it is" in Jupiter's universe does not resolve the issues the Knight has raised. Custance remains endlessly willing to sail off on a rudderless ship, content to accept "Goddes sonde," and Griselda remains gladly compliant to the Walter who torments her needlessly. Dorigen, finally, raises the issue as it surfaces in the "grisly rokkes blake" which menace her husband (V 859), but never returns to it. Nor can either Aurelius or his hireling magician remove the rocks and their (to Dorigen) inexplicable threat.

Chaucer doesn't remove the rocks either. Throughout the *Tales* he has raised the issue of the rocks; he can jest about that issue, as in the *Nun's Priest's Tale*, but he does not resolve it. In Chaucer's world as in Job's, the good man or the good woman may find him-/herself suffering pointlessly. Chaucer does not accept Theseus' Jupiter-solution: he has not made a virtue of necessity (I 3042). Instead, like Job, he has pointed out that the just suffer equally with the unjust—perhaps more, in fact (recall Griselda and Custance).[27]

Modern readers may be tempted to think of medieval Christians as unlikely to question as I suggest that Chaucer questions. One answer to that might be to point out that genius always questions; another, better answer might be to point out that skepticism was current in the Middle Ages, which saw at their inception Peter Abelard's justly-famed *Sic et Non* (ca. 1120), in the Prologue to which he writes that it is good to raise doctrinal questions which one cannot answer. As he puts it at the close of his Prologue, concerning questions raised by contradictory "dicta" of the holy Fathers of the church,

> These questions ought to serve to excite tender readers to a zealous inquiry into truth and so sharpen their wits. The master key of knowledge is, indeed, a persistent and frequent questioning. Aristotle, the most clear-sighted of all the philosophers, was desirous above all things else to arouse this questioning spirit, for in his *Categories* he exhorts a student as follows: 'It may well be difficult to reach a positive conclusion in these matters unless they be frequently discussed. It is by no means fruitless to be doubtful on particular points.' By doubting, indeeed, we come to examine, and by examining we reach the truth.[28]

---

[27]Sheila Delany has examined Chaucer's skepticism at some length, though chiefly in the *House of Fame* and *Troilus and Criseyde*. Her definition of Chaucerian skepticism, which she calls "skeptical fideism," seems to me right on the mark. She defines it as "that sense of the unreliability of traditional information which Chaucer deliberately incorporates into the style and structure of his poetry": *Chaucer's* House of Fame: *The Poetics of Skeptical Fideism* (1972; reprint, Gainesville, Florida: University Press of Florida, 1994), 2. See also her discussion (in the Epilogue) of skeptical fideism in the *Canterbury Tales*, 116–19. Delany does not discuss the tales I here explore, nor does she consider the problem of pain; nonetheless, her book and this essay have much in common.

[28]His praelibatis placet, ut instituimus, diversa sanctorum patrum dicta colligere, quae nostrae occurrerint memoriae aliquam ex dissonantia quam habere videntur quaestionem contrahentia, quae teneros lectores ad maximum inquirendae veritatis exercitium provocent et acutiores ex inquisitione reddant.Haec quippe prima sapientiae clavis definitur assidua scilicet seu frequens interrogatio; ad quam quidem toto desiderio arripiendam

If asked what conclusion he personally reached on the problem of pain, Chaucer would doubtless have cocked his head to one side, smiled quizzically, and said, "The answer to this let I to clerkys; I nam no divinystre."

* * *

Emerson Brown was important to me in many ways, and particularly as a scholar, a musician, and an example.

As a scholar Emerson not only exemplified for me the keen objectivity to which I aspire, he actually inspired much of my scholarship since 1987. It was in that year that he said to me, "We all ought to look more closely at how editors have punctuated Chaucer." That simple remark has been fruitful for me; many of my writings since have been extended footnotes to Emerson's statement.

I experienced Emerson's musicianship at a Southeastern Medieval Association Conference in New Orleans, when Emerson invited me to a local club where he joined the club's pianist to play his clarinet. I listened, delighted and astounded in equal measure; the pianist said to Emerson after he finished, "If you get tired of your day job, I think you could make it here." Anyone who ever heard Emerson play—which he did until well into his final year—would agree with the pianist. Emerson never wanted to quit his day job at Vanderbilt University, however.

Finally, Emerson was an example to me not only of scholarship, but of how to live. On February 26, 2002, he amended for me a recommendation for a former graduate student of his who was applying to my school. He telephoned the Vanderbilt career center, he re-wrote his letter of recommendation for the former student, and he sent me a lengthy and informative message by e-mail. This was not uncommon for Emerson; what made it uncommon for him or for anyone is the fact that he was just entering the Alive Hospice facility, and was to die three weeks later, on March 19. The Emerson I knew was a man who was thinking of another, and trying to help him, on the threshold of death. To use Iago's phrase in a better cause, "There was a daily beauty in his life" which inspired all who knew him.

---

philosophus ille omnium perspicacissimus Aristoteles in praedicamento Ad Aliquid studiosos adhortatur dicens, "Fortasse autem difficile est de huiusmodi rebus confidenter declarare nisi saepe pertractata sint. Dubitare autem de singulis non erit inutile." Dubitando quippe ad inquisitionem venimus; inquirendo veritatem percipimus. From *PROLOGVS Petri Abaelardi, Sic et Non*, ed. B. B. Boyer and R. McKeon (Chicago: University of Chicago Press, 1976). Downloaded from the web site noted below on 26 February 2004. http://homepages.wmich.edu/~johnsorh/MedievalLatin/Texts/AbelardSic.html. A second web site, http://www.fordham.edu/halsall/source/1120abelard.html (26 February 2004) has afforded much of the translation, modernized by Jerome S. Arkenberg. I have translated a few terms differently from Arkenberg.

Fables, *Cupiditas*, and Vessels of Tree
Chaucer's Use of The Epistles to Timothy

JOHN F. PLUMMER

What we have learned, following John Austin, to call performative language, or speech acts,[1] were in fourteenth-century England central to heated disputes over devotional practices, preaching, and the sacraments. Performatives, like oaths, curses, blessings, promises, thanksgivings, apologies and threats, differ from constative language in that rather than being true or false they "do" things, effect changes in states of affairs. In order for the performative actually to function, certain circumstances must apply. Only a judge in court may sentence someone to prison, for example; only certain persons under certain conditions are empowered to pronounce one "man and wife"; only I can bind myself legally with an oath. Whereas the truth or falsity of the constative utterance itself is independent of its speaker, the ability of the performative to work is radically dependent on the status of its speaker. A clear and contentious example of such concerns is seen in the claim by Wyclif and the Lollards that a sinful priest was not capable of performing the sacraments. Their argument was that the priest's language in consecrating the host during mass, or in conferring absolution in the sacrament of penance, or baptism, or last rites, for example, would fail, carry no effect, in the case of a priest not himself in a state of grace. In Austin's terms, the sacramental language would be infelicitous. A man who was not himself in a state of grace, the argument ran, could not confer grace on another through his language.

The performative nature of a sermon is self-evident; irrespective of the content of a sermon, even assuming it to be entirely and unproblematically orthodox, the nature of the preacher might affect its felicity. Strictly speaking, preaching was the exclusive privilege of ordained priests, all of whom were men, and here again the orthodox position was challenged by the Lollards among others, who encouraged lay preaching and preaching by women.[2] The Pardoner's response to the Wife of Bath's public glossing of Paul's ideas on marriage is prefaced by his statement "'Now, dame,... by God and by Seint John! / Ye been a noble prechour in this cas'" (III 164–65), drawing attention to her performance *qua* performance. Estate also determined the felicity (or not) of

---

[1] *How to Do Things With Words* (New York: Oxford University Press, 1962).
[2] Alcuin Blamires's "Women and Preaching in Medieval Orthodoxy, Heresy, and Saints' Lives," *Viator* 26 (1995): 135–52, explores the complexities and sometimes paradoxes generated by orthodoxy's attempts to justify its exclusionary positions.

237

preaching, as is underlined by Harry Bailly's impatience with the Reeve's moralizing in his Prologue: "What shul we speke alday of hooly writ? / The devel
made a reve for to preche, / Or of a soutere a shipman or a leche" (I 3902–4).
Whatever the quality, or truth value, of a discourse such as biblical citation or
preaching might be, its final value or validity was deeply affected by the nature
of its performance, including the quality / nature / ortho- or heterodoxy, class,
and gender, of its enunciator. Even a public citation or invocation of scripture
was and is itself performative, and open to varying responses.

The *Canterbury Tales* is deeply concerned with the many functions of language, beginning with the "forward" struck between Harry and the pilgrims to
tell tales to shorten their way to Canterbury. As an illustration, we might look
at some of the interchanges between Harry and pilgrim tale-tellers, the Pardoner and the Parson among others. Harry has two exchanges with the Parson,
in the *Epilogue* to the *Man of Law's Tale* and the *Prologue* to the *Parson's Tale*
proper. Both exchanges are marked by a concern for language—in the *Epilogue*
to the *Man of Law's Tale*, swearing, preaching, threatening, promising, glossing,
and tale-telling, to give just a partial list, and, in the *Parson's Prologue*, verse
and prose, fabling and preaching, chaff and wheat. In this last exchange the
Parson cites I Timothy as scriptural authority for his refusal to tell a "tale":

"Thou getest fable noon ytoold for me,
For Paul, that writeth unto Thymothee,
Repreveth hem that weyven soothfastnesse
And tellen fables and swich wrecchednesse."   (X 31–34)

The Parson presumably has in mind either I Timothy 1:4, which instructs Timothy to warn his flock "neque intenderent fabulis, et genealogiis interminatis"
("not to study fables and endless genealogies")[3] or I Timothy 4:7, "Ineptas
autem, et aniles fabulas devita: exerce autem teipsum ad pietatem" ("But avoid
foolish fables and old wives' tales and train thyself in godliness"). The Epistle
is invoked here not to command silence, but to
reject fabulation in favor of edifying textual production, the Parson's sermon.
Indeed, 2 Timothy 4:2–5 reads in part

Testificor ... *praedica verbum*, insta opportune, importune: argue, obsecra, increpa in omni patientia, et doctrina. Erit enim tem-
pus, cum sanam doctrinam non sustinebunt, sed ad sua desideria
coacervabunt sibi magistros, prurientes auribus, et a veritate quidem
auditum avertent, ad fabulas autem convertentur. Tu vero vigila, in
omnibus labora, opus fac evangelistae, ministerium tuum imple.

(I charge thee ... *preach the word*, be urgent in season, out
of season; reprove, entreat, rebuke with all patience and teaching.
For there will come a time when they will not endure the sound
doctrine; but having itching ears, will heap up to themselves teachers

---

[3]Vulgate citations are taken from *Biblia Sacra iuxta Vulgatam Clementinam* (Madrid: Bib-
lioteca de Autores Cristianos, 1977); English translations are from *The New Testament.... A
Revision of the Challoner–Rheims Version* (Paterson, N.J.: St. Anthony Guild Press, 1941).

according to their own lusts, and they will turn away their hearing from the truth and turn aside rather to fables. But do thou be watchful in all things, bear with tribulation patiently, *work as a preacher of the gospel,* fulfill thy ministry. [Emphases added.])

These two epistles to Timothy and also the epistle to Titus are called the pastoral epistles because, as one authority puts it, they "express a pastoral concern for the addressees, and because they exhibit a concern for the orderly pastoral care of Christian congregations."[4] The invocation of Timothy here by the Parson, at the end of the day and the end of the pilgrimage, seems apt, as he may reasonably think of his fellow pilgrims as his flock, whose itching ears and lusts have largely attuned them more to fables than to the sound doctrine he is about to offer.

Lawrence Besserman's admirable and useful *Chaucer and the Bible* lists seven general and thirty-four specific Chaucerian allusions to or quotations of the two epistles of Paul to Timothy.[5] In my estimation about half of these are questionable; many are statements about vice or virtue that could be connected to any number of other biblical texts. But what I notice in simply rereading I and II Timothy bearing in mind the distinction made by Chaucer and the Parson between good and bad, or at least useful and useless, language is a curious connection between these not-very-prominent biblical texts and three of his pilgrims, the Parson himself, the Pardoner, and the Wife of Bath—all three of them preachers. I will not argue that no other pilgrims allude to these Epistles: the hypocritical friar of *The Summoner's Tale*, that arch-penetrator of homes, is connected to them to his discredit, and the Second Nun has Cecilia echo them in her speech to Valerian and Tiburce before their martyrdom. Indeed, Cecilia's speech (VIII 383–90, echoing 2 Timothy 4:6–8) could itself be regarded as a sermon, and she another preacher, but for the purposes of this paper I will confine myself to the Parson, Pardoner, and Wife.[6]

In speculating on the possible significance of these three characters sharing a connection with the Epistles to Timothy, I argue that these texts might have occupied a place in Chaucer's imagination as well as that of many of his contemporaries precisely because they concern themselves with orderly pastoral care, healthy devotional practices, and preaching, at a time when these issues were very much a matter of public discussion.

As is well known, tension between secular clergy and the fraternal orders was at a high pitch in England during Chaucer's lifetime. The Epistles to Timothy were, as it happens, frequently cited in anti-mendicant attacks. As Penn Szyttia and others have documented, the most important anti-mendicant polemicist in terms of long-term influence was William of Saint Amour, writing in the 1250s in Paris. While the immediate impetus for William's attacks upon the friars

---

[4] *Harper's Bible Dictionary* (San Francisco: Harper and Row, 1985), s.v. "pastoral Epistles."

[5] New York: Garland, 1988, 377–79.

[6] Blamires, "Women and Preaching," 151, offers some suggestive comments on Cecilia as female preacher.

may be understood as a resistance to their successful incursion into the higher
ranks of the faculty of theology at the University of Paris, his eschatological
and apocalyptic reading of a number of New Testament prophetic texts ensured
that his ideas, "ecclesiological, eschatological, and theological," as Szyttia puts
it, "had a life and a language of their own."[7] William's most important treatise,
De periculis novissimorum temporum, condemned by Pope Alexander IV in
1256, takes its title from 2 Timothy 3:1–6:

> Hoc autem scito, quod in novissimis diebus *instabunt tempora*
> *periculosa*: erunt homines seipsos amantes, cupdi, elati, superbi,
> blasphemi, parentibus non obedientes, ingrati, scelesti, sine affec-
> tione, sine pace, crimnatores, incontinentes, immites, sine benigni-
> tate, proditores, protervi, tumidi, et voluptatum amatores magis
> quam Dei: habentes speciem quidem pietatis, virtutem autem eius
> abnegantes. Et hos devita: *ex his enim sunt qui penetrant domos*, et
> captivas ducant mulierculas oneratas peccatis, quae ducuntur variis
> desideriis: semper discentes, et numquam ad scientiam veritatis per-
> venientes.
>
> (But know this, that *in the last days dangerous times will come.*
> Men will be lovers of self, covetous, haughty, proud, blasphemers,
> disobedient to parents, ungrateful, criminal, heartless, faithless, slan-
> derers, incontinent, merciless, unkind, treacherous, stubborn, puffed
> up with pride, loving pleasure more than God; having a semblance
> indeed of piety, but disowning its power. Avoid these *For of such*
> *are they who make their way into houses* and captivate silly women
> who are sin-laden and led away by various lusts; ever learning yet
> never attaining knowledge of the truth. [Emphases added.])

William's title comes from the beginning of that passage, while at the end of
it he found one of the most striking images of his work, the false prophet making
his way into homes and leading the inhabitants, especially women, through
misplaced desire for learning, into heresy. This image, Sire Penetrans Domus, as
Szyttia documents fully, echoes through clerical and lay attacks on the friars for
the following century and a half. In secular literature one finds the figure in Piers
Plowman, the *Romance of the Rose*, and, allusively, in Chaucer's *Summoner's*
Tale.

In 1349–50, Richard Fitzralph, Archbishop of Armagh, took part in a papal
commission meeting to study the contentious question of poverty. The commission adjourned without reaching a conclusion on the question of Christ's
poverty and the claims of friars to imitate that poverty and the apostolic life,
and Richard was asked to study the matter further. Six years later he had
produced the treatise *de pauperie* in which he concluded, *inter alia*, that Christ
was not impoverished, and did not beg, and that the mendicant friars' claims
to emulate the apostolic life in poverty were misguided. In 1357, Fitzralph was

---

[7] *The Antifraternal Tradition in Medieval Literature* (Princeton: Princeton University
Press, 1986), 5.

invited to preach a series of sermons in London. These sermons, delivered in English, were directed against friars. The four major fraternal orders responded to Fitzralph's criticisms, drawing up an *Appelacio* purporting to identify twenty errors in the sermons, and noting with presumed indignation that the sermons had been attended by a "populous and exceedingly abundant multitude of men" (cited in Szittya, 128). In their *libelli* submitted to a papal commission at Avignon, the friars complained that Richard was "conducting a widespread propaganda campaign against them" in France, England, Germany, Spain, Italy, Hungary, and divers other Christian regions" (Szittya, 130 and n. 30.), and however much exaggeration this claim might contain, it is clear that the view that friars were the fulfillment of apocalyptic readings of 2 Timothy 3, as cited extensively in Fitzralph's fourth London sermon (Szittya, 150–51), had become very widespread, not only among their professional enemies but among the laity as well. The fourth sermon delivered in London attended by that "exceedingly abundant multitude" makes extensive and important use of 2 Timothy 3 (ibid.), and is the most eschatological and apocalyptical of the four sermons. Some years later, Wyclif's *de fundatione sectarum* also uses eschatological prophecies from the epistles to attack the friars, citing 1 Timothy 4's warning that in the last days many will depart from the true faith, and 2 Timothy 3, which had become the locus classicus of the *penetrans domus* teaching.

A further remarkable permutation of William of Saint Amour's apocalyptic reading of 2 Timothy 3 is to be seen in the writing of Henry Knighton, fourteenth-century chronicler of Leicester. Taking William's writings on "the latter age of the world" and the coming of Antichrists and false preachers, Knighton applies them not to friars but to the Lollards. The transformation of William's attacks upon the friars in the mid thirteenth century into an attack upon late-fourteenth-century followers of Wyclif proceeds in general along a broad avenue of complaints concerning false, misleading, heretical, self-serving, and/or deceptive *preaching*. The prize piece of evidence for William of the friars' devotion to false preaching had been the *Evangelium Aeternum* or *Eternal Gospel* of Gerard of Borgo San Donnino, based very loosely and outrageously on the writings of Joachim of Fiore. The Eternal Gospel, the idea went, was a third Testament, completing the sequence Old and New Testament, Old and New Dispensation, presided over respectively by God the Father and Christ. The Eternal Gospel would usher in a dispensation sponsored by the Holy Spirit, and administered by a new order, the friars. This mid-thirteenth-century heretical, even crack-pated, piece of writing would probably have sunk into obscurity quite rapidly if William of Saint Amour had not seized upon it as positive proof of fraternal ambitions and wrong-headedness. Knighton, facing in 1382 what he saw as an equally frightening heresy, transferred William's response, *de periculis*, into an attack upon Wyclif, in terms of false teaching in general and more specifically in terms of vernacular translations of the Bible. Rather surprisingly, then, the Eternal Gospel is seen as the antecedent to the equally threatening English Gospel:

Hic magister Iohannes Wyclif euangelium quod Cristus contulit clericis et ecclesie doctoribus, ut ipsi laycis et infirmioribus personis secundum temporis exigenciam et personarum indigenciam cum mentis eorum esurie dulciter ministrarent, transtulit de latino in Anglicam linguam non angelicam. Vnde per ipsum fit uulgare et magis apertum laicis *et mulieribus legere scientibus*, quam solet esse clericis admodum literatis et bene intelligentibus, et sic euangelica margarita spargitur et a porcis conculcatur.

(The Gospel, which Christ gave to the clergy and the doctors of the church, that they might administer it to the laity and to weaker brethren, according to the demands of the time and the needs of the individual, as a sweet food for the mind, that Master John Wyclif translated from Latin into the language not of angels but of Englishmen, so that he made that common and open to the laity, *and to women who were able to read*, which used to be for literate and perceptive clerks, and spread the Evangelists' pearls to be trampled by swine.[8])

Claiming that Wyclif was fulfilling the threat foreseen by William, of those who would change the Gospel of Christ into another which they claim to be more perfect, the eternal Gospel, Knighton concludes that "Eternal it might well be called, which now is common and in the vulgar tongue, and thus remembered for ever" (ibid., 245), and shortly thereafter, "the Lollards, who have changed the Gospel of Christ into the eternal Gospel, that is into the vulgar and common mother tongue, which laymen believe to be better and more worthy than the Latin tongue" (ibid., 249).

Later in the entry for that same year, Knighton reports the story of a certain priest, William Swinderby, also known as William the Hermit, who adopted Lollard positions and who, having been convicted by the Bishop of Lincoln for heresies and errors in his preaching, was first consigned to be burned, but later allowed to live after making public confession to having preached and taught falsely. Knighton offers a transcription of the confession Swinderby was required to make. The eleven points, some heretical, some erroneous, which Swinderby recants include typical Lollard ideas about the non-efficacy of the sacraments when administered by sinful priests, tithes considered as alms, excommunication, and accusations of simony. His eleventh point is particularly interesting because it illustrates that, in yet another permutation, allusions to Timothy, especially the idea of *penetrans domus*, originally hurled against friars, were evidently being used in the 1380s by Lollards against seculars as well: " . . . nullus sacerdos in aliquam domum intrat nisi ad male tractandum uxorem, filiam, aut ancillam, et ideo rogabat ut mariti caueant ne sacerdotem aliquem in domum suam intrare permittant." ("No priest ever enters a house but to defile a wife, a daughter, or a maid-servant, and that therefore he besought men to take care never to admit a priest to their houses." [Knighton, 322–23].)

---

[8] *Knighton's Chronicle*, ed. and trans. G. H. Martin (Oxford: Clarendon Press, 1995), 242–45; emphasis added.

To sum up, then, during the period of the *Canterbury Tales* the English community, clerical and lay, was engaged in a frequently heated series of debates, Lollard and anti-Lollard, Mendicant and anti-Mendicant, concerning "orderly pastoral care of Christian congregations," ranging over issues of clerical celibacy, translation of the Bible, the efficacy of the sacraments administered by sinful priests, the nature of the Eucharist, and preaching. And prominent among the scriptural texts adduced during these debates were the Epistles to Timothy.

To turn then to the three Chaucerian characters themselves, a preliminary observation about their citations of Timothy is that they *are* citations rather than allusions. By this I mean to distinguish them from Chaucer's more customary practices studied so ably by Emerson Brown in, for example, his explorations of Chaucer's biblical wives, or allusions to the *hortus conclusus*, or the Miller's promise to tell "a legende and a lyf / Bothe of a carpenter and of his wyf" (I 3141–42). In those allusive moments, Chaucer and (some of) his audience hear the biblical echo while the character, e.g., the Miller, is unaware that an allusion has taken place, let alone its implications. By contrast, the Parson, Pardoner and Wife are quite aware that they are citing a biblical text. A second preliminary observation is that in three out of four of these citations, there is no resort to gloss or the exegetical tradition.

There is certainly nothing unusual in the Parson's scriptural citation, and his use of the citation is orthodox and straightforward. No gloss or clever reversal or obliquity is offered, nor, so far as I have been able to determine, is any added meaning to be found in the exegetical tradition. The epistle is straightforward, and so is the Parson's use of it: no gloss, simply the letter: do not tell foolish tales.

The same could be said of the Pardoner's use of I Timothy 6:10, "Radix malorum est cupiditas" (VI 334 and 426). This is not to say that the biblical text is not elaborated upon, but simply to remark that it is not glossed. Here the text's value is of course undercut by the Pardoner's admission that his only intent in citing Paul is to extract money from his audience, to practice the vice he warns of. His citation is worse than nullified, for this performance raises the specter of other religious language, including the sacramental, being nullified by clerical corruption—exactly the charge leveled by the Lollards.

And thus it is not surprising that when the Wife of Bath refers to Timothy, she is also literal, though of course thoroughgoingly resistant. She understands perfectly well the plain injunction of 1 Timothy 2:8–10 to dress modestly, and she intends to refuse:

"And yet—with sorwe!—thou most enforce thee,
And seye thise wordes in the Aposteles name:
'In habit maad with chastitee and shame
Ye wommen shul apparaille yow,' quod he,
'And noght in tressed heer and gay perree,
As perles, ne with gold, ne clothes riche.'
After thy text, ne after thy rubriche,
I wol nat wirche as muchel as a gnat."

(III 340–45, emphasis added)

Indeed, on the basis of her apparent knowledge of clerical textual practice ("text," and "rubric") Alcuin Blamires has argued that "the Wife of Bath, being a lay person determined to confute clerical lore on the basis of unglossed scriptural evidence, is applying Lollard vocabulary in a Lollard manner."[9]

One must admit that in her citation of 2 Timothy 2:20–26, she is less accurate in her paraphrase, and her argument contrary to the standard gloss. As part of her defense of serial polygamy and deprecation of virginity, she opines that

> " ... wel ye knowe, a lord in his houshold,
> He nath nat every vessel al of gold;
> Somme been of tree, and doon hir lord servyse."   (III 99–101)

The passage to which she alludes reads "In magna autem domo non solum sunt vasa aurea, et argentea, sed et lignea, et fictilia" ("But in a great house there are vessels not only of gold and silver, but also of wood and clay"). Her implication seems to be that the married woman, the wooden vessel, can serve the Lord as well as the virgin, or golden vessel. Unfortunately for the Wife's argument, the next verse of the Epistle concludes that one must purge oneself of vice and become a golden or silver vessel, "Si quis ergo emundaverit se ab istis, erit vas in honorem santificatum, et utile Domino ad omne opus bonum paratum" ("If anyone, therefore, has cleansed himself from these, he will be a vessel for honorable use, sanctified and useful to the Lord, ready for every good work"); and the conclusion of the *glossa ordinaria* is that "there are also wooden and earthen vessels, that is, those who are in the house in such a way that they are not a part of the structure of the household nor in the peaceful community, but are nevertheless in the same organization with the good." As D. W. Robertson puts it, "the wife's reference to vessels thus puts her firmly among the evil who are in the church but not of it."[10] From the Parson's point of view, indeed, the Wife's performance in *Prologue* and *Tale* might align her more with the old wives' tales (aniles fabulas) of I Timothy 1:4 than with felicitous preaching.

Presumably, of these three preachers, Chaucer would consider only the Parson as legitimate. But because their respective sermons and their citations of Timothy are so different, we cannot compare and judge between them in terms of their content or interpretation of the Epistle (and we remember that the citations are essentially *not* interpreted). Returning to the interactions of the Host with the Parson with which I began, and remembering how those interactions were so marked by such speech acts as swearing, threatening, promising, glossing, tale-telling, versifying and prosifying, fabling and preaching, I propose to compare Parson, Pardoner, and Wife in illocutionary terms. A biblical citation, regarded as constative language, would always be "true," but a biblical citation can have any number of kinds of illocutionary force, from prophecy to parabolizing to admonition, among others. Whereas a prophecy or parable requires interpretation, exegesis, or gloss, an admonition (which is what most of

---

[9] "The Wife of Bath and Lollardy," *Medium Ævum* 58 (1989): 229.

[10] *A Preface to Chaucer* (Princeton: Princeton University Press, 1962), 327. The translation of the *Glossa* is Robertson's.

Timothy is) does not. So the speech act of citing Timothy consists essentially of voicing the apostle and his moral admonitions. A felicitous performance of such voicing requires the speaker to conform, him- or herself, to the admonition, and the Parson of course does so admirably: "Thou getest fable noon ytoold for me." We remember here the closing words of his General Prologue description: "Cristes loore and his apostles twelve / He taughte; but first he folwed it hymselve" (I 527–28). By contrast, the citations of both Wife and Pardoner are infelicitous, because, in two different ways, they fail or refuse to perform apostolically while voicing the apostle's words: the Wife cites the words and immediately announces her refusal to abide by them, while the Pardoner cautions against cupidity with only cupidity in his heart.

What I'd like to suggest, tentatively, here is that Chaucer's exploration of the problematic subject of preaching, and of doing things with words more broadly, focuses not upon doctrine (all of the citations of Timothy are perfectly sound doctrinally), but on preaching as illocutionary act, a performance which requires a consonance of speech and intent to be felicitous. In the words cited earlier from 2 Timothy 4:2–5, the apostle urges that he "*work* as a preacher of the gospel" (opus *fac* evangelistae). In placing the words of the Epistle to Timothy in these characters' mouths, Chaucer shows an awareness of the dispute over issues of pastoral care in his community and the role of performative speech in such issues. In the exchange between the Host and Parson in the *Epilogue* to the *Man of Law's Tale* mentioned earlier, the Parson objects to Harry's swearing "for Goddes bones" and "by Goddes digniteee" (II 1166, 1169), which provokes the following reaction:

> Oure Host answerde, "O Jankin, be ye there?
> I smelle a Lollere in the wynd," quod he.
> "Now! goode men," quod oure Hoste, "herkeneth me;
> Abydeth, for Goddes digne passioun,
> For we schal han a predicacioun;
> This Lollere heer wil prechen us somwhat."   (II 1173–77)

It is not necessary for us to believe, with Harry, that the Parson is a Lollard, but it is worth noting that Harry could believe it solely on the basis of the Parson's distaste for swearing, and that Chaucer would not find it implausible for Harry to be familiar with Lollard resistance to oaths. Harry's surmise, accurate or not, is a way of registering how commonplace was the consciousness of the disputes over performative language in the context of religious practices. The consonance between the Parson's words and his works both reminds us of the Lollard arguments that corrupt priests could not efficaciously 'perform' sacraments and simultaneously presses back against those arguments in that the Parson leads an exemplary life. The Parson's evident concern for his parishioners and pastoral care detailed in his General Prologue portrait makes his citation of the Epistle to Timothy a felicitous preamble to his "Moralitee and vertuous mateere" (X 38).

NOTES ON CONTRIBUTORS

Peter G. Beidler is the Lucy G. Moses Distinguished Professor of English at Lehigh University in Bethlehem, PA. The author of articles and books on Chaucer, Henry James, Ojibwe author Louise Erdrich, and others, Beidler has won a number of teaching awards, most notably the CASE Professor of the Year award for 1983. He was named the Robert Foster Cherry Visiting Professor at Baylor University for 1995–96. In 1987–88 he was a Fulbright professor at Sichuan University in Chengdu, Sichuan, China.

T. L. Burton (Reader in English at the University of Adelaide) is the Founding Director of the Chaucer Studio and General Editor of Boydell & Brewer's Annotated Bibliographies of Old and Middle English Literature series. He is the editor of *Sidrak and Bokkus* (EETS 311–12, 1998–99), and author of *Long Words Bother Me* (Sutton, 2004). He has a long-standing interest in historical and regional pronunciation, and is preparing a pronunciation guide for William Barnes's dialect poems.

Howell Chickering is the G. Armour Craig Professor of Language and Literature at Amherst College. He is the author of *Beowulf: A Dual-Language Edition* (1977) and frequent articles about Chaucer's poetry.

Holly A. Crocker is Assistant Professor of English at the University of South Carolina. Her articles appear in *Chaucer Review, Shakespeare Quarterly*, and a number of edited collections. She is currently editing an essay collection entitled *Comic Provocations: Exposing the Corpus of Old French Fabliaux* (Palgrave), and completing a book entitled *Seeing Chaucer's Manhood*. Holly was a graduate student at Vanderbilt University, where she was lucky enough to enjoy Emerson's teaching, mentoring, and kindness in his final years.

Alan T. Gaylord is Winkley Professor of Anglo-Saxon and English Language and Literature, Emeritus, at Dartmouth College. He is the editor of a collection of essays from divers hands on *The Art of Chaucer's Verse* (Routledge, 2001). For the Chaucer Studio he has published "The Poetics of Alliteration" (with CD), and recordings in Middle English of *Pearl*, and Chaucer's Knight's, Miller's, Friar's, and Monk's tales. His two volumes of "Adventures in Prosodic Criticism"—"Out Loud with Chaucer's Shorter Poems" and "Out Loud with *Troilus and Criseyde* and the *Legend of Good Women*"—are forthcoming from the Chaucer Studio Press.

D. Thomas Hanks, Jr., is a Professor of English at Baylor University. He has published chiefly on Chaucer and Malory, with excursions into children's literature. His most recent publication on Chaucer (with Wendy Allman) is "Rough Love: Notes Toward an Erotics of the *Canterbury Tales*," *The Chaucer Review* 38.1 (2003): 36–65.

Britton Harwood is Professor of English at Miami University, Oxford, Ohio, where he teaches Middle English literature and critical theory. He is at work on "Pluralist Chaucer: Synthesis and Difference in Contemporary Literary Theory." Recent essays of his appear in *ELH*, *Exemplaria*, the *Journal of Medieval and Early Modern Studies*, and *Studies in Philology*.

Thomas D. Hill has taught at Cornell since 1967 and has published books and papers on topics in Old English, Middle English, Old French, Old Norse–Icelandic and other medieval languages and literatures. In the fall of 1964 he met Emerson Brown in the English Department reading room in Olin Library and encouraged him to take R. E. Kaske's Middle English course, in which Em became inspired to become a medievalist. He is honored to be one of those paying tribute to Emerson, whose love of scholarship (and of Cornell) has always been an inspiration.

Michael Kensak (Emerson's last protégé) is an Associate Professor of Medieval and Renaissance Literature at Northwestern College, where he also teaches German and directs the Honors Program. Dr. Kensak has published articles on Chaucer, pilgrimage narratives, alchemy, medieval mythography, and the semiotics of inebriation in such journals as *The Chaucer Review*, *Studies in Philology*, and *Philological Quarterly*.

Josephine A. Koster is Associate Professor of English at Winthrop University, where she teaches courses in medieval literature, digital literacies, and professional writing. She received her M.A. and Ph.D. degrees from the University of North Carolina at Chapel Hill. Her research focuses on literacy, gender, and rhetoric in late medieval England, and she is completing a monograph on that subject.

John F. Plummer, Professor of English at Vanderbilt University, was a colleague of Emerson at Vanderbilt from 1979 until 1997. He has written on Chaucer, Middle English lyrics, drama, and the Arthurian Romance.

Daniel J. Ransom is Associate Professor of English at the University of Oklahoma and General Editor of the Variorum Chaucer. As a Stanford undergraduate he was converted to medieval studies by Emerson Brown, and sent by him to Cornell University to study with R. E. Kaske, Emerson's mentor. Subsequently he became a protégé, and successor, of Paul G. Ruggiers, another Cornellian. He has published on Dante, troubadour poetry, the Harley Lyrics, and Chaucer.

Lorraine Kochanske Stock, who teaches medieval literature at the University of Houston, has served as President of the Southeast Medieval Association and currently serves on the Council for the MLA Division of "Middle English Excluding Chaucer." She has published many articles about various aspects of Middle English and Old French literature and is completing a book project, *The Medieval Wild Man: Primitivism and Civilization*, whose subject reflects the topic of her essay honoring Emerson

Brown. She first met Emerson in the early 1970s when she was a graduate student in the Medieval Studies Program at Cornell, and fondly recalls hearing Emerson tinkling the piano keys at parties hosted by Robert E. Kaske, her mentor and Emerson's longtime friend.

Paul R. Thomas has taught English at Brigham Young University since 1980, and publishes articles, books, and recordings on medieval literature and drama, Chaucer, and Shakespeare. In 1988 he began assisting Tom Burton, the Founding Director of The Chaucer Studio (with whom he is now Co-Director), with production and marketing, and joined Chaucerians in recording the *Merchant's Tale* in Middle English with Emerson Brown, who narrated in a wonderful *sangfroid* way. Paul re-edited and digitized Emerson's recording as a CD in 2004.

Michael W. Twomey is Professor of English and Latin at Ithaca College, where he teaches medieval literature, Arthurian legend, Chaucer, Latin, and the history of English. His most recent work is about critical approaches to the *Gawain*-poet (in *Readings in Medieval Texts*, ed. D. Johnson and E. Treharne, 2005) and the fate of medieval encyclopedias in the early modern period (in *Schooling and Society*, ed. A. A. MacDonald and M. W. Twomey, 2004).

Winthrop Wetherbee is Professor of English and Avalon Foundation Professor in the Humanities at Cornell University. He is the author of *Chaucer and the Poets: An Essay on Troilus and Criseyde* (Cornell, 1984) and *Chaucer: The Canterbury Tales* (Cambridge, 1989) as well as articles on Chaucer, Gower, and the classical tradition in medieval poetry.

Joseph S. Wittig was a classmate of Emerson Brown's at Cornell University. Since then he has taught Old and Middle English and Medieval Studies at the University of North Carolina at Chapel Hill. His publications range across Old English, Middle English, Old French, and medieval Latin, although his work has focused principally on *Piers Plowman* and on the early Latin glosses to Boethius's *Consolation of Philosophy*.

R. F. Yeager is Professor of English and Foreign Languages at the University of West Florida. He has written widely on medieval and early modern literatures, especially Gower and Chaucer.